Imposing Harmony

Imposing Harmony

MUSIC AND SOCIETY

IN COLONIAL CUZCO

Geoffrey Baker

DUKE UNIVERSITY PRESS

Durham and London

2008

© 2008 Duke University Press
All rights reserved
Printed in the United States of
America on acid-free paper ∞
Designed by Amy Ruth Buchanan
Typeset in Quadraat by Keystone
Typesetting, Inc.
Library of Congress Cataloging-in-
Publication Data appear on the last
printed page of this book.

For Charlotte

Contents

Acknowledgments

I have been truly fortunate that three wonderful scholars of Spanish and Latin American music—Tess Knighton, Henry Stobart, and Juan José Carreras—have shown such belief in my work for many years. I deeply appreciate their involvement and support. For their help and encouragement, I am grateful to my colleagues past and present in the Music Department at Royal Holloway, University of London, and to the community of Spanish historical musicologists that has welcomed me at conferences and has engaged with my work.

Many archive researchers have offered their thoughts and advice when our paths have crossed. Gabriela Ramos, Jean-Jacques Decoster, Carolyn Dean, and Kathryn Burns have given me vital assistance at various stages of this project and have inspired me with their exemplary work. Pedro Guibovich kindly provided useful leads in Cuzco and Seville. I would particularly like to thank Donato Amado, my archival *maestro* and friend, who has helped me in more ways than I can remember, and who, along with Gabriela Ramos, located a number of early-seventeenth-century notarial documents cited in this study. I owe an intellectual debt not only to these scholars, but also to the work of Robert Stevenson and Samuel Claro, pioneers in the investigation of Cuzco's music history, and to that of Bernardo Illari and Juan Carlos Estenssoro, two inspirational musicologists of the Andean region. Bernardo has offered support and assistance since before the idea for this book was formed, and his work has always been an example to me. Estenssoro's unpublished master's thesis is a model of Latin American historical musicology, though its accessibility is sadly very restricted.

I am grateful to the directors and archivists of the Archivo Departamental del Cuzco; the Archivo Arzobispal del Cuzco; the Archivo Arzobispal de Lima; the Biblioteca Nacional del Perú, Lima; and the Archivo General de Indias, Seville. Diana Fernández Calvo and the staff at the Universidad Católica de Argentina kindly assisted me during my research in Buenos

Aires. The following bodies and institutions provided crucial financial support at various stages of my research: the Royal Academy of Music; the Music Department, Royal Holloway, University of London; the University of London Central Research Fund; and the Arts and Humanities Research Board. I was fortunate to receive an Early Career Fellowship from the Leverhulme Trust, which allowed me to complete this project, and I am very grateful to Valerie Millholland, Miriam Angress, and Justin Faerber at Duke University Press for seeing it through to fruition.

Thanks to my friends in London and Cuzco for distracting me, but not too much, and to the Bakers and Pimlotts for many tips and words of encouragement along the way. I am sad that Gordon did not live to see this book, but he is part of it. Special thanks and much love to Anne and to Charlotte, whose influence is on every page that follows.

An earlier version of chapter 3 was first published as "Music in the Convents and Monasteries of Colonial Cuzco," *Latin American Music Review* 24.1 (2003): 1–41. An earlier version of chapter 4 appeared as "Indigenous Musicians in the Urban *Parroquias de Indios* of Colonial Cuzco, Peru," *Il saggiatore musicale* 9.1–2 (2002): 39–79. I am grateful to the University of Texas Press and L. S. Olschki for permission to reproduce these articles. Material from chapter 5 has appeared in "La vida musical de las doctrinas de indios del obispado del Cuzco," *Revista andina* no. 37 (2003): 181–205, and chapter 1 includes material previously published in "Music at Corpus Christi in Colonial Cuzco," *Early Music* 32.3 (2004): 355–67.

Introduction

The center of the city of Cuzco, the Plaza de Armas, lies at the bottom of a shallow valley, with streets fanning out in three directions toward the surrounding hills. During my research in Cuzco's archives I lived in a house perched high on the hillside that leads down to the colonial center and up to the Inka citadel of Sacsayhuaman. As I looked out of my window beside the Cuesta San Cristóbal, the city spread out before me like a relief map, with the cathedral and churches of La Compañía, San Francisco, La Merced, Santa Ana, and Belén overshadowing the two-story buildings around them. It is not just the physical dominance of the church that continues to this day. Living in one of the former parroquias de indios, or Indian parishes, I became intimately acquainted with the city's "soundscape" alongside its townscape, and I soon learned that many of the sounds of the colonial city can still be heard in modern-day ceremonies. Confraternities process through the parishes to the sound of trumpets, drums, and fireworks, just as they did three or four centuries ago. Shawms and sackbuts have been replaced by clarinets and saxophones, but the city still echoes with music on saints' days and public holidays. In Cuzco, barely a week goes by without a parish fiesta or funeral procession, each with Andean musicians playing a leading role.

In the city center, the sounds of Cuzco are more diverse. Traditional Andean instruments feature in tourist restaurants and in civic parades in the main square, and there is even an Andean band that plays by the luggage carousel in the airport, ensuring that many visitors' first experience of the city is a musical one. But by night, in the bars and clubs where middle-class Cuzqueños mix with younger foreigners, the music takes listeners to different places. Peruvian DJs spin tunes—rock, salsa, trance, drum 'n' bass—that blend their cosmopolitan aspirations with those of the local dancing public. Foreigners, especially those on longer trips away, may think nostalgically of home.

Such musical imaginings are not new to Cuzco: they have been a feature of the city for nearly half a millennium, since its conquest by the Spaniards in 1533. Cuzco, a prime "contact zone" (Pratt 1992) between the Andes and Europe, has long seen musical interactions, exchanges, and appropriations. European music lay at the heart of the process of colonization and was widely perceived as the most successful evangelical tool employed by Spanish missionaries in the sixteenth century, but it was also incorporated into native responses to colonialism. Mission music gave way to the formation of a music profession that provided a route for Andeans, in particular members of the indigenous elite, to stake a claim to a key cultural, religious, and educational role in colonial society. The instrumentalists processing through the parish streets today are the descendants of the Andean musicians who ensured the spread of Spanish music throughout the diocese of Cuzco from the mid-sixteenth century onward.

For the early colonizers, the maintenance of European musical traditions provided an affective link to the Old World and a means of domesticating their new environment. Andean music, on the other hand, took on significance for the local criollo population—those of Spanish descent born in the New World—as a marker of distinction between colonizers and colonized, but it was also harnessed to the construction of local difference from Spain and even from Lima. Musical interactions both sharpened and blurred the boundaries between ethnic groups, feeding into impulses toward integration as well as differentiation. Music, then as now, was central to the ways in which Peruvians and others thought about Cuzco, themselves, and each other, and about their place within the city and the wider world.

The attention of colonial music historians was first drawn to Cuzco in 1953, when Rubén Vargas Ugarte published his article "Un archivo de música colonial en la ciudad del Cuzco." While brief, this article signaled the presence of a major archive of colonial music—one of the most significant on the continent—in the Seminary of San Antonio Abad. Vargas Ugarte's findings inspired two of the most eminent scholars of South American music, Samuel Claro and Robert Stevenson, to travel to Cuzco and follow up on his work. Their landmark publications (Claro 1969a; Stevenson 1980a) brought Cuzco's great musical treasure to the notice of the wider academic community. Claro's article included the first catalogue of the seminary holdings, an essential research tool, though he limited his analysis to a handful of dramatic works dating from the years 1743–50. Stevenson, meanwhile, traced the highlights of cathedral music until 1630, revealing this institution to have been a significant musical center in colonial Peru. The diocese of

Cuzco was created in 1536, just three years after the Spanish conquest of the city, and within a decade musical foundations had been laid in the principal church. After 1630, however, information is scarce due to the loss of some volumes of the cathedral chapter acts, and therefore few details emerge about the second or third centuries of colonial rule.

Immensely valuable as these early studies were, they were explicitly limited in scope, and significant lacunae in the city's music history remained. There were clearly temporal gaps: neither author addressed the final quarter of the colonial era (1750–1824), while the mid-colonial period from 1630 to 1740, although nominally covered by Stevenson, is passed over in just three paragraphs due to the lack of surviving cathedral records. Yet there was good reason to believe that musical culture blossomed during this "middle period." Cuzco was the center of a major school of art that flourished from the second half of the seventeenth century (Mesa and Gisbert 1982). The tenure of Bishop Manuel de Mollinedo y Angulo (1673–99) is widely considered to be a high point in the city's cultural history, and the bishop himself is unfailingly referred to as a patron of the arts (Villanueva Urteaga 1989; Viñuales 2004). Since this cultural apogee coincided with a period about which musicologists had been virtually silent, I was drawn to investigate the history of music during Cuzco's artistic heyday, as well as during its late colonial decline.

The omissions from these studies proved, however, more than simply temporal. Apart from fleeting references to convents, they focused exclusively on Cuzco Cathedral and the closely aligned Seminary of San Antonio Abad, leaving the rest of the city in almost total silence. In recent years, scholars of European music have begun to pay more attention to institutions and associations that were once marginal to mainstream musicology, such as monasteries, convents, hospitals, parish churches, schools, and confraternities, highlighting the importance of their roles in urban musical culture. This more inclusive perspective on the city seemed to hold out great possibilities for the study of music in Cuzco, where significant numbers of such institutions had been founded. As my research developed and previously neglected archival sources came to light, it became clear that virtually all the churches in the city and the surrounding villages played their part in the musical life of the region, and that confraternities based in even the smallest churches added immensely to this richly textured sound world. By focusing exclusively on the cathedral and seminary—centers of Hispanic ecclesiastical power—musicologists had painted an uneven picture of the musical life of the city and had barely touched on musical activities across the diocese. This picture did not tally with my own experiences of music and ceremony in Cuzco's parishes, which further encouraged me to believe that previous assumptions about centers and peripheries needed to be questioned. The centrality of the cathedral was both taken for granted and reinforced by colonial Hispanic elites, as it was the heart of Catholic colonialism in the diocese, and at the end of the seventeenth century almost one third of the Hispanic population of the entire diocese lived within a twenty-minute walk of this church (Garrett 2005, 66). Its preeminent role was not equally relevant to all the inhabitants of the city, however, much less of the diocese as a whole, the vast majority of whose lives centered on other institutions.

There is a need, then, for a broadening of social as well as spatial perspective and for a consideration of the musical experiences of a wider cross-section of Cuzco society. Looking at the musicological literature on Cuzco, one question became particularly pressing, the same question posed by Valerie Fraser (1990, 156) with respect to studies of colonial architecture: "Where are the Indians?" Cuzco's fame has for the past millennium rested largely on the achievements of its indigenous inhabitants. It was the capital of the Inka empire, the greatest ever seen in South America, and in spite of Spanish colonial rule it remained, essentially, a native Andean city. According to statistics collected in 1689, 93 percent of the population of the diocese was Andean, 6.5 percent white or mestizo, and the remaining 0.5 percent African. In the city, the percentage of Spaniards was higher, but there were still three indigenous inhabitants for every white or mestizo (Gibbs 1979, 79). A Spanish visitor in 1737 noted that "most of the inhabitants are Indians; although there are many Spanish families, they become lost in the majority of the former" (Lanuza y Sotelo 1998, 121).[1]

With such a numerical dominance, the Andean population, its traditions, and its history played crucial roles in the formation of colonial culture and society, for all its subordination to Spanish power. In the early years of the colony, Cuzco was granted the right to refer to itself as "the head of the kingdoms of Peru" (Dean 1999, 24): although Lima was the official viceregal capital, Cuzco stood symbolically at the head of the viceroyalty due to its glorious indigenous past. The Spanish colonists maintained and utilized the indigenous social structure in order to exercise power over the local population, more so in Cuzco than almost anywhere else in the Americas. Cuzco's churches and palaces were built on visible Inka foundations, suggesting that the colonizers' aim was not the total eradication of all traces of Andean civilization. Rather, it implies that this civilization was a necessary physical, social, and symbolic foundation on which the Spaniards might build the edifice of colonial culture.

It has long been established that indigenous artists played a central role in the development of the Cuzco School of visual art (Mesa and Gisbert 1982; Dean 1990; Damian 1995). Stevenson notes that Andeans were trained as instrumentalists in the cathedral in the late sixteenth and early seventeenth centuries, and he lists the names of a few seventeenth-century indigenous organ builders: overall, however, native musicians could hardly have occupied a more peripheral place in the musicological literature on Cuzco, which is devoted to the Hispanic musicians who filled the principal posts in the cathedral and seminary musical hierarchy. The Andean musicians so prominent in the city today are almost entirely invisible in historical studies, along with the institutions that patronized them and the parish streets and plazas in which they performed. A major thrust of my research was to discover whether Andeans had genuinely been marginalized in the musical life of the city or whether they had simply been silenced by omission from scholarly accounts.

In Cuzco, as elsewhere, the spatial and the social were inextricably linked: the indigenous majority of the urban population was sidelined to the geographical periphery. In the following pages, therefore, I attempt to decenter Cuzco's music history, expanding the focus from the Hispanic center—the cathedral-seminary axis—to include the geographical and social margins. The Spanish conquest of Cuzco entailed seizing control of the ceremonial center of the Inka empire and creating a Hispanic city in its place. As a result, the power bases of Andean society shifted to sites on the urban periphery: to the Andean parishes that formed a ring around the colonial center, as well as to rural areas of the diocese. If the Hispanic population thought of urban space in terms of a center of authority surrounded by concentric circles of diminishing status, Andean perspectives from the margins were undoubtedly quite different. An exclusive focus on central institutions has a distorting effect on our understanding of musical life in a society in which the indigenous elite, native musicians, and Andean cultural activity were concentrated in the peripheral parishes. Cuzco's musical life was in fact unusually decentralized, and there is therefore a particularly urgent need to problematize the widely accepted hierarchy of institutions in colonial society. Unlike their European counterparts, most colonial cities did not grow organically, but were constructed or reconstructed in order to reproduce a particular vision of social hierarchy in their urban layout. *Central* is thus an ideologically loaded concept in relation to colonial space, one inextricably linked to the reality of marginalization.

As will become apparent in the following pages, a broader perspective on the city reveals not only that indigenous musicians played a central role in Cuzco's music profession but also that the top posts in many churches were occupied by Andeans of high social standing who were important actors in the shaping of colonial society. Rather than being simply bit-part players in cathedral musical culture, as they have generally been portrayed in studies of colonial urban music, many native musicians were figures of considerable social and cultural significance, something that can only be grasped by encompassing the supposedly peripheral arenas in which they lived and worked. Indigenous church musicians outside the orbit of the cathedral were a distinct and distinguished social group, the study of which makes an important contribution to understandings of the mediatory roles of Andean elites in colonial society and their participation in the creation of Andean Catholicism and colonial culture, issues which have been at the forefront of recent historical studies (e.g., Decoster 2002).

The de-centering that I undertake in this study seeks to uncover the richness of urban musical life, a richness in large part due to the colonized Andean majority. One of my principal aims is thus to shed light on hitherto neglected indigenous musical practices. However, this is not a "decolonized" musicology: it is not the story of the subaltern masses, nor a tale of the survival of indigenous musical traditions in the face of Spanish domination. Such binarism is ill suited to the analysis of a society in which the power of the colonizers depended to a considerable degree on the cooperation of the elite ranks of the colonized, and in which the performance of colonial culture relied on indigenous participation. Many of the indigenous musicians who feature in these pages come from the ranks of intermediary figures who raised themselves, by dint of birth or occupation, above the mass of their fellow Andeans and used "European" music to profit, or at least to minimize their disadvantage, from the organization of colonial society. It is not, then, simply a case of "cheerleading for the subaltern side" (Krims 2002, 194).

Urban Musicology

Urban musicology as a discipline has attracted increasing interest in recent years. Reinhard Strohm's *Music in Late Medieval Bruges* (1985) is widely regarded as a pioneering work within the field, while the collection of essays

Music and Musicians in Renaissance Cities and Towns (Kisby 2001) provides both an excellent overview of urban approaches to musicology and an agenda for future research. Despite its focus on European urban centers, the latter volume offers many perspectives that are relevant to the New World: the examination of music in urban spaces, the reevaluation of the importance of parishes and confraternities in urban musical life, the "moonlighting" of musicians in other activities, even the use of notarial records to fill in gaps in the urban sound world. Yet these issues take on a distinctive slant in a colonial context. Civic ceremonies involving music constituted key moments in the production and reproduction of colonial power relations; parishes were not just where ordinary people lived but centers of native society, home to the indigenous majority whose experiences have been largely overlooked in studies of mid-to-late colonial musical life. Hispanic cathedral musicians, as members of a colonial elite, sometimes moonlighted to such an extent that they gave up their musical careers altogether, perceiving greater possibilities elsewhere, while many native musicians simultaneously fulfilled important social, religious, and educational roles in their communities. Notarial records, a valuable resource in any context, are in Cuzco the prime means of uncovering the existence of the indigenous music profession—one which was in fact central to urban musical culture. Urban methodologies thus have huge potential for challenging accepted views of the colonial music profession and of the place of music in the cities of the New World.

Such a focus on the urban social and cultural environment has been the exception rather than the rule in Iberian musical scholarship, though Miguel Ángel Marín's (2002) study of music in eighteenth-century Jaca, Spain, and the volume *Música y cultura urbana en la edad moderna* (Bombi, Carreras, and Marín 2005) have marked recent and significant advances in the field. Urban musicology has yet to make an impact on studies of colonial Latin American music, however, which have tended to center on key institutions (usually cathedrals) and their music archives (e.g., Sas 1971; Perdomo Escobar 1976; Stevenson 1980a, 1980b, 1980c) or, alternatively, on the larger scale of the region or viceroyalty as a whole (e.g., Stevenson 1960, 1976; Estenssoro 1990). Bernardo Illari (2001) provides important insights into urban musical culture in his magisterial study of colonial La Plata, yet the urban context features as a background viewed primarily through the lens of the cathedral, its music archive, and its documentary records. Egberto Bermúdez's (2001) brief essay, "Urban Musical Life in the European Colonies: Examples from Spanish America, 1530–1650," is a valuable sketch that hints at the possibilities of urban methodologies in the study of colonial music in Colombia and, by extension, other parts of the Americas. With regard to the Viceroyalty of Peru, only Juan Carlos Estenssoro's *Música y sociedad coloniales: Lima, 1680–1830* (1989) can be said to approach music from an urban perspective. The orientation suggested by the title is, however, undermined by the author's explicit decision to take the cathedral and its archive of scores as the focal point of his study. Furthermore, as a result of a dependence on printed sources, smaller institutions are given only the briefest of mentions, and the study is slanted toward the late colonial period, when newspapers emerged as useful primary sources. An examination of urban musical culture in colonial Latin America based on local documentary resources is therefore long overdue.

A key aim of urban musicology might usefully be seen as that of revealing interactions, exchanges, and conflicts on both institutional and individual levels in order to reconnect establishments and musical employees to their environments (e.g., Ruiz Jiménez 1997; Burgess and Wathey 2000). Such an approach encourages us to view institutions not as isolated islands but as part of urban networks and to ask questions about the place of musicians in urban society. Many musicians spent much of their time occupied in other fields, and urban musicologists have sought to make connections between their musical and nonmusical activities. The intention, then, is to move away from an excessive focus on a single church, on a handful of important musicians, or on a collection of music from an elite institution and toward a broader description of urban life and music making (e.g., Glixon 2003).

The need for such a widening of perspective with regard to Cuzco is illustrated by José Quezada Macchiavello's study of the seminary music archive, *El legado musical del Cusco barroco* (2004). While extremely valuable with respect to the preservation and description of the seminary's musical treasure trove, this study reveals the limitations of notated musical works as sources of information on urban musical culture. On the one hand, some useful information about the connections between the seminary and other urban institutions can be gleaned from the dedication of a number of pieces to the patron saints of the city's religious orders (see chapter 3). Given that the seminary's musicians were active outside its own walls, its archive sheds some light on the musical life of the surrounding urban environment, as well as on its own internal activities. Limited conclusions may also be drawn from marginalia in the music parts, though the texts and music tend to be less revealing. On the other hand, while Quezada Macchiavello updates and expands on earlier studies by Vargas Ugarte (1953) and Claro (1969a), he reveals little more about Cuzco's wider musical life than his predecessors, constrained as he is by the inherent limitations of his sources. As with the earlier studies, Andean musicians and most of the urban institutions that sponsored them play virtually no part in this account. The author clearly cannot be held responsible for the lack of evidence of indigenous music making in the seminary archive; indeed, his efforts to include the native population lead him to make the unsubstantiated and improbable claim that many indigenous musicians were educated in the seminary (his evidence relates in fact to the cathedral and dates from two decades before the seminary's foundation). More problematically, his desire for inclusiveness leads him to characterize the seminary repertoire as the legacy of a "mestizo musical culture," despite the fact that, as he is forced to admit, there is no evidence of such a hybrid culture in the written music, or indeed elsewhere (Quezada Macchiavello 2004, 83–86, 98).[2]

The texts in the vernacular that accompany many musical works in the seminary archive, like those from the cathedral of La Plata (Illari 2001, 442), are generally lacking in local specificity, many either borrowed from Iberian sources or closely modeled on them. In the entire Cuzco repertoire—some four hundred works—there are no textual or musical references to the Andean population. These texts do not simply represent a bland presence, much less a "mestizo culture," but rather mask an absence. The erasure of colonial reality in the musical repertoire is an act of violence, writing the colonial Others out of the script. While recognizing this type of (mis)representation as an integral part of the exercise of colonial power, we must also look beyond this music archive to gain a fuller picture of the place of music in Cuzco society. If there is any kind of mestizo barroco to be recovered in Cuzco, it is one of indigenous musical practices and performances that have left traces in historical documents, rather than one to be seen in the surviving musical works of the Hispanic elite, in which it is a criollo, rather than mestizo, identity that can occasionally be discerned. My contention throughout this study is that by focusing on musical practices rather than on musical works, we are better able to demonstrate the central role of music in colonial society, and thereby to combat any temptation to relegate cultural activities to the margins of historical inquiry. Tim Carter's contention that "the (f)act of performance can signify more than what is actually performed, and the musician may have greater value than the music" (2002, 14) is amply borne out in Cuzco.

If the seminary archive reveals only a few tantalizing clues about musical life beyond the confines of the cathedral-seminary axis, something that does emerge from studying these scores, however, is a sense of the impressive capacities of Cuzco's seminary musicians: the archive contains a Dixit Dominus (LCS 251) and a Laudate Dominum (LCS 287), both for seven choirs, while contemporary witnesses described ensembles of fifty musicians.[3] Sumptuous music was not limited to the seminary and cathedral but was also heard in monasteries, convents, and parish churches. Yet if we are to seek the roots of this musical splendor—more reminiscent of La Serenissima at the time of the Gabrielis than of most colonial Latin American cities—then we must look beyond narrow institutional explanations and investigate the musical economy of Cuzco as a whole. In order to understand how Cuzco Cathedral, whose successive bishops and chapters complained endlessly of their institution's poverty, was able to put on displays unrivaled in the Americas and how parish and monastic churches were able to aspire to cathedral-like ostentation, we must examine the distinctive forms of musical employment and institutional interaction that emerged in Cuzco's unique urban context. By exploring the city's musical culture as a whole, we may come to glimpse the mutual influences between the urban environment and the music that was produced within it.

While my focus is predominantly urban musical culture, due to the nature of the available records, I recognize that privileging the city over the countryside may constitute a further example of the valorization of centrality and risks perpetuating a colonial socio-spatial hierarchy based on polarized notions of urban civilization and rural barbarity (Rama 1996, 12). Furthermore, without examining the contours of rural music making, the definition of "urban musical culture" will remain unclear. The relationship between cities and their surrounding regions is arguably a facet of urban historical studies that has made insufficient impact on musicology. My investigation therefore seeks a balance between urban and rural perspectives by encompassing musical activities throughout the diocese of Cuzco, while concentrating on the influence of Cuzco's urban context on musical development and on the role of music in shaping urban experiences.

Although the emphasis of musicological research has been on major Hispanic urban institutions, Spanish-indigenous musical interactions in rural areas have also been the subject of investigation, but the focus has been on the early colonial period and the first encounters between missionaries and native populations (e.g., Stevenson 1976; Estenssoro 1990, 1992a; Turrent 1993). Relatively little attention has been paid to the later history of indigenous musicians under colonial rule, to the further development of musical organization after the missionary years, or to the place of native musicians in urban societies. A focus on the mid- to late colonial periods encourages an exploration of the ways in which European-derived music became fully assimilated into native communities, both urban and rural, which often became musically self-sufficient and even resisted control from Hispanic authorities as the colonial period drew to a close. During the seventeenth century, in particular, music was actively pursued as a source of social and professional opportunities, rather than being simply accepted in response to missionary efforts. In line with a number of recent historical studies (e.g., Lockhart 1992), I suggest that the aspects of colonial society and culture which flourished in the Spanish colonies were generally those which displayed continuities with the precolonial era and that the incorporation of European music is a sign that it was not, therefore, simply imposed on a passive Andean region, but that it offered particularly useful opportunities and attractions to individual Andeans.

For the musicians who appear in the following pages, music might be a career, an occupation, a source of income, a form of social climbing (Spalding 1970), but also a duty, an offering, a form of worship, a source of joy or satisfaction. Music permeated the city and was grounded in the lives of its inhabitants, yet it did not lose its capacity to transcend the ordinary. As Ruth Finnegan (1989, 339) observes, "musical enactment is at once a symbol of something *outside* and above the usual routines of ordinary life and at the same time a continuing thread of habitual action running in and through the lives of its many local practitioners." Both these threads are woven into the following pages, in which music is explored as a profession and a part of everyday urban experience, but also as a vital component of beliefs, aspirations, and social identities.

If European music offered distinctive attractions to the Andean population, native music, conversely, had its uses to the Spanish colonizers and their criollo descendants, and it was actively incorporated into important civic displays in order to dramatize the colonial social hierarchy. Music and musicians were bound up with the collective rituals through which colonial society produced and reproduced itself, and underpinned attempts by elites to bolster their status and by subordinates to open up spaces of opportunity. The impression of harmony that emerges from the seminary repertoire erases the discords that were an inescapable part of the colonial urban reality, and this elision of colonial tensions is largely perpetuated in musicological studies, in which Cuzco appears as a variation on a Hispanic theme, little different from a provincial Spanish city. The "colonial-ness" of the setting—the racial inequality, coercion, accommodation, and negotiation—is virtually invisible not only in musical texts but also in musicological commentaries. As racial and social stratification are generally considered to be two of the most characteristic issues of colonial Latin American history (Hoberman and Socolow 1986), studies that neglect these issues, treating the "colonial" in colonial music as little more than a temporal marker, will surely fail to grasp the role of music in the production of Latin American society and the elements that most distinguished the musical culture of the New World from that of the Old.

A Note About Archives and Sources

The distinctive view of colonial musical culture presented in the following pages is inextricably linked to the kinds of archival sources that I used. Whereas earlier studies concentrated on the holdings of the cathedral and seminary, I focused my attention on the Archivo Arzobispal del Cuzco (AAC), an archive devoted to historical documentation from the Cuzco diocese, and the Archivo Departamental del Cuzco (ADC) at the University of San Antonio Abad, an archive whose colonial-period resources comprise mainly legal and notarial records.⁴ The Archivo Arzobispal contains a series of account books from various Andean parishes of the city and the surrounding provinces that formed the bishopric of Cuzco. These *libros de fábrica*, as they are known, were supplemented by many *libros de cofradía*, or account books of confraternities based in the parish churches. Further research was carried out in Lima, at the Biblioteca Nacional del Perú (BNP), the Archivo Arzobispal (AAL), the Archivo General de la Nación (AGN), and in the Archivo General de Indias in Seville (AGI).

The resources of the AAC enabled me to focus my attention on institutions—parish churches and confraternities—that occupied a position so peripheral in the musicological literature of Spanish America that they had barely even registered. Notarial records, meanwhile, are a vast but virtually untapped source of information for musicological endeavor in the region. They illuminate the social and professional worlds of urban musicians in ways that other archival sources rarely do (Peters 1997). Musicians were often recorded in their nonmusical activities: buying or selling land or houses, engaging in financial transactions, writing their wills. Contracts also appeared in some numbers, providing further information about peripheral institutions such as rural parish churches, convents, and monasteries. Most importantly, the professional musicians who appeared in the notarial records were overwhelmingly Andeans, never previously documented in the city.[5]

If the Archivo Departamental frustrated me in any way, it was in its failure to reveal more than a handful of Spanish musicians. This was, I suspect, largely due to the issue of the perception and self-perception of Spanish musicians, who were almost always ordained or trainee priests and were normally described as such in documents, rather than as musicians. Marín (2002, 34) describes a similar situation with respect to cathedral musicians in Jaca. As many notarial records document musicians in their nonprofessional capacities, they can only be identified as such if their occupation is spelled out after their names. While this was usually the case with indigenous musicians, for whom music often constituted their primary professional activity, their clerical Spanish counterparts seem to have carried only their ecclesiastical tag, such as *clérigo presbítero*, with the exception of those who reached the posts of organist or choirmaster at the cathedral. As I had no access to alternative sources of information to help identify cathedral musicians—the cathedral archives had been closed to researchers for many years at the time of writing—in most cases they probably passed through my fingers without my knowledge. There is undoubtedly much more information on cathedral singers waiting to be unearthed in this archive if only new archival sources on cathedral music could be located.

Contracts to provide musical services are among the most prized gems in the notarial records, but they are limited in number. It is clear, however, that not every agreement between an institution and a musician or ensemble led to a notarized contract. Contracts formalized a particular kind of bond between an institution and a musician or ensemble, a bond that was primarily economic, but other types of bonds, in which religious or social duty played a primary role, were commonplace in the Andes. Financial and legal records clearly emphasize economic ties, and other kinds of relationship therefore have to be approached in a more elliptical manner. Account books, too, raise as many questions as they answer. The *libros de fábrica* and *libros de cofradía* reveal only a small part of the musical activities that went on in their respective institutions since they record payments from only one of several possible sources, and, like the notarial documents, they prioritize economic exchanges. In a society in which cash was in short supply, such exchanges were often of minor importance, and traditional Andean systems of reciprocity, payment in kind, or exchange of services predominated in many contexts.

The parish and confraternity account books held in the AAC date almost exclusively from the mid-seventeenth century onward. While notarial records survive from almost the whole colonial period, the majority of those of musicological interest date from 1620 to 1720, a century generally regarded as the most dynamic period of cultural production in the city's colonial history (e.g., Viñuales 2004). Since I was determined to focus my efforts on the holdings of local archives, I do not consider all parts of the colonial period in equal measure, but devote greater attention to the seventeenth and eighteenth centuries and to the musical organization and manifestations of a mature colonial society.

The sheer range of documentary sources employed opens up a broad vision of colonial Andean musical culture, outlined in chapter 1. This overview of the city soundscape is enriched by the observations of Diego de Esquivel y Navia, the dean of Cuzco Cathedral, whose *Noticias cronológicas de la gran ciudad del Cuzco* ([1749] 1980) is an invaluable source of information on the first two centuries of colonial rule. Ceremonies and processions appear to have occupied an important place in the mind of this mid-eighteenth-century churchman, providing cultural historians with a wealth of information about civic ritual.

In chapter 2 I explore some of the ways in which the functioning of the cathedral music establishment veered away from standard Hispanic models in the seventeenth to early nineteenth centuries. As all of my information was drawn from records held outside the cathedral, the picture that emerges differs from that of many Latin American studies, revealing distinctive developments in musical organization and illuminating the lives of some important cathedral musicians, most of whom were previously unknown to musicologists. I seek to answer some of the questions raised by Stevenson's original article: how, for example, did the cathedral musical organization develop after 1630? The first century of cathedral music making was dominated by the Sevillian model and by peninsular musicians who came to the Americas in search of professional opportunities. Did Cuzco Cathedral remain on the extended circuit of musical positions available to peninsular Spaniards, or did criollos begin to establish themselves in the musical hierarchy? The importance of the Seminary of San Antonio Abad had become clear from earlier research, but what was the exact nature of the musical relationship between this institution, the cathedral, and the multitude of other churches in the city? In the final part of this chapter, I shift my focus from the institution to an investigation of the lives of several senior musicians in an attempt to understand their place in Cuzqueño society and the changes that occurred in the Hispanic music profession during the seventeenth and eighteenth centuries.

The remaining chapters explore music in institutions that have not previously been investigated by musicologists working on Cuzco, such as convents and monasteries (chapter 3) and urban parish churches (chapter 4). As these establishments have attracted little attention across the continent as a whole, fundamental questions needed to be addressed. To what extent was music performed in these churches? How was the music organized, and who were the musicians—Spanish or Andean, professional or amateur? In many cases it is impossible to know whether the patterns that emerge were typical or atypical in the New World, given the paucity of research that has been undertaken on such institutions in other areas, but a comparison with the Iberian Peninsula gives a sense of the degree to which Old World models were adapted in this new environment.

Chapter 5 moves away from the urban environment into the Andean villages of the bishopric of Cuzco. The diocese was divided into fourteen provinces, each of which was subdivided into ecclesiastical administrative units known as *doctrinas de indios*, which were extensive rural Andean parishes. No investigation of music in these provinces had previously been undertaken, so it was necessary to establish the contours of rural musical organization and activities. By comparing music in urban and rural areas, a sense of their relationship emerges, one in which the cultural superiority of the city cannot be taken for granted. I pay attention throughout to the musical activities of confraternities, lay religious associations that sponsored music in rural villages, urban parish and monastic churches, and the cathedral. A focus on these lay societies greatly enriches our picture of the integration of European-derived music into the lives of the population of the diocese.

CHAPTER ONE

The Urban Soundscape

Every city and kingdom is like a fine, beautiful harmony and musical song, whose voices, diverse though they may be, are nevertheless brought to consonance and unity through the providence and art of the good singer.—Rodrigo Sánchez de Arévalo, Suma de la política, c.1454

Kublai reflected on the invisible order that sustains cities, on the rules that decreed how they rise, take shape and prosper, adapting themselves to the seasons, and then how they sadden and fall into ruins. At times he thought he was on the verge of discovering a coherent, harmonious system underlying the infinite deformities and discords.—Italo Calvino, Invisible Cities

The visit of Viceroy Francisco de Toledo to Cuzco in 1571 was a momentous event in the history of the city, and indeed of the viceroyalty as a whole. Though the Spanish under Hernando Pizarro had conquered the city in 1533, the next four decades were characterized by strife and political upheaval, rebellions and civil war. The Spanish conquerors fought among themselves, and several leaders were killed by their fellow countrymen. Diego de Almagro, returning from an unsuccessful attempt to subdue Chile, was defeated and executed not far from Cuzco. The Inkas, however, were also divided. Some remained in Cuzco and became vital allies of the Spaniards, while others retreated to the jungle near Vilcabamba, north of the city, where they continued to resist the disunited Spanish factions. These were dangerous and uncertain times: the first bishop of Cuzco, fray Vicente Valverde, was killed by native warriors on a missionary excursion. Viceroy Toledo, the king's supreme representative in Peru, had been appointed three years earlier, in 1568, to bring order to the viceroyalty. He had come to Cuzco to inspect his domain and to impose good government on the Spanish colonists in the former Inka capital, though he ended up directing the campaign to defeat the last Inka rebel, Túpac Amaru.

The city council was given ample warning of the arrival of the viceroy, whom it was keen to impress. When Toledo drew near to Cuzco, he was installed for the night in a house that the council had built just outside the city. The following day, he was taken up to a lookout constructed with a view down onto the plain below. First, a hundred Spanish horsemen appeared to the sound of trumpets and drums and enacted a mock cavalry battle under the gaze of the viceroy. They then made way for a display by Andean groups, who were just as keen to show their welcome as the Spaniards: forty years after the conquest, native leaders understood the importance of good political relations with the colonial authorities, though such performances of power were also vital to maintaining their status in the eyes of their own communities. They poured down the hillside opposite the viewpoint in great numbers, the Inka leaders first and their subjects from all four *suyos*, or quarters of the realm, behind them, each ethnic group carrying its flag and many multi-colored banners. Most wore breastplates of gold or silver, and many were decked in feathers, the colors and metals glinting in the sunlight. Each *suyo* then came before the viceroy and welcomed him according to its own custom, with its own distinctive dance. When the performances had finished, Toledo thanked the groups on behalf of the king for their display of allegiance to the crown.

The day of the official entry into the city dawned fine. The viceroy was again met by crowds of Andeans, who had constructed arches of many-colored flowers, birds, and animals over the road. So impressed was the eyewitness who recorded events by this Andean welcome that he added, "It should be noted that the city which can put on the finest display of these handicrafts is that which has the most Indians; and as they are so innumerable in this city, what a show they put on, with the different dances and *invenciones* [performances] that they brought out and the fine clothing in which the *kurakas* [native leaders] and *principales* [secondary Andean nobles] were attired." Toledo took an oath at an arch situated on the city limits, and then formally entered Cuzco. "The music of minstrels, trumpets, and other instruments that sounded as the gates were opened cannot be described," wrote the eyewitness. The viceroy was met by eight hundred finely dressed soldiers, and made his way into the city through streets decked with tapestries, through throngs of Andeans so thick that he could barely pass. Arriving finally at the main square and the cathedral, he opted to take a turn around the plaza, doffing his hat to the ladies who filled the windows and balconies. As he made his way back to the steps of the church, the chapter and canons came to meet him—the see was vacant at this time—and accompanied him inside to hear "a solemn mass with great music and clamor of voices, both of which are highly regarded in this holy church." Toledo had arrived at the cathedral of the oldest diocese in Peru, overlooking the Plaza de Armas at the heart of Cuzco (Torres de Mendoza 1867, 251–55).[1]

The Plaza de Armas, the physical and symbolic center of Cuzco, had been fashioned by the Spaniards out of the *haucaypata*—roughly one-third of the great civic square of the Inkas—and had thus been the scene of magnificent religious and political rituals since long before the Europeans' arrival in 1533. Inka Cuzco has been described as more of a ceremonial center than a city (Rowe 1967), and its layout differed substantially from European cities, for example in the dedication of extremely large spaces not only to ceremonies but also to cultivation (Viñuales 2004). In socio-spatial terms, Inka Cuzco was organized according to kinship principles and thus more closely resembled traditional village structures found in other parts of South America than European cities (Morse 1972, 370). After their military victory in 1533, the Spaniards therefore faced the dual task of urbanizing and Hispanicizing Cuzco. Their most obvious tool was architecture, and they constructed Spanish-style churches and municipal buildings on the exposed foundations of Inka temples and palaces in what was a highly visible show of domination. The transformation of the heart of the Inka center through the reshaping of the central plaza was of crucial symbolic importance to the colonial enterprise: Cuzco's magistrate, Polo de Ondegardo, saw this display of architectural power as the key to converting and acculturating not just Cuzco but the whole of the Andean region (Dean 1999, 30–31). The huge Inka plaza was carved up accordingly. The Watanay River, which divided the *haucaypata* from the larger section known as the *kusipata*, was filled in and houses built in its place, separating the colonial Plaza de Armas from the Plaza del Regocijo, as the *kusipata* was renamed. The Plaza del Regocijo was to be overlooked by the chambers of the colonial city council and thus to become the site of important civic ceremonies. The Plaza de Armas, meanwhile, was eventually chosen in 1552 as the permanent site for the cathedral, which was built on top of the palace of the Inka Viracocha in a final, graphic demonstration of the triumph of Spanish sacred power.

Acts of structural domination alone were not enough, however, to ensure total colonization of place, as the city plan produced by the early-seventeenth-century Andean chronicler Felipe Guaman Poma de Ayala ([1615] 1980, 970) reveals (fig. 1). This map of Cuzco shows "an almost untouched Inka city" full of pre-Hispanic sacred space, even though it was drawn some eighty years after the Spanish occupation (Locke 2001, 150). Inka shrines and landmarks, many noted with their Quechua names, are still prominent, with the *haucaypata* and *kusipata* labeled as such rather than as Spanish plazas, underlining that the contours and meanings of urban spaces were resistant to change despite the colonists' architectural program. Yet the Spanish mission to refashion Cuzco as a colonial city was not, of course, pursued solely at a spatial level: it was also fundamentally a cultural and ritual reinvention of Inka Cuzco, a process that began with the formal act of the city's foundation by Francisco Pizarro on 23 March 1534, marking a new, Hispanic beginning. Viceroy Toledo's turn around the Plaza de Armas in 1571 before he entered the cathedral might have been motivated primarily by flirtatiousness, but it could also be seen as a performance full of symbolic resonance for the inhabitants of Cuzco, his route tracing out the recent conversion of the key ceremonial space of the *haucaypata*.

The cultural construction of the Latin American city is the focus of Ángel Rama's influential work *The Lettered City* (1996), which explores the idea that urbanization and civilization in colonial Latin America—two processes inextricably linked, even on a semantic level (Waisman 2005)—entailed a transformation that was effected not only through architecture but also through the power of the written word. Rama (1996, 27) describes the Latin American city as two superimposed grids: a physical plane and a symbolic plane "that organizes and interprets the former . . . , rendering the city meaningful as an idealized order." He sees "the two cities—the real one and the ideal one—as entities quite distinct yet also inescapably joined. One could not exist without the other." Revealing how the city is not simply created out of stones but fleshed out by words and concepts, Rama emphasizes the role of wordsmiths (*letrados*) in the creation of "the lettered city" of colonial Latin America. Yet music, sound, and performance, I would argue, were equally integral to this process of colonization and urbanization in the New World, with the ordering of the city (so important to colonial *letrados*, and a focus of Rama's argument) conceived and enacted not only in verbal but also in sonic terms, exemplified by the concept and practice of harmony. European music, propagated by Spanish missionaries from the earliest years of the conquest of Peru, served both as a tool and as a metaphor for the harmonization of social forces. The imposition of musical organizational structures and the inculcation of European musical skills—especially harmony, previously unknown in the Andes—formed part of wider efforts to create temporal, spatial, and social order in the new colonial towns being founded across the viceroyalty (Waisman 2005), but they also contributed to the process of

CIVDAD
LAGRÃCIVDADICAVE

1. Felipe Guaman Poma de Ayala, 1613, folio 1051, *La gran ciudad y cabeza y corte real de los doce reyes Inkas, Santiago del Cuzco.*

urban transformation and redefinition in established centers such as Cuzco. While the attention of urban historians has focused on the verbal, visual, and olfactory dimensions of the city (e.g., Rama 1996; Dean 1999; Kinsbruner 2005), there is a strong case for considering the intersection of sound, urban form, and colonial power—la ciudad sonora, or "sonorous city," as it might be termed after Rama.[2]

The arrival of Viceroy Toledo in Cuzco in 1571 was heralded by Andean music and dance, minstrels and loud instruments, and sacred music in the cathedral. Indigenous cultural displays gave way to European sounds as the city gates were opened and the viceroy crossed the symbolic threshold from the Andean countryside into the Hispanic city. Three kinds of music, of increasing sophistication from a European perspective, announced the three stages of the entry: standing outside the city, crossing the boundary from barbaric (if colorful) campo to civilized ciudad, and arriving at the Hispanic heart of Cuzco. The deployment of musical resources was therefore highly figurative, and the progression underlined the urban/rural dichotomy that was central to the discourse and identity of colonial lettrados (Rama 1996). This account of a dynamic and carefully planned civic event exemplifies the ways in which music and sound—and their associated discourses—were implicated and employed in the cultural construction of urban identity and of the colonial city itself, offering a glimpse of the close relationship between sound and urbanism in the early modern Hispanic world.

Urbanism, harmony, and order

Urbanization lay at the heart of the Spanish conquest of the New World: "Of all the peoples that Rome had brought within its domain, the Iberians most closely imitated their conquerors in the significance they assigned to the city. In turn, Iberians reconstituted this prominence in the Indies, heightening it, in fact, in all matters social and cultural" (Szuchman 1996, 1). The Spaniards saw the Americas as a virgin territory onto which they might project their dreams and aspirations; a backward, natural, chaotic place, it demanded the rational organization characteristic of the humanist intellect (Eaton 2002). After the early exploratory expeditions, settlers began to arrive, bringing with them an approach to town planning that was both informed by and designed to promote a highly structured, hierarchical worldview. The famous grid plan, superimposed onto American population centers and empty spaces alike, represented "their sense of perfect order and the neat placement of people within a well-defined space" (Szuchman 1996, 5), its design symbolizing rational domination but also facilitating surveillance.

The physical concord of the European town plan was a spatial ideal created in the abstract, a bold attempt to construct a harmonious world from scratch and to harness urban design and architecture to the ideological subjugation of native populations (Fraser 1990; Rama 1996; Eaton 2002). In this sense the New World city was a coercive project as much as a physical location, the projection of an idealized, hoped-for future rather than the accumulation of past achievements that was the medieval European city, or indeed Inka Cuzco. Of course, not all these hopes were realized: the late-sixteenth-century "plan" of Cuzco, which circulated widely in Europe in the first volume of Braun and Hogenberg's *Civitates orbis terrarum* (1572), bore no relation to the way that the city actually appeared (fig. 2). It was, rather, an "iconic view" (Kagan with Marías 2000, 7) depicting a concept of the city that arguably reflects a will to order more than any physical reality, and its spare, geometrical appearance contrasts sharply with the dense, lived-in image by Guaman Poma de Ayala.

If its theoretical perfection was not always reflected in practice, the harmonious city plan was nevertheless emblematic of a Spanish colonial ideology that was urban in focus and in which the process of urbanization was key. The Spanish colonists in the New World drew on the Roman tradition of the city as a central tool of empire—one which the Spaniards had learned to use in the Iberian Peninsula through the experience of the *reconquista* of the Moors—but also on the Aquinian notion of the city as the repository of Christian virtue and piety and thus the ideal instrument of evangelization (Kagan with Marías 2000). These various impulses came together in the forcible resettlement of native American peoples into new towns, or *reducciones*, a policy that was regarded as an essential first step in converting them to the faith and ridding the land of disorder and idolatry. The city acquired, in short, a civilizing mission. At the heart of this mission was the imposition of *policía*, a complex term implying good government, law, order, peace, morality, and religion—all of which were seen as characteristic benefits of urban life. *Policía* had an architectural face, revealed in the many colonial prescriptions about town planning, but it could also, arguably, be expressed in (and implemented through) the sound and concept of harmony, a potent symbol of both order and the civilizing, Christianizing mission of the colonial church.[3]

The *Ordinances for the Discovery, New Settlement and Pacification of the Indies*

2. Georg Braun and Franz Hogenberg, *Civitates orbis terrarum*, book 1, no. 58, 1572, *Cuzco*. Reprinted by permission of the British Library (Maps C.7.d.1).

issued by Philip II in 1573 were a summary of earlier royal instructions concerning urban planning in the Spanish empire (Garr 1991, 3–31). They underline the interweaving of urbanization and religious conversion and also allude to the role of music in these processes. In a discussion of evangelical tactics, the authors of the regulations proposed a kind of religious ambush according to which priests should hide among friendly natives and then surprise those who were more resistant to the Christian message. Priests were instructed that "in order that they may be accorded greater respect and admiration they should be wearing at least white vestments, or surplices and stoles, and with the Cross in their hands . . . and, should they wish to generate greater admiration and attention among the infidels—and if available—they might use music, by way of singers and high and bass wind instruments, in order to entice the Indians to join them" (30–31).

Not only is this passage suggestive for its appearance in a collection of ordinances devoted primarily to urban planning, but it also echoes an earlier regulation in the same collection concerning architecture. The Spanish colonizers were instructed to keep the indigenous population away from new settlements during the construction process "so that when the Indians see [the completed buildings] they will be struck with admiration" (29). On the one hand, then, music might be considered as part of the third of the processes described in the title of the ordinances—discovery, settlement, and pacification—in which earlier urbanizing efforts were consolidated or intensified. On the other hand, both architecture and music are conceived as tools to provoke wonder among native populations; the belief in their power to move the observer or listener reveals a rhetorical spirit that manifests the urge to persuade, and thereby control, that lies at the core of José Antonio Maravall's (1986) conception of baroque culture. One of the functions of the city, then, was to convey messages and to demand attention (Kinsbruner 2005, 50): the city as statement. Music was not, therefore, simply an afterthought; like architecture, it was part of the process of communicating Spanish power to the indigenous population, a sonic corollary to the visual impact of construction. Early evangelization depended on this combination of sights and sounds, on architecture and music, more than on language (Fraser 1990, 82). In fact, the first attempts to impress native populations were often sonic before they were concrete. In Cuzco, where Inka architectural achievements had reached impressive heights, the rudimentary design and slow construction of the first Spanish churches may have had little rhetorical impact on the local population, so other techniques—music, ceremony, display—would have taken on particular importance.

The propagation of a Spanish urban vision in the Americas might thus be seen as part of a broader program of imposing order in which music, in the hands of the first Spanish missionaries, participated from the very beginning, sonic harmony encouraging and reinforcing the formation of a regulated social and physical world. Music provided a distinctive set of tools for shaping society, adding a particular dimension to the urbanizing, as well as the evangelizing, mission. The order and precision of the Spanish urban grid plan was mirrored in the organization of urban space through civic processions, in the structuring of time through the sounding of church bells, even in the perfect intervals of a harmoniously constructed polyphonic work—harmony for both eyes and ears.

The inextricable relationship between sonic, physical, and social harmony was well established in Renaissance Europe, as it had been in the ancient world which provided the inspiration for humanist scholars. Spanish music theorists of the fifteenth and sixteenth centuries, such as Bartolomé Ramos de Pareja, Juan Bermudo, and Francisco Salinas, display an indebtedness to well established classical concepts, above all to the ideas of Pythagoras and Boethius, in their adherence to the division of music into three categories: *mundana*, *humana*, and *instrumentalis* (León Tello 1962; Otaola González 2000). *Musica mundana* refers to the harmony of the spheres, *musica humana* to the relation between celestial harmony and the human soul, and *musica instrumentalis* to sounding music. The aim of the last was to reflect or reproduce the first two—to imitate the harmony of the universe and harmonize the human soul. Music thus had the power to create balance and order, to exert a beneficial influence on the human body and soul by helping to recuperate a lost inner harmony. The power of music derived from its intimate connection to the cosmos, in the image of which it was created; as such, it reflected the immutable laws of the universe.

According to Greek (and therefore Spanish) theorists, the beneficial effects of music could be felt in many realms: psychological, physiological, moral, educational, religious, but also sociopolitical, in the collective as well as the individual sphere (Otaola González 2000, 76). Rodrigo Sánchez de Arévalo, in his treatise on the activities suitable for princes, *Vergel de príncipes* (1456–57), discussed the role of music in fostering political virtues and disposing rulers toward good governance: he recommended music since "the kingdom is well ruled when it conserves musical harmony, that is to say, when out of its diverse and opposing members, by the art and ingenuity of the leader, emerges a harmony which is unity and concordance in the kingdom" (in León Tello 1962, 206–7). For Sánchez de Arévalo, a ruler should be like a good musician who elicits consonance from a diversity of voices. More than a century later, Francisco Salinas, in his *De musica libri septem* (1577), suggested that *musica humana* could be observed not only in the conjunction of soul and body, in the order of the arts and sciences, but also "in the constitutions of all the kingdoms and republics" (León Tello 1962, 563–64).

If the concept of harmony provided a model for social and political order in fifteenth- and sixteenth-century Hispanic thought, it was also rooted in the physical world and conceptualized in visual terms. Theorists wrote in terms of proportion and balance, for their understanding of harmonic principles was based on Pythagoras's exposition of the relationship between sound and number, exemplified by the mathematical ratios produced by a vibrating string. Behind such understandings of harmony was a belief in absolute patterns or essences that stood prior to and beyond the sensory world. Such essences manifested themselves in perceptible phenomena such as musical harmony and the mathematics of the monochord; perfect musical intervals thus had both numerical and spatial equivalents, with all three seen as differing but fundamentally unified expressions of a universal cosmic harmony. It was therefore but a small leap to the idea that such musical intervals and their expression as ratios corresponded to ideal architectural proportions, a theory explored by Leon Battista Alberti in his *De re aedificatoria* (c.1450) and put into practice by later architects such as Andrea Palladio and Francesco Giorgi (Wittkower 1998). Although most famously associated with the Venetians, the application of musical proportions to architecture was also well established in Renaissance and baroque Spain. Simón García expounded this theory in his *Compendio de arquitectura y simetría de los templos conforme a la medida del cuerpo humano* of 1681, and musical proportions had also been applied to the design of cathedrals in cities such as Segovia, Salamanca, and Valladolid in the sixteenth century. Harmony, then, was more than a vague metaphor to the early moderns, it was a concept that permeated understandings of society, of the physical world, and even of the human form, with beauty itself defined by Alberti as "that reasoned harmony of all the parts within a body" (Akkerman 2000, 275).

Harmony was also a guiding principle for utopian urban design, as it had been since the time of the ancient Greeks, who sought to fashion the city plan and urban society in the image of an orderly universe (Akkerman 2000). During the Renaissance, the notion of cosmic harmony again began to play a major role in urban planning as Pythagorean theories and a belief in the structured patterns of the universe returned to prominence. Like the ancients, the designers of "ideal cities" in the early modern world believed they were "capable of understanding the nature of these original patterns and hence of attuning the city as closely as possible to their perfect harmony" (Eaton 2002, 11). Central to this rebirth of ancient ideas about the link between harmony and urbanism was the rediscovery in the early fifteenth century of *De architectura libri decem*, a treatise by the Roman author and architect Vitruvius (Vitruvius 1999). In the first chapter of Book 1, Vitruvius stated that the architect ought to learn about music as part of his education, and to this end he devoted a later chapter (Book 5, Chapter 4) to an explanation of harmonic principles. The author's combination of writings on music, architecture, and urban planning reveals his debt to Pythagorean thinking, which was once again to play a major role in the Renaissance.

Though Vitruvius's work was best known in Italy after its rediscovery, his influence—and that of Alberti, who popularized his writings—was also felt in the Hispanic world (Kinsbruner 2005, 23). While he is not cited explicitly as a source, his shadow can be detected in the *Suma de la política* of Rodrigo Sánchez de Arévalo, published in around 1454 (Sánchez de Arévalo [c.1454] 1944; Antelo Iglesias 1985). In this volume, the author prefigures the arguments he was to develop further in his *Vergel de príncipes* about the relationship between music and civic order. In Book 1, Chapter 10, he makes repeated references to music and harmony in underlining the importance of pleasure and entertainment to good governance and the formation of virtuous and productive citizens. Most notably, however, he devotes Book 2, Chapter 9, to the topic of "how the city or kingdom should be united in concord [...] and how in it should reign consonance and musical harmony," exploring in full the analogies between music and urban society (Sánchez de Arévalo [c.1454] 1944, 111). He warns that the main problem facing cities, republics, and their rulers is discord among citizens, and he provides advice as to how to deal with such discord, spinning an extended metaphor of the ruler as a prudent musician and the tuner of a vihuela, loosening and tightening the strings of the civic instrument to create "perfect and sweet harmony and concord" (114). Foreshadowing his later work, he recommends that a good politician should follow the example of a skilled musician so that he might create "concord and unity and the sweet consonance of peace by his wisdom and musical prudence" (114). Sánchez de Arévalo draws explicitly on an ancient source, Scipio, "who said that every city and kingdom is like a fine, beautiful harmony and musical song, whose voices, diverse though they may be, are nevertheless brought to consonance and unity through the providence and art of the good singer. Just as, to refer to

Scipio, we see that a good organist strives so that there may be no dissonances in his instruments, ensuring that the voices make a melodious sound, so a good politician must work even harder to make sure that in all the parts or members of the city reigns concord and consonance of desires and deeds" (113).

It is apparent from Sánchez de Arévalo's work that the classical idea of the city as the embodiment of harmony left a strong imprint on urban theory in the decades before the Spanish colonial expansion into the Americas. While Sánchez de Arévalo showed an unusual degree of concern with the fine-tuning of the *civitas*, other urban theorists from the late fifteenth century onward drew more obviously on the practically oriented work of Vitruvius, which became hugely influential across Europe just at the time that urbanization took on an unprecedented importance within the Hispanic world with the discovery of the Americas. Although it appears that little attention was paid to urban planning during the first two decades of exploration and settlement in the New World, from 1513 the crown began to give precise instructions to colonial officials, instructions that bore the hallmark of classical ideals and, specifically, the writings of the Roman author. One of the architects of Mexico City owned a copy of Vitruvius's treatise and, as Dan Stanislawski (1947) has shown, the ordinances for the settlement of the Indies issued by Philip II in 1573, discussed above, reveal close parallels with this classical source. If Greek and Roman ideas of the city underpinned the urbanization of the New World from the early sixteenth century onward, then the concept of harmony resonates through the 1573 ordinances much more deeply than the sole overt reference to music might suggest.

Within the realm of urban theory, the principle of harmony was closely allied to those of order and symmetry (Akkerman 2000, 272): if cities were to be forged in the image of cosmic harmony, they were also "instruments for the creation and conservation of *order*" (Rama 1996, 14; emphasis original). The Spanish crown was obsessed with this notion; indeed, Ferdinand V's directive about town planning, quoted by Rama, includes the word *order* four times in a single sentence. Order meant, according to the received definitions of the day, "putting things in their places; concert and harmonious disposition among things" (Rama 1996, 4). Just as a desired function of architecture and urban design was to create a perfect, harmonious society (Eaton 2002, 49), the power to create order where it was lacking was widely attributed to music, and it was for this reason that the church placed music at the heart of its missionary efforts in the New World. The effectiveness of music on moral and religious planes, deriving from the link between harmony, virtue, and piety, is a recurrent theme in Spanish music theory and its ancient sources. Even animals were susceptible to the power of music to shape the world, again an idea that can be traced back to ancient Greece via Renaissance writers such as Sánchez de Arévalo (León Tello 1962, 215). The chronicler Diego de Esquivel y Navia ([c.1749] 1980, 2:146–47) tells of a miracle that took place in 1687 in the village of Guaroc, seven leagues from Cuzco in the province of Quispicanchis, after high mass in the parish church. When the singing of the Eucharist eulogy began, a dozen pigs that had been lurking in the middle of the plaza rushed to the steps of the cemetery, where they turned to the altar, knelt down, and lowered their heads as if worshipping the Lord. When the singing finished, they went back to their foraging, leaving witnesses amazed at the example shown by these lowly animals.

Music, then, was a powerful tool, capable of ordering the world in the image of the celestial harmony created by God. In a colonial context, this power takes on a coercive hue. The relationship between colonialism and Western music theory, with its discourses of science and immutable laws derived from the ancient Greeks, has been discussed by Richard Leppert (1987, 71–78), and while his example comes from a different empire (India) and a later century (the eighteenth), much of his argument pertains equally well to the imposition of harmony at earlier stages of European colonial expansion. The notion that music, like mathematics, obeys and is a manifestation of unchanging natural laws and cosmic order serves as a rational underpinning to the transplantation of European musical values, which, as more than "mere" cultural expressions, have right on their side. Within the concept of harmony thus lies a coerciveness born of the belief in its universality.

The imposition of harmony in the Americas was a multi-faceted program, effected on a variety of planes—physical, moral, religious, and cultural—though, in the light of the discussion above, it would be erroneous to regard these aspects as overly distinct. The Spaniards sought to recreate the harmony of the cosmos in strange lands, to make the New World resonate with the consonance of the Old (or, in the case of the more utopian Jesuits, to establish the concord lacking in the Old). In an urban context, the cultivation of polyphonic music might be viewed in the light of efforts to effect a harmonious ordering of society, creating a regulated soundscape to reinforce the transformation of the cityscape. Indeed, music was one of the means by which the context *was made urban*: if, as Marín (2002, 41) suggests, elaborate music was a distinctive marker of the city in early modern Spain, then the incorporation of European music in Cuzco may be seen as an essential part of the process of forging a Hispanic sacred city out of an Inka ceremonial center, an attempt to impose European urban values through sound. Sixteenth-century Cuzco saw the layering of one sacred topography on top of another, the superimposition of two physical and imagined cities. Because of the need to reshape an existing sacred geography, rather than building from scratch—as happened in many parts of the New World, including Lima—struggles over the meaning of Cuzco's urban spaces proved intensely important. The city's Catholic sacredness was more contested and less deeply rooted than that of Spanish cities or of newly created settlements in the New World; the reconfiguration of spaces through sound and movement, epitomized by the civic processions that transformed Cuzco's *haucay-pata* and *kusipata* into Spanish plazas, was therefore fundamental to colonial efforts to convert and control this most symbolic Andean place of memory. Newly founded cities offered the possibility of forging the urban structure in the image of harmony, but Cuzco's dense, pre-existing, and—from a European perspective—chaotic layout gave only limited opportunities for urban redesign. Filling the space with concordant sounds thus took on particular significance.

Uniting the City

The city of Cuzco housed a great number of religious institutions—parish churches, monasteries, convents, colleges—which sponsored music making of some kind. They were by no means entirely separate spheres of musical activity, but rather interacted in a variety of auditory ways. Indeed, it might be claimed that music and sounds served as prime urban connectors: they were the most effective form of mass communication and proved central to the colonial ceremonies that promoted a sense of urban identity, uniting the city in praise of, or mourning for, a religious intercessor or royal figurehead. On occasions important enough to warrant a civic ceremonial response, sound emanated from the cathedral—the geographical and, from a Hispanic perspective, symbolic center of the city—and was echoed back by the periphery, confirming its participation. When news of the death of Pope Benedict XIII was received in 1730, the cathedral emitted a distinctive peal of one hundred strikes of the main bell, and this signal was answered by all the other churches (Esquivel y Navia [c.1749] 1980, 2:248). Such communal bell ringing was a relatively frequent occurrence. In 1747, an alumnus of the Colegio de San Bernardo, Bernardo de Arbisa, was elected bishop of Cartagena; the college asked the cathedral and the other churches to ring their bells in celebration of this event, while in the same year, an earthquake precipitated bell ringing in all the churches to defend the city against after-shocks (395, 383).

The sound of bells, issuing from the heart of the Spanish establishment, was an aural reminder of the twin powers of church and state, reaching out to draw the city's inhabitants under their influence, connecting, defining, and possessing the urban spaces.[4] The responses of the other churches confirmed their obedience to these intertwined authorities, ritually unifying the city in joy, sadness, or—in the case of natural calamities—supplication. Bells were also an efficient means of imparting information: they sent out detailed messages from the center of colonial authority, messages expressed in an extraordinarily complex code. Chapter 11 of the 1780 *Regla consueta del cabildo eclesiástico de la catedral* of the cathedral constitutes a nine-page set of instructions for the ringing of the cathedral bells. The level of detail is astonishing, and it underlines the variety of meanings that were expressed through these sounds, far beyond simply setting the tone for civic events. It becomes clear that the peals of the cathedral bells have every right to be considered as music, for these instructions express minute concern with pitch, timbre, the duration of sounds and silences, tempo, and tone combinations.[5] There were sounds for celebration, sounds for mourning, sounds for the royal family, sounds for members of the church, and sounds for earthquakes, tempests, and other calamities "to remind the faithful to ask for God's mercy." The very detail of these instructions reveals the urge of the church to create and control an auditory system and thereby stamp its authority on the temporal and social structuring of the city (Garrioch 2003).

The associations of these sounds were, in fact, richer still: when eight bells were consecrated in the cathedral towers by Bishop Bernardo de Isa-guirre in 1663 in order to ward off the storms, thunder, and lightning that so frightened the populace, they were named after the Assumption and the Immaculate Conception of the Virgin, San Pedro, Santa Bárbara, Santiago, San Bernardo, Santa Catalina de Sena, and San Pablo (Esquivel y Navia [c.1749] 1980, 2:121). The first four divine intermediaries had all been chosen as patron saints and official protectors of the city or province, while San Bernardo and Santa Catalina were patrons of two important Cuzco institutions (the Jesuit college and the Dominican convent, respectively). The sounds that rang out from the cathedral towers appealed to divine authority through the city's chosen intercessors and were thus intimately connected with the voicing of a collective urban identity for the disparate inhabitants of the city. It is, of course, legitimate to ask to what extent these messages were understood by the general population. Bells encoded complicated signals and made for a powerful tool of communication, but only if the code was widely comprehended. It is worth noting, therefore, that research on bell ringing in provincial Spain and France has revealed that complex messages were both transmitted and received until very recently and that the auditory rhetoric of bells indeed constituted an effective communicative system (Marín 2002, 40–41; Corbin 1998, xi). Many of those who made and rang the bells in colonial Cuzco were Andeans, which may have affected how such signals resonated with the city's inhabitants.[6]

The ringing of bells was associated with extraordinary events but also, conversely, with regularity and normality, stability and harmony. As the principal markers of civic time, these sounds of authority conveyed the inviolability of the established order. That the bishop banned the ringing of bells during the terrible plague of 1720 reveals the unprecedented depth of this calamity: although bells were usually rung to ward off such disasters, on this occasion—the greatest catastrophe to befall Cuzco during the colonial period—they apparently only added to the suffering (Esquivel y Navia [c.1749] 1980, 2:221). Bells also reproduced the hierarchy of the city in aural form: the size of bells and the order in which they rang were significant, and breaches of protocol were taken seriously. On Easter Saturday 1747, the Mercedarians preempted the cathedral and the Jesuits followed suit, a violation of the established order prompting the cathedral to send out members of the chapter to bring the monasteries back into line (385). The quantity of regulations concerning bell ringing illustrates the degree to which sound manifested rights, duties, and social hierarchies. In spite of the occasional disruptions, bells had an unmatched capacity to communicate order and authority from one end of the city to the other. Societies across the early modern world "lived according to communitarian norms, everyone observing broadly the same timetable, which was marked largely by sound" (Garrioch 2003, 22). Music was used to mark the religious hours, the opening and closing of gates, morning and evening signals, and curfews, regulating and contributing to these communal patterns of behavior. Organized sound was "an auditory synchronizer" (Corbin 1998, xi) that imparted a rhythm to the functioning of the urban community and imposed a degree of harmony on the city.

Loud musical instruments, especially drums and trumpets, were also used to convey messages and moods over distance. The first recorded use of music in public announcements by Cuzco's town crier dates from 1570, when the city council received a royal decree concerning the establishment of Inquisition in Peru and "ordered that [the decree] be proclaimed on the eighth of the month [of March] in the squares of this city, with trumpets, shawms, and peals of bells from all the churches" (Esquivel y Navia [c.1749] 1980, 2:222). To judge from the author's account, such musical interruptions were a common feature of city life throughout the colonial period, underlining the importance of the *pregonero* (town crier) in preliterate Spanish America (Kinsbruner 2005, 34). Instructions from the viceroy in 1708 were proclaimed to the sound of war drums "in the usual places" (199), while even a royal decree about interest rates was announced in both plazas with shawms (11). Most striking, perhaps, was the repeated use of loud, dissonant sounds to express public mourning. On numerous occasions, Esquivel y Navia records the use of "discordant trumpets" (*trompetas destempladas*) and drums decked out in black to mark the death of a member of the royal family. In 1645, the death of the queen the previous year was announced in the city's public squares by a town crier "to the sound of drums and discordant trumpets, covered in black cloth" (81). News of the death of Charles II reached Cuzco in 1701; on 10 June, a group of municipal dignitaries went out wearing mourning and announced the news with "two drums, untuned and decked in mourning, [and] a trumpet" (182), while a similarly discordant sound broadcast news of the death of Philip V in 1747 (384). This must have been a distinctive and highly effective means of communicating information that reinforced the association of music with the rituals of death in colonial Cuzco (see chapter 4).

Royal births and nuptials, too, were announced by bells, drums, and trumpets, as were promotions of important churchmen. If these sounds of mass communication marked rites of passage of all kinds, they also heralded more literal arrivals. In common with many parts of the early modern world, Cuzco put on a display of unity in celebration of the entrance of important political or ecclesiastical figures into the city, a prime example being the arrival of Viceroy Toledo in Cuzco in 1571. A later viceroy, fray Diego Morcillo, also the archbishop of La Plata, visited Cuzco in 1719, and the city council named deputies to organize different aspects of the official entry. Some were in charge of street decorations and triumphal arches, others were to adorn balconies and plazas, still others created canopies over the ceremonial route into the city. One, Don Francisco Farfán de los Godos, was to hand over the keys to the city and organize the music (219). It was normal practice for the city council to organize these kinds of events in Latin America (Moore 1954, 202), and while specific evidence of musical provision is largely lacking in Cuzco, the chapter acts of the city council reveal some indirect involvement, appointing officials annually to oversee certain key feasts: those of Corpus Christi and San Sebastián, of Santa Bárbara (the patron saint of the council), and of the Fiesta de la Vera Cruz (the council was *patrón* of the confraternity of the same name). The city council was also involved in organizing and even funding musical-theatrical *comedias* that were put on to commemorate royal events. While the council itself probably employed only a handful of musicians, such as the drummers, trumpeters, and *ministriles* who accompanied important announcements, it played a leading role in organizing civic festivities in the city's central plazas, in which musicians from a range of institutions participated and which were key to producing and projecting a sense of urban identity.

Music and Civic Ceremonies

Shared public spaces such as plazas are central to discussions of urban culture. In the streets and squares of colonial Latin American cities, Lewis Mumford's "urban dialogue" was at its most evident and most dynamic, as different social sectors acted out rituals that reinforced or contested their status and their place in the urban hierarchy (Kinsbruner 2005, 120–26). It was here that civic fiestas brought together disparate urban communities, juxtaposing the various components of the city's society and soundscape in a spirit of collaboration but also of competition as they performed their histories, forged corporate identifications, and came together *as a city*. Cuzco's two adjoining principal squares—the Plaza de Armas and the Plaza del Regocijo—were the stage for many such colonial fiestas, among which the feast of Corpus Christi stood out as the principal annual civic ceremony. Across the Hispanic world, Corpus Christi constituted the epitome of the urban fiesta, in both a physical and a symbolic sense (Ramos López 2005). It crossed the city, its itinerary and stopping points marking out institutional and social hierarchies in space; it was organized and funded primarily by the city council, rather than by religious institutions; and it was a self-represen-tation of the city. In short, Corpus was performed "in, by, and for the city, qua city" (Ramos López 2005, 243).

According to the Spanish geographer Cosme Bueno ([1768] 1951, 95), "Fiestas are celebrated with the utmost solemnity and magnificence, with the procession of Corpus in Cuzco one of the most colorful and famous in all Christendom for the silver carriage, altars in the streets, arches, and the famous, joyful dances, in which the dancers are dressed in beaten silver, as are the others, while the statues of the patron saints of the parishes, which are brought out in the procession, are carried on sumptuous platforms of splendid, devout craftsmanship." Another, more detailed contemporaneous description of these festivities can be found in Don Alonso Carrió de la Vandera's 1773 travelogue, El lazarillo de ciegos caminantes, written under the pseudonym "Concolorcorvo." The author describes the elaborateness of the principal procession—despite the fact that Cuzco was, in his words, "the poorest town in all of Spain and the Indies"—which began with a solemn, sacred, Hispanic section:

> At short intervals are sumptuous altars where the bishop stops and de- posits the sacred monstrance so they can kneel down and worship the Lord, while the priests chant their prayers in which the people join, expressing themselves in their own way, although it is always pious and edifying. So the entire course of the procession is a continuous altar, and up to the end of the first three rows reigns a solemnity and a silence in which only holy praise is heard.

The second part of the procession, "the dances of the Indians who come from all the nearby parishes and provinces," is characterized as altogether more joyful, lavish, and heterodox (Concolorcorvo [1773] 1965, 264–65).

A third late-colonial observer of Cuzco's Corpus ceremonies, Ignacio de Castro ([1795] 1978, 57), concurred that the city's celebrations were un- rivaled in the Americas. These eyewitness descriptions illustrate that the Corpus Christi festival was considered by locals and outsiders alike as em- blematic of any given city (Ramos López 2005), and they bring the visual aspects of the eighteenth-century procession to life. All three emphasize the ornate ephemeral architecture, the splendid costumes of the native dancers, and the participation of the Andean parishes from the city and provinces, carrying the statues of their patron saints on their shoulders. Only that of Carrió de la Vandera, however, makes mention of the sonic aspect, and even he merely alludes briefly to the importance of ecclesiastical chant and si- lence in creating a suitable mood for the "serious" Hispanic part of the procession. Unfortunately, there are virtually no descriptive accounts dating from what might be regarded as Cuzco's artistic golden age, which lasted approximately from the mid-seventeenth century until 1720 and reached its apogee during the tenure of Bishop Manuel de Mollinedo y Angulo (1673– 99), a renowned patron of the arts who showed particular devotion to the Holy Sacrament and consequently to the feast of Corpus Christi. Neverthe- less, there are other sources that permit a partial reconstruction of the sound world of Corpus Christi in mid-colonial Cuzco, in particular the famous series of paintings of the Corpus procession dating from the early part of Mollinedo's era, probably from 1674–80, which provides vital clues about the musical aspects of the festival at this time of cultural florescence.[7]

One of the most prominent images of musicians appears in the canvas depicting the procession of the confraternities of Saint Rose and "La Linda," the local name for the image of the Immaculate Conception that had been adopted as the patron of the bishopric in 1651 (Esquivel y Navia [c.1749] 1980, 2:99–101) (fig. 3). This painting shows up to six Andean musicians playing shawms and a sackbut, accompanying the litter on which the statue of Saint Rose is mounted. This image underlines the contribution to the urban soundscape of confraternities, which have been almost entirely passed over by musicological studies of the region. As will be seen in subsequent chapters, music was required on a regular basis by confraternities based in the cathedral and the monastic and parish churches of the city, and these confraternities regularly employed indigenous musicians for their ceremonies, especially during Corpus Christi. The Cofradía del Santísimo Sacramento of the cathedral employed a similar ensemble—four shawm players and a *bajonero* (dulcian player)—in the mid- to late seventeenth century.[8] This group of Andeans was paid an annual salary of 126 pesos to provide music at the confraternity's weekly Thursday service, on those occasions when the Holy Sacrament was taken to the sick, and during the octave of Corpus Christi.

If this painting provides further evidence of loud instrumental music in the Corpus procession, another suggests the performance of sacred vocal polyphony. A second canvas centers on the Spanish magistrate, *corregidor* General Alonso Pérez de Guzmán, and depicts a triumphal arch and a temporary altar, to the left of which can be seen a harpist and some figures, both adults and children (fig. 4). They are gathered around the harpist, and their facial expressions suggest that they are singing; one adult and one boy appear to be holding sheets of music, implying the performance of polyphony. It seems highly probable that these singers are members of the Seminary of San Antonio Abad, accompanied by the cathedral *seises*, or boy singers. The seminary singers were particularly associated with processions of the Holy Sacrament, of which Corpus Christi was the most important. They are also recorded as singing polyphony on such occasions, and there are a number of villancicos (sacred compositions in the vernacular) in the seminary music archive dedicated to Corpus or to the Holy Sacrament (Quezada Macchiavello 2004, 206–8; see also chapter 2). An account of the Corpus festivities in Lima in 1630 reveals that the cathedral chapel master, Cristóbal

3. Anon., 1674–80, *Confraternities of Saint Rose and La Linda*, Corpus Christi series.

de Belsayaga, was injured by a firework while directing a villancico at an outdoor altar (Sas 1971, 2:41), supporting the contention that such works were performed at temporary altars during Cuzco's Corpus procession.

This series of paintings tells us nothing, however, about "traditional" Andean music making. Here, contemporary chroniclers prove more useful. One of the most distinctive features of the Corpus festivities, as late-eighteenth-century observers noted, was the participation of the Andean parishes, which processed to the city center with statues of their patron saints and participated in the Corpus parade to the accompaniment of music and dances, a practice dating back to the start of the colonial period. Garcilaso de la Vega (1964, 139) records the involvement of Andeans in the Corpus procession in the mid-sixteenth century, "each province singing in its own particular language . . . , to differentiate one ethnic group from another. . . . They carried their drums, flutes, conch shells, and other rustic musical instruments." After the foundation of the eight urban parishes between 1559 and 1572, the incorporation of indigenous dances and music at Corpus was required and regulated by the municipal authorities, as it was in other Latin American cities (e.g., Curcio-Nagy 1994). Indeed, the participation of the indigenous parishes of the city and province was central to the subsequent flourishing of this festival. In 1573 Viceroy Toledo gave instructions that each parish should take part in the principal civic processions of the year and should present two or three dances during the Corpus festival (Urteaga and Romero 1926, 200–201). This official regulation was reaffirmed in 1620, when the city appointed a new *corregidor* and chief justice, Don Nicolás de Mendoza Carvajal, who noted that the standard of the Corpus celebrations had declined and ordered that all the guilds and Andean parishes, both urban and rural, should participate with their "dances and performances" (Esquivel y Navia [c.1749] 1980, 2:41).

Indigenous displays of this kind appear to have become a staple element of important urban festivities. The 1610 *Relación de las fiestas*, a Jesuit account of the celebration in Cuzco of the beatification of Ignatius of Loyola, is particularly illuminating with regard to the ceremonial practices of the Andean parishes and reveals that their performances were not limited to the Corpus procession alone ("Fiestas Incas" 1986; Cahill 2000, 156–61). The eight urban parishes took turns on successive days to parade through the city with fine costumes, ceremonial objects, music, and dances. At the end of the procession, each parish performed *invenciones*; a polyphonic mass with instruments was then celebrated at the Jesuit church and a sermon delivered in Quechua. The first to process was the parish of Belén, which

4. Anon., 1674–80, *Corregidor Pérez*, Corpus Christi series.

was received at the church with peals of bells and music. The parish of Santiago sang a traditional song about a black bird called Curiquenque, adapted in honor of Ignatius: they were apparently inspired by the similarity between the bird's appearance and the habits of the Jesuit friars. The Hospital parish processed with a great clamor of music and dances, and they, too, presented a display of pre-Hispanic origin that had been tailored for the occasion. San Cristóbal contributed a majestic performance with music and dance, while San Blas brought an *invención* that celebrated a great victory achieved by their ancestors; as before, the songs were dedicated instead to the Jesuit founder and were accompanied by drums, trumpets, and other warlike instruments. The ethnic Cañari of Santa Ana performed a mock battle in the plaza to the sound of drums, and San Sebastián, eager to compete with the other parishes, processed with much Inka finery and visual display, impressing witnesses with the diversity of their dances and *invenciones*. Finally, the parish of San Jerónimo, the most distant of the city parishes, reenacted a famous victory over their ethnic rivals, the Chankas; once again, the songs were adapted to pay homage to the Jesuit order.

Andean music and dance traditions thus remained an important part of Cuzco's urban sound world for much of the colonial period, featuring alongside loud European instruments, polyphony, ecclesiastical chant, and the bells of the city's many churches. This same mixture of cultural elements was also a feature of civic ceremonies to mark significant events in the lives of the Spanish royal family or moments of importance in the city's history. The swearing-in of Philip III was celebrated in 1600 with days of festivities organized by the city council, including bullfights and "the inventions and celebrations of the parishes" (Esquivel y Navia [c.1749] 1980, 2:279). The birth of the infanta in 1625 was celebrated in Cuzco the following year in similar style: the news was proclaimed by the town crier, accompanied by peals of bells, and the festivities included three *comedias* and various *invenciones* organized by different urban groups such as the parishes, guilds, and different trades (57). In 1654, the new cathedral was consecrated, and the Holy Sacrament and sacred images were ceremonially transferred from the old church, known as El Triunfo, to the new in a procession involving the cathedral chapter, city council, and clergy through the two main plazas, "adorned with altars, triumphal arches, and many tapestries, with all kinds of dances, just as is the custom on the day of Corpus Christi" (110). Solemn vespers of the Assumption of Our Lady were celebrated later that day, and festivities then continued for more than two weeks with fireworks, masked entertainments, *comedias*, bullfights, and *invenciones* by the trades and guilds.

From this last description, it appears that Corpus Christi served as a kind of festive blueprint for other major ceremonial occasions.

Such accounts reveal that civic fiestas in colonial Cuzco were dynamic, multifaceted, polycultural events in which music played a central organizing role. These festivals featured Spanish and Andean musicians alike, with the latter performing both European-derived and native music, as well as fusions of the two. The description of the Jesuit fiesta of 1610 is particularly evocative: if songs of interethnic conflict under the Inkas were still being used (albeit in adapted form) almost eighty years after the conquest, then the Spaniards were not alone in believing in the power of music to shape colonial society.

PROCESSIONS

Perhaps the ritual that appears most frequently and prominently in Esquivel y Navia's diary of urban ceremony is the procession. Underlining the symbolic significance of urban spaces and impressing this significance on the local population, processions generally followed a sinuous route between city churches; their effects were both social—linking the religious communities dispersed throughout the city—and sacred. In response to an outbreak of typhus in 1585, the cathedral chapter decided to parade the statue of San Sebastián, a guardian against plagues, from the eponymous parish church to the cathedral in a solemn procession (Esquivel y Navia [c.1749] 1980, 1:251). The saint was later displayed in the main square and was witness to a sung mass in his honor in the cathedral. Processing to churches and collecting significant sacred objects constituted a key response to urban crises; by uniting the city behind certain locally significant divine protectors against a common threat, processions and the saints that they honored were intimately linked to the construction of an urban identity. San Sebastián featured prominently in early to mid-colonial ceremonies, while the crucifix of El Señor de los Temblores (the Lord of the Earthquakes) was the focus of later requests for divine intercession and continues to be the object of veneration and pilgrimages today (Locke 2001). An outbreak of plague in 1726 seems to have brought back memories of the terrible epidemic that had killed perhaps half the population of the diocese only six years earlier: El Señor de los Temblores was brought out from its side chapel into the main body of the cathedral for nine days, after which it was taken out in procession along with the two most revered images of the Blessed Virgin—the Immaculate Conception (patron of the bishopric) and Our Lady of Bethlehem—to the convent of Santa Catalina, where they stayed for nine days before returning to the cathedral via the monastery of San Agustín (Esquivel y Navia [c.1749] 1980, 2:239).

The Lord of the Earthquakes was seen as a protector against both plague and drought. Another similarly powerful and flexible symbol in difficult times was the image of Christ housed in the hospital of San Bartolomé. When an earthquake hit the city in 1649, the image of the Immaculate Conception was paraded to the hospital, where the Christ image was brought out (88). After a much larger earthquake the following year, the friars of San Juan de Dios took their image—described in a contemporary account as "the most venerated in Peru" (*Relación del temblor* 1651)—to the main plaza, where it sat alongside that of Nuestra Señora de la Soledad (Our Lady of Solitude), "owned" by La Merced. When there followed a drought a year later, the cathedral chapter responded by processing to San Bartolomé again: the ceremony included litanies, probably sung in the procession, and a sung mass (Esquivel y Navia [c.1749] 1980, 2:99). Although no musical details are recorded, the sung mass may well have been impressive: San Bartolomé saw regular large-scale polyphonic performances in the seventeenth century, and the confraternity which venerated the Christ image, based in the monastery church, was an important patron of music in mid-colonial Cuzco (see chapter 3).

Piecing together fragmentary evidence from Esquivel y Navia's account, from the record of the Corpus paintings, and from documents from Cuzco's archives, and by comparison with other parts of the Iberian world, we may conclude that music played a significant part in these urban rituals. The churches that punctuated the route of a particular procession were often the scene of sung masses, though Esquivel y Navia never elaborates on their musical content. Similarly, he provides no evidence of music during the processions themselves. The Corpus paintings, illustrating the use of shawms and sackbuts in procession and polyphonic singing at a temporary altar in the main plaza, therefore make for an important source of information on music in outdoor spaces, as do the various archival references to the seminarians singing polyphony and plainchant during their regular forays with the Holy Sacrament. Andean musical traditions also played a significant role in processions: according to the Jesuit description of the 1610 fiestas in honor of Ignatius of Loyola ("Fiestas Incas" 1986, 42), the Andean parishes "normally came through the middle of the city with many crosses, standards, dances, [and] music," leaving little doubt as to the richness and variety of the sound world experienced by observers of such urban rituals.

These complex, polycultural ceremonies demand examination in the light of the tensions and inequalities of colonial society. Why were processions so prominent in colonial Cuzco? Why, on the most important occasions, was it necessary that the Andean parishes should participate in these events? And what was the particular significance of music in processions?

As discussed above, the "imagined city" of Hispanic Cuzco was projected onto the Inka center through performance as well as construction. Processions mapped out a colonial vision, organizing and interpreting the urban space, in Rama's words (1996, 27), " 'rendering the city meaningful as an idealized order." It was not enough to build Cuzco as a sacred Hispanic city: architecture is slow to create, quick to dissolve (as earthquakes in 1650 and 1950 showed), and static. Nearly twenty years after their arrival, the Spaniards were still deliberating on the best location for the cathedral. Given the slowness with which the physical city developed, performance proved all the more important as a means of imposing the figurative meaning of the city on its inhabitants. Processions were powerful symbolic tools, ordering the city and its people. They marked out and integrated important religious and political sites, forging dynamic networks out of fixed urban spaces. They also created hierarchies of people (through inclusion or exclusion and placing in the procession) and of place (through emphasizing certain key institutions). Although processions to Andean parishes such as San Sebastián did occur, most civic displays served to reinforce a cognitive map of concentric circles of decreasing status radiating out from a powerful Hispanic center. Processions, like the written descriptions they engendered and other urban texts such as city plans, focused on the physical aspects of the city—above all, the churches of Hispanic institutions—thought to embody the nobility and virtue of the urban community (Kagan with Marías 2000).

Equally, and perhaps most importantly, processions served to discipline their participants. By walking the city streets in patterns preordained by ceremonial rules, city dwellers literally incorporated the lessons of power built into the cityscape. If Renaissance city planners had conceived of harmony in terms of static proportions, the organizers of baroque civic festivals focused on harmonizing the movement of people with the spatial layout (Akkerman 2000). The network of institutions, streets, and squares was brought to life through processions and other ceremonies that sought to impose a dynamic, if temporary, vision of harmony and order on the city's inhabitants: in the words of Italo Calvino (1997, 14), "the city says everything you must think, makes you repeat her discourse." In Cuzco, the Hispanic authorities sought to put Andeans in their place and inculcate ideology on a sensory level by requiring native participation in the most important ceremonies. The carnival festivities organized in 1631 illustrate how the city council created a symbolic performance of both unity and hierarchy in such civic events: "On January 24 the council ordered that the festivities in the week before Carnestolendas [the period just before Lent] should take place in the following form. The first day, the Indians from ten leagues away. The second, the parishes; the third, the guilds of tradesmen; the fourth, the merchants; the fifth, the city with jousting; the sixth, the city and gentlemen with bull-fights" (Esquivel y Navia [c.1749] 1980, 2:62). All social groups were included in the fiesta, but the activities in which they participated were spread over the week and took place in ascending order of importance (as perceived by the colonial elite), graphically reproducing the social hierarchy.

It is worth noting the socio-spatial distinctions that Esquivel y Navia, the archetypal Cuzqueño *letrado*, draws in this last account: not a duality of urban and rural, but a three-way division between city, parishes, and countryside. Here and elsewhere (e.g., 1:279; 2:41, 57) he employs the word *ciudad* in a specific way, to refer not to the *urbs* or physical space of the city (which included six of the eight Andean parishes examined in chapter 4) but to the elite group of Hispanic city councilors who represented the *civitas* (Kagan with Marías 2000). By using the word *city* as shorthand for *city council*, he excludes the Andean parishes and their residents from this socio-spatial category. This is more than a semantic detail. Esquivel y Navia's usage underlines the fundamental colonial division between Spanish citizens and Andean residents; the latter might have shared the *urbs*, but they were barred from the *civitas*, and were therefore not fully part of the city. Similarly, by insisting on the festive performance of difference between the (European) city and the (Andean) parishes, colonial administrators categorized the Andean "suburbs" as extraneous to the *ciudad* in the act of insisting on their inclusion in the fiesta. The marginal status of Andean city dwellers was dramatized in both word and deed.

The colonial fiesta thus united the city while simultaneously differentiating it. Sameness and difference were also enacted within processions: the former through the participation of many sectors of society, the latter through the careful allocation of position within the parade. The colonial hierarchy was therefore reproduced and reinforced through location according to social, religious, political, and ethnic status. Across the Hispanic world, from the mid-sixteenth century onward, the Corpus procession presented a stratified, hierarchical vision of the city in which individuals participated as representatives of social groups or institutions, not as individuals, and thus dramatized the desired social order (Ramos López 2005). In Cuzco, the Hispanic elite, increasingly concerned about the weakening of social distinctions as racial mixing blurred the clear dividing lines of the early colonial period, underlined the differences between and within the two "republics" through the organization of civic ceremonies. The incorporation of indigenous cultural displays provided a means of maintaining the illusion of clear distinctions between social and racial groups, while allowing all the city's inhabitants to share the festive environment and strive for a communal purpose that might override the tensions of colonial society. Corpus Christi in Cuzco was distinctive in that it performed the defeat of the non-Christian Andeans, the "festive opponent whose presence affirmed the triumph" (Dean 1999, 15). Corpus was a reenactment of the subjugation of Andean civilization by the Spaniards, an annual victory parade in which the participation of the defeated Inkas was required in order to reinforce the colonial power structure. Native music and dance were thus essential elements, from a Hispanic perspective, in marking out this "festive opponent." It is striking that although ecclesiastical music performed by Andeans was promoted by the church in native parishes (as discussed in chapters 4 and 5), "traditional" indigenous music was always required by the Hispanic authorities in civic festivities in the city center. Differentiation thus lay at the heart of the colonial fiesta: the contrasts between Hispanic and indigenous music reproduced boundaries and hierarchies in aural form.

Surveillance, too, constituted an important aspect of these public festivities. The colonial fiesta linked the social and the spatial, bringing colonial society into view and ordering it in space. Competition was also fundamental, for the organization of fiestas stimulated the markedly corporative nature of Cuzco society. The Spanish authorities obliged various groups within colonial society—parishes and guilds, in particular—to play an important part in festive occasions, and corporate rivalry was a frequent result. The competition between guilds and parishes certainly stimulated the splendor of the fiestas, but it also had political significance. The report that Viceroy Juan de Mendoza y Luna left to his successor, Francisco de Borja, the Príncipe de Esquilache, in 1615 reveals that colonial governors pursued a policy of controlled divisiveness through the fiesta as a means to preserve their hegemony. In a section on Africans and mestizos, in which he discusses the dangers of allowing the social mixing of races, the viceroy makes explicit the link between subaltern cultural displays, competition, and surveillance:

It is not to be underestimated what would happen if they attempted some sort of general uprising, for they greatly outnumber the Spaniards. . . . The Government is doing something to lessen the risk, and many decrees point to this end: the most important is to bring their gatherings and dances out into the open, so that everything takes place in public places, and to maintain the separation between ethnic groups that they already keep, because only bad will come of the joining together of diverse groups in search of unity. (Beltrán y Rózpide 1921, 169)

Visibility thus made for a key aspect of colonial ritual, for privacy limited the power of the state. As with so many aspects of colonial legislation, the path had been marked out by the great reformer Viceroy Toledo, who included in his 1575 *ordenanzas* the decree that dancing should take place by day, in public, and be authorized by the *corregidor* and the priest (Estenssoro 1992a, 363). This same emphasis on the public performance of ceremonies resurfaced in Cuzco in the mid-eighteenth century: Bishop Pedro Morcillo Rubio y Auñón ordered in 1743 that the Salve should not be sung in oratorios or in private houses (Esquivel y Navia [c.1749] 1980, 2:294), typifying the attitude of late-colonial Spanish authorities to popular religion in the New World (Viqueira Albán 1987).

Andean participation in civic ceremonies was also vital to the formation of a Cuzqueño criollo identity. As tensions between peninsular Spaniards and Peruvian-born criollos increased during the seventeenth century, criollos' self-definition came to depend less on a Spanish-indigenous cultural opposition and more on a peninsular-American distinction.[9] In order to define their difference in relation to peninsular Spaniards, Cuzco's criollos appropriated a mythologized Inka past and a folklorized present. After all, without its glorious imperial past, Cuzco was just another Spanish Andean city, sandwiched between the political power of Lima and the economic might of Potosí. Andeans were encouraged to perform their history in officially controlled festivities in order to present the criollo elite with a glorious mythical past on which to base their vision of the present and with which to underpin their rivalry with the Old World *peninsulares* and with the viceregal capital of Lima.

Indigenous culture and history were thus essential to criollos' sense of prestige: it was their equivalent of classical antiquity, a vital component in the construction and performance of the imagined criollo city. Due to cultural differences and the destructive effects of the Spanish conquest, Inka civilization left few fixed elements that could be incorporated into an in-

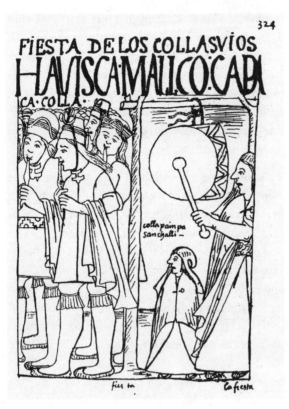

5. Felipe Guaman Poma de Ayala, 1613, folio 324, *Fiesta de los collasuyos.*

vented criollo tradition. Most buildings were razed, though foundations were often left poignantly visible, and there were no sculptures. Nor, indeed, were there works of literature, in a European sense; rather, Inka history (or mythology) was sung and enacted (Betanzos 1996, 166–67). It is for this reason that Andean performative culture was so central to the fiesta and that the authorities required and regulated not just native presence but also participation. Putting indigenous culture on display constituted the prime means of recalling the city's illustrious history and recreating the difference that was essential to the identity of the Cuzqueño criollo elite.

With respect to the regulation of Andean participation in colonial fiestas, it is important to note that inclusivity did not stretch to female musicians, who were not just marginalized but silenced from public music making. Female musicians had played drums before the Spanish conquest while men played wind instruments (fig. 5), and their absence in the colonial period reveals that indigenous music was restricted as it was adapted for civic ceremonies. It should be noted, however, that this was not simply a colonialist phenomenon, for women also disappeared from Corpus processions in sixteenth-century Spain, where the progressive institutionalization of the festival was matched by a parallel masculinization (Ramos López 2005). On the other hand, not all opportunities for public music making were closed to Andean women: as discussed in chapter 3, they participated in performances in convents and *beaterios*, and it was therefore their link with traditions of musical performance, rather than with musical performance per se, that was broken. Music might be an acceptable public activity for native women, but only as long as it evidenced conversion and piety, rather than the persistence of supposed idolatry.

What, then, of European-derived music? Sound was clearly integral to creating a sense of sanctity. The mobility of the sacred has been noted by scholars of early modern Europe: religion focused on moveable holy objects to a greater extent than on the spaces housing them (Muir and Weissman 1989, 94–95). Music may thus be considered as contributing to the "hallowed zone" surrounding the mobile sacred images that lay at the heart of the Catholic religion. Perhaps the most important duty of the city's premier music ensemble, the seminary choir, was to accompany the Holy Sacrament in processions. Spaces were imbued with sacred meaning because of the images that they housed and the activities that they permitted. Rather than serving simply as aural adornment, music formed part of the process of creating sacred places out of urban spaces. In a city that had been the seat of Inka "idolatry" and was constantly besieged by natural calamities—earthquakes, plagues, droughts, storms—the importance of sanctifying, cleansing, and protecting the urban fabric is clear.

Sounds, like processions, may also be viewed through the lens of Spanish efforts to create the colonial city of Cuzco. Bells, town criers, and elaborate music marked out and ordered European conceptions of civic time and space (Muir 1981, 5–6); polyphony, in particular, was characteristically urban music in Spain, and these sounds undoubtedly contributed to imparting an urban character to new American settlements. In Cuzco, sounds and music made sense of the alien space of the Inka ceremonial center, transforming it into a holy Spanish city. European cities grew more organically, and meaning accrued over centuries or millennia; in the New World, however, the Spaniards had to create "instant places," imposing meaning on strange land- or cityscapes. This may explain, in part, the urgency of their musical project: conversion was clearly fundamental, but there was also a haste to bring musicians and music from Europe to stock New World cathedrals and to train up native Americans for cathedral service, a haste born from the urge to create a harmonious and ordered Spanish city of the senses. In his landmark study, José Antonio Maravall (1986) characterized the culture of the baroque as urban, conservative, and controlling. Accordingly, baroque cultural forms might be considered not just as characteristic urban products but also as aesthetic means to shape and structure urban society, and thus as ideally suited to the Spanish project in the New World. Indeed, Rama (1996, 10) argues that "the American continent became the experimental field for the formulation of a new Baroque culture"; in other words, the new imperatives of the New World—above all, the rapid creation of "ideal cities"—led to a fundamental shift from the serenity of the Renaissance to the guiding hand of baroque culture. The Spanish urbanizing mission was a diverse program, in which music was extensively employed alongside other cultural tools: musicians played an integral part in the establishment of order and *policía*, constructing a *ciudad sonora* in parallel with the *ciudad letrada* and adding an aural dimension to the city's symbolic plane.

"Concord and Consonance of Desires and Deeds"

Reading Esquivel y Navia's history of more than two centuries of colonial rule in Cuzco, there are few signs of overt resistance to the reordering of the urban sound world precipitated by the imposition of Spanish hegemony. This is unsurprising, perhaps, in a record by the dean of the cathedral. There are reasons to suggest, however, that a high degree of consensus (or "concord and consonance," to quote Rodrigo Sánchez de Arévalo [c.1454] 1944, 113) may indeed have been achieved in the musical sphere during the mid-colonial period. The Jesuit account of the 1610 fiestas reveals that this religious order promoted certain forms of indigenous cultural expression and implies that these sounds could be turned to political advantage by both the friars and the Andean population: the city parishes used their cultural displays not only to score points against ethnic rivals but also to forge alliances with the Jesuits, a late-arriving order which missed the first wave of colonization but nevertheless became a powerful presence in colonial Cuzco. Instead of presenting a polarized view of domination and resistance, then, mid-colonial society reveals considerable cultural fluidity and flexibility, with Andeans often, to quote Eric Hobsbawm, "working the system to their minimum disadvantage" (quoted in Stavig 1999, 83) rather than rejecting it.

While the adaptation of native musical expressions in honor of the Jesuit founder serves as a perfect example of consensus achieved through flexibility, church music, too, offered particular opportunities for productive cultural boundary crossing and for exploiting the new possibilities afforded by colonial society. It is not for nothing that the "European" profession of church musician was practiced largely by Andeans in Cuzco: embracing Hispanic musical and religious culture opened doors in colonial society. One of the Corpus Christi paintings provides intriguing clues that for elite sectors of Andean society, blurring certain cultural differences—differences that were essential to Hispanic constructions of urban society in the colonial fiesta—may have been a more advantageous strategy than defiant cultural resistance.

The painting of the procession of the indigenous parish of Hospital de los Naturales includes a carriage in which three musicians of Hispanic descent are performing (fig. 6). It is a particularly intriguing image, given that carriages did not appear in processions in Cuzco until 1733, more than fifty years after this painting was completed. Carolyn Dean (1999, 84–85) has argued convincingly that the carriages in this and the other paintings of Andean parishes were copied from a seventeenth-century Spanish festivity book by Juan Bautista Valda, published in Valencia in 1663, which Bishop Mollinedo had probably brought with him to Cuzco in 1673. She concludes: "The five parochial canvases thus make a claim not only on the viewers' memory of Corpus Christi celebrations in which Inka *caciques* paraded in antiquarian costume, but also on their imagination—to a conceivable future in which elaborate Spanish *carros* rumble in procession around Cuzco's double-plaza." It is significant, I would add, that the future participation of this indigenous parish in the Corpus celebrations is envisioned, at least in part, through markedly Hispanic cultural symbols.

In considering the cultural significance of this curious artwork, it is important to note that most of the paintings in the Corpus series were probably sponsored by the individuals or groups who are their subjects. Not only were there a range of patrons but also a number of artists were responsible for their production (Dean 1999, 77). Artists in mid-colonial Cuzco, like musicians, generally belonged to the upper echelons of indigenous society, and some of their sponsors are also likely to have been well-born Andeans. The Corpus series therefore includes, in all probability, the perspectives of various members of the native elite on this central religious festival, realized on canvas by other members of their social group. Certain paintings may be seen as part of the festive discourse of these individuals,

6. Anon., 1674–80, *Hospital de los Naturales Parish*, Corpus Christi series.

along with the music, dance, and costumes that they sponsored, and as an attempt to impress on observers their key role in colonial ceremonies.

The imagined future scene depicted in the Hospital canvas, with its symbol of Hispanic modernity—a Spanish carriage complete with musicians of Hispanic appearance—occupying a prominent position, should thus be considered as constructing and projecting a particular self-image and vision of colonial culture on the part of the painting's sponsors, presumably elite members of the indigenous parish of Hospital de los Naturales. How might we interpret this vision of native participation in the Corpus Christi procession? It bears little relation to the eyewitness reports and official regulations composed by members of the Hispanic elite, which focused on the more "exotic" aspects of native cultural displays, in particular the traditional music, dances, and costumed performances. Yet the indigenous creators of this painting elided the Andean displays that they would presumably have sponsored and preferred to foreground a more Hispanic, "modern"—or rather, futuristic—vision of colonial Andean culture, identifying the depicted native subjects with European music.

In this canvas, like the confraternity painting discussed above, we see musicians playing European instruments; in neither case is musical culture imagined in terms of traditional native display. The reason may be sought in Dean's argument that the role assigned to the indigenous population by the Hispanic elite in the Corpus festivities was primarily to perform their indigeneity and thereby act out the role of the defeated Other in the triumph of Christianity over native religion. As such, the performance of native music and dances in Corpus Christi not only evidenced successful evangelization but also reproduced and legitimized the unequal power relations of colonial society. Native music was therefore inextricably linked to subordination. These paintings, I suggest, propose an Andean alternative to the Hispanic vision, in which religious conversion is not linked with submission: they envisage conformity to expectations of Christian devotion, but also a refusal to perform difference through a display of exoticized music. To show evidence of successful conversion and devotion—for example, by sponsoring religious paintings or musical performance—was undoubtedly useful to the native elite in their dealings with colonial authorities, whereas to perpetuate unequal power relations through externalizing difference was less desirable. These images thus provide a window onto subtle attempts by the indigenous elite to resist the orchestration of the colonial authorities, to step beyond a narrow Spanish definition of indigenous culture that threat-

7. Anon., 1674–80, *Hospital de los Naturales Parish*, detail of the musicians, Corpus Christi series.

ened containment within a folklorized past, and to construct more fluid cultural identities.

The emphasis placed by these paintings on the Hispanic elements of colonial Andean culture, both present and future, reveals a desire for equality through cultural assimilation, and a rejection of the subordinate status associated with cultural difference that lay at the heart of the Spanish colonial vision of Corpus in Cuzco. The paintings assert the indispensability of Andean musicians to the festival's success; rather than signifying otherness, however, they feature as a key element, even an equal partner, in the realization of the supposedly Hispanic sound world and the ritual performances of Hispanic confraternities. The familiarity with European music expressed in these works also draws attention to the cultural flexibility and high social status of their subjects. The prestige of the indigenous elite rested in part on its ability to draw on the symbolic resources of both European and indigenous cultures. While the maintenance of certain traditional trappings of power was key to the preservation of authority within indigenous society, displaying selected signs of acculturation was equally important to success in the Hispanic sphere. Hispanicization could be a positive choice, for "Europeanized clothing and objects spoke to the privileged interculturality of native nobles and other wealthy Andeans" (Dean 1999, 169), allowing such elite individuals to emphasize their distance from commoners, as well as their proximity to the colonists.

European music was arguably one such sign of distinction among the native elite. As will be seen in subsequent chapters, it formed part of the educational program in the Jesuit Colegio de San Borja, the school for the sons of native nobles, and the social status of leading indigenous parish musicians was often high. An identification with European religious music —either professionally, as a sponsor of musical activities, or even through visual images in paintings such as the Corpus series—may have been another such display of "privileged interculturality" on the part of aspirational native elites who sought to leave behind certain elements of their stigmatized "Indian" past, including, perhaps, native music, and assimilate into the upper strata of colonial society (Stern 1993, 170). Indeed, the implication of these paintings is that in the context of Corpus Christi in mid-colonial Cuzco, difference was performed visually, through ceremonial dress and headwear, whereas assimilation was performed musically.

This impression is strengthened by Esquivel y Navia's description of the celebrations in 1747 for the swearing in of King Ferdinand VI. On Sunday, 24 September, there was a masked parade of the eight Andean parishes, which finished with a squadron of more than twenty Inkas dressed in beautiful costumes and wearing the *mascapaycha* (headdress), followed by "a carriage in which there were musicians with harps, guitars, violins and bandolas, who sang various songs to the accompaniment of the instruments in front of the house of the [City] Council" (Esquivel y Navia [c.1749] 1980, 2:405). While the Andeans maintained their Inka dress as a symbol of distinction, their display was accompanied by Hispanic musical instruments. The fact that the Hospital parish's painted vision of the future was so closely realized in this civic event some seventy years later suggests that the familiarity with European music displayed in this canvas was indeed aspirational, and more than merely incidental.

I would argue, then, that European music features in these paintings as a symbol of prestige, religious devotion, modernity, and cultural flexibility, a symbolic element utilized by the native elite in the construction of collective identities that went beyond the category of *indio* created by the Spanish colonizers. Whether traditional music was seen as backward by such sectors of society is hard to determine, but its elision by European-derived music in these images suggests that the latter was viewed positively by the native elite as an attribute of a forward-looking, culturally mobile identity. By comparing these paintings with descriptions of Hispanic observers, we may glimpse the social and political maneuvers played out through colonial cultural performance and perceive the role of music in the projection of competing views of colonial society by different sectors of the urban population. It may be surprising at first that the Hispanic reports emphasize traditional native display while the Andean paintings downplay musical difference, yet if native elites "valued their Hispanism highly" (Stern 1993, 167), while Spaniards sought to accentuate social distinctions, then such a state of affairs is understandable.

For much of the colonial period there was thus a relatively high degree of consensus over the value of music making, and both European and Andean traditions were seen to have their uses by those outside their ethnic group of origin. Colonial historians such as James Lockhart (1992) have emphasized the ways in which colonial society developed under the influence of preexisting indigenous patterns and structures, relying on the "complementarity" of Spanish and native cultures (Stavig 1999, xvi). The Inka legacy of temples, festivals, processions, and a religious calendar—in short, the rich ceremonial life of the pre-Hispanic Andes—had numerous parallels with Catholicism, allowing a common understanding that civic and religious rituals played an important role in society. When Cuzco as a whole was threatened by natural disasters such as the 1650 earthquake or the 1720 plague, all sectors of society contributed to the ceremonial pleas for mercy, and music formed part of attempts to pull together for a genuinely common aim. *Misas rogativas* (supplicatory masses) were celebrated in all churches, while processions brought the urban population together in the streets. Certain divine intercessors and sacred icons, such as the Lord of the Earthquakes or the Christ image at San Bartolomé, united the population in defense or celebration of the city, smoothing ethnic differences and consolidating urban identity.

European-derived music was widely accepted by the native population: indeed, the musical life of the city, and even more that of the surrounding provinces, depended on the willing adoption of the European tradition by Andeans. European music provided Andeans with a sanctioned ceremonial outlet, and the music profession offered them a range of attractions, as I will discuss in subsequent chapters. Indications from Mexico and Peru dating from the sixteenth century suggest that if the Spaniards faced a problem with numbers of church musicians, it was superfluity rather than lack. The seventeenth century, too, saw large numbers of Andeans, including many minor nobles, participating in the music profession in and around Cuzco; it was apparently an attractive career path, and European music seems to have had considerable cachet. Many Andean leaders showed a striking enthusiasm for all things Hispanic and for the Christian faith, and the sounds of the church neatly encapsulated and exteriorized these two prominent facets of the aspirations of Andean elites. The century from 1650 to 1750, after the early seventeenth-century campaigns to extirpate idolatry had subsided, seems to have been a period of relative stability in terms of musical relations between the two republics, one marked by nuanced and fruitful cultural negotiations rather than the simple realization of, or resistance to, colonialist aims.

"Division and Internal Discord among the Citizens"

Consensus over the value of music did not, of course, equate to a broader social consensus. On many occasions, city residents identified primarily with the confraternities, parishes, and guilds that constituted the organizational units of public festivities, and music was harnessed to competition between these social groups. In Cuzco, parish- and confraternity-based ceremonies undoubtedly emerged as more important social unifiers than citywide rituals, and corporate loyalties were often stronger than civic bonds.[10] Beyond their communal purpose, fiestas in colonial Cuzco were designed to emphasize not only group solidarity but also cultural differences between the Andean and Spanish republics. Civic rituals were both "a venue for harmonizing contradictions" and "a battleground for social status" (Cahill 2000, 135), an opportunity to negotiate some sort of unity, but also a source of social differentiation and "division and internal discord among the citizens" (Sánchez de Arévalo [c.1454] 1944, 111).

The colonial elite did not demand that the city sing with one voice; instead, it sought polyphony, or, as Bernardo Illari (2001) has christened it, "polychoral culture." To push the analogy further, the colonial fiesta could even be conceptualized as heterophony: simultaneous variations on a common religious or political theme. This lent ceremonies a cultural richness, but also a polysemic character that opened the door to dissonant actions and interpretations. Civic ceremonies and processions did not always reproduce the social order in the way that the colonial authorities desired; indeed, Esquivel y Navia's history of the city is strewn with reports of disputes over precedence, almost entirely within the ranks of the Spanish population. The huge importance of perceptions of honor in colonial Cuzco is dramatically illustrated by the endless squabbles over primacy between the city and cathedral councils, the regular and secular clergy, and between Peruvian-born criollos and Iberian *peninsulares*. Clashes occurred frequently and sometimes turned violent: groups often walked out of, or refused to take part in, urban ceremonies because they were unhappy with the order of preference. If fiestas were richly symbolic affairs, vitally important to the reproduction of colonial order, they were also shot through with the tensions inherent in a factionalist society. They were certainly far more than entertainment.

Disputes and discordant voices were thus never far away. For all that music and dance are often characterized as sources of social harmony, rather than allowing for the temporary bridging of divides among competing groups, they may actually bring these groups together "into an intense and potentially explosive proximity" (Stokes 1994, 10). Corporations such as guilds, trades, and confraternities may have created bonds within colonial society, sometimes even across race, class, and gender lines (Hoberman 1986, 321), yet their juxtaposition in civic ceremonies meant that competition was a distinguishing feature of colonial life, with conflict among rival groups a constant possibility. Underlying tensions that simmered for years or decades might boil over at times of heightened intensity, such as during fiestas, and might be exacerbated by the sonic aspects of urban rituals.

A bitter rivalry, nominally focusing on the granting of university status but also fueled by class divisions, developed between the Jesuit Colegio de San Bernardo and the Seminary of San Antonio Abad and ran for most of the seventeenth and eighteenth centuries. It appears that neither side missed an opportunity for a noisy challenge to its rival. The Colegio de San Bernardo was given the title of *colegio real* (royal college) in 1620, and early the following year it announced the news in public places with shawms and drums. Indeed, in granting this title, Viceroy Don Francisco de Borja declared that on the feast day of San Bernardo and other important days in the calendar, college members had the right to go out into the streets and plazas of the city on horseback, accompanied by trumpets, shawms, and drums, without their celebrations being impeded by the city authorities or any other residents (Esquivel y Navia [c.1749] 1980, 2:38–39). The fact that this right was defended from the outset strongly implies the recognition that loud, colorful displays by particular urban groups had the capacity to upset members of rival communities. The dividing line between music/order and noise/disorder was therefore very thin. In 1696, when San Antonio Abad was finally granted the right to award university degrees, after decades of fierce opposition from the Jesuits, the seminary students celebrated with peals of bells and a procession around the main streets and plazas with trumpets and drums (163). A clearer example of musical revenge is hard to imagine. This behavior continued into the following century, as a report from 1709 details: a fight broke out between members of the two colleges after the seminarians repeatedly paraded past the gates of the Jesuit institution (200). Religious rivalries also found their way into musical texts and performances: Samuel

Claro (1969a, 27) found evidence that the same argument was pursued in a musical work in Cuzco—a festive duo for sopranos with the text, "Vitor, vitor, q.e ganamos a la Compañía" (Hurrah, hurrah, for we defeated the Company [of Jesus])—while bitter theological disputes between the Jesuits and Dominicans over the nature of human liberty spilled over into popular songs, dances, and the theater in colonial Lima (Martín 1968, 66).

Andean participants, meanwhile, undoubtedly read civic ceremonies in very different ways to the Hispanic elite. Just as fiestas came increasingly to articulate differences between the Hispanic sectors of society, there is also evidence that these occasions provided opportunities for the expression of rivalries between Andean communities (Dean 1993). The Inkas were an ethnic group that, like the Spanish, had been a colonial power: they had subjugated and ruled other ethnic populations, and antagonisms dating back to this period continued to surface in Spanish colonial fiestas. The often fierce rivalry between Inka and non-Inka communities was expressed in the cultural competition between the city's Andean parishes during fiestas (Dean 1999, 92–93, 183). Esquivel y Navia ([c.1749] 1980, 2:173) describes an outbreak of alcohol-fueled violence among Andean parish groups during the Corpus procession of 1700, a dispute that centered on the dancers. Music and dance were media through which competition was commonly expressed in Andean society (Spalding 1984, 57–59): the indigenous songs and dances performed in colonial fiestas, while encouraged by the Spaniards to mark out difference and subordination, might thus provide opportunities for public shows of strength that acted out or harked back to pre-Hispanic rivalries. The 1610 Jesuit fiestas were seized by the parishioners of San Blas and San Jerónimo as a chance to reenact famous victories over ethnic rivals, while the Cañari of Santa Ana parish, subjugated under the Inkas, took the opportunity for a militaristic display of strength. The Spanish were well aware of such internal divisions among the Andean population, having exploited them during the conquest, and the manipulation of ethnic tensions and distinct cultural expressions as part of a divide-and-rule strategy was not alien to the thinking of colonial governors such as the viceroy Juan de Mendoza y Luna.

Enough evidence of colonial disputes survives to confirm that conflicting conceptions of urban society coexisted within Cuzco: as the city plans illustrate, there was not one but many "imagined cities." For all that colonial authorities may have attempted to orchestrate the behavior of urban groups and the meanings of civic ceremonies, the 1610 Jesuit fiestas or the outbreak of violence in the 1700 Corpus procession suggest that other, conflicting views continued to be held and defended. Nevertheless, for much of the colonial period these contrasting and overlapping perspectives were held together in a more or less uneasy balance: while dissonances surfaced on occasion, the polychoral or heterophonic ordering of the colonial fiesta, based on inclusiveness and the externalization of difference, did not alter radically. In reading Esquivel y Navia's history of Cuzco it is striking that during the period up to 1750, cultural disharmony and competition, or at least that which was recorded, seem to have been concentrated on internal disputes within the Hispanic and Andean republics—between criollos and *peninsulares*, between Inkas and non-Inkas—rather than across these macro-ethnic lines. Around the middle of the eighteenth century, however, a different picture starts to emerge: just as with the church's campaigns to extirpate idolatry a century and a half earlier, a sea change in attitudes saw the Spaniards reacting against the fruits of their own policies and imposing an increasingly monophonic conception of colonial culture.

The second half of the eighteenth century saw greater emphasis on social and religious orthodoxy and a rising official disapproval of popular religious observances throughout the Spanish empire. Decrees and prohibitions began emanating from Spain around mid-century in an attempt to halt a perceived decline in moral standards and public behavior (Viqueira Albán 1987). Religious fiestas came under the scrutiny of new, rationalistic Enlightenment attitudes, and their popular elements were increasingly seen as heterodox, reeking of superstition and licentiousness. The Bourbon reforms began to bite in earnest in the Americas during the reign of Charles III (1759–88), a period commonly referred to as a "second conquest" by historians, but the spirit of the age can be detected slightly earlier in the growing official condemnation of secular influences on church music. In Peru, this sentiment was articulated by the reformist archbishop of Lima, Pedro Antonio de Barroeta y Ángel, who in a 1754 edict banned minuets, arias, and "secular songs" from church services, and who warned his *maestro de capilla*, Roque Ceruti, to ensure that church music was "grave, serious, and suitable to the holiness of the place" and "entirely devoid of the flattering ornamentation of theatrical music" (Sas 1971, 1:41–45; Estenssoro 1989, 1992b). While his efforts were not at first widely supported, and therefore had to be repeated over the subsequent decades, they had clearly influenced the bishop and chapter of Cuzco Cathedral by the time that the latter produced their *Regla consueta* in 1780, which railed against the introduction of theatrical and secular styles into church music and warned the *maestro de capilla* against following this path (see chapter 2).

The *Regla consueta* was far from the first attempt to reform church music in Cuzco. The king had banned the staging of religious *comedias* at the Seminary of San Antonio Abad a decade earlier, after a lengthy period of ambivalence about the genre (Claro 1969a, 27), illustrating that the reformers were focused initially on Hispanic, urban cultural expressions. However, attention also turned outward from the central Hispanic churches to the urban periphery and surrounding provinces around this time. An episcopal decree to reduce the number of local fiestas in the bishopric of Cuzco was issued in 1777, though while urban parish music making did decline from this time onward, there is little evidence that this policy succeeded in rural areas, where the combined effects of popular religious fervor, insufficient colonial authority, and the importance of fiestas as a source of income for parish priests conspired against the reformers' efforts (Cahill 1986, 49).

The year that the cathedral produced its *Regla consueta*, 1780, is primarily remembered as the moment at which official nervousness in Peru turned to outright fear with the eruption of the Túpac Amaru rebellion, the most serious outbreak of resistance to Spanish rule in the Andes. This revolt, although eventually suppressed, sent serious shock waves through the upper levels of the colonial hierarchy. Indigenous cultural manifestations, once regarded by the colonial government as politically useful in their potential for stimulating ethnic divisions, were now suddenly seen as containing the seeds of dissent, and there was a backlash against the display of Andean culture in public celebrations. The sentence pronounced against the rebel leader Túpac Amaru and his associates in Cuzco by the *visitador* (inspector) Don José Antonio de Areche on 20 May 1781 includes the instruction to ban indigenous instruments and *comedias* reenacting Inka history.[11] Attention soon turned back to Andean fiestas in general. In 1784, Don José Gallegos, *visitador general* of the Cuzco diocese, banned the scissors dance, threatening those who participated with hard labor in perpetuity in a textile mill and musicians who accompanied the dance with six months in prison (Cahill 1986, 50). Crown officials banned ceremonial dancing throughout the *real audiencia* (royal audiency) of Cuzco in 1793 (Espinavete López 1795, 152), while a viceregal edict issued the following year listed the penalties for those who sang "indecent, mocking, or rude songs," and banned dancing and musical instruments from *chicherías* (establishments where *chicha* [maize beer] was sold) (Estenssoro 1990, 589).

While the success of such policies is hard to judge, it seems that they were more effective in the city than in the countryside. Ignacio de Castro's

([1795] 1978, 57) account of the celebrations marking the foundation of the Audiency of Cuzco in 1788 makes only the briefest mention of the Andean dances and *invenciones* so characteristic of earlier fiestas, even though the event took place five years before the 1793 ban. Debates about indigenous culture had raged at earlier periods, above all in the early seventeenth century, but the post-1780 rebellion period marked the first time that concerted moves were made to limit Andean dancing in the city. Indigenous cultural expressions had continued to form part of civic ceremonies during the earlier period of the extirpation of idolatry, even if cultural differences were blurred somewhat as ethnic groups imitated each other's dances (see chapter 4). The account of the Jesuit 1610 fiestas, the council records of the native parish of Hospital de los Naturales, and the insistence of the city's *corregidor* in 1620 that the native parishes contribute "dances and performances" to the Corpus festivities all reveal the continued presence of native music and dancing in the second decade of the seventeenth century, generally perceived as a high point of extirpatory fervor. It appears that the urge to perform social distinctions and to encourage ethnic rivalries overcame the suspicion of native culture within the urban context. The late-colonial political climate, however, led to marked changes in urban culture. Castro ([1795] 1978, 151) innocently remarks that military music was "all the rage" in Cuzco in the 1780s and 1790s, a time when, as Kathryn Burns (1999, 171) notes, the Túpac Amaru campaign and its aftermath had converted the city into "an armed camp, full of regular troops, militiamen, weapons, and ammunition." The effect of stricter attitudes toward music in the cathedral are also evident in Castro's description of the music performed during the thanksgiving mass to celebrate the entry of the royal seal of the *audiencia* in 1788: despite the joyousness of the occasion, "the music was of the serious and respectable kind that is used in that magnificent church, directed and performed by the students of the Seminary of San Antonio" ([1795] 1978, 88). This commentary, like the various prohibitions in the cathedral's *Regla consueta*, suggests that the lively, sometimes comical villancico repertoire with strong secular leanings found in the seminary archive was no longer heard in the cathedral by this time.

This growing Spanish fear of popular culture reflected not just class and ethnic but also gender prejudices. The *Regla consueta* twice links the frowned upon theatrical influences with femininity, warning the chapel master against "bringing worldly songs into the choir, with their trilling of effeminate voices," while the official who complained in 1819 about the proliferation of dances in religious fiestas—a custom that clearly had not been eradicated, despite earlier decrees—began his argument with the words: "As persons of both sexes are mixed together in these dances, or at least, the dancers are followed by a bunch of women, many of them half-naked, and all of them burdened with an excess of *aguardiente* [eau-de-vie] and *chicha*, I hardly need to refer to the impurities that must be committed in such gatherings."[12] The defensiveness of the male Hispanic elite in the closing years of the colonial period could hardly be clearer. To judge from such descriptions, the crackdown on indigenous cultural forms had given impetus to a hybridization of Spanish and Andean dances and music that arguably challenged the status quo more than the traditional forms they replaced. The older dances might be regarded as relatively conservative and unchallenging, their point of reference fixed in a defeated past. Popular dances of the late eighteenth century were different; their anti-authoritarianism spoke of a new social order, of class upheaval from below. As Andeans absorbed these dances into their culture, they also took in their codes and messages: the mixing of men and women, sometimes with the switching of gender roles and costumes, the licentious movements, the seditious song lyrics, all signs of the popular "countertheater" (E. P. Thompson) that blossomed across the Spanish empire in the late colonial period.

Spanish cultural policy, however, was becoming ever more restrictive under the Bourbon reforms, and so, as the 1819 report reveals, elite prescriptions and popular culture only grew further apart. The inclusiveness that for much of the colonial period had characterized public festivities and, on a smaller scale, musical style gave way to a nervous exclusiveness and even repression. Official regulations in the late eighteenth century increasingly undermined the communal aspect of religious fiestas by segregating or removing undesirable elements. The integrated civic fiestas of the seventeenth century, during which viceroys and rural Andeans, bishops and African slaves might all participate in the same events, ceded to increasing supervision and exclusion. The elements of these events most appreciated by the ordinary public—Andean costumes, dances, instruments, theatrical performances, comic villancicos—were suppressed or restricted. Similar processes occurred in relation to musical style, with attempts to banish the "theatrical" features from sacred music. The effect of these repressive measures in some contexts was the separation of popular and elite culture, rather than the suppression of the former; in Lima, at any rate, the theater flourished as it took over the elements that had been eliminated from religious celebrations (Estenssoro 1989, 96–97). In Cuzco, Spanish efforts to purge the heterophony of urban musical culture through the reimposition

of a narrowed conception of harmony—a musical "second conquest"—
seem to have brought more serious consequences as the church had been
the main provider of public entertainment (including staged musical-theatrical performances) throughout the colonial period, but the continued vitality of popular religious celebrations in rural parishes speaks of the limited effectiveness of these endeavors outside the city.

Secular and Domestic Music

The histories of Cuzco's musical life that can be recovered today generally
revolve around ecclesiastical institutions and the musicians they employed.
The church was the only musical patron of note in Cuzco, for there was no
court; theatrical performances were put on most frequently by ecclesiastical
institutions such as the seminary and the convent of Santa Catalina, and no
evidence has emerged of private music ensembles sponsored by wealthy
individuals. Historians have observed a preponderance of churchmen
among the middle and upper sectors of Cuzco society, and a corresponding
dearth of merchants (Brisseau Loaiza 1981, 156; Gibbs 1979), factors that
undoubtedly affected the patronage of music. However, the surviving records also undoubtedly reflect the general exclusion of nonhegemonic musical styles and disenfranchised historical actors from the archives (Carter
2002, 17). For all that this is fundamentally a history of church music and
musicians, then, it is important to highlight the limited evidence of secular
and domestic music making in Cuzco in order to counter the marginalization of such activities in archival records and historical accounts.

There is evidence of widespread private ownership of stringed instruments such as guitars, harps, and vihuelas, which are found frequently in
the wills of Spaniards and Andeans, men and women. The priest of the
parish of Belén, Don Luís de Pedroca y Bustamente, owned a vihuela, while
the Andean Doña Catalina Quispe Sisa Uscamayta left a harp and a guitar in
her will.[13] Instruments were sometimes included in women's dowries:
Doña Luisa Carrasco included a harp worth fifty pesos in her dowry to
Tomás Pabón.[14] Domestic performance did not necessarily imply a secular
orientation: an inventory of the house of Doña Antonia de Arbiza includes
the contents of an oratory, where a harp was found.[15] Although a number of
houses in the city had oratories (Viñuales 2004, 39–40), private worship was
not always well regarded by ecclesiastical authorities. The city's bishop
issued a decree in 1743 banning the singing of the Salve in oratories and
private houses (Esquivel y Navia [c.1749] 1980, 2:293), suggesting that do-

mestic religious music making was in fact commonplace. This prohibition reflected the preoccupation of mid-eighteenth-century ecclesiastical authorities with the separation of sacred and secular culture, for private houses were also the settings for somewhat earthier musical gatherings. The records of a court case dating from 1741 relate how a dance organized in the house of one María Mercedes, known as "The Blonde," turned into a brawl among the participants after a disagreement on the dance floor led a musician to strike one of the dancers with his guitar.[16]

Secular music making was a feature of both public and private spaces, indoors and outdoors. One place where music might have been heard is the *pulpería*, a cross between a general store and a bar. An inventory of the contents of the *pulpería* of Andrea Portilla, drawn up after her death, included a bandurria and two old guitars.[17] Open-air public spaces were also the scene of many kinds of music and impromptu performance. There is evidence that some prominent individuals, both Spanish and Andean, were accompanied by personal musicians. In addition to the Spaniard Joseph García Catalán, who hired an Andean named Juan Bautista from the village of Chinchero to play the trumpet wherever his master went, there is also a late-eighteenth-century illustration of the area around San Cristóbal and Sacsayhuaman in which a noble Andean couple can be seen taking a stroll, accompanied by servants with a parasol and musical instruments.[18]

In colonial records, secular music making is often portrayed as morally dubious. One of Felipe Guaman Poma de Ayala's ([1615] 1980, 802) drawings shows an *indio criollo* (creolized Indian), included as an example of the Andean *yanaconas* who worked as servants in Spanish institutions, whose adoption of Hispanic cultural traits is illustrated by his strumming on a guitar (fig. 8). The author was not sympathetic to such acculturated Andeans or their musical activities, accusing them of "doing nothing but drinking and idling, playing and singing."[19] In 1737, Don Gregorio Maita, a *maestro organista*, began legal proceedings against his wife, alleging adultery. According to a witness, Maita's wife and her lover had been causing a scandal by performing around the town on public holidays, playing the harp and the guitar.[20] Frescoes dating from the end of the eighteenth century in the convent of Santa Catalina include a pastoral scene of a group of musicians playing the harp, guitar, recorder, and violin, surrounding a woman they are either wooing or accompanying as she sings (fig. 9). Another fresco shows a gentleman with a guitar in one hand and a drink in the other. The depiction of these musical scenes has a particular purpose here: the mural as a whole concerns the theme of penitence as a route to salvation, and the

8. Felipe Guaman Poma de Ayala, 1613, folio 324, *Criollos y criollas indios.*

musicians are symbolic of the world and its temptations (Sebastián López, Mesa, and Gisbert 1985–86, 2:555–56). Angelic musicians appear on different arches, their physical separation speaking eloquently of the polarization of sacred and secular in official late-eighteenth-century attitudes to music. Secular music, which the church was taking great pains to excise from its institutions by this time, is represented not as a harmless diversion but as embodying the dangerous lure of worldly pleasures.

Those of a religious calling were not, however, immune to such temptations, either musical or corporeal, judging from an inspection made by the bishop to the parish church of Hospital de los Naturales in 1751. Witnesses were questioned about whether priests "have women in their houses or elsewhere, if they go to dances or fandangos, and if they use secular dress or prohibited weapons."[21] This was no idle question, according to Jorge Juan

9. Tadeo Escalante (?), c.1800, fresco in the convent of Santa Catalina.

and Antonio de Ulloa ([1749] 1978, 285–86), two Spanish scientists who spent eleven years from 1735 to 1746 in the *audiencias* of Lima and Quito, recording many observations of social life and customs in the Andes:

> Fandangos or dances are normally sponsored by members of an order, or to state it more properly, those nominally called friars. The regular clergy bear the cost, participate themselves, and with their concubines hold these functions in their own homes. The fact that these fandangos are held in a friar's house is sufficient to prevent civil officials from daring to violate its sanctuary. Although clerical sponsors of these dances masquerade in laymen's clothing, they are so well known that they cannot go unrecognized.

The predilection of priests for secular musical entertainments dates back at least to the late sixteenth century, to judge from the prohibition which formed part of Bishop Antonio de la Raya's *Constituciones sinodales* of 1601, in which priests were banned from carrying guitars or other musical instruments at night, and from playing or dancing at public gatherings (Lassegue-Moleres 1987, 62). Another prohibition from the same set of constitutions threatened priests with a fine of eight pesos and two days in prison if they attended nonreligious *comedias* (53). However, even the highest reaches of the ecclesiastical hierarchy, responsible for such restrictions on the enjoyment of secular music, were susceptible to its attractions: the dean of the cathedral invited the bishop and prebends to his country residence in 1745, where he put on such a rich spread of food, drink, and music that none of the gathered dignitaries made it back to the cathedral for the evening services, which had to be directed by the chaplains (Esquivel y Navia [c.1749] 1980, 2:323).

The early ecclesiastical prohibitions serve as a reminder that while most documentary records focus on daytime activities, Cuzco's music history also encompasses the hours of darkness. Some church services took place at night or early in the morning—midnight mass in the cathedral might finish as late as 4:30 a.m. (318)—and nighttime vigils were common. Popular music and dances often occurred at night (Illari 2001, 378–79), though they are generally silenced in colonial records, dismissed as unruly and disordered by colonial elites and thus beneath mention. When nighttime music making does surface, it is usually only to be prohibited or criticized, or for a participant to be castigated. Castro ([1795] 1978, 57) waxes lyrical about the official daytime Corpus Christi festivities, which he describes as the best in the Americas, but he was clearly disturbed by the more carnivalistic aspects of the unofficial fiesta and was especially critical of the eve of the main event, contrasting "such a holy day" with "a night of utter licentiousness."

The popularity of music and dancing—whether by day or by night—provided opportunities for teachers, instrument makers, and merchants. Teaching contracts are often ambiguous, as they do not usually specify the intentions of the pupil. Some, however, do give indications as to the ends pursued—principally, a dowry reduction for girls planning to enter a convent—while others suggest study for purely personal purposes. At least some of the many owners of instruments must have sought instruction for no other reason than for their own amusement. Doña Juana Francisca de Olarte hired an Andean from San Sebastián named Diego Quispe Tito to teach her the harp for six months; since she was married, this could not have been a strategy for gaining entry into a convent.[22] In a contract dating from 1634, an Andean *maestro de enseñar arpa* (master harp teacher) named Felipe Guari Tito was hired by a local merchant for five pesos a month to provide two daily harp lessons to his sister-in-law, Tomasina de Perales, so that she might learn to play and tune the instrument within a year.[23] Such a level of commitment on the part of both teacher and pupil is remarkable, perhaps suggesting more than an amateur interest.

The prevalence of the guitar in the home, at dances, in open-air performances, and even in church implies a flourishing trade in instruments.[24] The profession of guitar maker seems to have been well established, and references to *maestros guitarreros*, generally Andeans, appear repeatedly in Cuzco's archives. There was a guild of guitar makers, and there is further evidence of professional solidarity in the form of notarized debt guarantees.[25] As with other trades, masters took on apprentices: in 1754 the *maestro guitarrero* Don Joseph Otalora took on an apprentice named Joseph Guaypar for a period of two years. Otalora undertook to house and clothe his young charge and agreed to be paid in kind through the work that Guaypar would carry out during his apprenticeship.[26] Although the trade of guitar maker generally entailed a lower social status than the profession of *maestro cantor* (master singer), in at least one case a *maestro guitarrero* was also *principal*, or deputy leader, of his parish.[27]

There is evidence from the seventeenth century to suggest that merchants acted on occasion as middlemen between guitar makers and the purchasing public. In 1629 Juan de la Cruz contracted an Andean *maestro carpintero* (master carpenter) named Miguel Poma to make three dozen *discantes medianos*, a dozen vihuelas, and six harps over the course of the following year.[28] De la Cruz may have been a traveling merchant who aimed to sell the instruments outside the city, or he may have been a shop owner like Francisco de Valencia, who died in 1659: an inventory of the contents of his shop included nearly seventy guitars, as well as guitar strings.[29] Valencia was not, however, a specialist music vendor. His shop is described in the inventory as a clothes and merchandise shop (*tienda de rropa y mercaderias*), and among the other items that it contained were hardware, haberdashery, and food. This implies that musical instruments were neither regarded, nor priced, as luxury or specialized items, but were bought off the shelf in large numbers by the general public.[30]

Instrument ownership was therefore widespread, and the city was permeated by musical sounds. Evidence emerges of a lively musical world outside the orbit of the church, and of a wide variety of performance styles and spaces: secular music, music as recreation as well as devotion, music heard in homes, at private dances, and in public places. Nevertheless, there is no question that the information that can be found in archives in Cuzco, Lima, and Seville is weighted heavily toward the performance of church music, and it is to the musical functioning of ecclesiastical institutions and their interrelations that I now turn, beginning with the bastion of Catholic colonialism and a central pillar of the Spanish "lettered city," the cathedral.

CHAPTER TWO

The Cathedral and the Seminary of San Antonio Abad

On 17 June 1747, a funeral peal of one hundred strikes rang out on the cathedral bell to announce the death of Philip V (Esquivel y Navia [c.1749] 1980, 2:396). The signals that followed, known as *clamores* and *dobles*, were echoed by the bells of all the other churches in Cuzco. Answering this call, the city council, military companies, citizens, and merchants processed to the cathedral to the sound of discordant drums and trumpets. They were joined at the principal church by representatives of the religious orders and colleges, where all heard funeral vespers, sung polyphonically by the musicians of the Seminary of San Antonio Abad (Santander 1748, H1). The following day,

> from six o'clock in the morning, the communities [of friars] came to the cathedral to sing the Office of the Dead and mass for His Majesty, each one in the chapel designated by the master of ceremonies, and the office was distributed in the following manner: Santo Domingo, the first nocturn. San Francisco, the second nocturn. San Agustín, the third nocturn. The Mercedarians, the lauds. San Juan de Dios, the Bethlemites, the colleges of San Antonio and San Bernardo, the customary vigil and the mass. (Esquivel y Navia [c.1749] 1980, 2:398).

At eleven o'clock the vigil was sung polyphonically with the cathedral clergy and representatives of the city's religious communities all still present. The vigil finished at midday, and the ceremony ended with a solemn mass.

In sixteenth-century Cuzco, as in virtually all other cities of the Hispanic world, musical life revolved around the cathedral. Despite its early organization along Sevillian lines, however, from the early seventeenth century onward it was not the cathedral's own *capilla de música* (music chapel) that dominated the soundscape of central Cuzco, but the musicians of the Seminary of San Antonio Abad, located one block behind the principal church in what is today known as the Plaza Nazarenas. Within a few years of the drawing up of the seminary's constitution in 1605, its students were playing an important role in the music performed both inside and outside the walls of the cathedral, and by the middle of the century they constituted the premier music ensemble in the city, both in terms of size and prestige. The seminary singers not only solemnized ceremonies such as the funeral vespers of Philip V, but they also acted as musical ambassadors for the cathedral, extending its influence into the city by performing polyphony in other churches and during processions with the Holy Sacrament.

The cathedral was therefore no isolated island of musical activity but a central point in a rich and dynamic network that linked urban institutions and communities. On many occasions this network was brought to life through the ringing of bells, the echoing of central rituals by churches on the periphery considered a sufficient declaration of allegiance and unity. At more important moments, however, sonic participation from afar was not enough, and the physical presence of important groups was required. The grandest civic ceremonies, such as Corpus Christi and major events in the royal family, saw the city's monastic communities, students, and guilds, along with representatives of the Andean parishes—including dancers and musicians—make their way to the Plaza de Armas to participate in the occasion. Although held primarily in the open air, ceremonies usually began or ended with a service in the cathedral. In 1746, the marriage of the Spanish infanta was celebrated in the cathedral with a thanksgiving mass at which "the whole city" was present, and, as the description of Philip V's funeral reveals, this presence might take a participatory form.[1]

If the urban population was drawn into the cathedral, the religious and political heart of the city, at the crux of such ritual occasions, then the cathedral, conversely, extended its influence out into the surrounding spaces through architecture, both permanent and ephemeral, as well as music. The arch, a feature unknown to the Inkas, was reserved for ecclesiastical buildings, with the exception of the arched colonnades on the Plaza de Armas (Fraser 1990, 144). This expansion of church authority into the principal square on its doorstep was enhanced during festivities by the erection of temporary altars and triumphal arches (Dean 1999). Sound, too, was a means through which the church reached out to appropriate the secular urban space on its doorstep. Music—bells, fanfares, chant, and polyphony—allowed effective and richly symbolic communication with the masses that thronged the main plaza on the principal feast days: neither the written nor the spoken word had the same capacity in this linguistically divided, largely illiterate society.

The Organization of Music in Cuzco Cathedral

In his pioneering article "Cuzco Cathedral: 1546–1750," Robert Stevenson (1980a) covers the history of music in the principal church from its foundation until 1630 in some detail. However, several volumes of the cathedral chapter acts, on which his article is based, had been lost. Samuel Claro's (1969a) article on dramatic music in Cuzco was much more limited in scope, covering just the decade 1740 to 1750 in depth. As a result, the long middle century of colonial rule from 1630 to 1740, when urban culture was arguably at its most fertile, has been passed over in virtual silence, and nothing is known about cathedral music in the final quarter of the colonial period.

Due to the severe limitations imposed by the availability of archival sources in Cuzco, any attempt to write a comprehensive history of music in the cathedral or seminary during the colonial period would be doomed from the outset, and this is not my aim. Nevertheless, even the patchy documentation that is accessible reveals that the organization of music in Cuzco Cathedral grew to differ from the Hispanic models on which it was initially based, principally through an unprecedented level of dependence on musicians from San Antonio Abad. Rather than regarding the cathedral as an isolated cell of musical activity, as has often been the case in Hispanic and Latin American musicology (Marín 2002, xiv; Carreras 2005, 34), I will seek to understand the ways in which this institution and its musical personnel were integrated into the urban environment and connected to other local institutions and individuals. The divide between sacred and secular space, the cathedral and the Plaza de Armas over which it looms, was permeable and fluid, constantly blurred by processions that started or ended at the principal church. Music within the walls of the cathedral was frequently performed by representatives of other religious institutions, while the seminarians accompanied important figures or ritual objects as they went forth into the streets. The cathedral may have been the dominant urban institution, but its musical life was entwined with, and dependent on, the surrounding city.

THE PRINCIPAL MUSICIANS

Stevenson's study confirms that the musical structure of Cuzco Cathedral was initially created along traditional Spanish lines. Like other New World cathedrals (Perdomo Escobar 1976, 4–5), it was founded on the Sevillian model. By the 1550s, the musical infrastructure of the cathedral had been put in place: books of plainchant and polyphony had been acquired, and skilled musicians had started to arrive from Spain.[2] The nominal head of music in the cathedral was the *chantre*, one of the five senior dignitaries of the cathedral, whose duties were laid down in the 1538 *bula de erección* of the see of Cuzco (Hernáez 1964, 169). Although by the end of the sixteenth century this was usually an honorary position in Spain, the *chantre* of Cuzco Cathedral was still expected to be capable of directing the choir as late as 1591, especially in the absence of a *maestro de capilla*, or chapel master (Stevenson 1980a, 5). Around this time, the cathedral adopted the Spanish convention of appointing a deputy, or *sochantre*, to take on the *chantre*'s musical duties, though the *chantre* was supposed to maintain quality control over cathedral music, according to chapter 4 of the *Regla consueta del cabildo eclesiástico de la catedral* (1780).[3] The main duty of the *sochantre*, who was generally paid out of the *chantre*'s prebend, is noted as teaching plainchant to the choirboys and any other singers required to perform this music, which presumably included the chaplains known as *capellanes de coro*; this was usually the case in Spanish cathedrals as well (Suárez-Pajares 1998, 63).

In practice, most musical instruction fell to the *maestro de capilla*, who was next in line in the musical hierarchy. As far as can be determined, his duties and terms of employment were essentially the same as in other cathedrals in the Ibero-American world. The *maestro de capilla* was expected to teach and rehearse the choirboys and adult musicians, to conduct and manage the choir, and to compose villancicos, motets, and other music required for calendar feasts (Stevenson 1980a). A detailed description of these duties as perceived in the late eighteenth century can be found in chapter 30 of the 1780 *Regla consueta*, and they appear to have changed little over the previous two centuries. However, the number of rehearsals had dropped from seven to two a week, and the creative duties of the *maestro de capilla* had changed with the times: whereas the composition of villancicos—lively, sometimes comic, vernacular works with marked secular musical influences—had once been a primary obligation, the *Regla consueta* rails against the so-called theatrical style, the use of which had now become a punishable offence.[4] A lowering of standards and the imposition of a narrower stylistic orthodoxy can thus be observed between the late sixteenth and late eighteenth centuries.

The post of cathedral organist was also important and well remunerated. It was filled by some of Cuzco's most eminent musicians, including three members of the prominent Herrera family, discussed below, and Basilio de Pancorbo, who occupied this position after serving as *maestro de capilla* for three years in the early eighteenth century. In terms of status, the organists occupied the level below maestro de capilla, and they often assisted the maestro with his musical duties.

THE CATHEDRAL SINGERS

It is when we come to the provision of singers that the distinctiveness of Cuzco Cathedral begins to emerge. There were, in fact, several groups involved in singing in the cathedral during the colonial period, and their combinations changed over time, though there were also certain stable elements of the singing establishment.

During the whole of the colonial period, the cathedral supported *seises*, or boy singers. It hired a full complement of six *seises* in 1552 (Stevenson 1980a, 2), and was still doing so in the first decade of the nineteenth century.[5] It also maintained the *coro* (choir), made up of chaplains known as *capellanes de coro*, whose main function was the performance of plainchant. Six *capellanías* (endowed chantry funds) were established at the cathedral's foundation, the holders of which were to attend the nocturnal and diurnal hours and sing at the choir stand at solemn masses. More were founded over the course of the colonial period, such as that established by Diego Arias de la Cerda, a canon of the cathedral of Huamanga, in 1681.[6] The duties of each *capellán de coro* were spelled out in the foundation of his chantry. As well as saying twelve masses each year, the holder of Arias de la Cerda's *capellanía* was obliged to attend sung masses, Prime, Terce, Sext, None, vespers, and compline every day in the cathedral. These musical chaplains were therefore a mainstay of cathedral music, singing plainchant whenever such music was required and, in many cases, contributing to the performance of polyphony on more solemn occasions. The number of *capellanes de coro* varied during the colonial period: Arias de la Cerda alone endowed six *capellanías de coro*, according to Esquivel y Navia ([c.1749] 1980, 2:145). Cosme Bueno ([1768] 1951, 93), however, writing less than two decades later, states that the cathedral had eight *capellanes de coro* in total, suggesting that *capellanías* had been suppressed as well as created.

Esquivel y Navia ([c.1749] 1980, 2:341–42) gives an evocative account of the performance of plainchant by the *capellanes de coro* during the ceremonies for the publication of edicts by the Inquisition in 1746. The ritual began with a procession of clerics and chaplains with candles, "singing the major litany in a low, dark tone" (en tono lúgubre y bajo). The candles were later extinguished and the *sochantre* and *capellanes* sang "in a low, dark tone (as they normally sing the Miserere) the psalm 'Deus laudem mem ne tacveris, etc.'"

This description, an unusual evocation of the atmosphere of a ceremony in the choir of the cathedral, confirms that the *capellanes* performed separately from the polyphonic singers.

The history of polyphonic performance in the cathedral goes back at least to the 1550s, when its library included masses by Cristóbal de Morales (Stevenson 1980a, 2). Virtually nothing is known about the singers who performed this music until the 1590s, when the cathedral was employing between three and five salaried, clerical singers (Stevenson 1980a, 6–7).[7] This arrangement continued into the early seventeenth century, but after this point there is no information about the organization of this group. If one were to infer from the examples of other cathedrals, there would be no reason to suppose that practices changed substantially. Local evidence, however, suggests otherwise.

THE SEMINARY OF SAN ANTONIO ABAD

The salaried cathedral singers were supplemented from the early seventeenth century onward by *colegiales* from the Seminary of San Antonio Abad. The seminary's constitution, drawn up in 1605, reveals the intention of its founder, Bishop Antonio de la Raya, that the seminarians should play a significant part in the ceremonial life of the cathedral.[8] The musical duties of the *colegiales* are not, however, mentioned specifically; it was simply decreed that "all will learn to sing." This much conforms to peninsular patterns (Martín Hernández 1964). Singing was part of the religious profession, and musical instruction, generally in plainchant, was thus a normal part of the curriculum of any Spanish seminary.

As for serving the cathedral, this was one of the principal functions of a number of Spanish seminaries; indeed, seminary scholarships were often given in preference to *seises* or altar boys as they already had experience of cathedral service (Ramos López 1994, 61; Martín Hernández 1964, 321). Granada's seminary seems to have been held up in Spain as a model, and San Antonio Abad in Cuzco was set up along similar lines as a provider of cathedral assistants (Ulloa [1748] 1990 2:153).[9] It may be significant that Antonio de la Raya, the founder of San Antonio Abad, was consecrated as bishop of Cuzco in Granada Cathedral (Stevenson 1980a, 8). An Andalucian by birth, he was also well enough acquainted with the city and its musical establishment to have appointed a native of Granada, Pedro Bermúdez, as *maestro de capilla* at Cuzco Cathedral.

In cases such as that of Granada, where the seminarians played an important role in the functioning of the cathedral, the students were the equivalent of *monaguillos* (altar boys or acolytes), and their musical duties probably extended no further than carrying music books to and from the music stand. In Cuzco, however, San Antonio Abad seems to have adopted a much more significant musical role within a few years of its foundation. According to Stevenson (1980a, 10), Bishop de la Raya was "the first to set aside an endowment in a New World seminary specifically for the teaching of vocal and instrumental music," and students learned to sing both plainchant and polyphony. The seminary formed its own *capilla de música* that was soon to play a fundamental part in cathedral musical activities. In 1625, twenty years after the seminary's constitution was drawn up, the bishop wrote that its *colegiales* had been serving the cathedral for more than fourteen years, attending vespers, Salve, and mass every day, accompanying the Thursday mass, and processing with the Holy Sacrament when it was taken out to the sick, singing psalms and polyphony, "which is very edifying for the people."[10] By participating in the Saturday Lady Masses as well as the Thursday masses for the Holy Sacrament, the seminarians took on two of the principal roles normally assumed by the cathedral singers in Latin America, and they also became responsible for taking the church's message to the wider urban population in musical form (Esquivel y Navia [c.1749] 1980, 2:26–27, 40; Illari 2001, 207–8). A relatively rapid and comprehensive shift toward dependence on the seminary musicians is implied by the cathedral chapter's report in 1621 that "it is the seminary which sustains the choir and attends to the service of the church, as there are no chaplains or other ministers."[11]

A musical link between seminary and cathedral was not without precedent in the New World: evidence for such a relationship has been found in La Plata, Caracas, and Quito, where cathedral *maestros* were obliged to teach music in the seminaries, though there is no sign in any of these cases that seminarians performed as a group in the cathedrals (Estenssoro 1990, 212; Stevenson 1978, 37; 1980c, 26–27). The musical organization of the cathedral and seminary in Cuzco also differed notably from that in Spain, where seminarians did not normally perform polyphony or take part in cathedral musical activities. The case of colonial Tucumán, in modern-day Argentina, shows the greatest similarities with that of Cuzco: the city's seminary was the main center of music education and provided singers for the cathedral (Illari 1996, 26–27). This is, however, the only example that has so far come to light which mirrors the reciprocal arrangement extant in Cuzco, which was apparently unique among Peruvian cities in the high musical profile of its seminary.[12]

The role of the seminarians of San Antonio Abad in the musical life of the cathedral, already significant in the early seventeenth century, only increased with time. In 1648, Bishop Juan Alonso de Ocón wrote to Spain: "These *colegiales* serve the cathedral with great ostentation and solemn music, which is envied throughout the realm."[13] Meanwhile, in the same year, the institution's rector, Don Juan de Cárdenas y Céspedes, stated that the seminary had its own *capilla de música*, with more than thirty musicians and a *maestro de capilla* who sang at the Thursday masses, accompanied the Holy Sacrament on its forays out to the sick, and attended the cathedral with such skill and dedication that it was "the best served and most distinguished in the whole realm of Peru." He highlighted the consoling and edifying effect of the seminary musicians on the urban population, and a witness to this report added that seminary musicians took part in the celebrations on the feast days of the patron saints of the city's monasteries and convents.[14]

This glowing opinion of the role of the seminary was shared by the cathedral chapter, which wrote in a 1658 letter to the king of "its assistance in the divine offices of this cathedral, in which it maintains two admirable musical choirs."[15] A decade later, in 1669, the rector again eulogized about the musical splendor of the processions to the sick, claiming that the seminary had more than fifty singers who served the cathedral and confirming that they also sang in the churches of the city's monastic orders.[16] The seminary *capilla de música* must have constituted one of the most formidable musical forces in the Hispanic world at this time, and it not only played an increasingly prominent role in the music performed within the cathedral but was also firmly established as the mobile arm of the cathedral's musical forces, singing in processions through the city and going forth to represent the cathedral at external functions.

For a cathedral *capilla de música* to be overshadowed in this way was highly unusual in the world of Spanish music, yet the impression that the musicians of the seminary were gradually supplanting the cathedral's own singers increases further in the eighteenth century. Bishop Melchor de la Nava ordered that the rosary should be sung every Wednesday evening by the seminarians as they processed through the central plazas, and when Don Gaspar de la Cuba was appointed as dean in 1719, the ceremony was accompanied by the *colegiales* singing in the *coro alto* of the cathedral (Esquivel y Navia [c.1749] 1980, 2:208, 216). Joseph Antonio Santander (1748) chronicled the ceremonies to mark the funeral of Philip V and the accession to the throne of Ferdinand VI in 1747; in his florid yet disappointingly vague description of the music at vespers in the cathedral, he mentions only the exquisite harmony of the seminary musicians. Ignacio de Castro ([1795]

10. Anon., 1674–80, *Corregidor Pérez*, detail of the singers and harpist, Corpus Christi series.

1978, 88), in his account of the events surrounding the official foundation of the Audiencia del Cuzco in 1788, refers to a mass in the cathedral in which "the music was grave and respectful, as is the custom in that magnificent temple, directed and performed by the students of the Seminary of San Antonio." There is little doubt, then, that the *colegiales* became primarily responsible for providing music in the cathedral on important occasions. Indeed, there is no mention of cathedral singers other than the seminarians in eighteenth-century accounts, so it seems that by this time, the seminary *capilla de música* had become the de facto cathedral choir.

THE SEMINARY ARCHIVE AND *COMEDIAS*
That Cuzco's extensive collection of colonial music is held in the seminary archive rather than in the cathedral is another indication of the increasing identification between these institutions as the colonial period wore on. This archive, incomplete though it may be, reveals much about the multiple roles of the seminary musicians. It is dominated by vespers psalm settings and villancicos for feasts of the Virgin and Christmas, suggesting that the seminarians were expected to solemnize vespers on these important religious occasions, while the large number of Lamentations reveals a significant role at Easter. Given the seminary's close relationship with the Cofradía del Santísimo Sacramento and its prominent role in ceremonies involving the Holy Sacrament, it is unsurprising that there are a number of villancicos

dedicated to Corpus Christi or the Eucharist. The institution's responsibility for honoring the feast days of the city's convents and monasteries is reflected in pieces dedicated to their patron saints, a number of which show signs of having been performed in the monastic churches. Perhaps most striking, however, is the inclusion of a number of mid-eighteenth-century musical-theatrical compositions. As well as performing in the cathedral, processing outside it, and accompanying occasional visits to the monastic churches, the seminary had another important role in urban musical life as the group that became increasingly responsible for the performance of *comedias*.

While the nature, location, and role of these musical-theatrical performances changed over time, it is clear that *comedias* played a prominent part in Cuzco's cultural life for much of the colonial period. To judge from the 1601 *Constituciones sinodales* of Bishop de la Raya, *comedias* were a loosely defined genre in the late sixteenth century, performed both inside and outside churches, sometimes during services, and incorporating both sacred and secular themes (Lassegue-Moleres 1987, 63).[17] Dramatic, semistaged performances of various kinds continued to take place inside Cuzco's churches for the following 180 years: the prohibitions that emanated from Lima and the metropolis in the eighteenth century (Claro 1969a, 28) seem to have been slow to take effect in Cuzco. In 1780, the cathedral *Regla consueta* banned the performance of *loas* and *entremeses* in the church on Christmas Eve "because of the disorder they bring to the church, with the mix of women and men, and the din which disturbs the Choir,"[18] a prohibition that is highly revealing about actual practice at that time.[19]

The communal sound world of the city was thus characterized by frequent musical-theatrical performances in which, from the late seventeenth century onward, the seminarians played an increasingly prominent role, though this brought changes in both location and purpose, as well as a certain narrowing of parameters. In 1688, Doctor Don Juan Bravo Dávila y Cartagena was elected as bishop of Tucumán. Born in Cuzco, he had studied at the seminary and had moved through the ranks of parish priests to become *chantre* of the cathedral. When news of his election arrived, the seminary presented him with *comedias*, dances, and music (Esquivel y Navia [c.1749] 1980, 2:150). The bishop of Paraguay passed through Cuzco in 1723, and he, too, witnessed the performance of two *comedias* in front of an audience of the city's Hispanic elite (229). Claro (1969a) relates that two *comedias* were performed in the seminary on consecutive days in 1743 in honor of the city's new bishop, Don Pedro Morcillo Rubio y Auñón. The audience was again made up of high-ranking ecclesiastical and secular figures. The promotion of the seminary's rector, Don Fernando Joseph Pérez de Oblitas, to the see of Paraguay in 1749 was marked by the performance of an *Opera Serenata* in his honor, while the celebrations the following year for the new bishop, Juan de Castañeda, included a *comedia* in the seminary.

Seminary *comedias* thus focused on events of local significance and were generally dedicated to an important ecclesiastical figure often present at the performance. They were encomiastic works, performed in the seminary to a select audience. The only public *comedia* performance recorded by Claro took place in the Plaza del Regocijo and was put on as part of the funeral ceremonies for Philip V by the city's leading merchants, not by the seminary. Similarly, the swearing in of the prince of Asturias, Luis Fernando, was celebrated in 1712 with three *comedias* presented in the Plaza del Regocijo by the city's *corregidor*, Don Rodrigo Venegas (Esquivel y Navia [c.1749] 1980, 2:205). From the late seventeenth century onward, *comedias* commemorating royal events were generally staged by leading citizens in the Plaza del Regocijo—home to the city council, which no doubt oversaw the events—while those celebrating the achievements of leading churchmen were presented in the seminary. While the civic *comedia* entertained a cross-section of the city population in a public square, the seminary *comedia* became an art form for the city's criollo elite, its purpose to sing the praises of members of this group (as well as of the institution and the city) rather than to entertain or edify the public.[20] The *comedia* was also the face that this elite chose to show to important outsiders; indeed, the connection between *comedias* and the flattery of dignitaries seems to have become widely recognized. In a decree banning such performances in the seminary, sent to the bishop of Cuzco in 1770, King Charles III wrote of "the severe harm that results from putting on *comedias* and other theatrical displays when a new rector arrives, or a viceroy or bishop passes through the city" (quoted in Claro 1969a, 27).[21] The seminary repertoire thus serves to underline this institution's links with ecclesiastical figures of authority and with other religious houses in the city. Music was more than just adornment or entertainment; it was a means for the seminary and for the criollo elite to forge social, political, and religious connections.

SEMINARY SINGERS AND *CAPELLANÍAS DE CORO*

The *colegiales* of the seminary not only took part in polyphonic performances in the cathedral but they were also the clerics of choice to take up *capellanías de coro*. These chantries, which required the frequent performance of plain-chant in the cathedral, were destined for priests. Given that they received both the religious and musical instruction that these posts demanded, semi-nary teachers and students were prime candidates for such *capellanías*, and in filling these positions they were able to contribute to the performance of music in the cathedral. Seminarians had to demonstrate that they had sufficient income to support themselves before they could be ordained as priests, and the main way that they did this was by obtaining one or more *capellanías* (Ganster 1986, 146). By ensuring that a seminary singer was given a *capellanía de coro* in the cathedral, the ecclesiastical authorities allowed the individual to take the next step in his church career while retaining the services of a trained musician without having to pay his wages as a singer out of the cathedral *fábrica*.

Diego Arias de la Cerda, the canon of the cathedral of Huamanga who founded a *capellanía de coro* in 1681, specified that in future the cathedral chapter should choose an ordained *colegial* of the seminary with a good voice and knowledge of plainchant to fill the post.[22] In this foundation, a clear distinction is made between *capellanes de coro* and the cathedral's polyphonic singers: Arias de la Cerda insisted that the chantry was not open to salaried musicians because his aim was to increase the total number of singers (whether of chant or of polyphony) in the cathedral. The cathedral singer Agustín Cortés de la Cruz, who founded several *capellanías* in his will in 1696, stated that these foundations were specifically intended to support the per-formance of both plainchant and polyphony on important occasions. He indicated his preference that one of these chantries should be filled by a current or former seminarian.[23] Providing a salaried singer with a *capellanía de coro* would not have had any positive effect on the number of cathedral musicians, thus one might assume that Cortés de la Cruz, like Arias de la Cerda, intended the chantries to be filled by musically trained seminarians who did not have another musical post. According to his will, however, he was himself simultaneously a *cantor* and *capellan de coro* in the cathedral. The priest Antonio González was both *maestro de capilla* at San Antonio Abad and a *capellán de coro* in the cathedral in 1675, suggesting that while some chan-tries were used to boost the number of singers, others were destined to supplement the income of musicians who were already employed.[24]

While some founders thus saw their *capellanes* as additional plainchant singers, others perceived them as potentially contributing to polyphonic music making. Don Francisco de Sosa y Aspitia established a chantry in

1746 with the instructions that candidates had to be current *colegiales* who taught either music or *gramática* at San Antonio Abad; his first chaplain was the priest Francisco Vaca de Castro, who was a *maestro de música* at the seminary at that time.[25] Similarly, Don Felipe Gallegos, a dignitary of the cathedral, founded a *capellanía de coro* in his will in 1765 in which he specified that candidates should be *colegiales* of the seminary who were proficient in music so that they might be able to "help in the choir at the music stand."[26] We can only assume that musicians as skilled and experienced as Vaca de Castro and González, the latter a composer of two pieces in the seminary archive (LCS 311 and 325), would not have refrained from joining in polyphonic performances, and that *capellanes de coro* would regularly have been found singing alongside the cathedral and seminary *cantores*.

The seminary, aside from bringing its *capilla de música* into the cathedral on a regular basis, therefore also became the prime source of cathedral musicians since musically trained seminarians took up permanent musical posts in the cathedral either as *capellanes de coro* or as salaried singers (Stevenson 1980a, 16). By the late seventeenth century, the picture is thus somewhat complex, with members of the seminary, salaried cathedral singers, and *capellanes de coro*—singers with a variety of sources of income and institutional connections—performing separately and in various combinations in the choir of the cathedral.

The eighteenth century presents a slightly different picture, for no evidence of salaried Hispanic cathedral singers has emerged after 1700.[27] The most likely explanation for the disparate eighteenth-century evidence is that the cathedral post of *cantor*, financed by the cathedral *fábrica*, was eventually eclipsed by the post of *colegial cantor*, funded by a scholarship from the seminary. Certainly, almost every eighteenth-century Spanish cathedral musician who appears in Cuzco's archives was a *colegial* of the seminary. It seems that the minimal cathedral *capilla de música* of just three to five singers recorded around 1600 was retained throughout the century, but was supplemented by the large seminary forces on important occasions when more elaborate music was required. This would have been a way to maintain the splendor of music in the cathedral, which did not have the economic resources of La Plata or Lima, without bankrupting the *fábrica*. It may have been that in the eighteenth century, the availability of an extremely large, highly trained ensemble of seminary singers, at no cost to the cathedral, led to the eventual elimination of the salaried singers' posts in the cathedral, which had been looking for ways to reduce the burden on its *fábrica* from the late sixteenth century onward.

To complicate further the definition of the "cathedral musicians," there is ambiguous evidence that the singing forces, which were exclusively Spanish in the seventeenth century, were complemented by Andeans at some point in the early eighteenth century. This is suggested by an oblique and well-hidden reference in a document dating from 1730 to "the lands of the Indian *cantores* of the cathedral."[28] Another, almost equally oblique reference in a second document dating from 1765 concerns the assessment of the tribute due to be paid by the Andean *ayllu yanaconas*[29] of the Cathedral parish, which included "the sacristans, bell-ringers, and *cantores* who are serving in the cathedral."[30] No other references to a group of Andean singers in the cathedral have been found. The ambiguity of these documentary traces resides in the meanings of the word *cantor*. In cathedral documents, *cantor* invariably indicates a singer, while the word *ministril* is used to designate an Andean instrumentalist. In other sources, however, *cantor* is often used more loosely to mean "musician." These documents concern the cathedral, but were not produced by its employees; thus the word *cantores* may in fact refer to the cathedral's corps of Andean instrumentalists.

The earliest evidence for Andean involvement in cathedral music is a 1571 contract to provide *ministriles* for cathedral services (Viñuales 2004, 68). The cathedral's wind players in the 1580s were sons of *yanaconas*. The fact that the *ayllu yanaconas* of the Cathedral parish still included cathedral *cantores* in 1765 implies a consistent practice of training and employing members of this *ayllu* to serve as musicians in the principal church over much of the colonial period. The link between *yanaconas* and musical service was not limited to Cuzco, nor to the colonial period. At least some native instrumentalists employed by La Plata Cathedral also came from this social group (Illari 1997, 94–95, 101), while there is evidence that *yanaconas* had been involved in music before the Spanish conquest in Cuzco (Betanzos 1996, 79).

From the early colonial period on, certain musical posts in the cathedral were reserved for Spaniards, others for Andeans: there was a sharp dividing line between Spanish clerical singers and Andean lay instrumentalists. The post of *maestro de capilla* was only ever occupied by Spaniards, and the same was true of the post of organist until halfway through the colonial period. The cathedral eventually acquired two organs, however, and it appears that the chapter countenanced the appointment of an Andean to play the role of second organist or understudy, judging from the fact that in 1666 the cathedral had a salaried native organist named Pascual Tito.[31] An Andean harpist named Don Joseph Ygnacio, considered below in detail, was also recorded as a cathedral employee in 1687.[32] There was thus limited penetration of Andean musicians into the solo instrumentalist posts in the seventeenth century. Most native musicians, however, were confined to the lowest rank of the cathedral music establishment, that of ministril.

From the evidence provided by Stevenson, it would appear that the post of ministril was occupied exclusively by Andeans, at least until 1630. In 1607, the cathedral supported eight native ministriles, while accounts of the Cofradía del Santísimo Sacramento of the cathedral show regular payments to five Andean instrumentalists between 1640 and 1673.[33] It is unclear whether the latter were the same musicians employed by the cathedral itself. The duties of these players were focused on the ceremonies of the Holy Sacrament—the Thursday masses, Corpus Christi, and the processions to the sick—and so they must have accompanied or played alongside the seminary singers. After this date, no information about instrumentalists emerges until the early nineteenth century. At this time, the cathedral employed two harpists and two bajoneros, while on major feasts (generally Christmas Eve and Holy Week) these musicians were supplemented by two to four violinists. The surnames of the salaried musicians, such as Chuqui, Tecsetupa, and Livisaca, are clearly Andean, while Vicente Flores, bajonero, is listed in another document as indigenous.[34]

Although there is very little information to go on for the mid- to late colonial periods, there is nothing to suggest that the indigenous character of the profession of ministril changed substantially. Distinction, or discrimination, between white singers and indigenous instrumentalists was a feature of the cathedrals of La Plata, Santafé, and Lima during the seventeenth century, although in the case of Lima there was a small degree of flexibility (Illari 1997, 98–99; Bermúdez 1999). As Bernardo Illari (2001, 112–13) writes of La Plata Cathedral, "the opposition between the Caucasian Self and the Ethnic Other was mapped onto the music chapel in terms of singers (cantores or músicos) and instrumentalists (ministriles, minstrels or wind instrument players). . . . Singers were part of the dominant group; they were 'we' in colonial La Plata. Minstrels were the Others and held a subaltern rank within the group." This racial distinction presumably has its roots in the social division between singers and ministriles in the Iberian Peninsula. Ministriles comprised a somewhat separate group among the musicians of the cathedral in seventeenth-century Sigüenza, for example, and received lower salaries and occupied a lower social position (Suárez-Pajares 1998, 85). If playing instruments was a kind of "manual labor" of the music profession across the Hispanic world (Illari 2001, 129), then it is unsurpris-

11. Anon., 1674–80, *Confraternities of Saint Rose and La Linda*, detail of the Andean wind players, Corpus Christi series.

ing that indigenous musicians were generally chosen to fill such posts in the New World. Social categorization and racial discrimination are a more convincing explanation for the widespread restriction of native musicians to instrumental roles in prominent New World cathedrals than any vocal "deficiency" as perceived by Spanish ears (Stevenson 1960, 95).[35]

It remains to be confirmed to what extent Andean musicians made limited inroads into the cathedral musical establishment as the colonial period progressed, and to what extent they remained largely confined to the lowest posts. There is a small amount of evidence that the late seventeenth century, a time when the fortunes and social status of indigenous musicians in Cuzco were at a peak, may have seen a greater degree of prominence of Andean instrumentalists in and around the cathedral. If there were indeed Andean singers in the cathedral, they may have joined native instrumentalists such as the organist Pascual Tito and the harpist Joseph Ygnacio and performed on occasions like the so-called Sunday morning Indian Mass, while the musicians of the seminary sang at events that were directed primarily at the Hispanic population.[36] Even if this were true, however, it would be going too far to suggest that there was a significant ideological shift or weakening of the institutionalized racism of the cathedral establishment. A more convincing explanation would be that as the financial situation of the city and the cathedral declined in the eighteenth century, and all sections of the population were decimated by the 1720 plague, the cathedral took the pragmatic step of marginally increasing the role of its cheap, plentiful, and skillful Andean musical labor force, without fundamentally upsetting the hierarchy of the establishment.[37]

Africans were not numerous in colonial Cuzco, where slaves were an expensive luxury, though a few worked as house servants for the city's elite (Van den Berghe and Primov with Velazque and Ccuhuata 1977, 45–46). They may, however, have been relatively audible. Several African slaves appear in Cuzco's archives as trumpeters, including one who was donated to the cathedral confraternity of the Holy Sacrament with the specific instruction that he should play at confraternity services and accompany the processions when the Holy Sacrament was taken out to the sick.[38] African trumpeters had a notable presence across Renaissance Europe (Lowe 2005, 39), and Pilar Ramos López (2005, 251) describes a certain predilection among the peninsular Spanish nobility for hiring African *ministriles* as a sign of distinction, citing the example of black trumpeters who performed during Corpus Christi in Seville in 1740. In addition to the trumpeters recorded in Cuzco, two African horn players performed at the hospital of San Andrés in the late eighteenth century, suggesting that a certain association between Africans and brass playing was maintained in the colonial Andes.

INSTITUTIONAL INTERACTION

Given the reliance of the cathedral on seminary musicians from the 1610s onward, it is clear that interaction between the city's ecclesiastical institutions was integral to urban musical life. Both the cathedral's own musicians and those of the seminary were active outside the walls of their institutions at different times during the colonial period, and there is also evidence that musicians from other institutions participated in services within the walls of the cathedral. Music making thus helped to forge and maintain institutional connections and to shape relations between urban religious communities.

The *Constituciones sinodales* of Bishop Gregorio de Montalvo, issued in 1591, include the earliest information about the participation of the cathedral *capilla de música* in the celebrations of other churches. Chapter 38, a section encouraging good relations and mutual support between secular and regular clergy, exhorts "that we should honor their feast days, especially those of their patrons, such as Santo Domingo, San Francisco, San Agustín, the Nativity of Nuestra Señora de la Merced and the Transfiguration of the Lord, the advocation of the church of the Company [of Jesus], and the days when they celebrate the feast of Corpus Christi, and send the musicians of this church on such days" (Lassegue-Moleres 1987, 55). This appears to have been a response to a dispute that arose three years earlier, when the Jesuits and the friars of Santo Domingo, San Francisco, and San Agustín refused to preach in the cathedral unless the secular authorities attended the four monastery feast days accompanied by singers, rather than celebrating them in the cathedral (Esquivel y Navia [c.1749] 1980, 1:256). Despite the conciliatory tone of the 1591 regulations, however, the willingness of the cathedral dignitaries to lend out their musicians to other institutions seems to have declined rather than increased. Whereas the relevant chapter of the 1591 constitutions is phrased in positive terms, the cathedral choir constitutions adopted in 1610 are rather more negative in tone: the bishop and chapter insisted that the cathedral singers were not to sing polyphony at non-cathedral festivals, burials, or funerals without their special permission (Stevenson 1980a, 11–12).

From this period onward the role of musical ambassadors was taken over by the seminary musicians, who became sufficiently identified with the cathedral to represent it in outside functions. Several observers testified to the fact that the seminarians took part in the celebration of the feast days of the patron saints of the city's convents and monasteries in the seventeenth century, and a number of works in the seminary archive bear dedications to these saints, as well as evidence of performances in the monastic churches. This archive is thus suggestive of the institutional links of the seminary, which was responsible for the musical connections between the cathedral and the surrounding city on key days in the church calendar. On the other hand, dedications to the patron saints of the urban parishes remain almost entirely absent from the works in the seminary archive, and no evidence that the seminarians took part in parish celebrations has emerged. Furthermore, the participation of the seminary musicians in the monastic churches seems to have been restricted to one annual event in each institution, with additional performances only on occasions of great importance. The two principal convents had impressive musical capabilities themselves, and the monasteries tended to hire musicians from the Andean parishes for both regular services and major feasts. From the mid-seventeenth century onward, the cathedral musicians, in the broadest sense of the term, had a limited role in the musical life of the city's other churches, though they still had an important role to play in civic events.

The picture that emerges in Cuzco differs considerably from that in Spain. The cathedral was the dominant musical establishment in most Spanish cities, and it exerted its influence over most, if not all, the other churches in the city. The capilla de música of a typical Spanish cathedral participated regularly in the celebration of important dates in the religious calendar in other institutions, including parish churches (Bourligueux 1970; Casares Rodicio 1980; Siemens Hernández 1975; Gembero 1995). Research into the musical organization of such smaller institutions in Spain is still at an early stage, but a study of a parish in Pamplona reveals a core group of clerical musicians, capable only of performing plainchant, supplemented by cathedral musicians for polyphonic performance on important occasions (Gembero 1998). As will become clear in subsequent chapters, this Spanish model —which could be crudely summarized as a dominant cathedral *capilla de música* surrounded by weaker, dependent institutions—is far from applicable to colonial Cuzco. The records of Cuzco's parish churches make no mention of receiving musical groups from the cathedral or the seminary; indeed, they provide ample evidence that the parishes had their own fully formed *capillas de música*, capable of performing polyphony, and were therefore in no need of external assistance. A more balanced picture thus emerges in Cuzco, where many churches strove for a high degree of musical self-sufficiency and no single group dominated the city's musical life. Several institutions sent out their musicians to perform in other churches, including the seminary, the Jesuit college of San Bernardo, and the parish church of Santiago.

The strength of music in Cuzco's peripheral churches was a direct result of the evangelical drive that underpinned the Spanish colonial enterprise, and specifically of the musical policies of the church and crown that had been formulated in the early days of the colonization of the Americas. Music was seen as central to efforts to convert the native inhabitants of Peru, and the organization of music in indigenous parishes was therefore a priority. The result of these policies was the creation of sizeable and capable musical ensembles in the majority of churches, as will be seen in subsequent chapters. The disposition of musical forces in Cuzco, which created a decentralized musical panorama that differed markedly from that found in equivalent-sized Spanish cities, did not therefore emerge by chance but resulted directly from Spanish colonial policies.

Although Cuzco Cathedral did not dominate the urban soundscape to the same extent that other Hispanic cathedrals did, it was nevertheless the ceremonial center of the city, and on certain important occasions, rather than imposing its musical forces on other institutions, it was the scene of communal music making as the urban religious communities came together to celebrate important rituals. When news of the death of Charles II arrived in 1701, there was the customary procession to the cathedral with discordant trumpets, followed by funeral vespers and a solemn mass. Delegations from the monasteries and urban and rural parishes made their way to the cathedral in the surrounding days to mark the king's funeral "with all the pomp that they could muster" (Esquivel y Navia [c.1749] 1980, 2:182–83). If the author's description here leaves much to the imagination, he provides more precise details about the 1747 funeral ceremonies of Philip V, described at the start of this chapter. A very similar collaborative arrangement had been made when news of the death of Pope Benedict XIII was received in 1730. Representatives of the religious orders, parishes, and the seminary began singing masses and holding vigils in the cathedral from seven o'clock in the morning, and "the Office of the Dead was distributed among the orders in the following way: the Dominicans sang the first nocturn, the Franciscans the second, the Augustinians the third, and the Mercedarians sang the lauds" (248).

These accounts reveal a standardized ceremonial procedure for the incorporation of the regular orders in the celebration of sung funeral offices in the cathedral, in which the city's friars reciprocated the presence of seminary musicians in their churches on their feast days. The sequence of performance is intriguing: the 1747 account, in particular, suggests that the monasteries sang in descending order of antiquity and that the order of precedence of the city's ecclesiastical institutions was thus performed in this ritual. The ceremony was crowned by the polyphonic singing of the vigil at the end of the morning, the cathedral asserting its primacy by trumping chant with polyphony. The only flaw in this picture is that the order of precedence of the Augustinians and Mercedarians has been reversed in relation to their foundation dates, for reasons unknown. But ceremonies often dramatized symbolic hierarchies in colonial Cuzco: the notion that the sequence of the offices symbolized a descending order of seniority is supported by the organization of the 1610 Jesuit fiestas, in which the city parishes paraded on successive days "according to their antiquity" ("Fiestas incas" 1986, 42). A reverse order can also be seen in the Carnestolendas fiestas of 1631, organized in a sequence of rising importance (Esquivel y Navia [c.1749] 1980 2:62). It therefore seems highly likely that the participation of various Spanish religious communities in the Office of the Dead acted out not only their allegiance to the higher authorities of crown and church but also their relation to each other. These communal performances were undoubtedly symbolically charged, uniting as they did a broad range of religious groups under one roof in one ritual. Their involvement in music and ceremony in the cathedral lends weight to Miguel Ángel Marín's (2002, 156) insistence on the mutual interdependency of urban institutions in the Hispanic world, rather than total dependency on the cathedral.[39]

Diego de Esquivel y Navia, in his account of the funeral of Philip V, relates that the groups of friars were distributed around the cathedral, "each one in the chapel designated by the master of ceremonies." This is a reminder that the cathedral should not be regarded as a single, unified ceremonial or performance space. The cathedral musicians, *capellanes de coro*, and *colegiales* of San Antonio Abad ruled the choir, but side chapels hosted performances by other musicians, especially during confraternity ceremonies. There are regular payments during the 1780s and 1790s by the Cofradía de Nuestra Señora de Belén "to the musicians who watched over Our Lady during the Octave of Corpus in the cathedral."[40] The Cofradía del Señor de los Temblores, based in the cathedral, also made use of music in its functions, hiring cathedral *maestros de capilla*, singers, and instrumentalists for the *novenario* (nine days) and feast day of the Lord of the Earthquakes in the late eighteenth and early nineteenth centuries.[41] An organ was also commissioned for the confraternity's chapel by its *mayordomo* (majordomo) in 1761.[42] Such evidence of musical activity in side chapels by friars and confraternity members reveals that the decentralization of Cuzco's musical culture was echoed even within the walls of the cathedral.

Cathedral Musicians: Case Studies

Some sense of the complexity of the musical organization of the cathedral has emerged above. A variety of groups performed music within different spaces inside the cathedral, while the category of "cathedral musician" breaks down into a variety of subgroups—salaried singers, choirboys, seminarians, *capellanes de coro*, Andean *ministriles*, African brass players—revealing a complex array of personal, economic, and institutional connections. It is only through examining the lives and career paths of a few individual cathedral musicians that we may come to understand in more detail the contours of this variegated professional group.

THE HERRERA FAMILY

Three members of the Herrera family, a father and his two sons, all named Tomás, dominated the post of cathedral organist for most of the seventeenth century, presenting a prime example of a colonial music dynasty. The establishment of a family at the heart of a cathedral's musical life over a considerable period of time seems to have been more common in the New World than in the Old (Sas 1971; Stevenson 1978; Stevenson 1980a). Such situations were certainly not unknown in the Iberian Peninsula, but family connections were of more importance in small towns and peripheral areas than in cities (Marín 2002). It seems probable that many colonial cathedrals received fewer or even no applications from external musicians when musical posts became vacant, perhaps due to the large distances between major urban centers, and that a pronounced localism led to a preference for internal candidates. The circulation of musicians in search of better posts, a notable feature of Cuzco Cathedral's musical life between 1590 and 1610, seems to have ended altogether after the early seventeenth century as the seminary began to guarantee a steady supply of local talent and a new generation of criollo musicians with firm (and lucrative) roots in their hometown began to emerge.

The first reference to Herrera *père* serving as cathedral organist dates from 1610, while the second son was appointed to the same post in 1682 after the death of the first, a priest (Stevenson 1980a, 12). More information about the family can be found in a *filiasión*, or document about his parentage, prepared by the elder son on 10 June 1678. In this document, a series of witnesses were asked five questions about Herrera and his parents: the third and fourth request confirmation that the father "was a noble person who served in the cathedral of this city in the post of organist for more than sixty years, giving good account of his person," and that the elder son had served in the same post for more than thirty years. One witness, Don Lucas de Berassa, gave revealing answers to the third question. He described Herrera's father as close to Cuzco's bishops Hernando de Vera and Juan Alonso de Ocón, and claimed not only that the father had served as organist for over sixty years but that his fame had spread to Spain, where his portrait hung in El Escorial "as a man distinguished as both composer and organist." Herrera *père* had been esteemed by Cuzco's dignitaries and appeared in his portrait "as a noble person, accompanied by gentlemen and leading lights of this city."[43] Such exalted social status for a cathedral organist was highly unusual in the Hispanic world, yet it would appear that the most senior musicians in seventeenth-century Cuzco formed part of the city's elite.

The younger Herreras' musical careers were not restricted to the cathedral, for they were hired both by other institutions and by individuals to teach music, sometimes on a daily basis. In 1646, for example, the younger son was hired as a private music tutor for a student at San Antonio Abad. The contract stipulated that he was to provide Alonso López Ponce with a year of daily lessons, which were to include singing, composition, and the improvisation of counterpoint, for which he was to receive 280 pesos.[44] He was also hired by Juan de Pancorbo, the administrator of the convent of Santa Catalina, to teach organ, composition, singing, and counterpoint to a convent girl; the two-year contract for daily lessons, signed in 1654, was renewed on termination, constituting a significant commitment and additional source of income. The elder son also had convent connections and was contracted for two years by the nuns of Santa Clara to give daily lessons to the convent singers, organists, and harpists and to provide the necessary music for all the festivities organized within the convent.[45] Another function fulfilled by the members of the Herrera family was to check the quality of newly constructed organs, or of repairs to old instruments, on behalf of the institutions that commissioned them. The monastery of San Bartolomé, for example, hired Pedro Guaman in 1662 to spend two months repairing its organ. It was written into the contract that at the end of this period the organ was to be checked "to the satisfaction of Tomás de Herrera, *maestro mayor de órganos*."[46] Such activities were, however, normal for cathedral musicians in Spain; in their professional lives, if not socially or economically, the Herreras thus differed little from their peninsular counterparts.

ALONSO FERNÁNDEZ DE VELASCO AND
ALONSO DE ZÚÑIGA Y ANAYA

Alonso Fernández de Velasco, hired as *maestro de capilla* in 1626, sent an *información de servicios* (a kind of curriculum vitae) to Spain in 1642 in which he sought one of the two vacant *raciones* in the cathedral.[47] At the time of writing, Fernández de Velasco was priest of the parish of San Cristóbal as well as cathedral *maestro*, and he had also held a post in the Holy Office of the Inquisition for ten years. In 1647, his request was granted. Rather than helping to finance the post of *maestro de capilla*, however, this *ración* seems to have been a goal in itself, for in the very same year, Fernández de Velasco gave up his musical career: his ambition to climb the cathedral hierarchy appears to have outweighed his musical calling. In 1652, the cathedral chapter asked the king to grant him a vacant canonry, and he was finally promoted to this higher post some five years later.[48]

Details of the handover to his successor as *maestro de capilla* appear in the *informaciones de oficio y parte* of Alonso de Zúñiga y Anaya, a young seminarian who was elected to this post by the cathedral chapter on 23 March 1647.[49] Zúñiga started at 250 pesos per year, which was soon raised to 400 pesos "as *el bachiller* Alonso Fernández de Velasco, who used to occupy the post, has been promoted to a *ración* in the cathedral." The use of the word *promote* confirms that Fernández de Velasco received a *ración* as a reward for his twenty years of service as *maestro de capilla* rather than as means of funding his musical post. When he gave up his position as *maestro de capilla* in 1647, he was only forty-six years old; he was in good health and had plenty of his working life ahead of him, judging from the fact that he was promoted to canon after a recommendation from the chapter in 1652, in which he is described as serving the cathedral as *racionero* "with enthusiasm, punctuality, and good example."

Fernández de Velasco used his musical career as a stepping-stone en route to the upper tiers of the cathedral hierarchy, apparently thinking of advancement in terms of ecclesiastical promotion rather than seeking a more prestigious or better paid post as *maestro de capilla* in another cathedral, as was generally the case with leading musicians in Spain. The same attitude was manifested by his successor, the longest-serving *maestro de capilla* in the history of Cuzco Cathedral, Alonso de Zúñiga. Born in 1625, he began serving the cathedral, presumably as a *seise*, in around 1635, from which time he was also studying at the seminary.[50] In 1647, at the age of just twenty-two, while still a *colegial* at the seminary, he took over the post of *maestro de capilla* on the promotion of Fernández de Velasco. He was still occupying this post in 1703, fifty-six years later, at the age of seventy-eight, in marked contrast to his predecessor.[51] In 1657, after ten years in his post, Zúñiga sought to emulate Fernández de Velasco and gain promotion to a prebend in the cathedral. In this case, however, the reward was not forthcoming, and Zúñiga was still seeking this same promotion twenty-one years later. In 1678, Don Juan Bravo Dávila y Cartagena, a canon in the cathedral, petitioned for a prebend on Zúñiga's behalf. After listing the latter's services to the cathedral and summarizing his career, the canon wrote: "He is no longer young and is exhausted by his musical duties, and he is worthy that Your Majesty should honor him with a prebend in this cathedral so that, seeing this example, others may work and pursue music in order to be able to occupy this post."[52]

The awarding of prebends to musicians was a consistent feature of cathedral organization in the Iberian Peninsula, but they were generally used as the foundation of musicians' salaries rather than as rewards. In some cases musicians actually received the prebends, while in others the prebends were suppressed and the income that was generated was put toward their salaries (Llordén 1965; Bourligueux 1970; Siemens Hernández 1975; Casares Rodicio 1980; Gembero 1995; Suárez-Pajares 1998; Marín 2002). Attempts were made from the 1550s onward to bring Cuzco Cathedral in line with this Hispanic model, but these requests remained unsuccessful, and Cuzco's cathedral musicians did not receive prebends at this time or, with the exception of Fernández de Velasco, at any later stage, primarily because of the cathedral's precarious economic status and its consequent difficulty in maintaining even its core prebends.[53] For all that he was the only musician to be awarded such a post, Fernández de Velasco's career path was in fact very unusual by Hispanic standards, for he saw his *ración* as superseding his musical calling rather than as a means of funding it. Zúñiga's 1678 petition, cited above, underlines that both Fernández de Velasco and Zúñiga, as well as, more importantly, the bishop and chapter of Cuzco, saw a *ración* as a golden handshake rather than a signing-on incentive.

Despite repeated requests, backed by the entire cathedral chapter, it appears that Zúñiga never received his reward; he is still described simply as *maestro de capilla* in a 1703 document, and no mention of him as *racionero* has been located. Attempts to organize the funding of music along Spanish lines thus generally foundered for a lack of income to support prebends, and from the late sixteenth century onward, the cathedral sought alternative solutions to the problem of financing musical posts. The solution that was most commonly adopted in order to supplement the somewhat meager salary available from the cathedral *fábrica* was to grant musicians a curacy in one of the city parishes.[54] Zúñiga, like Fernández de Velasco before him, was a parish priest; his *doctrina de indios* was, however, some distance from the city, in the province of Canas y Canchis, whereas his predecessor had been based at the rather more desirable urban parish of San Cristóbal, within sight of the cathedral. Given that Zúñiga's *doctrina* was one of the more distant ones in the bishopric, it is perhaps legitimate to question whether his parishioners saw him with any degree of regularity. In 1663, he had attempted to take over the city parish of Hospital de los Naturales, but it appears that here, too, he was unsuccessful.[55]

This solution was not unique to Cuzco, since documents relating to the *audiencia* of Quito and to the cities of La Paz and La Plata show that this was customary in other parts of the continent in the early seventeenth century.[56] Urban parish benefices were highly prized, and competition was intense: the fact that they were given to cathedral singers is an indication of the priority that was given to these church servants.[57] Evidence that this was common practice in Cuzco, but that it was not necessarily seen as *good* practice, comes to light in two letters written by Cuzco's arguably most musically minded bishop, Antonio de la Raya. Although de la Raya himself ordered that the *maestro de capilla* Pedro Bermúdez be installed in one of the Cuzco parishes in 1597, he made this decision before he had arrived in the city in person. It seems that almost as soon as he saw the situation in Cuzco for himself, he had second thoughts, to judge from letters written to the king in 1598 and 1601.[58] The cathedral could not afford to pay the singers a complete salary out of the *fábrica*, but de la Raya decided that he preferred the solution that had been proposed half a century earlier by Bishop Juan Solano —to grant them *raciones*—rather than continuing to provide them with a second job in the form of a curacy. When Fernández de Velasco petitioned for a *ración*, he supported his request by quoting directly from these reports that Bishop de la Raya had sent over forty years earlier.

Under de la Raya's proposal, the singers would have been both "rewarded and honored," for they would have received the added status of becoming prebendaries of the cathedral. One of the principal benefits of employment as a cathedral musician throughout the Hispanic world was the social status attached to the post, in large part precisely deriving from the fact that it was commonly accompanied by a prebend. That musicians were virtually never granted *raciones* in Cuzco, and were therefore never "honored," should be borne in mind when we come to consider their lives and career paths; it may have contributed in the long term to the decline of the post of salaried singer in Cuzco Cathedral. Indeed, the failure to obtain prebends for musicians may have been a crucial factor in the overall development of music in the cathedral, limiting its capacity to attract distinguished musicians from other cathedrals, pushing ambitious priests toward other kinds of ecclesiastical post, and leading some highly skilled musicians to abandon their artistic vocation.

Despite the efforts of Cuzco's bishops in the sixteenth and early seventeenth centuries to modify the financing of cathedral musical posts, the example of Zúñiga reveals that the practice of cathedral singers doubling up as parish priests continued at least into the second half of the seventeenth century, for no prebends were forthcoming. Furthermore, financial pressures increased dramatically just a few years after de la Raya's petitions to the crown. The year 1609 saw an event that was to have a major impact not just on the cathedral's general economic situation but also specifically on the funding of music: the diocese of Cuzco was divided into three to create two new bishoprics, Huamanga (now Ayacucho) and Arequipa. From this date onward, successive Cuzco bishops and cathedral chapters sent a steady stream of letters to Spain complaining about the financial condition of the cathedral, underlining the drastic decline in tithe revenues.[59] This decline led to cuts in cathedral musicians' salaries in 1610 and again in 1615, when the division of the diocese was given explicitly as the reason (Stevenson 1980a, 12; Esquivel y Navia [c.1749] 1980, 2:26–27). Thus the practice of joint appointments for parish priest-musicians—the only way to ensure that they received a respectable salary—continued, despite opposition from some senior figures. Some musicians held other posts as well: Zúñiga served as an inspector and ecclesiastical judge in the province of Canas y Canchis, where he was a priest.

If Zúñiga was frustrated by decades of unsuccessful attempts to secure a cathedral prebend, he was rather more fortunate in other spheres. The limited documentation on his life, like that on the Herrera family, suggests unusually high social and economic status for a musician in the Hispanic world. One of his great-grandfathers was a conquistador, and the others were among Cuzco's first *encomenderos*, an elite Hispanic group that received enormous grants of native labor and tribute in the earliest days of the colony. In the *informaciones* that he presented in 1657, the witnesses that he brought forth spoke at length about his grandparents and great-grandparents, urging the king to reward him for the great deeds of his family. One of these witnesses was his uncle, Don Juan de Cárdenas y Céspedes, the rector of the Seminary of San Antonio Abad and one of the most influential ecclesiastical figures in the city.

He was not only well born but also landed and wealthy. His haciendas in the valley of Mollepata in the province of Abancay, inherited from his parents, generated income in the form of rent, and Zúñiga thus owed his financial security directly to his illustrious ancestors.[60] Toward the end of his life, he donated the haciendas to the convent of Santa Catalina; in return, the convent allowed Doña Rosa de Santa María, an orphan whom he had brought up there, to profess as a fully fledged "nun of the black veil" without the payment of a dowry.[61] He was also prosperous enough to be involved in the lending of large amounts of capital: four documents from the period 1688 to 1696 detail loans that he made totaling 10,500 pesos, a considerable sum for a man with an annual salary of 400 pesos.[62] He may not have been honored by the cathedral, but he was still a wealthy man of considerable social standing.

AGUSTÍN CORTÉS DE LA CRUZ

One of the most intriguing and influential musicians in colonial Cuzco was a contemporary of Zúñiga named Agustín Cortés de la Cruz. Although he apparently sang for decades in the cathedral, little is known about Cortés de la Cruz's musical activities other than that he appealed against being stripped of his scholarship as a seminary singer in 1672, and that he was a cathedral singer on a salary of three hundred pesos a year at the time that he drew up his will in 1696.[63]

Cortés de la Cruz was the epitome of the Cuzqueño priest-businessman-musician. He was exceptionally well connected and occupied a place at the heart of the city's Spanish establishment. He was one of the witnesses and executors of the wills of the cathedral *chantre* Juan de Espinosa Medrano, perhaps the most important Cuzqueño *letrado* of the seventeenth century, and of Juan de Cárdenas y Céspedes, the rector of San Antonio Abad (and Zúñiga's uncle).[64] Juan de Pancorbo, the administrator of the convent of Santa Catalina and an important ecclesiastical and musical figure, named Cortés de la Cruz as sole heir and executor of his will, and Cortés de la Cruz was given power of attorney by a number of prominent Cuzco citizens, a clear indication that he was considered influential by his peers.[65] An extremely wealthy and prolific businessman, Cortés de la Cruz owned a considerable amount of land near Yucay that he both bought and inherited from Pancorbo, and he also inherited a hacienda near Lamay. He had property in the city, buying land, houses, and shops in the parish of Hospital de los Naturales in 1683 to a value of ten thousand pesos, and acquiring more property in 1690, this time within a stone's throw of the cathedral, for a further eight thousand pesos.[66] His income was boosted by rent from both rural and urban properties, to the tune of hundreds, possibly thousands, of pesos each year.[67] He operated almost as a one-man bank, lending considerable sums of money to other Cuzco citizens, and he was a prolific buyer of (expensive) African slaves.[68]

At the time that he drew up his will in 1696 (which was actually many years before his death), he possessed six *capellanías*. Five of these gave him a combined annual income of fourteen hundred pesos, in comparison with his salary of three hundred pesos as cathedral singer. One was based in the chapel of Santa Bárbara, attached to the city council, from which he obtained an annual income of four hundred pesos per year from before 1691 to 1713, when he died.[69] The city council voted for the incumbent, who was their chaplain; Cortés de la Cruz must therefore have had close ties to the highest secular authorities in the city. Indeed, he left money for the decoration of the chapel of Santa Bárbara in his will.

Cortés de la Cruz founded an annual mass at the Jesuit college in honor of the Immaculate Conception. His donation of two thousand pesos gave an annual sum of one hundred pesos as interest to be spent on the celebration, which he specified should include music.[70] In his will, he founded four new *capellanías* aimed at members of the seminary, demonstrating his concern for the financial security of his successors. That his interest lay in the well-being of cathedral music, and not just in his own salvation, is made clear in the clause in which he stresses that the *capellanías* in the cathedral choir remain free from any obligation to say masses for his soul (which was a standard requirement) and are intended solely for the support of musicians who participate in important celebrations. He had even patronized an individual musician, Juan Antonio Munsibay de Chávez, an organ builder and *maestro bajonero*, who gave him a harpsichord as a token of gratitude for a host of favors.[71] However, he requested that his burial should be "without any pomp or coffin, but in the very earth, and without music, except that of the Fathers," an austere instruction for a wealthy musician who had performed polyphony as his profession and who had left chantries to support polyphonic singing.

Agustín Cortés de la Cruz was thus an active participant within Cuzco's material, spiritual, and musical economies.[72] He was clearly an exceptional figure, but in many ways his career shows features that were probably common, if less exaggerated, among Spanish musicians in Cuzco in the seventeenth century, and he must have served as an example of the heights to which a musician could rise in Cuzco society. That said, it is questionable to what extent he should be classified as a "musician" at all; while, as *cantor* in the cathedral, he occupied one of the city's prime musical posts, music provided little of his income and probably occupied little of his time. In the surviving documentary records, he refers to himself as the chaplain of the city council or simply as a priest. Like Fernández de Velasco and Zúñiga before him, he sought a cathedral prebend: his ambition was primarily to ascend the ecclesiastical hierarchy rather than to pursue a musical career.[73]

It is instructive to compare seventeenth-century figures such as Cortés de la Cruz, Zúñiga, and the Herreras with their counterparts in Spain. Cathedral musicians on the Iberian Peninsula were notoriously impoverished, complaining constantly to their respective chapters about their meager income, and this made for a major contributory factor in the high mobility noted among these musicians. Emilio Casares Rodicio (1980, 197) estimates that about 40 percent of music-related entries in the chapter acts of Oviedo Cathedral are complaints about salaries, petitions for raises, loans, and so on. Cathedral musicians all over Spain suffered economic difficulties in the seventeenth and eighteenth centuries, turning many *maestros de capilla* into peripatetic musicians who went from cathedral to cathedral in search of better economic conditions (e.g., Gembero 1995, 136; Siemens Hernández 1975, 74, 85). Most musicians had few possessions and no money when they died, and many therefore did not make wills.

Cortés de la Cruz, Zúñiga, and Herrera père stand out clearly from their metropolitan brethren. They did not move from Cuzco, and they were wealthy and influential figures. Whereas Spanish musicians complained constantly about their salaries and often died in debt to their employers, Cortés de la Cruz remarked nonchalantly in his will that the cathedral owed him four years' salary, requesting merely that the money be collected in order to found a chantry in the *coro* to support future musical activities. Here, it is the musician who finances the cathedral music establishment, not the other way around.

JOSEPH YGNACIO

It is much more difficult to gather precise information about Andean musicians who worked in the cathedral, as the vast majority had neither the social nor the economic standing to leave significant documentary traces. One exception, however, is the cathedral harpist Don Joseph Ygnacio. Like many of his Spanish colleagues, Ygnacio led a double life, though in this case it consisted of two professions: master candle maker and harpist.[74] There are many more archival references to Ygnacio as *cerero* than as *arpista*; it appears that his career as a cathedral musician was subsidiary, at least in economic terms, to his candle-making activities. Most of the information that survives about him appears in his will and an accompanying codicil, drawn up in 1697.[75] He was a wealthy and generous man who owned a house in the barrio of Matará (an area in which a number of musicians lived), as well as a wax and candle shop, and he declared 1,380 pesos in cash. He also listed many thousands of pesos that he was owed by a wide range of individuals and institutions, either for his services as candle maker or for loans that he had made, including one to the prominent musician and organ maker Juan Antonio Munsibay de Chávez.[76]

His generosity and economic status are evident in the bequests that he made to monasteries and confraternities, which include fifty pesos to the Cofradía del Santo Cristo de Burgos in the monastery of San Agustín, fifty pesos to the Cofradía de Nuestra Señora de la Soledad de los Españoles in La Merced, and one hundred pesos to gild the frames of the paintings in the chapel of Christ in San Juan de Dios. He also wrote off the debts of two priests from San Agustín, leaving the money for whatever work seemed most urgent in the monastery, and he left a harp and a clavichord to the

Seminary of San Antonio Abad. He declared that he was owed fifty pesos from his salary, presumably as cathedral harpist, and donated this money to the cathedral to be used in whatever manner was seen fit, mirroring a gesture in the will of Agustín Cortés de la Cruz the previous year.

One of the most noteworthy features of Ygnacio's will is that he asked to be buried in the church of the monastery hospital of San Bartolomé, where he was being treated at the time, specifically in the crypt of the Cofradía del Santo Cristo de la Coluna de los Españoles. This hospital, and in particular this confraternity, which I discuss in the following chapter, contracted large musical forces on a regular basis in the late seventeenth century, and therefore it is probably not coincidental that Ygnacio wished to be buried in the confraternity crypt and left money for decorating its chapel. It may be that the membership of the brotherhood consisted of a high percentage of musicians, or that Ygnacio had served it in a professional capacity. Whatever the case, he clearly felt an affinity with this particular lay society, and he put his faith in its patron saint and members to ensure the salvation of his soul.

The case of Don Joseph Ygnacio shows an indigenous musician of relatively high social and economic standing who moved easily in Spanish social and institutional spheres. Ygnacio requested to be buried in the crypt of a "Spanish" confraternity, despite being a parishioner of Hospital de los Naturales, and he was being treated in San Bartolomé, officially a hospital for Spaniards. The three confraternities to which he donated money—perhaps suggesting that he was himself a cofrade—were all distinctively Spanish, as were the institutions that benefited from his generosity. He could therefore be regarded as both culturally mobile and a colonial success story. He was apparently not of noble birth—he stressed in his will that he was a self-made man—yet he carved out a comfortable niche for himself in mid-colonial society. It would be a mistake, however, to assume that a musical career ensured a path to financial success, for Ygnacio's wealth seems to have derived primarily from his extramusical interests. His earnings as a harpist would have ensured a respectable standard of living, but not the kind of economic standing evident from his will, which contrasts markedly with the poverty generally associated with peninsular Spanish musicians around this time. This begs the question, why pursue a musical career at all? In the case of Ygnacio, the answer might well have been a mixture of social prestige and religious devotion. Music was a high-status profession during this late seventeenth-century cultural florescence and would also have been a useful point of entry into the world of religious institutions on which his career as a candle maker depended. Ygnacio's pursuit of the profession of church musician undoubtedly contributed toward his status as a Christian *indio ladino* (Hispanicized Andean) and toward his notable degree of integration into the Hispanic sectors of colonial society.

Joseph Ygnacio is recorded as cathedral harpist in 1687, and he bequeathed musical instruments to the seminary. Given that he drew up his will in 1697, it is reasonable to suggest that he was active as a musician by the mid- to late 1670s, when the Corpus Christi paintings were produced. Is Ygnacio the Andean harpist portrayed accompanying the seminary singers and cathedral *seises* in the Corpus Christi canvas *Corregidor Pérez* (fig. 10)?

LAURENCIO NÚÑEZ DE PRADO

Laurencio Núñez de Prado was appointed *maestro de capilla* at the cathedral on 30 September 1758, for which he was paid an annual salary of 550 pesos in the 1770s. In 1781 he was also serving as *maestro de capilla* at the seminary. In his role as *maestro de capilla* of the cathedral, he examined a candidate for the post of cathedral organist in 1785; the examination took place, however, in the seminary, suggesting that there was little distinction between the two institutions in terms of musical personnel and organization by this stage.[77] Like many of his predecessors, Núñez derived his income from various sources. He received payments for musical services to the cathedral Cofradía del Señor de los Temblores, and he also carried out piece-work such as organizing the music at the funeral of the *chantre*, Don Joseph de Segura y Melo, in 1776.[78] He was given a *capellanía* worth 200 pesos a year at the Beaterio de las Nazarenas in 1769, and another of the same value by the rector of the seminary in 1781.[79] He also served as the secretary of the University of San Antonio Abad from 1769 to 1786 (Valcárcel 1953, 6), and prior to that he had acted as an administrative assistant for the dean and chapter of the cathedral, his duties including renting out cathedral properties.[80] He died at some point before mid-1788.[81]

The case of Núñez is instructive, for it contrasts with the seventeenth-century examples examined above and hints at some of the changes that occurred in the music profession during the course of the eighteenth century. Despite his salary and chantries, Núñez's financial position was somewhat insecure, to judge from a claim made against him in 1781 by Doña Tomasa Medina, who sought repayment of a debt of 103 pesos: Núñez blamed the Túpac Amaru rebellion and the failure of his debtors to pay him, and asked for two months' grace.[82] In general, the financial and social status of musicians dropped during the eighteenth century. The cathedral *maestro de capilla* Juan Lázaro Gallegos died in 1724 with few possessions and sizeable debts.[83] The remunerative possibilities of the music profession seem to have declined in the early eighteenth century as the work load increased. Tomás Pérez de Vargas, who may have been Gallegos's predecessor, served simultaneously as *maestro de capilla* and *sochantre* in the cathedral and *maestro de capilla* in the seminary, yet he was not paid for the latter two positions, despite the seminary's acknowledgment of his excessive workload.[84]

It seems that Núñez had served as *colegial cantor* in the seminary as a young man prior to his appointment as *maestro de capilla*, for his name appears on the back of parts of two Beati Omnes in the seminary archive, dating from 1751 and 1752 (LCS 203 and 204). Although nothing concrete is known about his earlier years, the standard career path for Hispanic musicians in Cuzco was to begin as a *seise* in the cathedral while still a child, then to take up a singing scholarship at the seminary as *colegial cantor*, and finally to attempt to graduate to one of the paid musical posts at the cathedral such as that of *maestro de capilla* or organist, though many clearly ended up in other ecclesiastical roles that had a more tenuous connection to the musical establishment.

Eighteenth-century musicians, like those of the previous century, did not live on their salaries alone, but their complementary careers were often more humble. The University of San Antonio Abad provided a useful source of additional employment not only for Núñez but also for Gallegos before him, while the former had previously worked as a cathedral administrator alongside his musical duties.[85] Chantries continued to provide important additional funds to support musicians: the seminary *maestro de capilla* in 1756, Francisco Vaca de Castro, served a *capellanía* that appears to have been attached to his post, while Núñez held a chantry administered by the rector of the seminary.[86] These two cases also shine more light on the shifting of the burden of funding musicians toward the seminary during the eighteenth century, a period when the economic fortunes of the city and the cathedral took a marked turn for the worse.

A catastrophic epidemic of the plague in 1720, combined with the disintegration of the system of credit based on mortgage-type loans, or *censos*, left the diocese facing serious economic problems by the 1730s (Burns 1999). In 1751, the cathedral chapter wrote that tithe, chantry, and *censo* income had declined so dramatically that "Cuzco, once one of the most populous of Your Majesty's cities and the most adorned with illustrious families, is today desolate, and reduced to the miserable state of a mere twenty citizens of quality."[87] With trade hit by the increasing dominance of the Potosí–Rio de la Plata route, Cuzco had by the late eighteenth century descended from its early colonial status as "the head of the kingdoms of Peru" to "the poorest town in all of Spain and the Indies" (Concolorcorvo [1773] 1965, 265). This eighteenth-century economic decline accelerated the process of devolving responsibility for the financing of music to the seminary that had begun a century earlier. It seems that the cathedral paid salaries only to the *maestro de capilla* and the organist, while the seminary supported its singers through specific music scholarships (*becas de cantores*) and offered various discretionary rewards, including chantries, to the more senior musicians.

MATÍAS BARZENA

Detailed information about cathedral musicians and their social, economic, and professional milieu in the late eighteenth and early nineteenth centuries can be gleaned from a group of *oposiciones* (competitions) for the posts of *maestro de capilla*, *sochantre*, and organist.

Don Matías Barzena applied for the post of cathedral organist in 1804, attempting to conclude a process that had begun twenty years earlier.[88] In his original petition in 1784, Barzena stated that he had been raised in the seminary, had studied philosophy and theology, and had subsequently been appointed as a professor of arts at San Antonio Abad. He had served the cathedral for more than twenty years as a seminary singer, as well as playing the organ. Having made clear his own suitability for the job, he launched into a lengthy and vitriolic attack on the current incumbent, fray Joaquín Toledo, arguing that he deserved to be given the friar's position. Barzena was examined in polyphony and plainchant by Laurencio Núñez on 1 January 1785 and received the enthusiastic endorsement of the cathedral *maestro*, as a result of which he was awarded the post of organist the following day.

At this point the document shifts forward nearly twenty years to 14 May 1804, when Barzena was again to be found applying for the post of organist. He explained that he had been given Toledo's position in 1785, but that the friar had then engaged in some surreptitious politicking with the Audiency of Lima as soon as the bishop had left for Madrid, and as a result had managed to regain his post. Barzena therefore had to wait another twenty years until Toledo died, after at least thirty-two years' service as cathedral organist, in order to have a second chance.[89] On this occasion, Barzena gave more information about his musical formation and abilities: he had studied music in the seminary under Núñez, singing both polyphony and plainchant in the cathedral; he played the organ on important occasions when both instruments were required; and he composed polyphonic Latin-texted pieces that were performed in the cathedral. In 1778 he had been awarded the post of master of students of theology at the University of San Antonio Abad—the same position that the *maestro de capilla* Juan Lázaro Gallegos had held some seventy years earlier—as a reward for his many years of service as *cantor seminario* in the cathedral, and by 1781 he had received a chair in philosophy (Valcárcel 1953, 148). This evidently brought him neither satisfaction nor economic security, however, as he bemoaned his "miserable fate" and extreme poverty in his *oposición* at the cathedral.

The cathedral chapter agreed to award him the post of organist (for a second time), but with certain conditions. He had to play at a range of masses, some of which were seriously marred by the poor singing of the clerics. Furthermore, he had to resign his *capellanía de coro*, as his duties as organist would prevent him from singing in the choir.[90] Barzena's reply to this offer reeks of twenty years of frustrated ambition: he complained about the chapter's conditions and criticized them for "vulgarizing" the organ through overuse, but accepted the offer because of the lamentable position in which he found himself and through concern that a more compliant but less competent candidate might otherwise be chosen.

This document is worth examining in some detail as it illustrates a number of key points about musicians who worked in the cathedral orbit around the end of the eighteenth century. As for much of the previous two centuries, the classic educational path for Spanish musicians remained to serve as a *seise* in the cathedral for a minimum period of three years, then to seek a scholarship in the seminary as *colegial cantor*.[91] Their studies included music, but as seminarians, they were also provided with a general arts and humanities education. Many went on to occupy teaching or administrative posts at the University of San Antonio Abad or to pursue ecclesiastical careers, whether or not they continued to serve as musicians. There are numerous cases of *colegiales cantores* who received university posts as a reward for their musical services, suggesting that the scholarships funding them were not overly generous. There were very few paid musical posts, and many musicians ended up giving their services for free or for minimal compensation; as a result, music was dying out as a viable career for Spaniards in Cuzco. Barzena had to wait some four decades to obtain an official, salaried post with title; up to that point, he had performed and composed essentially as an amateur, claiming that "even though I was not obliged to turn up and play, I did so." Having spent most of his life waiting for some reward for his services, Barzena had less than four years to enjoy the fruits of his labors before he died.

Because of the scarcity of paid musical positions, most late-eighteenth-century cathedral musicians were very poor, indeed virtually destitute, in marked contrast to their seventeenth-century counterparts. Barzena's pleadings of poverty are typical of this period. He was reduced to begging for a paid post, arguing that he should be given Toledo's job because he needed the money more than the friar, who was supported by his monastery. The bitter tone of Barzena's appeals is characteristic of late colonial documents on cathedral music. Candidates and salaried musicians not only bemoaned the poor state of music in the cathedral but also blamed each other for this state of affairs; the effects of intense competition for scarce resources are evident. Unsurprisingly, these economic pressures affected artistic standards, and Barzena's brief as organist included covering up the mistakes of the cathedral singers. This marked late-colonial artistic decline has been noted in several New World cathedrals, including Quito, Caracas, and Guatemala (Stevenson 1978; 1980b; 1980c).

Many features of Barzena's *oposición* are repeated in a similar document dating from the same year of 1804 concerning the competition for the post of *maestro de capilla* in the cathedral after the death of the incumbent, Andrés Corsino Dávalos, and in the records of the *oposición* for the position of organist after Barzena's death in 1808.[92] The picture of cathedral music and musicians that emerges from these late-colonial sources is one of falling musical standards, declining economic status, ever-increasing insularity, and bitter internal discords. The cathedral was forced to appoint an organist who was ignorant of polyphony, while funding, too, was in disarray: a receipt from 1802 shows that the cathedral delayed almost two years in paying the organist Joaquín Toledo the paltry sum of twelve pesos for lack of funds, during which time he had to pay the Andeans who pumped the organ bellows out of his own pocket.[93] All the candidates for *maestro de capilla* came from the ranks of the seminary musicians, and most were or had been holders of *becas de cantores*. Thus despite the unfavorable conditions, the seminary continued to train and provide singers for the cathedral, and the *becas* that supported these singers were still in demand. Toward the end of the colonial period, however, there was a process of casualization of musical labor in the cathedral: the seminary production line continued to produce trained musicians, but there were few paid jobs for them. The early-nineteenth-century *oposiciones* reveal a group of musicians who spent years on the fringes of the *capilla de música*, assisting with music in an unofficial, unpaid capacity, waiting to seize their slender opportunity to obtain a salaried post.

Conclusion

Some major differences can be observed between Spanish musicians in Cuzco between the mid-seventeenth and early nineteenth centuries and their peninsular counterparts. Many of these differences revolve around the issue of low mobility. Whereas the metropolitan model of urban musical organization was one of frequent circulation between posts, the picture that emerges from mid-colonial Cuzco is one of localism and stasis: it has more in common with a Spanish town like Jaca (Marín 2002), which had approximately 10 percent of the population of Cuzco, than a comparably sized Spanish city. Peninsular *maestros de capilla* sometimes moved between churches and cities several times in the course of their career. The contrast with musicians in Cuzco from the time of Zúñiga onward, most of whom were born and died in the city and whose training and working life revolved around the cathedral and the seminary, could not be starker.

Nevertheless, Cuzco's insularity in terms of musical personnel was the result of a gradual development. The musicians who filled posts in the cathedral during most of the first century of its operation were products of the peninsular Spanish music profession in search of better pay and working conditions; Cuzco Cathedral initially formed part of the Hispanic music circuit. While Cuzco faced competition for musicians from the richer cathedrals at La Plata and Lima, to which a number of its employees defected (Stevenson 1980a), the bishop and chapter made considerable efforts to attract Spanish musicians and to retain their services. Major changes in the organization of music in the cathedral occurred in the early seventeenth century, however, with the foundation of the Seminary of San Antonio Abad and the division of the bishopric, giving rise to the marked localism of Cuzco Cathedral's music establishment in the mid- to late colonial period.

The dramatic cut in revenues that resulted from the split of the diocese in 1609 had a direct effect on musicians' salaries. Given the cathedral's lack of prebends for musicians, it is clear that the conditions were hardly ideal for attracting qualified musicians from other cathedrals. Fernández de Velasco remains the only musician known to have received a prebend, and it is therefore probably not coincidental that he was the last musician of note to be lured from another cathedral during the colonial period, in 1626: for the following two centuries, local musicians occupied the post of *maestro de capilla*.[94] The conditions favored musicians who had already established a role in the city's social and economic life and who could compensate for the somewhat meager rewards offered by the cathedral by developing their nonmusical activities. Such musicians were generally disinclined to leave the city as their socioeconomic status derived from their integration into the urban social fabric rather than their salary as *maestro de capilla*. Cristóbal de Belsayaga is the last senior musician known to have left Cuzco in order to take up an equivalent post elsewhere, moving to Lima in 1621 (Stevenson 1980a, 14). He was not a native of Cuzco, and his five years in the city were apparently insufficient to put down lucrative roots.

The division of the diocese coincided closely with the foundation of the city's seminary, and these two events were to alter fundamentally the musical panorama of the city. Just at the time when the economic basis of the cathedral *capilla de música* was seriously undermined, its salaried musicians started to be supplemented by locally born seminarians who provided their musical services for free as part of their vocational training. As a result, the burden of financing music was both reduced and shifted away from the cathedral *fábrica* and was supported instead by seminary scholarships. The bishop reported in 1625 that the seminarians had been singing in cathedral ceremonies for more than fourteen years, which would date the start of their involvement in the cathedral's musical life to around 1610, a year after the division of the diocese and the very year that the cathedral musicians' salaries were first cut. The timing and nature of these developments suggest that the enhanced musical role of the seminary, which was not set out in its 1605 foundation document, was a response to a musical crisis precipitated by the division of the diocese just four years later, and that the rapid development of the seminary as a training center for musicians was intended to resolve the problems that had arisen with the more conventional model of musical organization in the cathedral. Cuzco had been losing out to the cathedrals of La Plata and Lima since at least 1590, and with the blow to revenues in 1609, the bishop and chapter must have realized that they could no longer compete in attracting leading musicians with large salaries, so they decided to pursue a more inward-looking strategy, but one that would ensure a regular supply of trained musicians without a crippling financial outlay. In this way, the Spanish model was adapted to suit local circumstances in Cuzco: the seminary continued to provide cathedral servants, like many of its peninsular counterparts, but these servants were trained to address musical needs that arose shortly after its foundation.

The early seventeenth century was thus marked by a localization of the music establishment. The seminary became the key source of Hispanic musicians, with a seemingly endless stream of *seises* becoming *colegiales cantores*, some of whom subsequently maintained a connection with musical performance, either as salaried musicians or as *capellanes de coro*. They came from criollo families and had local roots, and they enjoyed the possibilities that went with them. The social and economic circumstances of these musicians differed substantially from those of their counterparts on the Iberian Peninsula, where financial pressures were the principal motivating factor in circulation among institutions and towns. Cuzco's criollo cathedral musicians, who developed outside interests and parallel or even substitute careers, did not generally face such pressures in the mid-colonial period, and many appear to have been financially secure, their economic status based primarily on property ownership and business dealings rather than on salary. This was a clear disincentive to seek a post elsewhere. Consequently, even a Hispanic-dominated institution like Cuzco Cathedral should not be regarded merely as a kind of provincial Spanish outpost.

Fernández de Velasco's receipt of a *ración* in the cathedral was described in 1647 as a promotion, and he was thus seen to be making an upward career move by abandoning his job as *maestro de capilla*. Indeed, several musicians who reached the level of *maestro de capilla*, including Tomás Pérez de Vargas, peaked early in musical terms and moved on to other ecclesiastical careers; others, like Alonso de Zúñiga, sought repeatedly to do so without success. This is the strongest indication that the music profession was viewed in a different way by its practitioners in Cuzco than in Spain, where a *maestro de capilla* generally saw promotion as moving to the equivalent post in a richer or more prestigious institution. Many Iberian cathedral *maestros* and organists were prebendaries, as were some singers, and they therefore enjoyed the social status commensurate with this rank in the ecclesiastical hierarchy, even though their financial means were generally much more modest. The opposite was the case in Cuzco, and this may be of crucial importance in understanding how musicians viewed themselves and were viewed by others. The fact that a number of Cuzco's musicians sought promotion within church ranks, a pattern also observed by Illari (1996, 44) in Tucumán, would seem to suggest that Javier Suárez-Pajares's (1998, 145) claim that social climbing was more of a driving force than artistic vocation within the Hispanic music profession holds particularly true for Cuzco. For many of its incumbents, the post of *maestro de capilla* seems to have been simply one of a range of ecclesiastical posts that *colegiales* of the seminary might seek to fill, more of a stepping-stone on the ecclesiastical career path than a vocation or end in itself.

Looking further down the musical hierarchy, the post of *colegial cantor* must have been attractive to budding churchmen. Whereas the Jesuit college and university were dominated by the better-off members of the criollo elite, San Antonio Abad attracted mainly poor students from good families (Villanueva Urteaga 1992, xv–xvi). The post of *colegial cantor* provided these students of limited means with accommodation, food, and clothing; thus involvement with music from an early age, particularly as a *seise* in the cathedral, improved the educational and career possibilities for such individuals. The financial and educational incentives available to talented young singers must have encouraged many to pursue the *seise–colegial cantor* route, whatever their ultimate goals. Music opened up a path into the cathedral hierarchy, keeping musicians close to the heart of the local ecclesiastical power structure. If training as a *seise* was a means to a scholarship in the seminary, occupying the position of *colegial cantor* improved a young prospective clergyman's chances of remaining at the center of the Hispanic ecclesiastical world once he was ordained, either in a dedicated music post or with a chantry in the cathedral choir, rather than being shipped off to a *doctrina* at the far reaches of the diocese. The colonial church was a centripetal organization: most clergymen sought proximity to the center, as this increased the chances of career success, with cathedral prebends the highest prizes and urban parish benefices much sought-after staging posts on the route (Ganster 1986, 148, 152). Occupying a cathedral post allowed individuals to develop and maintain the kinds of social and professional networks necessary for promotion, and thus following a musical career path may have been attractive to Spanish clerics, despite its modest financial rewards, because it kept them at the center of the "lettered city," in close contact with the highest ecclesiastical authorities.

The first criollo to become *maestro de capilla* in Cuzco, Alonso de Zúñiga, embodies the differences between the Peruvian and Iberian music professions. Descended from a conquistador and from Cuzco's first *encomenderos*, he enjoyed the wealth and social status that derived from this lineage, and he was a member of the local ecclesiastical elite. He repeatedly sought promotion to a *ración*, clearly envisaging a future as a cathedral dignitary rather than as a composer and director of music. Thus the characterization of music as a profession among Cuzco's Hispanic residents becomes somewhat problematic during the seventeenth century. Many rank-and-file musicians were seminarians, while the senior posts were occupied largely by priest-landowner-businessmen who did not regard themselves primarily as musicians. It was normal practice for Latin American clergymen to diversify their sources of income and to take on a range of ecclesiastical posts while also engaging in business activities and pursuing interests in mining, real estate, farming, and textiles (Ganster 1986; Gibbs 1979; Marzahl 1978).

Thus, rather than regarding the cathedral employees studied in this chapter as musicians who took on extramusical duties to support themselves, we should perhaps view them as priests who were engaged in a variety of activities, one of which was music.[95]

One of the positive consequences of the move away from a purely professional model of musical organization in the cathedral was that the scale of cathedral music making expanded dramatically. Whereas the church had only a handful of polyphonic singers at the start of the seventeenth century, half a century later it could call on ten times as many musicians. There are pieces in the seminary archive written for twenty voices, compositions for seven choirs, and reports of an ensemble of fifty musicians: imposing harmony indeed, especially for a provincial cathedral. The capacity to perform such huge works was a direct result of the abandonment of the traditional Hispanic cathedral model of musical organization in the early seventeenth century in favor of dependence on seminary musicians. It was because of this partial deprofessionalization that Cuzco Cathedral was able to outshine its wealthier rivals, such as La Plata and Lima, in the splendor of its music making, at least in terms of scale, and to maintain much of this splendor into the late eighteenth century, by which time economic woes had led many provincial cathedrals to experience a terminal decline in musical standards.

CHAPTER THREE

Convents and Monasteries

In 1673, three Andean *maestros cantores* were hired to provide their musical services to the monastery of San Juan de Dios. They agreed to perform at five weekly masses and a range of annual feasts including the Fridays in Lent, Holy Week, Easter, Palm Sunday, and the feast days of San Bartolomé and San Juan (the patron saints of the monastery's hospital and of the order), as well as at the funerals of any friars who died. On certain occasions they were required to bring their shawms (the Fridays in Lent and the monthly *misa de renovación*, or mass of renewal), on others to take part in processions (Maundy Thursday and Easter Day), and they were expected to bring twelve singers and four instrumentalists—an organist, harpist, *bajonero* and cornettist—on each day.[1]

Five years later, Don Alonso Merlo de la Fuente, the dean of Cuzco Cathedral, expressed his wish to take his niece and goddaughter, Doña Josefa María de Santa Cruz y Padilla, a novice in the convent of Santa Catalina, away with him to Lima. However, his niece was a talented singer and a key member of the convent's musical forces. So keen was the prioress of Santa Catalina to keep the girl in the convent that she not only offered the novice the chance to profess as a "nun of the white veil" and to take her place in the *coro* without payment of a dowry but she also guaranteed her certain privileges: Doña Josefa would only have to sing on important occasions when polyphony was performed, and she would be exempt from all other convent duties, even if for some reason "God saw fit to take away her voice."[2]

These two cases underline the considerable importance that Cuzco's convents and monasteries attributed to their musical activities. The nuns of Santa Catalina placed a high monetary value on the musical abilities of this particular novice, so reluctant were they to lose her: the dowry payment for taking the white veil was around 1,660 pesos. The monastery and hospital of San Juan de Dios, meanwhile, emerges as a significant patron of music in the late seventeenth century, the frequency and scale of the performances detailed in the contract mentioned above rivaling those of smaller Latin American and European cathedrals. An investigation of the role of music in the houses of Cuzco's religious orders will clearly be essential to building a picture of the city's musical life, yet these institutions have been almost entirely overlooked by musicologists throughout the Viceroyalty of Peru.[3] The use of music by the religious orders in Lima has been noted in general studies by both historians and musicologists, but there are no detailed studies of the musical functioning of such institutions or of their place in urban musical culture.[4] The problem of sources is acute in Cuzco, as it is elsewhere on the continent: the city's monastic and conventual archives are either closed to researchers or have been lost entirely. Nevertheless, evidence from other sources, such as the notarial documents quoted above, sheds light on various aspects of musical organization, training, and performance within the institutions of the city's religious orders and hints at the role of nuns and friars in the musical life of the city.

Convents, Culture, and Urban Identity

The convent of Santa Clara, founded by the Franciscan order in 1558, is the oldest in Peru.[5] It was established initially as a center for the education and Hispanicization of the mestiza children of the early Spanish settlers and Inka women. The first mixed-race entrants were taken in as full-fledged nuns, yet within a few years a wider backlash against mestizos in Cuzco led to the emergence of an internal hierarchy based on race. Spanish nuns began to wear the black veil (*el velo negro*), while mestizas took the white veil (*el velo blanco*): as such, a feature distinguishing professed nuns from novices took on the added connotation of marking the perceived superiority of the Spanish nuns over their mixed-race sisters. A second convent, Santa Catalina de la Sena, was established in 1605 by Dominican nuns who moved from Arequipa after their convent was seriously damaged by volcanic eruptions in 1600 and 1604. This institution was not intended primarily for mestizas: they were allowed to enter, but not officially to take the black veil. A third convent, Santa Teresa, was established in 1673. Little evidence of musical activity at Santa Teresa has emerged, perhaps reflecting the fact that it was founded in response to the perception that the lifestyle of the city's nuns had become excessively lavish; it may therefore have tended toward austerity in its external displays.

Convents, like the colleges of San Bernardo and San Borja for the male children of the region's elites, were at the heart of the reproduction of Hispanic culture and values in the Andes and thus proved important in establishing and maintaining Spanish hegemony in the New World. Santa Clara was, according to Kathryn Burns, a "school of Spanish culture"; its purpose "was not simply to create nuns, but to create culturally Spanish young women" (1999, 27–30). Young mestizas were a kind of cultural capital, and the convent pursued a program of acculturation in order to incorporate these women into the Hispanic social sphere. Music education and performance in convents were thus initially intended to advance the twin aims of evangelization and Hispanicization, as they were throughout the hemisphere. Yet convents also appear to have played a unique role in the consciousness of Peru's prominent Spanish citizens. Unusually, both Santa Clara in Cuzco and Santa Catalina's first incarnation in Arequipa were founded by their city councils, rather than by elite families or individuals, indicating that convents were seen as potential symbols of municipal status and pride. Prominent local figures, by placing their daughters in a convent, sponsoring an orphan, or playing a role as an administrator or benefactor, could invest in the "spiritual economy" of the city and in the future and prestige of their culture. Just as convents were symbols of the spiritual (and economic) well-being of the city's Hispanic elite, their performances had the potential to reproduce and project the cultural vision of this urban group. Their practices were thus viewed in highly symbolic terms. Convents were considered "a reflection on the communities around them; Spanish ideals of honor and feminine purity were powerfully represented and reinforced by these bulwarks against evil, dishonor, stain. If the nuns' honor was upheld, a city could hold itself in esteem" (Burns 1999, 24). Convents thus lay at the heart of Spanish efforts to construct "ideal cities" in the heart of South America, and their cultural activities—above all, the performance of polyphony—were symbolic resources used by the local elite to maintain the status and privilege of the institution, the city, and their social class within this highly stratified society (Kendrick 1996, 415–16).

Convent culture appears, however, to have become a site of struggles over differing visions of the colonial city and the activities and performances of nuns came under particular scrutiny by church authorities, especially in Lima. Successive eighteenth-century archbishops made efforts to suppress the more carnivalistic elements of convent festivities and thereby to defend the honor of the viceregal capital, issuing a stream of decrees aimed at controlling the musical activities of the nuns, which made for a constant source of friction. The religious authorities sought to restrict what kinds of music the nuns performed—there were bans on villancicos and polyphony in processions—and the locations of performances, with repeated edicts attempting to eliminate music in convents' *locutorios* (visiting rooms) and entryways. There were regular complaints about excessive expenditure, the hiring of external musicians, dancing, costumes, and other forms of festive behavior (Sas 1971; Martín 1983; Estenssoro 1990). Convent culture was the object of such controlling impulses because of the unique reproductive role of these institutions in Peruvian cities and the symbolic associations of female music making: if nuns were dancing and making merry, then Spanish culture might be perceived as having mutated in the colonies. Convents were a barometer of Hispanic culture, and the impression that they conveyed was significant to the self-image of various elite sectors of the European population.

It is notable that those who frowned on the musical practices of Lima's convents were primarily the archbishops, who were usually outsiders, whereas the local criollo elite was generally delighted by these florid expressions of baroque culture. Encouraged by local dignitaries, the nuns regularly defied repeated accusations and prohibitions by archbishops: one Lima abbess defended her convent's displays by reporting "the approval of many officials of this *real audiencia* and other serious, circumspect citizens of good judgment who were present" (quoted in Estenssoro 1990, 414–15). The archbishops saw an excess of spectacle and the intrusion of the secular world, but Lima's residents simply enjoyed some of the finest musical entertainment on offer in the capital, and convent performances regularly drew crowds of the city's religious and secular elites.[6] In the seventeenth and eighteenth centuries, as the ideological split between locally born criollos and peninsular Spaniards became more entrenched, the former may have come to identify more with their convents—institutions dominated by local families and interwoven with the spiritual and economic life of the city—than with the cathedral. A symbol of metropolitan power, headed usually by a nonlocal archbishop, the cathedral was the scene of state-sponsored ceremonies, often precipitated by events that were distant both in place and time and that in themselves had little direct effect on the lives of the local populace. The symbiotic relationship between convents and the local elite, however, brought economic, spiritual, and cultural benefits to both parties; convents' artistic activities could therefore be a source of civic pride as well as concern.

Convent culture appears to have been a sphere in which power relations between the secular church and the convents, between *peninsulares* and criollos, were constantly renegotiated. The intensification of official suspicion of convent music in the late colonial period may well reflect unease at the growing sense of criollo pride and cultural autonomy. The repeated show-downs, meanwhile, reveal the stubbornness, even rebelliousness, of the nuns and their resistance to interference. In his study of Milanese convent music, Robert Kendrick (1996, 421) regards such disputes not as simple miscalculations about episcopal power but rather as "conflicts necessary to the continued projection of female monastic ritual and music in the public life of Milan." The fact that episcopal decrees were repeated frequently suggests their ineffectiveness: nuns were backed by their influential fam-ilies, so bans tended to be short lived. Many nuns in Cuzco, too, came from important families, and their displays of cultural independence were perfor-mances of their status and autonomy as members of the local criollo elite. Records of disputes over music, for all that they tend to reflect the perspec-tive (and the authority) of the episcopate, in fact serve to underline that nuns, while separated physically from the city, were not marginalized or powerless. Music provided them with a voice and a presence in colonial society by attracting, and in some cases flattering, the local elites that played such vital roles in convents' political and economic functioning. The influ-ence of the nuns in the city depended on their participation in such social networks (Monson 1995), and their participation was boosted by their cul-tural, as well as economic, activities. Musical performances behind the convent walls allowed nuns to ally themselves with leading criollo citizens and religious dignitaries while asserting their independence from the secu-lar, metropolitan church hierarchy, and thus to shape their own distinctive space in colonial cities.

Convent Music

In her magisterial study of Cuzco's convents, Kathryn Burns (1999, 106) describes the churches of Santa Clara and Santa Catalina as "among the most brilliant theaters in the region for the staging of one of the most lavish, spectacular cultural events of the day, the Roman Catholic mass." She also points out that musical activities within the convents were not confined to the churches: "As Santa Clara and Santa Catalina grew into *conventos grandes*, their entryways and locutorios became alive, even bois-terous, with activity . . . . [They] might ring with the choral and instrumental music of an evening's entertainment" (103). Despite their modern image as islands of calm and silence in the middle of the noisy, hectic city, Cuzco's convents were important centers of musical performance, education and, to a lesser extent, employment in the colonial period, as indeed they were in Spain. Sumptuous, large-scale performances in church, exuberant fiestas, musical-theatrical performances, and private music making were all characteristic features of life in the *conventos grandes*, as these "cities within the city" were known.

An account of musical activities in Santa Clara can be found in a mid-seventeenth-century chronicle by the Franciscan Diego de Mendoza. According to the author ([1665] 1976, 70), ceremonies in the convent were suitably lavish for the senior institution in Peru, and the nuns devoted considerable effort and study to ensuring that both plainchant and polyphony with instrumental accompaniment constituted a regular feature of these occasions.[7] Documents in Cuzco's archives confirm that musical performance was a central element of convent life. In 1664, Tomás de Herrera— the older of the two Herrera brothers who worked as cathedral organist— was hired by the convent of Santa Clara for a period of two years to teach music to the nuns. He was to instruct a group numbering up to twelve on a daily basis, teaching them singing, organ, and harp, as well as providing "all the music that might be required in the festivities organized by the convent."[8] Among the music preserved in the archive of the Seminary of San Antonio Abad are polychoral works whose parts are inscribed with the names of nuns, indicating that such complex pieces formed part of the convents' repertory. The archive includes an anonymous thirteen-part Lauda Jerusalem for four choirs (LCS 278): all the parts have female names on them, such as "soror francisca" and "soror maria," and the piece is dedicated to Santa Catalina. Another, even larger work, a twenty-part Magnificat by "Maestro Sanz" (LCS 333), also has many parts marked with female names, revealing the nuns' participation in the performance of polyphony on a grand scale.

Nonliturgical music making was also commonplace in Cuzco's convents. Music played a significant part in festivities within the cloister walls, and the evidence from prohibitions issued in late colonial Lima reveals that convents knew how to throw a party.[9] The priest Juan de Pancorbo stated in his will that he had lent a harpsichord worth three thousand pesos to Santa Catalina, where he had been the administrator, for a fiesta.[10] Outsiders, too, were witnesses to the splendor of the convents' festivities; indeed, important visitors were sometimes the very excuse for these fiestas. When the bishop of Paraguay passed through the city in 1723, Santa Catalina put on a performance to celebrate his arrival (Esquivel y Navia [c.1749] 1980, 2:229).

The visit of a prominent Spanish Franciscan friar, Alonso López de Casas, to Santa Clara in July 1737 occasioned a special concert that included a *loa*, some *juguetes* (a lively, generally comic type of villancico), and other "excellent musical works" (Lanuza y Sotelo 1998, 122). Music was clearly not always a solemn affair in convents. Several playful villancicos in the seminary archive appear to have been performed by nuns: the comic Christmas villancico "Un pastor y un estudiante" (LCS 153) has the name "soror francisca" on its harp part, while "Va de xacara" (LCS 164) and "Escuchen los jacareros" (LCS 162) reveal conventual connections through references to an abbess or "madre vicaria" in their texts.

Such musical displays, like *comedias* performed in the seminary, were often designed to impress or flatter their audience, not merely to entertain them. In 1743, the arrival of the recently appointed bishop Morcillo Rubio y Auñón in Cuzco precipitated a week of festivities in his honor, which included an afternoon of music, theater, and dance in Santa Catalina attended by the bishop himself (Esquivel y Navia [c.1749] 1980, 2:294). One of the works performed was a zarzuela in praise of the bishop, written by the abbess of the convent (Claro 1969a, 14), revealing that convents' cultural performances, while potentially a means of marking independence, could also serve to establish a good relationship with the highest church authorities. Cloistered nuns were not able to participate in civic events, so official visits were key opportunities to make a favorable impression on local or visiting ecclesiastical dignitaries who might play an important future role in the convent's affairs. Encomiastic music was a characteristic feature of Cuzco's cultural life, allowing urban communities and institutions to forge potentially fruitful links with powerful individuals, and the nuns did not hesitate to sing the praises of their distinguished guests when it suited them.

Convents offered the opportunity for female musicians not only to engage in communal music making but also to shine on the semipublic stage as individuals and achieve recognition for their skills. The Dominican friar Thomas Gage wrote of a nun whom he heard in the convent of La Concepción in Guatemala City: "This Doña Juana de Maldonado y Paz was the wonder of all that cloister, yea, of all the city for her excellent voice and skill in music" (Thompson 1958, 190). On an institutional level the skillful performance of elaborate polyphony was a way for convents to project their belief in their elevated status in the city. A symbolic hierarchy of colonial society was enacted more commonly in spatial form, principally in the order of precedence of various groups in public processions and the seating arrangements at ceremonies, but the cloistered nuns were unable to participate in such visual enactments of prestige, making their aural presence in the city even more important. Music was a vital means for nuns to record their presence and display their status on the urban stage from which they were physically excluded by courting local elites and drawing the city into the convent, where they could be heard, if not seen (Monson 1995, 11; Kendrick 1996, 416). Finally, on an urban level, performances in front of important ecclesiastical visitors from outside the city were opportunities to represent and glorify Cuzco in the eyes of the world.

If the aims of most performances were relatively benign, amounting to little more than the projection of a positive image of religious dignitaries or institutions, and thereby of the city itself, on other occasions the nuns used the convent walls as a barrier behind which to carry out more overtly political campaigns with virtual impunity. Lima's nuns satirized their political opponents in songs composed and performed within the cloister: convent music emerges here as a tool for female self-expression in a male-dominated and -regulated world (Monson 1995, 9–10).[11] Music was also used as part of the internal political processes of convents. In 1644, the winning candidate in the election of the prioress in the convent of Santa Catalina in Cuzco, Doña Mencía de San Bernardo, was accused by her defeated rival of a range of underhand electoral tactics, including courting votes by putting on musical entertainments.[12] Victory, too, might be celebrated in song: the villancico "Escuchen los jacareros" (LCS 162) includes a number of verses that lavish praise on the abbess of an unnamed convent, including one lauding her election.[13] The mixture of music and politics within convents was particularly controversial, for the nuns were appropriating and subverting an art form that was supposed to embody, at least in the eyes of the ecclesiastical authorities, all that was pure and unworldly. The fact that edicts were issued at regular intervals throughout the seventeenth and eighteenth centuries in an attempt to control the convents' independent spirit indicates both the longevity of the controversy and the stalwart resistance of the nuns to outside intervention.

MUSICAL INTERACTIONS

Despite the restrictions of the cloister, music afforded nuns considerable contact with the city beyond its walls. Not only were many performances directed at outside audiences, forging connections with local elites and visiting dignitaries, but convents also hired external musicians to train the nuns, to write music for them, and, possibly, to direct their music making. The presence of a number of pieces in the seminary archive marked with nuns' names suggests that *maestros de música* from the seminary supplied their services and their music to the convents.[14] As well as the pieces mentioned above, a twelve-part Lauda Jerusalem (LCS 274) is marked with many female names; a four-part Miserere by Pedro Vidales (LCS 194) has the name Doña Catalina de San Gabriel on the cover; the villancico "Ya no mas cupido hermoso" (LCS 034) has female names on all the vocal parts; and "Enigma soy viviente" (LCS 143) is marked with the name Doña Francisca Gamarra. The regular borrowing of seminary music by the convents is also implied by the note on a heavily used villancico, "Buen viaje, leva la mar" (LCS 018): "Hombre ô muger seas quien fueses / quien aqueste papel cantares / advertid que nescesita / mucho donayre y gracia" (man or woman, whoever it may be who sings this part, be aware that it requires much grace and charm).

Further evidence of the connection between the seminary and Cuzco's two oldest convents may be found in a number of other pieces in the seminary archive. "Atended escuchad" (LCS 087), two polychoral Dixit Dominus (LCS 241 and 247), a Laudate Pueri (LCS 299), and an eleven-voice Lauda Jerusalem (LCS 275) are all dedicated to Santa Catalina. Two Laetatus Sum (LCS 252 and 253) are dedicated to the same saint, and the performing forces—one or two sopranos and harp—suggest that these pieces were written especially for the convent (Marín 2002, 134–35); one of the dedications ("Dedicado a mi M.e S.a Catalina de Sena") implies that the composer may actually have been a nun. Two villancicos, "Queditito quedo" (LCS 159) and "Para entrarse monja" (LCS 114), are dedicated to Santa Clara. The former has the name Señora Doña Gabriela written on one part, while the title of the latter is particularly suggestive, implying that villancicos were written and performed for the ceremony of the taking of the vows, as they were in Spain (Burns 1999, 109; Marín 2002, 131). "Para lograr las gracias" (LCS 124) is dedicated to Nuestra Señora del Carmen, the patron saint of the convent of Santa Teresa, and a Laudate Pueri (LCS 300) was sung, according to an annotation, in the same convent on the saint's feast day in 1754. "Pues que nace en Belén" (LCS 057) and "Albricias que en la insigne" (LCS 083), although not dedicated to convent saints, were apparently reused in convent settings, to judge from variants in their texts. While the pieces annotated with female names were incontrovertibly performed by nuns, those which are dedicated to the convent saints are possibly more ambiguous. However, it seems highly likely that they were performed in the institutions to which they are dedicated, given the evidence presented in the previous chapter that seminary musicians took part in the celebrations for the patron saints of the city's monastic institutions.

The fact that pieces with convent connections are preserved in the seminary archive suggests that they were written or directed by seminary *maestros*. It seems likely, however, that full music ensembles were brought in from outside only rarely, as there is every indication that for much of the colonial period, the two principal convents had large and complete musical forces capable of performing complex polychoral works. These institutions apparently aimed for, and generally achieved, a high degree of musical self-sufficiency. While the evidence suggests that they relied on seminary *maestros* to supply them with some of their music, and perhaps to train and direct their choirs, additional performers from outside were probably only needed to provide maximum splendor on key occasions such as the feast day of the titular saint or the election of an abbess. Santa Teresa may also have received ensembles on occasion, especially as its own musical capacities were seemingly limited. Two surviving villancicos, "Ay que portento ay que prodigio" (LCS 016) and "Oy cielo y tierra" (LCS 106), were sung in honor of the convent's saint, to judge from textual variants, while the Wednesday evening processions instituted by Bishop Melchor de la Nava, which included the singing of the rosary by the seminarians, began and ended at the Carmelite church (Esquivel y Navia [c.1749] 1980, 2:207–8). The canonization of San Juan de la Cruz in 1729 was marked by a large procession with the saint's image from the cathedral to Santa Teresa, where solemn vespers were sung (245); Bishop Bernardo Serrada was a member of the Carmelite order, and so the ceremonial life of this church may have blossomed at this time.

The nuns provided employment opportunities for outside composers, as well as for directors and performers. The will of the indigenous *maestro compositor* Don Matías de Livisaca, discussed in the following chapter, refers to a debt of thirty-five pesos owed by Doña Francisca Olaya, *vicaria* of Santa Catalina, to the musician for two psalms that he had composed, presumably for the convent musicians.[15] In addition, the convents provided work for organ builders and repairers, as well as for makers of other common instruments such as the harp and the *bajón*. The organ builder Juan Antonio Munsibay de Chávez came to a creative agreement with the convent of Santa Catalina: he offered to provide the convent with an organ in lieu of his daughter's dowry as a nun of the black veil, worth 3,312.5 pesos.[16]

MUSIC EDUCATION IN THE CONVENTS

Convents had a variety of musical connections with other institutions and individuals, but their educational programs provided some of the most regular interaction with outsiders. Not only was the elder Herrera son hired to instruct the nuns of Santa Clara in 1664 but his brother had been contracted in 1654 by Juan de Pancorbo, the administrator of Santa Catalina, to teach a young girl named Ana María Carillo, whom Pancorbo was bringing up in the convent. Herrera was required to give her a daily lesson in keyboard playing and singing polyphony for two years.[17] He was rehired by Pancorbo when this contract expired to carry out the same duties for a further two years, though on this occasion he was also required to teach composition, which suggests that at least some of the music performed within convents was composed by the nuns themselves.[18] There is also an indication that convents hired indigenous music teachers alongside Spaniards. In 1676, Diego Achasa, an indigenous *maestro bajonero* and a resident of the parish of San Sebastián, was hired to teach two girls in Santa Catalina: one was to learn the *bajón* and the organ, the other just the *bajón*, and they were to be given two lessons a day.[19]

That convents were the prime centers of female music education is underlined by Diego de Mendoza ([1665] 1976), who writes of the central role of instruction in plainchant, polyphony, and the playing of instruments in the education of novices in Santa Clara.[20] The beneficiaries of this education were not just ordinary novices but also, on occasion, orphans or foundlings who had been brought up in the convent by a senior nun. Josepha del Carmen, a "nun of the black veil" in Santa Catalina, left accommodation in the convent to a girl known simply as "Josepha the *bajón* player," whom she had raised since childhood, so that the girl might continue to serve in the choir.[21] The musical forces of convents therefore consisted of more than simply nuns: disadvantaged girls who were part of the household of senior nuns could forge a more prominent role for themselves within the institution by learning and providing musical skills. Those of lesser means could support themselves, or even pay off their dowry in part or in whole, through their musical services. Musical talent therefore provided a route to climbing the social ladder of the convent since it enabled poorer members who might otherwise have spent their lives as servants to senior nuns to participate in convent ceremonies or even to profess as nuns of the white veil. An Andean novice in Santa Clara named Antonia Viacha was granted a reduction in her dowry when she took the white veil in 1708, in return for many years of service both performing and teaching the *bajón*. The tone of the abbess's statement makes clear that she was highly appreciative of this service, and she offered Viacha the opportunity to pay only 1,000 pesos of the 1,656 pesos 2 reales that she owed.[22]

Musical ability thus had considerable financial value: it was highly esteemed by the convent authorities, who were prepared to make generous offers to talented musicians. In 1770, the convent of Santa Catalina offered the black veil to a sixteen-year-old girl for half the usual cost (1,662 pesos 4 reales) in return for her service as organist in the convent choir. The girl had clearly been preparing for this moment, as she had been brought up in the convent and had already served one year as organist.[23] This case, like the one presented at the beginning of this chapter, underlines the extent to which convents valued musicians of talent and reveals that such talent could bring not only economic benefits and other privileges but also the advantages of high status within the convent.

The practice of providing financial incentives to talented musicians is well catalogued in both the Old and New Worlds. Convents in Lima regularly waived part or all of the dowry for girls who showed musical skill, and La Encarnación had a particularly fine reputation for music, maintaining its standards through an admission policy favoring those who would be able to contribute to its musical life (Stevenson 1960, 56; Lizárraga 1987, 111–12; Vásquez de Espinosa 1992, 601; Martín 1983, 182). This custom had its roots in Europe, where it was standard practice in the convents of Spain and Italy, and no doubt in many others across Europe (Marín 2002, 127; Monson 1995).[24]

TRAINING GIRLS FOR CONVENT SERVICE

In the cases detailed above, the girls who were offered financial incentives by Santa Catalina had received their musical education within the convent. However, many parents or guardians, fully aware of the advantages that such a musical training might bring, gave their daughters a thorough grounding in ecclesiastical music as a precursor to their entry into a convent in order to improve their chances of reaping these economic and social rewards. Such practices have also been noted in Spain (e.g., Gembero 1998, 284). Investing in music education was a wise choice for parents of limited means who hoped to place their daughters in a convent and for whom a sizeable dowry might have proved a stumbling block; but even wealthier citizens saw that musical skills would allow their daughters to stand out within such institutions. In 1645 a merchant named Juan de Vega Buerres hired Juan Candidato de Cárdenas to teach music to his daughter. The contract specifies that Candidato should teach her how to lead both polyphonic and plainchant masses as well as vespers, and should instruct her in a variety of keyboard forms and techniques required by church organists, so that "any master of this art or nun who may hear her will confirm her skill."[25] A century later, Don Agustín Apumayta, *maestro organista* and *principal* of the parish of Hospital de los Naturales, agreed to teach music, including "verses of all the psalms," to the daughter of Don Miguel Cano de Contreras; the contract was for two years of lessons every morning, whether or not the girl should enter a convent during this period.[26] Other contracts do not specifically mention that the pupil was destined for one of the city's convents, but training in church music would have been of little use to a girl outside these institutions, and the intentions of the parents are therefore implicit. Don Bartolomé Padilla, *maestro organista*, was hired in 1768 to teach a girl named María Teresa Juana de Dios Olazábal the skill of accompanying vocal music on the organ.[27] A similar agreement was struck between Doña Bernarda Salazar and Don Gregorio Viracocha Ynga, *maestro músico organista*, to teach the former's daughter, María Pacheco, the organ every day for a year, so that at the end of the year she "could play in any choir."[28]

While most of these musicians were hired by Spaniards, who were more likely to be able to afford to invest in their children's musical education—and it was clearly a good investment, given that the return on two years of lessons at between 50 and 150 pesos per year might be a dowry reduction worth over 1,600 pesos—there are also cases of Andeans entering into such agreements. Don Gaspar Viacha, the governor of the village of Colquepata, hired Juan Antonio Munsibay de Chávez to teach singing, *bajón*, and everything relevant to "his profession of *cantor*" to his two daughters, at one hundred pesos for six months' instruction.[29] Viacha's niece, Antonia, was the novice and *bajonera* who professed in Santa Clara in 1708; music seems to have been a favored occupation among the female members of this indigenous family. Another Andean named Juan de Samudio declared in his will that he had spent 185 pesos on instruments and musical education for his daughter Catalina.[30] It appears, then, that Andean elites too were aware not just of the socioeconomic advantages of having family connections within convents but also of the greater opportunities for advancement within these institutions for musically skilled novices.

Beaterios

Indigenous women are all but invisible in studies of colonial music, not least because of their exclusion from public performance in civic ceremonies. Felipe Guaman Poma de Ayala ([1615] 1980, 767), however, includes music among the skills possessed by devout Christian Andean women, and some evidence of their musical education and performance activities within convents has emerged in these pages. The two daughters and the niece of Don Gaspar Viacha all learned to play the bajón, while the Andean Diego Achasa was hired to teach the same instrument, suggesting that the organizational model of the cathedral—indigenous players of wind instruments accompanying Hispanic singers—may have been replicated to a certain degree in the city's convents. If they had a musical presence in Santa Clara and Santa Catalina, Andean women were also audible in beaterios, centers of female religious education that were smaller and more informally organized than convents, but that responded to women's aspirations to live as a pious community and to devote themselves to mutual support and educational activities. Beaterios were often founded under the auspices of a male institution and beatas took some of the vows of the religious order in question, but they were not usually cloistered. In many parts of the New World, the Spanish-indigenous dichotomy was mapped onto convents and beaterios, but in Cuzco the lines seem to have been less clearly drawn. As we have seen, Andean women had a place—if a subordinate one—in Cuzco's convents, while the beaterio of Las Nazarenas, which stood next to the seminary in the plaza of the same name, was founded for Spanish women to raise orphans. Most beaterios in Cuzco, however, were occupied primarily or exclusively by indigenous women, having been established for this purpose by members of the native elite. Indeed, these were the only religious institutions that could be both founded and funded by Andeans. They allowed prominent Andeans to exercise a degree of control and responsibility that they never had in convents, where even the most noble could only profess as nuns of the white veil; in beaterios, on the other hand, some Andean women came to hold the position of abbess (Burns 2002, 128–29).

Evidence of music making in beaterios is extremely scarce yet nonetheless suggestive. According to an early-nineteenth-century inventory, Las Nazarenas had an admirable chapel with an organ (Viñuales 2004, 186). Given that some of Cuzco's beaterios aspired to become convents—Las Nazarenas attempted to upgrade its status repeatedly in the eighteenth century, though without success (180–82)—the performance of religious ceremonies with suitable decencia (propriety) undoubtedly bolstered their efforts to convince the ecclesiastical authorities of their respectability. Decencia was especially important to Andean beaterios, which often struggled against Spanish prejudice (Burns 2002). The Beaterio de la Santísima Trinidad was founded in 1674 by three Andean nobles who stipulated that the beatas should learn "to read and write and sing and play some musical instruments with the aim that, with the brightness of their voices, the unbelieving Indians who have still to be conquered may be drawn into the Christian faith" (Burns 2002, 127). According to an inspection four years later, the *beaterio*'s chapel contained musical instruments including an organ, harp, guitars, *raveles* (a kind of string instrument), shawms, *bajones*, and trumpets. A witness was impressed with the instrumental skill of the *beatas*: "Having finished singing, the *beatas* played the instruments, creating great harmony, admiration, and devotion" (Burns 2002, 127). Music was thus central to the mission of the *beaterio*'s founders to exteriorize their faith and to reinforce piety among the Andean population.

There were many *beaterios* in the city, though precisely how many is unclear: nine were recorded in just two Cuzco parishes in 1689, and there were still at least eight in the city a century later (Burns 2002, 123; Castro [1795] 1978, 54). If Santísima Trinidad was in any way representative, *beaterios* added another significant dimension to Cuzco's musical life. Further information on their music making is unfortunately lacking, but evidence from La Plata suggests that these institutions played a notable part in the soundscape of colonial cities (Illari n.d.). The *beatas* of San Francisco in La Plata performed polyphonic repertoire of cathedral origin, and because they were not cloistered, they had a higher musical profile in the city than nuns. On occasion they performed in other churches, posing a threat to the monopoly of the cathedral *capilla de música* over urban religious institutions and thus provoking censure. The musical activities of *beatas* also attracted the attention of the religious authorities in Lima, where the archbishop Melchor Liñán y Cisneros, a vocal critic of female religious musical practices who had banned villancicos among the city's nuns and restricted their performances of polyphony with instruments, decreed in 1702 that men and women should not go to *beaterios* "to play and sing . . . with harps and vihuelas and *violones* and other instruments" (Sas 1971, 1:36). *Beaterios*, like convents, apparently exercised a pull as centers of musical activity, though their more relaxed rules allowed men and women to sing and play music together more readily than in convents.

Whereas cloistered nun-musicians were invisible to audiences, since they performed behind a grille, *beatas* could be both seen and heard in public performances, and they therefore offered a unique and appealing musical spectacle within colonial society. As female Andean musicians, both their sound and their appearance were distinctive. Their performances were richly symbolic for Spanish audiences, enacting what Bernardo Illari (n.d.) calls a "mission musical tableau"—converted Andeans performing European sacred music, and thus justifying Catholic colonialism in the eyes of

Hispanic observers. A missionary impulse was explicit in the musical instructions that accompanied the foundation of Cuzco's Beaterio de la Santísima Trinidad, which suggest that these *beatas*, too, were intended to be heard by "unbelieving Indians" outside of their community. In a mirror image of the male Andean parish musicians to be examined in subsequent chapters, female Andean *beatas* were seen as potential musical intermediaries in the propagation of the Catholic faith.

From the perspective of Andean communities, however, the acquisition of musical skills by indigenous women reveals that female musical education in colonial Cuzco was not simply a question of the reproduction of Hispanic culture by and for the Hispanic populace. Learning European music was bound up with individual and collective strategies for advancement: joining a *beaterio* choir was a potential source of prestige and even money, and it allowed indigenous women a voice and a presence they otherwise rarely had in colonial society. When they challenged the cathedral *capilla de musica* in La Plata or came up against episcopal authority in Lima, singing *beatas* showed themselves as capable of pushing against the limits imposed by colonial power and of negotiating their space in the city. In the case of *beaterios*, as in that of convents, musical performance was a prime interface between religious women and the wider urban population, and the disputes in Lima and La Plata reveal that music provided an avenue for such women, both Spanish and Andean, to test the boundaries of their circumscribed social worlds.

The performance of music by *beatas* is also tied up with the production of a collective, "decent" (i.e., honorable) Christian identity by the region's Andean elites (Decoster 2002; Burns 2002). Roberto Choque Canqui (2002, 336) describes the case of a Bolivian cacique who built a *beaterio* at which daughters of the native elite studied music, became accomplished performers, and accompanied religious services. The instructions for music education and performance in Santísima Trinidad in Cuzco were drawn up by the institution's noble Andean benefactors. If this appears to be a symbol of the success of the Spanish evangelical program, it also reveals that the adoption and propagation of Catholic religious and cultural practices had become important to the self-definition of Andean elites. The patronage of music in *beaterios* formed part of the broader performance of authority by members of the native nobility via these institutions, which were founded to manifest their piety and provide a "decent" place for their relatives and other members of their social and ethnic group. Church music was a sound of high status in colonial society; it reflected positively on both performers and sponsors, hence its explicit inclusion in these ordinances. The performance of European-style sacred music by indigenous women in an Andean religious institution was a potent expression of the aspirations of a new native nobility that emerged in the second half of the seventeenth century and sought to construct an honorable Christian identity. The sounds of voices and instruments that resounded in the *beaterio*'s chapel were richly meaningful to its founders, encapsulating their urge for *decencia* and piety, the allure of modernity and Hispanism, and their desire that they and their kin should actively participate in the Catholic faith.

Music in Monasteries, Hospitals, and Schools

Franciscan and Dominican friars were among the first Spaniards to enter Cuzco, establishing their houses in 1534, the year of the formal Spanish foundation of the city. The Franciscan monastery in Cuzco was not only the order's first in Peru but also the head institution of the province of San Antonio de los Charcas. In the following year the Mercedarian order founded what was eventually to become the largest monastery in the city, the head of the province of La Visitación de Nuestra Señora, and the Augustinians followed suit in 1559. The Jesuits established themselves in Cuzco in 1571 and spelled out their ambition by buying the former palace of Huayna Capac on the main plaza, within a stone's throw of the cathedral; in the aftermath of the 1650 earthquake, the cathedral chapter was displeased by the ostentation of the order's new church, and a lengthy dispute ensued (Esquivel y Navia [c.1749] 1980, 2:98). The Jesuits were to play important cultural and educational roles, setting up two schools, San Borja for the sons of caciques and San Bernardo for Spaniards, as well as the University of San Ignacio de Loyola. Another order that subsequently gained a high profile in the city was that of San Juan de Dios, which entered the city in 1617 and took over the rundown hospital of San Bartolomé for Spaniards, as well as founding its own monastic house, commonly known by the name of the order. The order of the Bethlemites, which took over the semi–parish church of Nuestra Señora de la Almudena, was the last major order to install itself in Cuzco, arriving in 1690 and founding the hospital and monastery of La Almudena in 1698.

In the previous chapter, we saw that the religious orders came together to sing plainchant in the cathedral as part of the Office of the Dead for kings and popes. Indeed, it seems that there was a connection between the communal identity of the regular clergy and the sounds of plainchant in such urban ceremonies. The participation of the male orders in civic processions is well documented—for example, in the series of Corpus Christi paintings —though evidence of musical performance is unfortunately lacking. During Holy Week in 1745, the four senior monasteries and San Bartolomé put on "magnificent processions" on successive days from Monday to Friday, illustrating their prominence in urban rituals, but leaving open the question of their aural impact (Esquivel y Navia [c.1749] 1980, 2:322). It is nonetheless entirely possible that they sang plainchant at some point during such processions. The friars also participated in events of critical importance to the city or the Spanish empire by replicating the ceremonial activities of the cathedral within their own institutions. In 1649, when an earthquake shook the city, the bishop and cathedral chapter ordered that a misa rogativa be celebrated in the cathedral with the religious orders present, and that the following day the friars perform the ceremony in their own churches "with the same solemnity" (88). More commonly, the monasteries echoed the cathedral bells when they were rung to mark extraordinary events, and the cathedral reciprocated the favor by ringing its own main bell to mark the feast days of the orders' patron saints.

Cuzco's monasteries, like its convents, thus played a notable role in the musical life of the city. However, key differences can be observed between the musical activities of these two types of institution. Whereas convent music was often sumptuous and on a grand scale, with complex vocal and instrumental polyphony performed by the nuns themselves, the music of the friars appears to have been more restrained, probably limited to plainchant with organ on most occasions. No documents equivalent to the contracts to teach sophisticated music to convent novices have been located in Cuzco's archives, nor has any evidence to suggest that the friars placed the same importance on musical talent and education as their female counterparts. The only relevant music contracts that survive are agreements between monasteries and organists or organ builders. The implication from what is missing, as well as from what survives, is that friars were trained within the monasteries by a vicario de coro, or choirmaster, who was a member of the community and whose principal duty was to teach and direct plainchant. The impression that elaborate musical performances played a lesser role in Peruvian monasteries than in convents arises not only from archival sources but also from the accounts of contemporary witnesses. It is instructive to compare their comments—and, above all, their silence—about music in the male establishments with their praise of the musical abilities and achievements of the nuns.

The Franciscan chronicler Diego de Mendoza ([1665] 1976, 42–43) makes various references to music and ceremony in the monastery of San Francisco in Cuzco, but he mentions nothing more elaborate than plainchant. Yet his descriptions of the musical activities of the Franciscan nuns of Santa Clara, discussed above, refer repeatedly to polyphony and instrumental music. He clearly recognized and appreciated sophisticated music; it seems probable, therefore, that the contrast between his two accounts is not coincidental. A similar impression arises from contemporary descriptions of Lima's religious houses. The Dominican friar Reginaldo de Lizárraga (1987, 111–14) enthused about the musical abilities of the nuns of La Encarnación and La Concepción around 1600. In his description of the monasteries of the five main orders, however, he makes no mention of music; he even reveals that many friars would attend the Saturday Salve Regina at the convent of La Encarnación, which strongly implies that the nuns' ceremonies outshone those of their male counterparts. Antonio Vásquez de Espinosa (1992, 594–602), another chronicler of Lima's religious establishments in the early seventeenth century, is also full of praise for the nuns' musical capacities. While he goes on to describe the monasteries of the capital in some detail, painting a picture of ceremonial splendor that could compete with the best that Europe could offer, music again remains conspicuously absent from his account.

EXTERNAL MUSICIANS IN CUZCO'S MONASTERIES

This does not mean that more complex music was not performed in monasteries; it simply implies that such music appears not to have been performed by the friars themselves. In Spanish cities it was normal practice for the cathedral *capilla de música* to supplement the musical forces of monasteries on important days in the religious calendar, and there is evidence that cathedral musicians and, later, singers from the Seminary of San Antonio Abad participated in the musical activities of Cuzco's monasteries (see chapter 2). As in the case of the convents, there are pieces in the seminary archive that suggest performance in monasteries, though it is probable that a full complement of polyphonic seminary singers would have been required in the male institutions. There are villancicos dedicated to three of the principal monastery saints: San Agustín (LCS 095, 105, 107, 111, 115, 131, 149), Santo Domingo (079, 092, 101), and San Francisco (091). The villancico "Festejese la iglesia" (LCS 098) was clearly heavily used, to judge by the variants in its texts: it was apparently performed in honor of various senior religious figures, as there are references to a *racionero*, a prebendary, and a father superior in the text. The tenor part of choir 1 has been altered to refer to a father who was made provincial (head of his order's province). Another piece, the comical Corpus Christi villancico "Un monsiur y un estudiante" (LCS 152), was also apparently performed in a monastery, possibly to celebrate the election of a provincial.[31]

Seminary musicians thus attended the city's monasteries on the feast days of their patron saints, in all probability performing the repertoire dedicated to these saints in the seminary archive, and supplied encomiastic music for the celebration of occasional events. For more day-to-day musical services, however, the monasteries drew on the numerous Andean professional musicians in the city. In 1653, the monastery of San Francisco took on the Andean organist Juan Flores Usca to play the organ in its church for one year on a salary of 100 pesos, soon to be raised to 120 pesos.[32] The following year, Flores Usca was contracted by San Agustín, again at 100 pesos for the year, "to serve the monastery as organist, turning up punctually to play the organ at the usual times."[33] He seems to have been quite in demand during this period: two months after his first contract with San Francisco, he signed a second one with fray Luis Ramos, *vicario de coro* of the same institution, again to play the organ in the monastery's church, this time on an improved annual salary of 130 pesos plus food and lodging.[34] However, Flores Usca did not complete this contract, for some five months later the monastery hired a new organist, another Andean named Pedro Miguel from the parish of Hospital de los Naturales, to serve in the church for a year in return for 110 pesos and meals in the monastery.[35]

It is perhaps surprising that these monasteries did not have a friar capable of playing the organ, as this seems to have been the normal arrangement in Spain (Marín 2002, 139). While it is difficult to generalize in the case of Cuzco due to a lack of documentation, there is further evidence that monasteries hired outsiders. The Andean organist Joseph Ygnacio Mayta is recorded as *maestro organista* of the church of Santo Domingo in 1742.[36] The monastery of La Almudena had an anonymous salaried organist for much of the eighteenth century, while La Merced was employing an outsider, Don José Arrisabal, as organist in 1813.[37] One issue may have been that a friar skilled in organ playing might attract the attention of another institution, forcing his monastery to hire an organist from outside to fill his place. Fray Joaquín de Toledo served as cathedral organist from 1772 to 1804 "without ever turning up at his monastery, so that due to his absence, a considerable amount is expended on paying a secular to play the organ in his respective church." These were the words of his bitter rival Matías Barzena, who coveted Toledo's cathedral post and who went on to recommend Toledo's "confinement to the cloister, using his ability in the service of a monastery which gave him his education and sustenance."[38] Barzena's wish was never fulfilled, however, and monasteries' organists continued to look toward the cathedral: another friar, Damian Donayre from San Agustín, applied for the post of cathedral organist in 1808.[39]

Monasteries were a valuable source of work for organ builders, as well as for players of the instrument.[40] It appears from the large quantities spent that it was de rigeur for these institutions to have a fine instrument and to maintain it in good working order. Gabriel Cabezas, *maestro de hacer órganos* (master organ builder), was contracted by the monastery of Santo Domingo to repair their organ in 1631. The prior of the monastery lavished 1400 pesos just on these repairs, which indicates the importance that he placed on this instrument.[41] In 1662, the Arequipa-born Pedro Guaman, *indio organero, ladino en la lengua española* (Spanish-speaking Andean organ builder), was hired to carry out repairs on the organ of the monastery of La Merced; these included replacing seventy pipes, thirteen trumpets, two drums and a bird-whistle, as well as cleaning and tuning the instrument. His work was checked by Tomás de Herrera, the organist at the cathedral.[42] The following year, the same maker sold an organ to the monastery of San Agustín for 700 pesos. The instrument was unfinished, but Guaman agreed to finish, tune, and install it in the *coro* of the monastery within four weeks, after which it, too, was to be checked by Herrera.[43] Either the organ was not particularly well made or it was heavily used, for only eight years later the monastery paid 550 pesos to another indigenous maker, Pedro Romero, to carry out full repairs on the instrument.[44]

Players of instruments other than the organ were hired for occasions on which greater musical splendor was required. The accounts of San Agustín for the years 1781–85 show a regular monthly payment to an organist, but also occasional larger payments for "music," drummers and trumpeters, and other such expenses.[45] These extra musical forces were drafted for important annual fiestas such as the feast days of San Agustín and San Juan, indicating that the monastery was prepared to pay for occasional musical reinforcements. Another, unusually descriptive, document provides further evidence that Cuzco's monasteries were capable of putting on a lavish musical display when so inclined and that they might draw on Andean musicians instead of the seminary singers for important occasions. A ceremony took place in the monastery of San Francisco on 2 August 1678 to mark the election of fray Cristóbal Daza Dávalos as provincial of the order. According to a witness, "at around one o'clock in the afternoon I saw the whole community and all the friars of the monastery coming out of a door in the main cloister that leads to the church; they came in procession with a tumult of drums, trumpets and shawms, letting off fireworks . . . , and as they processed they sang the *Te Deum*, arriving eventually at the main chapel." At the end of the ceremony the friars "paid their respects with a great noise of drums, shawms, peals of bells, and the organ."[46]

Like the textual traces in seminary villancicos, this suggests that the election of a provincial was commonly used as an excuse for musical celebrations in monasteries. The noise and exuberance of this particular festivity are notable—accounts of such displays in monasteries are found much less frequently than those of similar events in convents—as is the distinction between the music of the friars, who processed while singing a hymn, and the clamor of the instruments, which were undoubtedly played by Andean musicians hired especially for the occasion from outside. Wind instruments were normally the preserve of indigenous musicians in colonial Cuzco, as they were in other Latin American cities with a large native population. This account seems to reflect a subtle line between the sacred and the secular features of the fiesta; the friars organized the event and sang in it, yet they maintained a certain separation from the more worldly musical elements, performed by Andean professional musicians.

It seems reasonable to conclude, therefore, that musical activities of the friars themselves were limited in scope and that the monasteries were largely self-sufficient on a day-to-day basis, apart from the need to hire an outside organist in some cases, but that they did occasionally bring in musicians for important events. There is clearly a distinction between the music performed by the friars and the music performed within the monasteries. For example, confraternities based in the monasteries would have brought in musicians on some occasions: the Cofradía de Jesús Nazareno in the monastery of San Francisco hired a full complement of musicians to attend its masses in 1670, creating the impression that elaborate music was not an unusual occurrence within this institution.[47] The evidence that Andean ensembles were hired on important occasions—a feature absent from the surviving material relating to convents—suggests that if Cuzco's nuns created the musical spectacle themselves, playing the leading parts during their fiestas, the friars were happy to leave these activities to others. Monasteries appear not to have hired outside music teachers or directors, depending instead on their own *vicario de coro*, which implies a more modest program of music education among the friars.

The ready availability of Andean musicians, a notable feature of Cuzco's musical life that will be explored in subsequent chapters, may explain the discrepancies that emerge between this picture and that of the only other comparable institution to have been studied, the monastery of La Merced in Santiago de Chile, which owned a variety of instruments and music books and appointed a *vicario de coro* who taught both chant and polyphony (Vera Aguilera 2004). While these differences may simply reflect the types of sources used—the Mercedarian archive in Chile is open to researchers, unlike its Cuzco counterpart—it may be that the proliferation of highly trained seminarians and professional Andean musicians in Cuzco meant that it was easy for monasteries to secure reinforcements, and that they therefore elected to concentrate on plainchant and to leave polyphony to musicians brought in from outside. In a smaller, more peripheral city like Santiago, musical life probably depended to a greater extent on the activities of Hispanic churchmen such as the Mercedarian friars, and self-sufficiency—in other words, polyphonic capability—may have been necessary for such institutions. It is perhaps unwise, therefore, to assume that friars in larger cities performed more elaborate music than those in smaller centers. The breadth and depth of musical culture in Cuzco may have reduced the friars' need (and opportunity) to perform music other than plainchant. There is enough evidence of the borrowing and hiring of outside musicians to suggest that monasteries in Cuzco chose not to be self-sufficient, but rather opted to leave musical extravaganzas to professional musicians and seminarians. Instead, the friars participated in urban musical culture by performing plainchant both within and outside their institutions and by stimulating the city's musical economy.

MUSIC IN MONASTERY HOSPITALS

More information on the musical world of the monastic houses is available in the records of the monastery hospitals of San Bartolomé and La Almudena and the hospitals of San Andrés and Hospital de los Naturales. The friars of San Juan de Dios and the Bethlemite order, later arrivals in Cuzco, appear to have offered greater opportunities to external musicians than those of the older monasteries.

The contract between three indigenous musicians and the monastery hospital of San Juan de Dios with which this chapter began reveals that this institution was home to regular, large-scale polyphonic performances with instruments in the late seventeenth century and was therefore no musical backwater. Like many monasteries in Spain, San Juan de Dios relied on outside musicians for the performance of elaborate polyphony; unlike most of its peninsular counterparts, however, it did not hire cathedral musicians, but instead drew on the city's Andean musical workforce, based primarily in the city's parish churches, and as a result could employ musicians to perform with a regularity that was impossible in Spain. The *capilla de música* of a Spanish cathedral often became overcommitted, since it was the principal, and sometimes the only, group in a given city capable of putting on large-scale polyphonic performances. In Cuzco, the strength of parish music meant that many more polyphonically trained musicians were available, and outside assistance could therefore be hired more regularly. The contract with San Juan de Dios reveals that the ensemble performed polyphony almost on a daily basis, something that is inconceivable in most Spanish monasteries. As if this were not enough to fill the cloisters with music, there are also contracts showing that the Cofradía de Santo Cristo de la Coluna, based in the same monastery, insisted on lavish music at its ceremonies. This confraternity, examined below, hired Andean parish musicians over a period of some seven decades to provide vocal and instrumental music at its Friday masses and all its annual feasts.

There is further evidence that music occupied an important place at San Juan de Dios and that the monastery consistently brought in musicians over a period of many years. The foundation stone of monastic music was of course the organ, and in 1649 the friars hired Antonio Cabezas, the younger of a prestigious father-and-son team of instrument makers, to build them an organ identical to that in the Jesuit church for 550 pesos, suggesting that they planned to take music seriously.[48] Bishop Mollinedo made an inspection of the hospital in 1680, during which the institution's accounts were presented. Over the previous two decades, the friars had spent 3,033 pesos on paying musicians to participate in masses in their church and in the funerals of those who had died.[49] This document indicates an impressive and continuous commitment to music, especially given that the bishop wrote in his summary at the end of the report that the hospital had neither a doctor nor a surgeon, having given both jobs to friars who knew nothing in order to save on salaries. The pharmacy had few medicines, and the patients complained that the friars did not look after them properly, but musical activities were apparently unaffected. This case illuminates the importance of music to religious institutions, and particularly to hospitals: the fact that the monastery dedicated such financial resources to music while simultaneously cutting other costs—music was the second largest expenditure by the hospital after medical care—indicates that it was central to the friars' activities, rather than a luxury or a simple adornment. If the friars preferred to spend money on musicians than on doctors, it suggests that they believed wholeheartedly in the healing, or at least consolatory, power of music, and in its capacity of music to boost the effectiveness of the religious rituals that were central to medical practices.[50] When such efforts failed, a funeral with music provided further spiritual assistance after death.

Evidence from the mid-eighteenth century indicates that music continued to play a part on important dates in the religious calendar at San Juan de Dios, but that the scale of the performances had declined by this time.[51] Most documented masses were sung by a single priest. They were celebrated on certain saints' days and at the burial of anyone who died in the hospital, and they were paid for by families in memory of deceased relatives or by guilds. Exceptionally, groups of musicians performed. The *novenario* of San Juan de Dios was the most important period of the year in the monastery; in 1759, for example, there were payments to drummers, trumpeters, and those who organized the fireworks. Singers were brought in for the Friday masses in Lent in 1772 and 1773, and for the funeral mass of a friar who died in 1768, both the kind of occasion at which musicians had been required a century earlier. The monastery was still employing an organist at the very end of the colonial period, indicating that its musical traditions might have faded but had not disappeared.[52]

The Bethlemite monastery and hospital of La Almudena organized regular musical activities from the earliest days after its foundation—surviving accounts begin in 1705—until the end of the eighteenth century, and these records give a sense of the kind of musicians hired by the monastery and of the occasions on which they were expected to perform.[53] Throughout this period, the monastery had a salaried organist, and in 1720 the monastery spent four hundred pesos on a new organ, suggesting that musical performance was a regular feature in the church. There is also a payment of thirty-eight pesos to the organist, named Miguel, for "six months of teaching and playing" in 1722. It is not clear who or what he was teaching, though he may have been instructing one of the friars in organ playing, as is implied by another ambiguous payment, dating from 1706, "to the organist who teaches Brother Joseph." In 1732 a salaried *maestro cantor* is also noted, but there were also regular and irregular payments to a range of other musicians including singers, drummers, trumpeters, shawm players, *ministriles*, a harpist, *colegiales* or *cantores del colegio*, and sometimes a general payment for "music for the fiesta." During the period 1763–70, a distinction appears in the accounts between *músicos menzales* (salaried musicians) and *músicos sobresalientes* or *músicos independientes (del mensal)* (freelance musicians), with the former presumably performing at the regular masses and the latter hired for important feasts. This may well have been true at other times as well, since variations in the accounts often appear related to changes in scribal rather than musical practice.

Two names are mentioned in these accounts: there are several payments for musical services to "D. Ignacio" between 1712 and 1718, and one, in December 1711, for "Musica, de libisaca, noche buenas" (Music, by Livisaca, Christmas Eve). It seems probable that "Ignacio" was the same Don Joseph Ygnacio who organized the annual musical event at the hospital of San Andrés between 1709 and 1723 (see below). Meanwhile, "libisaca" may well have been Don Matías de Livisaca, the Andean composer and musician from the parish of Santa Ana who sold psalms to the convent of Santa Catalina and who also owned a house on the plaza of La Almudena. If these suppositions are correct, then the monastery of La Almudena hired two of the most influential indigenous musicians in early-eighteenth-century Cuzco to organize its events.

Although the accounts vary considerably from year to year, the two most important feasts from a musical perspective emerge clearly as Easter and Christmas. The latter was invariably followed by another large celebration with music on December 28, the Feast of the Holy Innocents—often referred to as "aguinaldos" or "misa de aguinaldo"—which was sometimes celebrated with music throughout its *novenario*. The vespers of the Nativity of Our Lady, on September 8, and its *novenario* were also regularly commemorated with musical reinforcements: the monastery spent thirty pesos on music during this period in 1709. In the early part of the century, singers from a *colegio* performed at these three principal feasts, though the identity of the college is unclear. Cuzco's most famous singing *colegiales* were those of the Seminary of San Antonio Abad, but the students of the Jesuit college of San Bernardo also sang in other institutions, as we shall see below. Other major feasts in the church calendar appear more sporadically in the accounts, though whether this unevenness reflects actual practice is a moot point. The feasts of Epiphany, San Antonio, Santiago, the Assumption, and San Andrés all saw payments to musicians in some years. In 1752, detailed expenditure on the fiesta of San Antonio is noted: among the many festive costs are payments to musicians, drummers, and trumpeters for every day of the *novenario*, to musicians who participated in the procession and throughout the day of the feast, and a further payment to four drummers, two trumpeters, and two shawm players for the vespers and feast day itself.[54]

Detailed accounts from the late eighteenth century show that musicians were also hired for regular services, usually once or twice per week. Irregular payments to musicians by the monastery appear for a variety of reasons, most commonly for the funerals of friars, but also for one-off occurrences that precipitated festivities in the monastery: thanksgiving masses with lavish music were celebrated in May 1735, in the name of the *prefecto general* of the order, fray Joseph de San Estevan, and again in September 1747 for the swearing in of King Ferdinand VI. As was the case at San Juan de Dios, music making in the church of La Almudena was augmented by the activities of confraternities. The Hermandad de Esclavitud de Nuestra Señora de la Almudena was founded in 1689, a year before the Bethlemites arrived in Cuzco and thus while the church was still designated a semi-parish. The constitutions of the brotherhood provide a detailed list of the occasions on which a sung mass was to be celebrated, including a range of saints' days, weekly masses, feasts of Our Lady, and the funerals of confraternity members (see chapter 4).[55] The participation of musicians and a harpist on all these occasions is specified in the constitutions, implying that the sung mass was polyphonic.

A sense of smooth and regular functioning emerges from the monastery's accounts. This impression is undermined, however, by a demand made in 1795 by the organist, Don Tomás Arcos, for fifty-eight pesos that he claimed the institution owed him in unpaid salary.[56] This allegation was, perhaps unsurprisingly, denied by the head of the monastery, but it was supported by various witnesses including Don Mariano Arias, a sergeant in the fifth cavalry regiment and *maestro violinista*, and Don Carlos Cusiguaman, *maestro arpista*, both of whom also claimed that they were owed money for services lent to the same church. The latter said that all the musicians apart from the organist had resigned after the monastery stopped paying their salaries, suggesting that La Almudena seems to have succumbed to the general crisis that engulfed Cuzco's musical life in the late colonial period.

Despite this breakdown in relations, it is clear that the hospital provided a steady source of income for a number of external musicians for almost the whole of the eighteenth century. Taken together, these account books show a considerable amount of regular musical activity and expenditure, demonstrating the monastery's notable role in the musical economy of the city. But, as in the case of other monastic institutions, not all music was contracted from outside: the Bethlemite friars themselves sang plainchant, both within and outside the monastery. According to a 1751 inspection, "every day at the correct hour a conventual mass is said, with the community present—and on Thursdays, Saturdays and Mondays it is sung." In addition, a chaplain was required to sing a mass every Monday, with the responses sung by the community of friars.[57] The Bethlemites also participated in the Office of the Dead for Philip V in the cathedral in 1747.

The Hospital de San Andrés for Spanish women, founded in 1649, was governed by a brotherhood rather than by one of the regular orders. Documents detailing the expenditure of the hospital between 1708 and 1730 indicate a modest musical program involving the hiring of outside musicians only on the feast day of the patron saint.[58] There is considerable consistency in the forces that were hired, and even in the precise personnel. The entry for 1715 records expenditure on preparing the organ and buying harp strings, on two drummers, two trumpeters, and a group of shawms, and a larger payment for music to "Don Ygnacio," maestro músico (who presumably brought a group of musicians with him). These musicians performed at vespers and later the same evening, as well as on the day of San Andrés itself. This pattern was followed every year during this period, and despite the fact that this event occurred only once a year, certain musicians appear to have been regulars. Don Joseph Ygnacio Mayta, the Andean organist and harpist who was also employed by Santo Domingo and La Almudena, was paid to organize the music every year from 1709 to 1723, while the organ repairer Carlos Cuyotopa was hired from 1709 to 1717.[59] Other sources suggest that ceremonies in the hospital were occasionally attended by elite musical and social groups. When Bishop Mollinedo visited San Andrés in 1680, his inspection began with a mass of the Holy Spirit, sung "with full solemnity" in the choir by the colegiales of San Antonio Abad, while the feast of San Andrés in 1746 was celebrated in the hospital with solemn sung vespers in front of a sizeable congregation that included the city council (Esquivel y Navia [c.1749] 1980, 2:365).

Records from the end of the eighteenth century reveal that considerable sums continued to be spent on musicians, drummers, and trumpeters for the feast of San Andrés; shawmers and two African horn-players also appear in the accounts.[60] Easter, too, saw annual payments of thirty to forty pesos to singers and instrumentalists. This account book appears to illustrate unequivocally that there were just two large musical events each year at this time. However, some intriguing footnotes added to the accounts by the hospital's administrator, Don Josef Agustín Chacón y Becerra, reveal just how misleading this impression is. In a note in 1789 he declared that masses were also celebrated every Thursday, once a month (the misa de renovación), and during the Forty Hours devotion in Holy Week, the novenario of Corpus Christi, and the week of "Dolores," with the attendance of priests, altar boys, and musicians, the playing of drums, trumpets, and shawms, and with fireworks; yet he had not charged the hospital for these services for two years and intended to continue paying for them out of his own pocket and with the help of other pious contributors. He also added that he had paid for music, food, and flowers on the saints' days of hospital patients.[61] In 1792, he added further notes to the records, stating that every Thursday throughout the year there was a sung mass in the hospital church at six o'clock in the morning with "complete music," drums, and trumpets, and that there was also "very full music" during the three days of Carnestolendas before Lent. Again, he stressed that he did not charge the hospital a centavo for these services.[62]

Four important points emerge from these entries by the hospital administrator. First, even San Andrés, one of the smaller hospitals, in fact made a significant contribution to Cuzco's musical life and provided a considerable amount of work for musicians: on average, there would have been two masses with music each week in the hospital church. Second, individuals as well as institutions patronized music in colonial Cuzco. While this is not entirely surprising, evidence for such patronage is in very short supply due to the kinds of historical records preserved. Third, music was one of the principal services provided for hospital patients, and it might thus be considered a form of medical care. Fourth, and this is a point that I will take up at length in subsequent chapters, account books can be misleading: they may provide some evidence of music making, but much information may be omitted. These hospital records demonstrate clearly that music was subsidized from more than one source, a common occurrence in Cuzco's churches, and thus regular musical activities frequently do not appear in account books, which record only institutional outlay. In the case of San Andrés, it was only on the two most important religious occasions of the year, when particularly large numbers of musicians were required, that the hospital itself contributed to the cost, while musicians for all other feasts and regular masses were covered by the administrator. Were it not for the zealous record-keeping of this particular individual, the true extent of musical activities in San Andrés would have remained invisible. Account books, then, may reveal only extraordinary expenditure, the tip of the iceberg of musical activity.

The order of San Juan de Dios was given control of the Hospital de Naturales for Andeans in 1622, but the decision was reversed a year later and the hospital returned to the hands of the city council, by which it had been founded in 1556. The only sources of information that could be located concerning music in this hospital were accounts for the years 1787, 1792, and 1793. In the first year, the hospital paid the considerable sum of sixty-five pesos to Gabriel Altamirano for the music during the seven days of Easter, the key feast in this parish; it also recorded a payment of sixty pesos to the musicians for the festivities of 1792, and fifty pesos the following year.[63] The hospital was attached to the parish church of the same name, and according to the priest's report of 1689, the parish church "is used together with the hospital for burying the friars and the poor who come to be treated, and for its festivities" (Villanueva Urteaga 1982, 228). This hospital therefore contributed to the active musical life of one of Cuzco's eight parish churches, no doubt patronizing the parish musicians. Although the surviving evidence is scarce, the size of the payments for music indicates an impressive annual festivity, and regular funerals would have added to the musical functions in the parish church.

The apparent richness of the musical life of Cuzco's hospitals may simply reflect the random survival of historical records, as only one equivalent account book for an older monastery (San Agustín) could be located. The fleeting archival traces do suggest that elaborate music was performed at important celebrations in the senior institutions, and it is entirely possible that records, if they existed, might reveal more musical activities and the patronage of Andean parish ensembles. San Agustín was the smallest of the city's senior monasteries in the late eighteenth century (Castro [1795] 1978, 49–50), so the larger institutions may have seen more extravagant musical displays, such as that recorded in San Francisco in 1678. There are, however, reasons to suspect that greater emphasis was placed on music in the monastery hospitals than in the monasteries of the mendicant orders. The most obvious difference between the two types of establishment revolves around sickness and death. Hospitals were places where the sick went to be healed but also consoled and, in many cases, to "die well"; religious services and music were part of the comfort and medical assistance offered to the sick and the dying, and funerals were a regular occurrence in these institutions. Friars who died were standardly buried with full pomp, with musicians hired for the occasion. Spaniards or mestizos of reasonable financial means who died in hospitals might also request a solemn sung funeral in the hospital church, which included candles, incense, bells, and various rituals of death including a sung mass with vigil.[64] As this service cost sixty pesos in the late eighteenth century, and given all the other evidence of hospital music making, it seems entirely reasonable to suggest that a proportion of this sum would have been set aside for musicians to attend the funeral mass and burial. As places of healing, illness, and death, hospitals thus required musical performance with considerable regularity. The relationship between sacred music and healing was not, however, confined to these institutions: it was seen in the previous chapters that one of the most elaborate public musical events in Cuzco was the regular procession with the Holy Sacrament to the sick, involving the seminary singers and *ministriles* from the cathedral Cofradía del Santísimo Sacramento. Ecclesiastical reports stress the edifying and consoling effects of plainchant and polyphony on the public in this most emblematic of the seminary's duties.

The provision of elaborate music may also have been a projection of the wealth or aspirations of the newer institutions. The Bethlemite order was the last to arrive in Cuzco and may therefore have embraced lavish display as a way to establish itself and make its presence felt in the city. The earliest surviving records, dating from 1705, seven years after the foundation of the monastery, show that a musical program was already in place by this time. The order acquired nine haciendas in the forty years after its arrival, which provided a sizeable income and allowed the Bethlemites to run one of the largest and most efficient hospitals in the Viceroyalty of Peru (Glave and Remy 1983, 275–82). The order was suppressed in the mid-nineteenth century and is now largely forgotten in Cuzco, but it made a significant impact on the city's society and economy in the eighteenth century. Ignacio de Castro (1978, 55) was impressed by the monastery's physical structure and the amount of money that had been lavished on fine buildings, paintings, and decoration; indeed, he questioned whether such magnificence was really suitable for an institution dedicated to the care of the sick. The attention paid to music may therefore reflect the considerable resources and desire for status of this late-arriving but successful institution.

The strict order of precedence in colonial Cuzco placed the hospital orders behind the older monasteries, which occupied prime positions in urban rituals because of their antiquity: as a result, internal festivities may have taken on greater importance in the newer monastic houses. The willingness of the hospital orders to spend considerable sums on musical extravaganzas on their feast days probably reflects the fact that such events constituted the high point of their visibility and audibility within the city. Impressive musical displays within their institutions allowed the hospital orders to leave their mark on the city's cultural life despite their secondary status in the religious hierarchy.

The musical instruction of girls and novices in the city's convents was directed internally, in the sense that the nuns' primary intention was to ensure their continuing musical self-sufficiency and excellence. Monasteries, too, undoubtedly trained their own personnel in music within their institutions: the religious orders in Cuzco had *casas de noviciado* where future generations of friars were educated, and novices must have been instructed in music by the *vicario de coro* in order to maintain a supply of suitably trained plainchant singers. Evidence of more specialized music instruction of the kind received by convent girls and young women is, however, lacking in the case of the male institutions, implying a more limited degree of musical ambition.

The regular clergy were, on the other hand, involved in wider educational projects outside their institutions. They undertook the task of educating certain sectors of Cuzco's population, and music formed a core subject within their educational programs. The Jesuits were at the forefront of efforts to instruct both the Spanish and the Andean elites in the city of Cuzco, and they ran two schools, the Colegio de San Bernardo for the sons of Spaniards, and the Colegio de San Borja for the sons of caciques. Although little research has been undertaken on San Bernardo, founded in 1619, there is some evidence that it included music in its curriculum. The college hired Juan Candidato de Cárdenas in 1638 to teach its pupils to sing; he was to attend every day except Sunday and on feast days, and was paid 120 pesos for a one-year contract.[65] In 1645, the Andean *bajonero* Juan Blas from the parish of San Blas was hired by the rector of the college for one year, on virtually identical terms: he was to be present at the college between midday and one o'clock every day except Sundays and feast days to play the *bajón* and teach the pupils. As an Andean, his salary was considerably lower, at twenty-four pesos for the year, but he had the right to go to the college to eat whenever he wanted.[66] He also agreed to accompany the *colegiales* whenever they went to sing outside the school. Another Andean, Don Francisco Auca Tinco, is recorded as *maestro cantor* in the Jesuit college in 1691.[67] Nearly a century later, in 1799, music was still sufficiently important at the college that it spent seven hundred pesos on a new organ by the maker Francisco Andia.[68] The evidence of daily instruction and of external performances reveals that musical training was taken seriously at the Colegio de San Bernardo and suggests that the students achieved a high standard. Indeed, its *capilla de música* was praised by a mid-seventeenth-century observer as "the best in the realm," quite a compliment at a time when the musical capacities of the rival seminary of San Antonio Abad were at a peak (Viñuales 2004, 146).

The Colegio de San Borja, like the other *colegios de caciques* that the Jesuits established in South America, was founded with the express intention of indoctrinating and acculturating the future leaders of native communities (Galdo Gutiérrez 1970; Martín and Pettus, 1973; Alaperrine-Bouyer 2002). Even when San Borja was just a glimmer in the eye of a few Jesuit priests, music was already destined to become a central feature of the program designed to mould young Andean nobles according to a Hispanic Christian vision. The college was not actually founded until 1621, but as early as 1567 the Jesuit Juan de Matienzo wrote that instruction in singing and playing recorders should be aimed at the sons of caciques, while the sons of commoners should be directed toward trades such as carpentry and building (Galdo Gutiérrez 1970, 31). Regulations for the planned *colegios de caciques* were drawn up in 1576 by José de Acosta and Juan de la Plaza; according to the second of these regulations, "they will learn to read, write, sing, and play the music commonly used in churches" (Martín and Pettus 1973, 127). Just one year after the foundation of the college, one of its teachers wrote that the students were learning to sing and to play keyboard instruments (Vargas Ugarte 1948, 151), while music was also part of the curriculum in the *colegio de caciques* in El Cercado, Lima, around this time (Vásquez de Espinosa 1992, 610). Thus the teaching of music formed part of the overall program of religious indoctrination of native leaders, just as it had since the first missionaries arrived in the Americas.

It is likely that the Jesuits intended that some of their young charges should take up posts as *maestros de coro* in their communities on finishing their education. The theory behind the colleges was that after a period of intense acculturation, the sons of caciques should be returned to their communities, where they would serve as positive role models to their subjects.[69] The eldest sons were normally destined for political positions, but second sons were often trained in European professions (Dean 1990, 84); it would seem, therefore, that the younger sons of caciques would have been ideally suited to the influential post of *maestro de coro*, to be considered in depth in the following chapters. This was a position of considerable authority that combined musical and general teaching duties with religious leadership, and none would have been better qualified to fill these posts than graduates of the *colegio de caciques*, who inherited authority as their birthright and acquired the necessary skills through their Jesuit education.

Although the Jesuits emerge as the prime promoters of music education in Cuzco, the Franciscans also traditionally placed considerable emphasis on music, having been at the forefront of musical instruction during the first wave of colonization in Mexico and having made it a principal subject at the Colegio de San Andrés in Quito (Turrent 1993; Córdova Salinas [1651] 1957, 1035–36). They were active in the training of Andean musicians soon after the foundation of the first native parishes in Cuzco; the Franciscan Jerónimo de Oré was a great advocate of music education in the late sixteenth century, and Gregorio de Zuola, a friar who left a commonplace book with excerpts of polyphony, was a musically literate member of the order who ran the Franciscan *doctrina* of Urquillos a century later (Stevenson 1976; Esquivel y Navia [c.1749] 1980, 2:145). Traces of Franciscan musical instruction can also be found in Cuzco's archives. The friar Joseph Cortés made an apprenticeship agreement on 6 October 1714 with an Andean named Juan Quispe from the village of Chinchero. Cortés agreed to take on Quispe's son, Ignacio, for a period of ten years and to teach him the art of organ playing; Quispe was to live in the monastery under Cortés's roof.[70] In a second contract dating from the same year, the Franciscan Estevan de Aramburu hired the *maestro bajonero* Don Lorenzo Tambocoro to teach his art to five boys in the friar's care, who were to be able to perform in church functions without guidance within a year.[71]

CONFRATERNITIES IN THE MONASTIC CHURCHES

Confraternities were lay religious brotherhoods of European origin that have been defined as "carefully constructed death societies" (Flynn 1989, 13) and "a cult of the living in the service of the dead" (Davis 1974, 327). As lay associations, they were important channels for popular religious practices, uniting members in the veneration of a particular saint or holy image. They offered support and assistance in practical ways, fostering social cohesion and functioning as welfare organizations for their members, but also interceded for recently departed brothers and sisters—arguably their most important role. Many dozens of confraternities housed in Cuzco's churches sponsored musical performances, and widespread popular affiliation with these societies ensured that the majority of the city's adult population was exposed to sacred polyphony and loud instrumental music through their ceremonial activities. Indeed, despite the fact that confraternities have generally been omitted from musicological studies of Latin America, they were at the center of many individuals' experience of Catholicism. Their functions were among the most important religious occasions in the lives of both Spaniards and Andeans, and they were key to bringing the sounds of the church into the lives of the populace and investing these sounds with meaning.[72]

The Jesuits not only educated the indigenous elite but they were also active in promoting the formation of Andean confraternities in their college churches and training the confraternity musicians. The Jesuit chronicler Antonio de la Vega refers to daily performances by the Cofradía del Niño Jesús in the Jesuit Andean church in 1600. On Saturdays, the Salve Regina was sung polyphonically, and these services, along with fiestas and processions, were accompanied by the confraternity ministriles.[73] His description of confraternity processions is particularly striking:

> In their processions and fiestas they walk with candles lit, carrying the arms of the name of Jesus, and the Indian men wear white shirts and yacollos [colored cloaks], some made with cochineal, others with crimson damask, and the women wear llicllas and ascus, which are their cloaks and dresses, or basquiñas [skirts], of the same colors. There are more than five hundred of them, confraternity leaders and members, men and women. It is a great and edifying spectacle to see this confraternity on the day and octave of Corpus Christi, and on the days of their fiestas and celebrations, of which there are three or four in the year, when it processes publicly in the plaza with its singers and ministriles playing, and as there is such a wonderful display, with so many people and so many candles, it must be the most splendid sight in the whole city. (Vargas Ugarte 1948, 43–44)

The Jesuits also drew on these large and diverse musical forces to satisfy their own ceremonial needs, and the Cofradía del Niño Jesús performed at Jesuit college fiestas, according to Vega. Cuzco was not alone in witnessing the splendors of Jesuit confraternity music. At the school in Arequipa, the Salve Regina was sung on Saturday evenings by the native confraternity to the accompaniment of many instruments (Mateos [1600] 1944, 2:248). These Jesuit-sponsored musicians were hired by the maestro de capilla of the church that was later to become the cathedral to provide their musical services on all important occasions, such was their ability (Stevenson 1976, 286). The Colegio de San Pablo in Lima trained and maintained groups of Andean and African confraternity musicians who performed at festivities within the college and who were also in demand at outside functions, offering the public some of the best entertainment available in the capital (Martín 1968, 137). Thus the Jesuits' zeal for music education bore fruit not only at festivities within their institutions but also across the city.

Music was required on a regular basis by confraternities based in the churches of the other religious orders, and considerable musical forces were sometimes employed at confraternity functions. The Cofradía del Santo Cristo de la Coluna, founded in San Bartolomé to honor the venerated Christ image housed in the monastery's church, was apparently an organization that prided itself on providing large-scale, high-quality music at its ceremonies. Documents spanning sixty-six years reveal the consistent patronage of Andean musicians. Juan Quispe Yupanqui, maestro cantor, was paid 120 pesos by the confraternity's mayordomo in 1641 to attend all the sung masses and vespers throughout the year, as well as processions, novenarios, and the whole of Lent, with all the necessary ministriles including bajón, cornett, and harp.[74] In 1666 the confraternity hired the musicians of the parish of Santiago to provide vocal and instrumental music at its Friday masses and at all its annual feasts, for which it paid eighty pesos.[75] This link between the confraternity and the musicians of Santiago was still in place twenty years later when Don Tomás Chauca, maestro cantor of this parish, was hired by the mayordomo of the confraternity at sixty pesos for one year to serve with "the necessary officials" and "all their musical instruments" at their Friday masses, on Easter Monday, and on Easter morning.[76] Another twenty years on the confraternity again hired musicians to perform at the Friday masses, during Lent, and at Easter. This time the contract, also at sixty pesos per year, was to last for six years, giving a strong indication of the confraternity's unswerving patronage of musicians: such a long-term contract for musical services is unprecedented in Cuzco. On this occasion, the organist and bajonero of Santiago were joined by two musicians from other parishes, and the group agreed to provide "all the necessary singers and sopranos."[77]

While this cofradía may have been particularly music minded, it was not the only such musical patron, nor did it have a monopoly on the musicians of the parish of Santiago. In 1670, Don Cristóbal Chauca, maestro de capilla of Santiago, was hired by the Cofradía de Jesús Nazareno in the monastery of San Francisco to provide "complete music" at the confraternity's masses; he was to be paid sixty-five pesos for the year, and this was to be shared with his "officials."[78] The accounts of this confraternity from the years 1720 to 1763 have also come to light.[79] Music was always required during the three days of the confraternity fiesta, at which time a sung mass was celebrated each day and drummers and trumpeters performed. During the first six years of the accounts, singers, harpists, unspecified musicians, and an organist were also paid, not only for the fiesta but also for the Sundays in Lent. Most striking is the fact that from 1740 to 1753, there are annual payments of four pesos to the *vicario de coro* for the fiesta. The term *vicario de coro* was apparently only used for the musical director of a monastery; thus San Francisco hired its musical services—presumably plainchant sung by the friars—to a confraternity based in its church.

Another confraternity that had links with the monastery of San Francisco was the Cofradía del Santísimo Sacramento of the cathedral. According to its accounts, the confraternity was "founded in Cuzco Cathedral and San Francisco," and this link entailed the celebration of a sung mass on the third Sunday of every month in the monastery (Mendoza [1665] 1976, 43). Given that no payments to musicians are noted for these masses, it seems probable that the monastery's friars also provided the music at this monthly ceremony.[80] Nuns, too, may have provided confraternity music, though no evidence of such a custom has been found. Nevertheless, one might assume that the Cofradía del Santísimo Sacramento and the Cofradía de la Purísima Concepción in Santa Clara would have required music on occasion, and that the musically trained nuns might have been called on in such cases.[81]

Although very few confraternity records from the monasteries survive in accessible archives, their paucity is compensated for somewhat by their detail. The monastery of San Francisco alone had fourteen confraternities in the mid-seventeenth century—five Spanish, eight Andean, and one African (Contreras y Valverde [1649] 1982, 176). Considering that information about just two of them has been located, and that both included music in their ceremonies, we may be able to imagine the part played by such associations in the sound world of the monastic churches.

Conclusion

It is clear that the enthusiasm of the religious orders for music had a significant effect on the development of Cuzco's musical life. The Jesuit order ensured that a considerable proportion of both the Spanish and the Andean elites received musical training as part of their general studies at the *colegios* of San Bernardo and San Borja. The Spanish alumni of San Bernardo often went on to occupy important ecclesiastical and municipal posts and they would therefore have shaped policies concerning the subsidy of musicians by churches and the performance of music in civic ceremonies. The indigenous elite, meanwhile, was to play a key role in the promotion and financing of music in Andean parish churches, as will be seen in the following chapters, and some of its members went on to become professional musicians themselves. In the seventeenth century, at least, there was therefore a strong association between ecclesiastical music and Cuzco's ruling classes, whose musical education undoubtedly left its mark on patterns of private and institutional patronage in the city and the surrounding region.

Convents, *beaterios*, and monasteries were of central importance from the viewpoints of two groups—women and Andeans—that have been marginalized in musicological studies. Convents promoted the wider musical education of girls through their preferential treatment of musically talented novices, and, along with *beaterios*, they provided both Spanish and Andean women with their prime opportunities for musical training and performance. Since the nuns were cloistered, they could not participate in civic events; lavish musical displays by the nuns themselves within their convents, often performed for the benefit of local audiences and distinguished visitors, were therefore the only way that they could make their presence felt in the city's ceremonial life. Music was a means of reaffirming connections with local elites but also, at times, marking autonomy from ecclesiastical authorities. Both monasteries and convents, meanwhile, shaped the development of the music profession in Cuzco, creating work for musicians and instrument makers alike. The employment opportunities offered by monasteries and by the confraternities they housed stimulated the city's musical economy and helped to sustain the indigenous music profession, the subject of the following two chapters.

CHAPTER FOUR

The Urban Parishes

Surrounding the central Cathedral parish of colonial Cuzco were the eight *parroquias de indios*, or Indian parishes, that housed the vast majority of the city's indigenous population. The parishes of Hospital de los Naturales, Belén, Santiago, Santa Ana, San Cristóbal, and San Blas were contiguous with the Cathedral parish, forming a ring around it, while to the southeast of the city lay the remaining parishes of San Sebastián and San Jerónimo. These parishes were conceived as ethnically exclusive zones. Laws and edicts prohibiting Spaniards from living in *pueblos de indios*, or native settlements, were repeatedly passed during the sixteenth and seventeenth centuries, and these restrictions also applied to urban *parroquias de indios* such as those in Cuzco (Sebastián López, Mesa, and Gisbert 1985–86, 1:362–63). Many priests saw their fellow Spaniards, and particularly mestizos, as a pernicious influence on their Andean charges and therefore strove for racial exclusivity within their parishes. Information collected as part of Bishop Mollinedo's inspection of the diocese of Cuzco in 1689 (Villanueva Urteaga 1982) reveals that while this policy had been relaxed somewhat by the mid-colonial period, the *parroquias de indios* were still largely, and in some cases exclusively, indigenous zones.[1]

The parish was the day-to-day focus for most of the city's Andean inhabitants. The indigenous majority would have been more familiar with the regular ceremonies of the parish church and processions in the plaza and surrounding streets than with the occasional civic displays in the city center. Parish churches were musically autonomous for much of the colonial period, and the parishes themselves constituted largely independent soundscapes. Their musicians might contribute to civic ceremonies in the Plaza de Armas, but there is no evidence that those influences were reversed or that Hispanic musicians from the cathedral or seminary performed in the parishes. The church and its musicians played a dominant role in the sound world of the parish, and important events in the religious calendar such as

Holy Week, Corpus Christi, and the feast day of the patron saint were generally celebrated with masses, vigils, and processions accompanied by music. A rare eyewitness account of a procession in San Cristóbal in the mid-seventeenth century gives a flavor of these occasions:

> Today, Wednesday the third of October 1660, between eight and nine in the morning, I was in the parish of San Cristóbal of the city of Cuzco, Peru, where the parish priest, el licenciado Joseph Hurtado de Mendoza, was carrying the Holy Sacrament beneath a canopy; he was dressed in his surplice and cape, carrying it in his hands as is customary, accompanied by much music of shawms, candles, and choirs of singers; the cere-monial maces were carried by two solemn Indians, Inkas from the par-ish, and the banner by Don Cristóbal Carlos, alcalde mayor de naturales; the procession climbed to the small plaza of the parish, accompanied by many men and women . . . and the Sacrament was taken into the church with music, candles, and a peal of bells.[2]

Another unusual documentary source, from the parish of Hospital de los Naturales, provides evidence of the involvement of the parish council in organizing the festivities for the annual Day of the Purification in the early seventeenth century and implies the performance of non-European music at this important fiesta. The council issued instructions that each ayllu, the basic social unit of Andean society, should contribute dances and perfor-mances to the fiesta and the procession on that day. Various words for dance are used, including the Spanish terms danza and baile, but there are also repeated references to taquis, the word used specifically for indigenous dances. The council expressly requested a wide range of taquis, which were presumably accompanied by indigenous dance music, from different ethnic groups for inclusion in the festivities and processions. Intriguingly, some ayllus were asked to provide not their own traditional dances, but rather those of other indigenous groups: there are requests for dances of jungle-dwelling ethnic groups ("chunchos") and even for a "mexicano."[3] Ob-servers in the parish plaza would thus have seen colorful costumed displays and heard the sounds of the Catholic Church mingling with a variety of traditional musics.

Confraternity processions were also a prominent feature of parish life. With a number of these associations based in each church, there were occasions throughout the year on which confraternity-sponsored music sounded in the parish church, in the square, and on the streets. The music on these occasions appears to have been chosen for volume, with loud instruments such as trumpets, shawms, and drums predominating. Such impressive music would have allowed confraternities to project their voice on the urban stage, reinforcing corporate solidarity, boosting recruitment, and reflecting prestige on the confraternity and its *mayordomos*. Occupying a high confraternity office and sponsoring music brought honor to members of the Andean elite who sought to affirm and perform their status in the *parroquias de indios*.

Parish fiestas had many elements in common with civic events, but the associated meanings were undoubtedly quite different (Del Río Barredo 2005). The parish fiesta was a celebration of the individuals or corporation in charge of the cult as much as of the image or object at its center, and it temporarily claimed the urban space in which it took place. As a ritual of social promotion of, for example, a confraternity and its *mayordomo*, or the parish and its native elders, it was much more than a simple performance of colonial authority, and it thus disrupts José Antonio Maravall's (1986) conception of the baroque fiesta as a culture of control in which the urban population was largely passive and followed lines set out from above. Power was certainly at stake in parish fiestas, but to a greater extent than in the civic ceremonies discussed in chapter 1, the local native elites were the primary actors.

Confraternity music was performed for the benefit of the dead as well as of the living, as it formed part of rituals for deceased members. As Christopher Black (1989, 104) writes:

> Remembering dead brothers and sisters was a predominant concern amongst all confraternities. The living and the dead were part of one brotherhood. The living prayed to help the departed; the departed once they reached heaven might intercede for the living. Probably the main motivation behind many people joining the confraternities was that the society would help them to die well, provide them with a fitting passage into the afterlife through a decent funeral, and then organize corporate assistance with prayers for relief in and from Purgatory, and for a final favorable Judgment.

Evidence from account books indicates that many of Cuzco's confraternities celebrated a sung requiem and three to four sung memorial masses for each *cofrade* who died, as well as singing a response in his or her house. Thus, although music formed part of occasions that were celebratory in nature, within the parish soundscape it was also strongly associated with the rituals of death. When a parishioner died, the parish priest would go to the house of the deceased, accompanied by singers and other Andean church assistants, to collect the corpse and take it for burial. This practice was regulated in the 1591 *Constituciones sinodales* of Bishop Gregorio de Montalvo (Lassegue-Moleres 1987, 45), and two eyewitness reports from the parish of San Cristóbal in 1660 confirm that it was still customary seventy years later.[4] According to these accounts the parish priest and musicians made several stops along the route to sing responses over the body of the deceased. The early seventeenth-century Andean chronicler Felipe Guaman Poma de Ayala ([1615] 1980, 589, 767) wrote that if the priest was absent, singers might watch over the dying and then bury them with litanies, prayers, and responses.

Music in the streets and squares of the parishes was connected with celebration, with death, and also with unusual natural phenomena. Diego de Esquivel y Navia ([c.1749] 1980, 2:380) evokes the sounds of the city on the occasion of a lunar eclipse in 1747: "It was something to see, how the common people were so shocked, with their screams and cries at that moment; what is more, the priest of the parish of San Cristóbal descended through the streets with many people singing the rosary." Music and church bells were considered means of warding off disasters. Guaman Poma de Ayala ([1615] 1980, 631) believed that daily performances by church singers served to assuage God's wrath as manifested in the form of natural calamities. The great plague that struck Cuzco in 1720 inspired many religious ceremonies: the city authorities asked priests to perform *misas rogativas* and processions, sung masses rang out, and the public redoubled its spiritual efforts (Esquivel y Navia [c.1749] 1980, 2:221).

Each Andean parish of the city thus had its own ceremonial life, with residents accustomed to hearing vocal and instrumental polyphony, both indoors and outdoors, sponsored by the parish church or by the confraternities that it housed. Processions brought European-derived music to most of the inhabitants of the *parroquias de indios*, and for those who attended church regularly—whether as performers, confraternity members, or simply as part of the congregation—this music constituted the backdrop to their daily lives.

PARISH CHURCHES AND THE HISTORIOGRAPHY
OF URBAN MUSIC

The tendency of musicological studies of colonial Latin America to focus on the activities of cathedral musicians has produced a skewed picture since, in many cities, this is the only detailed research that has been undertaken. Such studies focus on the Spanish musicians who dominated cathedral music making; as a result, indigenous musicians, who made up the majority of the wider urban musical workforce in Cuzco (and, quite possibly, in other Latin American cities as well) and many of whom had little or no professional contact with the cathedral, have been largely neglected.[5] This approach has led musicologists to give detailed accounts of only a small (and, in the case of Cuzco, unrepresentative) proportion of the musicians who lived and worked in the colonies and, by extension, of only a fraction of their audiences. Recent Spanish musicology has begun to criticize the cathedral-centered approach that has long dominated research on the Iberian Peninsula and to explore the musical careers and experiences of a broader cross-section of city residents (e.g., Bombi 1995; Gembero 1998; Marín 2002; Bombi, Carreras, and Marín 2005). Similarly, scholars have been moving toward a more decentralized vision of English musical life, reassessing the importance of music in parish churches in particular (e.g., Burgess and Wathey 2000; Kümin 2001). The need for such a shift of focus is arguably even more acute in Latin America, where the selectivity of the musicological approaches transplanted from Spain to its colonies has often served to reinforce the historical marginalization of native populations.

In the case of Cuzco, one of the principal ways in which this imbalance can be redressed is to investigate the musical organization of the churches of the city's eight indigenous parishes. Drawing on neglected archival sources such as notarial records and the account books of parish churches and confraternities, I will focus on institutions that have thus far featured only as fleeting references in colonial music historiography and aim to resituate their musicians in the central role that they played in the city's ceremonial life.

The Organization and Financing of Music in Cuzco's Parish Churches

The bases of musical organization in Cuzco's parishes were laid down by Spanish missionaries in the first few decades after the conquest of the city. There were obvious precedents: music had quickly been recognized during earlier missionary campaigns in Mexico as an effective means of capturing the attention of native populations, involving the new converts in religious ritual, bypassing the language barrier, and teaching doctrine in easily memorable form (Stevenson 1976; Turrent 1993). Such a tactic was not developed in the New World, but grew out of Spanish evangelical efforts in parts of the Iberian Peninsula that had formerly been controlled by the Moors (López-Calo 1963, 1:254). In the Americas, Spanish music was seen as a powerful acculturative tool; it was the sugarcoating on the pill of religious doctrine. The power of traditional music to ensure the survival of indigenous culture was also recognized, however, so many Spanish missionaries made a conscious effort to replace native American songs and dances with new ones composed by the friars themselves, or at least to change the texts and objects of worship of traditional musical forms. As they set about the task of building a firm musical base in indigenous communities in Mexico, their expectations were exceeded. Music became so popular among native communities in parts of Central America that it threatened to escape the control of the church, and a decree was issued in Guatemala in 1565 in order to rein in the "great excess and superfluity of music in the churches" (Stevenson 1976, 167–71; Van Oss 1986, 20).

The lessons that the Franciscans had learned in Mexico were subsequently applied in Peru, though the greater military and political uncertainties meant that musical organization was slower to develop in the Andes. The Franciscan Jerónimo de Oré, in his *Symbolo catholico indiano* ([1598] 1992, f.56), recommended that in each Andean parish "there should be a school, with a master, and selected singers who are paid a sufficient salary, where the children may learn to recite the doctrine, and to read and write, sing, and play instruments." To judge from an earlier report, however, the Franciscans were already training singers and instrumentalists in at least one Cuzco parish by the 1560s.[6] Indeed, De Oré claimed in 1598 that the friars of his order had been instructing Andean musicians for more than forty years; his exhortations were thus based on well-established practice.

The first five urban parishes in Cuzco—Santa Ana, San Cristóbal, San Blas, San Sebastián, and Belén—were founded in 1559 by the city's *corregidor* Polo de Ondegardo with the primary intention of indoctrinating the Andean population. The remaining three parishes (Santiago, San Jerónimo, and San Pedro) were established in 1572 by Viceroy Toledo.[7] Although musical activities apparently began within a few years of their creation, specific regulations for parish musical organization in Cuzco can be traced back only as far as 1591, when the *Constituciones sinodales* of Bishop Montalvo laid down instructions for the training and employment of native musicians in the parish churches of the diocese: "As it is so important that the Indians are brought up in the Christian faith, there should be a school for children in every village. . . . Therefore we order that from now onward this must be the case, and that the children should be taught Christian doctrine and customs, to read and to write, and those who have decent voices should be taught to sing so that the churches may be better served." Andean musicians were to sing first and second vespers on Sundays and feast days, and they were to be paid two reales each for every mass sung (Lassegue-Moleres 1987, 45, 48). There are precedents for such regulations: the Third Council of Lima had issued a similar decree in 1583, encouraging the establishment of music ensembles and schools for singing and playing instruments in all native parish churches.[8] Earlier still, Viceroy Toledo, in a report drawn up after an exhaustive inspection of the viceroyalty between 1570 and 1575, had also specified that churches should maintain a sufficient number of singers and instrumentalists for their needs.[9]

According to Toledo's instructions, only the head musician—the *maestro de capilla*—should receive a salary, and this should be paid by the community, while the other musicians were to be rewarded with exemption from community services. These orders differ from the constitution drawn up a few years later by Bishop Montalvo, complicating our picture of the organization and financing of music in parish churches. The discrepancies concern both the nature of compensation to musicians for their services—whether cash or exemption from taxes and community services—and the source of any payments, either from the church or from community funds. Guaman Poma de Ayala, writing about Andean church organization at the start of the seventeenth century, mentions a standard number of four *cantores* (literally, singers) who received a salary, food, and exemption from tribute and labor levies, paid by the *mayordomos* and priest of the church. His drawing shows five such *cantores* playing the Salve Regina on recorders (fig. 12), indicating a flexible definition of the word *cantor*, as well as of the optimal number of musicians.[10]

Arguments between religious and secular authorities concerning those sectors of the Andean population from which these exempted individuals should come led Philip III to confirm the earlier order of Viceroy Toledo and to decree that in every village of more than one hundred people there should be two or three *cantores* free from tribute and personal services (Estenssoro 1990, 96–101).[11] Inconsistency in the practice of exempting musicians from tribute continued, however: in a 1645 document listing the tribute payers in the Cuzco parish of Santiago, only two *cantores* are specifically mentioned, one of whom was a *tributario* (tribute payer), the other a *reservado* (exempt from tribute).[12] Nevertheless, the system of exemptions sometimes worked in textbook fashion, for example in the parish of Belén, which had four *ayllus* in 1689, each of which provided the church with two tax-exempt *cantores* (Villanueva Urteaga 1982, 227).

Variation in the forms and sources of musicians' compensation is reflected in the account books from three of the eight parishes which are

12. Felipe Guaman Poma de Ayala, 1613, folio 666,
Los cantores de la santa iglesia impedidos de tasa.

preserved in the Archivo Arzobispal del Cuzco.[13] There is much evidence that musical activities constituted an important feature of parish church life, yet there are few signs of musicians' salaries. The church of Belén made annual payments to musicians at Easter and Corpus Christi in the last third of the eighteenth century, while drummers and trumpeters made sporadic paid appearances, but the only signs of rewards that could be regarded as a salary are those to the drummers and trumpeters who played at the monthly *misa de renovación* between 1743 and 1748, and to the drummer who was paid 3 pesos 6 reales for his presence "throughout the year" from 1768 to 1771. Inventories made between 1788 and 1807, however, show that the church possessed an organ, *bajón*, harps, violins, various drums and bird-whistles, and also employed a female *vicaria del coro*.[14] It seems unlikely that the church acquired all these instruments for a mere two performances a year.

The accounts of the church of San Jerónimo, the most outlying of

Cuzco's city parishes, paint a similar picture. Occasional payments were made to musicians, yet the true extent of music making only becomes clear from the frequent purchases and repairs to a range of instruments, from passing references such as five pesos spent "on a sackbut for the singers" or the purchase of sixty pesos' worth of vocal music from Lima, and from a number of inventories dating from between 1683 and 1740 showing that the church owned an organ, shawms, sackbuts, *bajones*, recorders, and harps.[15] After 1740 there are payments to musicians at Christmas in many years, but this appears to have been a "Christmas bonus" rather than a salary. The church organ was the object of repeated expenditure, but organists are mentioned only very rarely.

The church of San Pedro did pay salaries to an organist, a harpist, and a *bajonero*, all of whom clearly performed regularly, in the late seventeenth and early eighteenth centuries. It had purchased a magnificent organ in 1649 at a cost of over three thousand pesos, only to see the instrument destroyed along with the church in the great earthquake of the following year (Esquivel y Navia [c.1749] 1980, 2:95). Within two months, however, a replacement had been ordered, indicating that the resumption of musical services was considered a high priority.[16] Other signs of musical activity include the purchase or repair of harps, shawms, a *bajón*, and music stands for singing the offices of Holy Week in 1699. There were also annual payments to *cantores* at Easter: this feast, a focal point in the religious calendar throughout the Hispanic world, was the most important occasion in the year in the parish of Hospital de los Naturales, where celebrations were particularly notable. Vasco de Contreras y Valverde, in his *Relación de la Ciudad del Cusco* ([1649] 1982, 185), describes the three-day Easter fiesta in the parish, with perhaps just a touch of hyperbole, as "the greatest celebration in this realm and even in all Christendom." The singers must have performed more often than this, however, judging from the evidence of salaried continuo players and the references to repairs carried out in 1695 on a clavichord "that the *cantores* use for practicing" and to payments in 1701 and 1704 to the *bajonero* who "accompanies the musicians of this church."

While the process of reconstructing the musical organization of Cuzco's urban parishes is aided by the survival of these *libros de fábrica*, it is nevertheless far from unproblematic. These account books allow us to determine certain features of parish musical organization from the late seventeenth to early nineteenth centuries, but they pose as many questions as they answer. The basic problem can be stated simply: tangential evidence from a variety of sources points to the existence of permanent, regularly performing music ensembles based in the city's parish churches, yet payments to musicians appear only sporadically in the church accounts. These books are a record of payments made by the church *fábrica*; as such, any payments from other sources, or payments in kind, are almost always omitted. Unpaid musical performance, of which there was a considerable amount, is also very rarely recorded. This complicates the musicologist's task, since payments in kind and from sources other than the church itself can be very hard to detect, and much musical activity can easily go unnoticed. It is therefore necessary to flesh out the information from the *libros de fábrica* with details from other sources if a fuller picture of musical activities is to emerge.

The relative infrequency of payments to musicians in the *libros de fábrica* has several possible explanations. According to some of the sources noted above—the *Constituciones sinodales* of Bishop Montalvo, for example—salaries were supposed to be paid by the church *fábrica*; according to others, however, such as the *ordenanza* of Toledo, they were to be paid by the *caja de comunidad* (community chest). There is also evidence in Cuzco's archives that parish musicians were sometimes paid by the caciques (see chapter 5). It is entirely logical that musicians who were supported by their communities or caciques would have left few traces in church accounts. Furthermore, musicians were generally excused from paying taxes or any other kind of labor levy, and therefore many may not have received a salary at all. Tax and labor exemptions would serve as the equivalent of a base salary, on top of which they could earn cash in the form of occasional bonus payments from participation in certain parish, confraternity, or hospital ceremonies, or from private endowments.[17] Such exemptions undoubtedly boosted the attraction of the music profession, as they removed the obligation to participate in the wage economy in order to pay tribute, one of the most significant burdens that the colonial system imposed on the Andean population.[18]

Senior musicians were often paid in forms other than cash: a 1676 entry in the accounts of San Jerónimo, for example, notes that the harpist was paid in land, food, clothing, labor, and harp strings.[19] Evidence of such "mixed" salaries goes back to the *ordenanzas* of Toledo to the province of Charcas in 1575, in which the viceroy recommended an annual salary for *maestros* of two items of clothing, six *fanegas* (1.5 bushels) of corn or potatoes, and twelve rams (Levillier 1925, 359–60). Guaman Poma de Ayala ([1615] 1980, 635) stated that head musicians should receive an annual salary of twelve pesos, six *medias* (half a *fanega*) of corn, six of potatoes, and six alpacas, and examples of this kind of salary can be found in some contracts for musical services to rural churches, presented in the following chapter. The case of the harpist of San Jerónimo, while instructive, is perhaps unusual in that the church rented land for him, and that his remuneration in various forms other than cash was provided, and therefore recorded, by the church *fábrica*. In many cases the community would have provided food, goods, and labor directly to musicians and would have allocated them communal lands. Much musical activity would therefore have fallen outside the cash economy and the remit of Hispanic colonial documentation. This type of reciprocal arrangement was a characteristic form of Andean exchange, yet one that left few archival traces.[20]

Payment in forms other than cash is recorded in Spain during this period (e.g., López-Calo 1990, 429, 437; Stevenson 1961, 144). It may be more pertinent, however, that religious assistants under the Inkas were supported by the agricultural produce of their communities. Michael Moseley (1992, 65) describes pre-Hispanic "agricultural taxation," a custom that has resonances in colonial documentation: "It was Inca practice to divide conquered agricultural land into three categories, ideally of equal size, all of which the peasantry was obliged to farm. The first category was dedicated to the support of the gods, including the imperial pantheon and huacas [sacred objects] of local importance. These lands were cultivated first, before other categories of fields. Yields went to support religious functionaries, priests, and shrine attendants. Stores were also held to provide food and drink on holidays when particular gods, huacas, or ancestors received public veneration." There are manifold examples of colonial church musicians whose salaries were paid in agricultural produce and whose participation in confraternity ceremonies was rewarded with food and *chicha*, clearly echoing the Inka practices discussed by Moseley.

If musicians were often supported by their communities in such ways, it was because a sense of social obligation played an important part in their "contract," and this obligation was mutual. Service to the community and its deities was a key feature of life under the Inkas, and colonial-period musicians may therefore have regarded their duties at least in part as a form of tribute to the church, to the priest or cacique, to a holy image or saint, and as a service to their community, and as such they may have expected only occasional financial rewards. To regard the relationship between musicians and the parish church in the colonial period as purely commercial would therefore be erroneous. For many musicians, and especially for rank-and-file *cantores*, musical activities were as much a means of fulfilling social, economic, and religious obligations as a form of employment.

Historians have for some time embraced the idea that many aspects of colonial organization developed as they did due to the colonizers' acceptance and retention of pre-Hispanic models. The prevalence of musicians in indigenous parishes despite the relative lack of financial rewards from the church may well have its roots in long-standing Andean traditions of communal support for temple personnel via agricultural taxation and individual service in the interests of the community. While the model of parish musical organization was imposed by the Spanish colonists, and therefore usually included provision for the payment of *cantores*, its implementation was shaped by the Andean concept and practice of reciprocity that continued to underlie the relationship between religious servants such as musicians and their communities. If it is a truism that colonial Latin American economies were cash poor, as they exported their silver to Spain (Burns 1999, 135), then it was in the interests of institutions and communities to reward musicians in forms other than cash, if at all possible. The evidence that musicians were commonly compensated in nonmonetary ways reveals how the organization of musical provision was adapted from a professional European model to a more flexible one better suited to the different local traditions and economic conditions in the Andes.

Music might, then, be regarded as a "profession" only for key figures—the *maestro de capilla*, the organist, the harpist, and the *bajonero*—although even these prominent musicians were often recompensed with mixed salaries in which cash played only a part, especially in rural areas. The generosity of the rewards that musicians received no doubt varied according to the wealth of the individual church, as well as the will of the priest, the cacique, and the community. Nevertheless, the *maestro de capilla* and principal instrumentalists often received a salary, as they were more highly trained than the *cantores*. Contracts detailing the skills to be taught by a *maestro organista* to his apprentice show that this was not a profession quickly learned: contracts for two to four years of daily lessons are not uncommon, and two musical apprenticeship agreements of ten years' duration have been located in Cuzco's archives. It is reasonable to assume that such dedication and investment of time would normally have been rewarded with a salaried post, however that salary was paid. Music therefore seems to have offered genuine professional opportunities to some leading indigenous parish musicians, though they worked alongside other Andeans employed on quite different terms.

Although musical posts sometimes brought material benefits, it was often the intangible advantages of musical service, invisible in economic records, that carried most weight. Serving the church was considered an honor for much of the colonial period, and church servants, particularly senior ones, derived power from their position within the colonial hierarchy as intermediaries between the Andean and Spanish worlds. Church service offered protection from the most oppressive aspects of the colonial system: not only from the burden of taxation and forced labor but also from rapacious officials such as the *corregidores*. The Spanish scientists Jorge Juan and Antonio de Ulloa ([1749] 1978, 72–73), writing about the *audiencias* of Lima and Quito in the mid-eighteenth century, noted that "of all the Indians given special privileges by the king, only the caciques, mayors, and persons employed in the parish church are free from this oppression. If those serving in the church are not affected, it is only because the *corregidores* cannot touch them." Powerful figures in Andean parishes, such as the priest or the cacique, could provide protection for their followers; musicians sometimes benefited from this patronage and even came to exercise authority over other Andeans, being accused by Guaman Poma de Ayala ([1615] 1980, 857) of behaving as if they were Inkas.

As parish musicians were not full-time employees of their churches, they could expect to earn money from other sources, as well as providing for themselves through small-scale farming on church or community lands. Most of Cuzco's churches housed a number of confraternities, which almost invariably employed musicians on certain key occasions throughout the year; indeed, it seems that many indigenous musicians earned a considerable proportion of their income through this route. The musicians of the parish of Santiago, for example, were much in demand by confraternities in the late seventeenth century. As seen in the previous chapter, Andean parish musicians were also hired by the city's monasteries, hospitals, and convents, and they were involved in teaching prospective novices, students at the colleges, and private pupils. Many musicians also had interests outside music, in property, agriculture, or manufacturing; diversification of income was apparently key to their financial security.

The church *fábrica* should therefore be regarded only as a starting point in an investigation of the financial basis of the music profession.[21] Indeed, we should perhaps regard the silences in parish records, potentially a source of frustration to the musicologist, as revealing as much as they conceal, for they hint at the diverse sources of funding of parish music. When a range of sources such as inventories, *libros de fábrica*, wills, and contracts are read together, we can begin to glimpse the variety of musical organization, with funds and material goods provided by the church, the priest, the cacique, other local dignitaries, and the parish community. The extensive gaps in accounts simply point us away from the church as the sole or even primary patron of music in Andean parishes. The parish *libros de fábrica* give tantalizing glimpses of musical activities occupying a gray area between profession and religious observance in a world where cash was not at the heart of every exchange.

CONFRATERNITY MUSIC IN THE URBAN PARISHES

Given the irregularity of payments from the church *fábrica*, one of the prime means of support for parish musicians was undoubtedly confraternities. These lay associations were promoted by the Spanish clergy as part of their evangelical mission and were initially seen as an effective means of propagating Christianity. The indigenous inhabitants of the Andes apparently took to the confraternity system with enthusiasm, with a dozen or more being founded in some parish churches, and they became one of the prime channels for Andean involvement in Catholic ritual and ceremony. Andeans quickly threw themselves into the festive side of confraternity ceremonies, and this exuberance came to the attention of the church authorities in Cuzco. The *Constituciones sinodales* of 1591 included a warning to *doctrina* priests to clamp down on excessive drinking and unauthorized meetings by *cofrades*. By the time of the next set of *Constituciones*, ten years later, the church was trying not only to suppress the festive activities promoted by confraternities but also the number of confraternities themselves (Lassegue-Moleres 1987, 54, 67). Drunkenness, native dances, excessive expenditure, and extortion by priests were of particular concern, leading to the order to restrict confraternities to a maximum of four per parish—a limit that seems rarely to have been respected. The tensions that lay at the heart of these associations in Europe therefore resurfaced in the Americas. They were promoted by ecclesiastical authorities as a means of combating heresy and promoting religious orthodoxy and control over the laity, but they were also the prime vehicle for expressions of popular devotion: they simultaneously constituted an officially propagated mechanism of religious and social supervision and a source of official suspicion (Black 1989).

Two surviving confraternity constitutions, numerous account books, and contracts between musicians and confraternities reveal that a number of these lay societies housed in the city's parish churches were important sponsors of music. The Cofradía del Santísimo Sacramento in the parish of San Cristóbal specified that sung masses should be celebrated on the following occasions: Corpus Christi; every Thursday of the year; the first Sunday of each month (the *misa de renovación*); four for each *cofrade* who died; one on the *día de los finados* (Day of the Dead, i.e., All Souls); and eight during the following days. The priest was also required to go to the house of each dead *cofrade* and sing a response, a rite that involved the parish *cantores*, judging from the mid-seventeenth-century description of San Cristóbal quoted above.[22] The confraternity's constitution is confirmed by its accounts, which include payments to musicians for many of its functions.

The Hermandad de Esclavitud de Nuestra Señora de la Almudena was established in 1689 in the then recently founded semi-parish church of La Almudena in the parish of Hospital de los Naturales.[23] The first eight sections of the constitutions of this confraternity are all detailed instructions concerning sung masses, which were to be celebrated on the following occasions:

- four requiem masses for each member who died, as well as a response sung in the *cofrade*'s house
- all the feasts of Our Lady
- throughout the Octave from the first day of September to the Nativity of Our Lady
- every Tuesday (a requiem mass), Thursday, Saturday (Salve), Sunday, and on fiestas
- the days of San Pedro, San Pablo, San Andrés, San Joseph, San Isidro Labrador, San Fernando King of Spain, San Roque, San Felipe, and Santiago
- an annual day in memory of dead *cofrades*

That the sung mass involved musicians, rather than just a priest, is made explicit: the constitutions stipulate that the *músicos* should be paid two reales for each mass, vespers, Salve, and response, and the harpist one real. The quantity of musical performances organized by the confraternity is impressive—if the constitutions were adhered to, there would have been almost one sung mass per day throughout the year—and it is notable that the constitutions begin with this information rather than any other, a sign that sung masses were a high priority for the confraternity's founders.

The only notarized contract between a parish confraternity and a musician that has been found was agreed between the Andean organist Lucas Cañare of the parish of Santiago and the Cofradía de Nuestra Señora de Monsarrate in the same parish church; the musician agreed to play the organ in church on "the customary days" for an annual fee of twenty pesos.[24] However, the *libros de cofradía* from the city parishes reveal extensive musical activities. While the records of just one confraternity from each of the parishes of Belén, Santiago, and Hospital de los Naturales survive, these contain numerous payments to singers, *maestros cantores*, organists, harpists, violinists, drummers, trumpeters, shawm players, and so on.[25] Unfortunately, these payments are often noted in the form of an annual entry such as "one peso to the singers," and therefore it is impossible in many cases to determine any information beyond the basic fact that the confraternity hired musicians on at least one occasion in the year. Sometimes the occasions on which the musicians performed are, however, specified. These were most often: Corpus Christi; Easter; the feast day of the patron saint of the confraternity; the days of *aguinaldos* (offerings) and *finados* (the dead);[26] the weekly Thursday mass; the monthly *misa de renovaciones*; and at the funerals and memorial masses of deceased *cofrades*. The accounts never confirm that all these occasions were celebrated with music by one confraternity in any one year. Nevertheless, on a few occasions payments are noted as an annual salary, as in the case of the payment of twelve pesos to the shawm players of Hospital de los Naturales in 1692 "for all the fiestas during the year, at one-and-a-half *reales* per day," or the four pesos to the harpist of Santiago from 1710 to 1718 "for his salary for the year and his attendance in the choir," both of which imply a certain regularity.

It might be expected that masses for the dead would feature prominently in the musical expenditure of these "death societies." The records of the Cofradía del Santísimo Sacramento in the parish of Hospital de los Naturales do not disappoint, and between 1680 and 1695, singers performed at the funeral and three memorial masses of each *cofrade* who died, which totaled seventy-two masses in just one year. However, different confraternities had different musical priorities: the payments to musicians of the Cofradía de Nuestra Señora de Belén in the parish of Belén focus on the *novenario de aguinaldos*, while those of the Cofradía de la Purificación de Nuestra Señora in the parish of Santiago are concentrated on the confraternity's feast day.

Inconsistencies and vagueness mask every aspect of the recording of musical activities, even their very existence, since confraternity officials were usually more concerned with accounting for the money spent than giving accurate details of what it was spent on. The entry for 1733 in the accounts of the Santiago confraternity is typical of those found throughout the *libros de cofradía*: "12 pesos—mass and vespers on the feast of Our Lady." Far less typical is the note that follows immediately after: "And this expenditure includes payment for all the singers and music." This confirms the suspicion that much outlay on music is concealed in more general payments, and that the visible musical activities, sometimes in themselves impressive, are only the tip of the iceberg. Another problem relates to the use of the word *cantores*. For example, the Cofradía de Nuestra Señora de la Natividad in the village of Yucay includes the payment in 1772 of three pesos "to the *cantores* in this manner: one peso to the *maestro*, one to the organist, and one to the harpist." Much of the time, this loose definition of the word *cantores* to mean "musicians" can make it hard to discern exactly which musicians were taking part. The distinction between *cantores* (singers) and *ministriles* (instrumentalists) was applied in the cathedral, but the latter term is never used in parish church records.

More information is available from the parishes of San Jerónimo and San Cristóbal. The accounts of seven confraternities survive from San Jerónimo, and each paid musicians on at least one occasion during the year, sometimes more. Three of them made small donations in around 1680 toward buying a *bajón* for the church, something that was relatively common in cases in which the *cofradías* used church instruments. Two, the Cofradía de San Jerónimo and the Cofradía de la Santísimo Vera Cruz, paid for musicians to come from Cuzco to participate in special events, while the former stipulated that a sung mass should be celebrated for every *cofrade* who died. Payments appear to all the usual musicians—*maestro cantor*, organist, harpist, singers, drummers, and trumpeters—though the quantities expended indicate few paid performances.

The accounts of the Cofradía del Santísimo Sacramento of the parish of San Cristóbal are particularly detailed.[27] Singers were paid on a regular basis, with Corpus Christi, unsurprisingly, the most important musical event of the year. The entry for 1716 gives a detailed breakdown and shows that the singers were paid ten pesos for singing at Thursday masses, two reales for the *misa de finados*, three pesos for the mass and vespers at Corpus, and that they were also given nine pesos to buy shoes for the year. The confraternity also had material assets: a 1667 inventory shows that it owned two sets of shawms and a *bajón*. It sold one of the sets of shawms in 1669, raising twenty-five pesos, but these were more than replaced by their alms collector, Francisco Guaraca, who was given four pesos as a reward for bringing in three sets of shawms that had been donated as alms. Expenditure on music continued into the late eighteenth century, and despite the claims of the scribe in 1762 that the confraternity was in a state of "extreme poverty," it still managed to pay thirty-nine pesos each to the harpist, the violinist, and the organist who officiated at the weekly Thursday mass, as well as four pesos each to the drummers, trumpeters, and other unspecified musicians who participated at vespers and on the day of Corpus Christi.

The Cofradías del Santísimo Sacramento were generally the most lavish in their expenditure (and the most detailed in their accounting) and therefore should not be taken as typical; they do, however, give a glimpse of the upper limits of parish confraternity music making.[28] The accounts of the Cofradía del Santísimo Sacramento of the parish of Hospital de los Naturales, too, provide evidence of musical expenditure in the late seventeenth century. The fiesta of Corpus Christi might involve hiring drummers, trumpeters, singers, a harpist, and shawms, and often included fireworks. Sung masses were performed on Thursdays and on the first Sunday of the month, and from 1684 to 1695 a harpist was paid a salary for attending these masses throughout the year; the confraternity even purchased a harp in 1687.

The accounts of parish confraternities are both enlightening and frustrating—enlightening because they give a rare glimpse of confraternity music, frustrating because of the impossibility of establishing consistent patterns of musical performance over time even within a single confraternity due to the erratic nature of the accounts themselves. Nevertheless, the overall quantity of references to musicians of every kind in the confraternity records confirms that elaborate music was almost certainly a feature of at least one annual ceremony performed by each confraternity. In many cases, polyphonic performance was a far more regular occurrence, and confraternities thus made a significant impact on the musical economy and the soundscape of the city parishes, dramatically increasing the quantity of polyphonic music that was heard both inside and outside the churches.

PARISH MUSIC IN THE OLD AND NEW WORLDS

Despite the archival lacunae detailed above, the basic outlines of parish musical organization for most of the colonial period can nonetheless be drawn. The evidence suggests that parish churches had an active *capilla de música* consisting of four to eight singers who doubled on wind instruments including shawms, recorders, cornetts, and sackbuts, together with a *maestro de capilla* and some combination of organist, harpist, and *bajonero*. This *capilla de música* was a permanent, independent, and self-sufficient ensemble capable of performing polyphony. The model of Cuzco's urban parishes seems to have been the exception rather than the rule in Spain; while some Spanish parish churches supported comparable musical forces, most maintained smaller ensembles, such as an organist, possibly a *maestro de capilla*, and a group of nonprofessional, clerical plainchant singers. On important occasions in the Spanish church calendar, musicians were hired from outside—usually from the cathedral—to supplement the parish forces and to perform polyphony, but financial and logistical constraints limited the regularity with which such musical assistance could be sought to a few important annual feasts. Spanish cities tended to be dominated by one or, at best, a small handful of ensembles that took on musical duties in monastic, parish, and rural churches on major feasts.[29]

Cuzco's parish churches, however, were musically independent and could therefore perform complex music with whatever regularity they wished. Even in 1796, when the city had long been in economic and cultural decline, the eight parish singers of Hospital de los Naturales performed on four occasions every week, not including feast days.[30] The performance of polyphony was therefore a much more frequent occurrence in the parish churches of Cuzco than in most of their Spanish counterparts. There is no evidence that Cuzco's parish churches sought musical reinforcements, nor is there any reason to suppose that they were needed. Whereas parishes in Barcelona hired freelance "music companies" to bolster their musical forces on important occasions (Madurell 1948; Kreitner 1992), the parish *capillas de música* in Cuzco were not only self-sufficient but sometimes even themselves acted as freelance groups available for hire by other institutions. As a result, the sound world of colonial Cuzco was remarkably decentralized, since the city had a large number of permanent ensembles relative to its size, many of them located on the urban periphery.

So why did the organization of parish music develop in this way in Cuzco? How did the colony come to surpass the metropolis in the development of music in its smaller churches? In answering these questions it is important to bear in mind a simple but fundamental difference between the desired function of ecclesiastical music in the Spanish and Andean worlds.[31] In the former, music served as an ornament, a means of enhancing the *decencia del culto divino* (propriety of divine worship), to borrow a common phrase from colonial documents. In the indigenous New World, however, European music was introduced as a missionary tool, and some of the most encouraging results of the first friars in the Americas centered on the enthusiasm of their new charges for this music. The elaborate celebration of Christian rituals in indigenous parish churches was, in the eyes of many churchmen, a reflection of the efficacy of evangelization, a sign that the native population was embracing the new religion.[32] Yet the widespread survival of elements of indigenous culture in Peru throughout the colonial period cast frequent doubts on the priests' achievements, and music in parish churches therefore never lost its missionary edge. So-called idolatry continued to flourish, so Christian priests needed to keep their evangelical weapons sharp and trumpet their successes.

There was also reluctance on the part of the church, and especially the mendicant orders, to accept that the evangelical phase of the conquest might end. Native peoples were relegated to the status of "perpetual neophytes" because the privileges and exemptions of the orders were dependent on the continuation of this phase (Van Oss 1986, 161): as such, the justification for evangelical methods also continued. Indeed, it has been argued that "idolatry" was as much a Spanish invention as a set of native practices, created and sustained by European colonists for whom maintaining the distinction between Andeans and Spaniards was fundamental to the colonial enterprise (Estenssoro 2003). Nevertheless, whether idolatry was real, imagined, or both, colonial Peruvian religion maintained its evangelical mission and music retained its place at the heart of the "spiritual conquest" for much of the colonial period.[33]

Given that the Andeans took to church music with such skill and enthusiasm, it served as an outward symbol of success that might cover deeper deficiencies in the methods and achievements of certain churchmen. In 1682, the caciques of San Sebastián went to Cuzco to complain about their former priests and to request a Jesuit as their next doctrinero. The viceroy, Melchor de Navarra y Rocafull, the Duque de la Palata, sympathized with Jesuits and therefore with the request of the caciques, claiming that the secular clergy cared only about a superficial image of a well-run church: "[The priest] thinks that his obligation is fulfilled if the church is adorned and well served with music, ornaments and altars, which are visible and which bring credit to the priests, and he can do this, as they have done, from Cuzco; but caring for souls, succoring the poor, consoling the sick, warning and admonishing about vice, these cannot be done properly without their permanent presence in the village" (quoted in Colin 1966, 103). According to this skeptical view, music could serve as a high-profile, low-maintenance, even long-distance way for priests to appear to be fulfilling their parish duties while devoting a minimum of time and effort to their charges. Music, in the opinion of the viceroy, was an outwardly directed smoke screen as much as a genuine evangelical tool.

The proliferation of music in native parishes was thus in part the result of religious policy in the New World, since the provision of music was organized and regulated by the highest religious and secular authorities. Music was officially viewed as being among the most effective means of drawing

Andeans into the activities of the church and, given that they were in effect barred from taking holy orders until the mid-eighteenth century, of ensuring their continued involvement and participation. The church placed music at the heart of its evangelical efforts and promoted the results as a shining and attractive symbol of its own achievements, while Peru's viceregal government—the skepticism of the Duque de la Palata notwithstanding—supported musical activities by defending musicians' rights to exemptions from tribute and labor levies. First formalized by Viceroy Toledo in the 1570s, these exemptions were confirmed by Philip iii in the 1618 *Recopilación de leyes*, in 1675 by Baltasar de la Cueva Henríquez, the Conde de Castellar, and again in 1774 by the viceroy Manuel de Amat y Juniet (Tibesar 1953, 84).[34] That viceroys, bishops, and the crown intervened over such matters is a strong indication that music retained its position at the core of Spanish policies toward the cultural conquest of Peru's indigenous inhabitants throughout the colonial period. Just as Spanish colonialism entailed the projection of an idealized urban vision onto the perceived tabula rasa of the New World, the repeated efforts of religious and secular authorities to regulate musical provision in Cuzco—by stocking every church with its own *capilla de música*—might be interpreted as a relatively successful attempt to create a utopian musical environment, an "ideal city" whose harmony pleased the ear as well as the eye.

Spanish policy alone cannot, however, explain the strength of parish music. The cooperation and active participation of indigenous communities was essential to maintaining musical activities in their churches. Without the willingness of indigenous leaders and their communities to support musicians—whether through paying their salaries or taxes, carrying the extra burden placed on the community by their labor exemptions, or providing them with food or land—Spanish efforts to promote ecclesiastical music among Peru's indigenous communities would have failed. A detailed examination of parish music and musicians reveals that the imposition of harmony turned out to be more of a negotiation between the Spanish and Andean republics in which the upper strata of indigenous society took on a vital mediatory role in return for substantial benefits, and through which parish music reached unprecedented heights.

TRAINING, EMPLOYMENT PATTERNS, AND THE
CIRCULATION OF MUSICIANS

One of the most significant aspects of Andean involvement in the absorption of European music was the widespread dependence on indigenous *maestros de capilla* to pass on musical skills to the younger generation in their parishes. The *maestro*, a parish employee, normally taught music as part of the general education provided in church schools; as a result, parishes were often able to maintain relatively stable ensembles of local musicians. This custom of training Andean musicians within the orbit of the parish church led to a clear distinction between the cathedral and the parishes, with the latter operating as separate organizational units. In Spain, by contrast, contact and cooperation between parish and cathedral *maestros* seems to have been more normal, and parish musicians may often have been taught in cathedrals, as parish churches were not important centers of musical instruction (Bombi 1995).

This emphasis on training within the parish suggests a marked degree of localism in musical organization, an impression reinforced by a series of entries in the accounts of the parish church of San Jerónimo that indicate a certain reluctance to hire musicians from outside the parish and a preference for training local boys to fill musical posts. The first such payment is recorded in 1676, when a *maestro de capilla* was brought in from Cuzco—San Jerónimo was the most distant of the urban *parroquias de indios*—as none was available in the parish, and was paid a mixture of cash and food to teach the choirboys of the church.[35] This entry is notable because it is the only mention of a *maestro de capilla* in the accounts around this time, because the scribe explicitly mentioned that the *maestro* had been brought from outside due to the lack of a local alternative, and because the *maestro* was paid to train local musicians on a short-term basis rather than to direct music as a permanent appointment. The aim of this temporary arrangement appears to have been long-term self-sufficiency, something made clearer in a 1691 entry that notes a payment of ten pesos "to a harpist, both for playing in church festivities, and also for teaching some of the parishioners, which he did for four months until *a harpist from the village was taken on [se reduxo un arpista del pueblo]*" (emphasis mine). Again, this is almost the only mention of a payment to a harpist around this time, and it, too, involves an outsider. After this date, the *fábrica* made regular payments for harp strings, and even bought a new harp in 1706, but it made no cash payments to a player of the instrument. It thus becomes clear that the parish church aimed at musical self-sufficiency for economic reasons, since it was only obliged to pay cash to musicians brought in from the city. The 1691 entry states that the parish took on a local harpist after paying an outsider for four months, yet the accounts from subsequent years show no payments from the *fábrica* to this local musician. The expression *se reduxo* is key, implying that the musician was in some way obliged (the same verb was used for the forced resettle-ment of Andeans in the sixteenth century). The harpist no doubt joined the ranks of singers and instrumentalists who performed the music brought from Lima and who played the organ, shawms, sackbuts, and *bajones* listed in the church inventories, but who were rewarded in the form of benefits that did not register in the parish *libro de fábrica*.

More than a century later, the same process is still apparent. In 1799 the parish paid twenty-four pesos to the organist Matías Holgado for a year's salary. He took over from an indigenous organist who was too old and infirm to continue in the post—and who had been absent from the accounts for previous years. Despite the fact that Holgado, as a member of the parish, accepted a low salary, the *mayordomo* of the *fábrica* sought to avoid even this small outlay: "Considering it necessary that the church should avoid in future the cost of a salaried organist, I decided that it would be wise to train a boy named Ignacio Rocca, *indio noble*, in this art and therefore sent him to Cuzco, where I handed him over to the organist Francisco Altamirano, to whom I paid two pesos a month, which added to another two pesos for the boy's maintenance, make four pesos, and for the year, forty-eight." After paying forty-eight pesos a year for four years to train Rocca, the scribe noted in 1802 that "this year the boy's training finished, and from next year the organist's salary will stop, relieving the church of the cost of such an important em-ployee." The church clearly valued its musicians, but it simply could not afford to reward them properly. Having invested the equivalent of eight years' salary for Holgado on training Rocca, the church apparently expected many years of free service from the latter. However, in 1810 it was obliged to pay eighteen pesos to another organist, Lorenzo Benavente, for three months' work after "Ignacio Rocca declined to continue in the post, claiming that although he had been trained at the church's expense, he had served more than seven years without any salary, that he was now married and had a family, and that he had to devote himself to working and to support-ing them."

The church decided that it would be better to rehire Rocca on a low salary than to continue paying Benavente six pesos a month. Rocca was given two pesos a month as organist, and another peso for teaching two local boys: the former apprentice was now to take on his own apprentices. This teach-ing did not go altogether smoothly. In 1813, both boys were sent off to other teachers (one to the organist of the neighboring parish of San Sebastián, the other to the organist of the monastery of La Merced) as they were learning little with Rocca, and payments for their training continued for five years until 1815, at which point one was considered sufficiently skilled to serve the church. Whether he did so or not is unclear, but yearly payments to Rocca continue uninterrupted until 1854, by which time he had been working as an organist for fifty-two years.

The church's preference for investing in the training of young local musicians rather than contracting experienced performers and directors from outside the parish is understandable if locals could be paid less than outsiders or paid in kind, reflecting the fact that money was rarely overflowing in parish coffers.[36] Again we see that music occupied a gray area as a profession; musical skills had value, but not a "market value." Parishes seemed to rely on the fact that local musicians felt some degree of social or religious obligation to their churches and would therefore settle for lower wages, payments in kind, or, indeed, no payment at all, and in this sense, music fell somewhere between profession and duty. As a result, the circulation of Andean musicians between different churches seems to have been limited. Urban musicians did sometimes take up short-term positions in rural areas in order to train local boys—a process that will be examined in the following chapter—but long-term relocation and movement between urban institutions, of the kind seen among ambitious musicians in Spain, were rare. The economic constraints on parish churches and Andean communities meant that the hiring of expensive musicians from outside was kept to a necessary minimum and that cheaper (or free) local labor was preferred. There seem to have been more incentives and pressures to remain in situ than to move, as parish authorities showed a reluctance to allow musicians to leave after subsidizing their musical education.

At the level of the ordinary *cantores*, the lack of geographical mobility in Cuzco also relates to the fact that the principal benefit of such a post was often the exemption from tribute and labor levies. Differences in remuneration and working conditions between institutions, which stimulated the circulation of musicians throughout the Iberian Peninsula, would generally have been minimal in the Cuzco region. The chief stimuli for indigenous migration were the demand for labor in mines, in textile mills, and on haciendas, excessive tax burdens, and the need to seek work in order to earn cash to pay taxes; in theory, at least, none of these factors would have affected musicians. The movement of *cantores* was also constrained by limited opportunities, since the fact that Andean parishes, both rural and urban, tended to have educational programs ensured the constant provision of singers for their churches.

The marked localism among the singers in Cuzco's Andean parishes is mirrored in one of the few parishes to have been studied in detail in Spain, that of San Nicolás in Pamplona (Gembero 1998). Unlike in Spain, however, localism in Cuzco seems to have extended to the upper musical posts.[37] With regard to higher-ranking musicians, there appears to have been a glass ceiling that limited the professional advancement of indigenous musicians in Cuzco. Whereas in Spain, an ambitious parish *maestro de capilla* might aim for the equivalent post in a cathedral or another prestigious institution, the racial discrimination practiced by Peruvian cathedrals meant that this was effectively out of the question. It is not clear, therefore, that the notion of promotion would have had any meaning for an indigenous parish *maestro*, who was already at the top of his profession. From a more positive perspective, many senior musicians occupied positions of authority and came from elite families with a long history in their parishes, as will be discussed below; it is thus hard to see how a parish *maestro de capilla* would have benefited from moving to another post. As such, there are clear differences between patterns of mobility among musicians in the Old and New Worlds. In Spain, they were an unusually mobile professional group in an otherwise highly static society (Suárez-Pajares 1998, 157). In Cuzco, musicians appear to have been a relatively static group in a society that is now recognized to have been far more mobile than historians once thought (Wightman 1990), tied to their parishes by the lack of opportunities for advancement but also, and just as importantly, by the social advantages afforded by such posts.

The Socioeconomic Status of Urban Parish Musicians

The precise contours of the music profession are harder to determine than those of almost any other in colonial Cuzco, since its lower strata blend into community service and religious duty and its upper strata fuse with community leadership and religious authority. A number of Cuzco's indigenous musicians belonged to the social rank of *principal*, a position of leadership among indigenous parish communities one rank below the cacique. A *principal* was thus a member of a local elite: he might be the son of a cacique other than the firstborn (who would normally take over the *cacicazgo*), or a legitimate nephew (Díaz Rementería 1977, 45–46). The indigenous status structure was maintained in Cuzco more so than almost anywhere else in the Spanish colonies, and such titles were therefore more than honorific (Van den Berghe and Primov with Velazque and Ccuhuata 1977, 47). Musicians who have left traces in Cuzco's notarial records include Don Joseph Topa Ynga Guaraca, *principal* of the parish of San Cristóbal and *maestro cantor*;

Tomás de Santa Cruz, *principal* of the parish of Santiago and *maestro organista*; and Don Agustín Apumayta, *principal* of the *ayllu* of Matará in Hospital de los Naturales and *maestro organista*.[38] Many of the native musicians who appear in Cuzco's notarial records used the title "Don"—an indicator of high social status—as was often the case with the city's indigenous artists and skilled artisans, among whose ranks Andean minor nobles were also prominent (Garrett 2005, 42, 85; Dean 1990, 84). It will be recalled that the parish of San Jerónimo trained and employed the organist Ignacio Rocca, *indio noble*, in the early nineteenth century, revealing that even when the profession's fortunes had declined drastically, as they had by the late colonial period, it still attracted high-born individuals.[39]

This connection between high status and the music profession was in fact to be found across the Spanish colonies. Antonio Vásquez de Espinoza, in his *Compendio y descripción de la Indias Occidentales* (1992, 556), wrote of his visit to Cajamarca in northern Peru in 1615: "In this town there are many officials of every trade, excellent scribes, singers, and a *maestro de capilla* who instructs them; they participate every day in church as canons, celebrating the Hours and the mass of Our Lady. They take part in the mass, and play their shawms and other musical instruments in the divine offices, as is common throughout the Indies; normally they are the sons of *principales* and caciques, and they regard it as a great honor." The cathedral of La Plata, another important Andean city, instituted a special post at its foundation for a cathedral canon whose role was specifically to teach music to the sons of caciques (Illari 1997, 78), while *maestros cantores* were also drawn from the upper levels of indigenous society in early colonial Mexico, especially in Yucatán (Turrent 1993, 121–22; Collins 1977).

In Cuzco, the Andean elites were the focus of educational efforts coordinated by the Jesuits, who ran the Colegio de San Borja for the sons of caciques from its foundation in 1621 until the order's expulsion from the continent in 1767. The role of music in the general educational program of the college was discussed in the previous chapter, where it was suggested that while most, if not all, the students at the college received a thorough grounding in ecclesiastical music, those who showed particular aptitude may have been natural choices to take up posts as *maestros de coro* in their communities on finishing their education.

The role of *maestro de capilla* or *maestro de coro* in indigenous communities differed in key respects from its counterpart on the Iberian Peninsula. The distinctive nature of the post in Latin America was shaped by two intersecting sets of interests, those of the colonial church and of the native nobility.

After the social upheavals that followed the Spanish conquest, hereditary Andean leaders sought to consolidate their status and maintain their privileges in the new social order by obtaining positions of responsibility within the colonial power structure. The church was unwilling to sanction the establishment of a native priesthood in Peru—Charles II granted the right of ordination to Andeans in 1697, but this right was rarely recognized by the viceregal authorities before the mid-eighteenth century (O'Phelan Godoy 1995; Garrett 2005)—so the music profession became a substitute ecclesiastical career, a power base for native leaders within the colonial church. In the words of Vásquez de Espinosa, the musicians "participate every day in church *as canons*" (emphasis mine). The church was understaffed in Peru and struggled to convey its message to the indigenous population alone; in 1572 there were nearly 1,800 people per priest in the Viceroyalty of Peru (Spalding 1984, 250). The church's interests were therefore also served by the *maestro de coro* becoming the priest's native deputy.

In the case of the priest's absence, which was a regular or even semipermanent occurrence in some parishes, above all in distant parts of the diocese, the *maestro* was de facto head of the church.[40] Guaman Poma de Ayala ([1615] 1980, 631) clearly felt that some musicians abused their position as surrogate priests, writing that "the *cantores* of the church are very free in the absence of the fathers. They do not celebrate vespers nor matins nor None nor *alba* [dawn mass] nor the Salve nor do they bury the dead." When musicians and other indigenous assistants did lead church services, they sometimes had ulterior motives: "The *fiscales* and sacristans and singers, in the absence of the priest, lead the Salve, and on Wednesdays and Fridays they perform the service at night with the aim of committing sins with the girls and single women" (626). The author had contradictory views about musicians, however: elsewhere he presented them not only as fine polyphonic singers and instrumentalists ("grandes cantores y mucicos de canto, de organo y llano y de uigüela y de flauta, cherimia, corneta y bigüela de arco, organista") but also as prime examples of good, loyal Andean Christians, worthy even of joining the priesthood (764). In either case, it is evident that the *maestro de coro* and singers were expected to, and frequently did, officiate in church rituals when the priest was away.

The *maestro de capilla* not only wielded power over the church musicians and congregation but he also came to occupy the position of *maestro de escuela*, or schoolmaster. The lack of a free school in Cuzco for Andeans along the lines of the Colegio de San Andrés in Quito meant that responsibility for the education of those who did not attend the elite *colegio de caciques* fell within the

13. Felipe Guaman Poma de Ayala, 1613, folio 670,
Los maestros de coro y de escuela de este reino.

orbit of the parish church, and the key educational role was often filled by the
maestro de capilla. The fact that responsibility for education had passed into
the hands of Andean *maestros* in the early colonial period is made clear in
Viceroy Toledo's *ordenanza* to the neighboring province of Charcas in 1575
(Levillier 1925, 359–60). For the following century and a half, musical training was linked to general education and formed a core part of the school
curriculum. The importance of music in primary education is made clear in
chapter 15 of the 1591 *Constituciones sinodales* of Cuzco's Bishop Montalvo, and
it is echoed a few years later by the Franciscan Jerónimo de Oré ([1598] 1992,
f.56): "The school is like the soul of a village, that it may be better instructed
and governed, and where there is no school, the doctrine, music, adornment
and service of the churches, altar and choir will all be lacking." Primary
education was thus concerned not just with teaching skills like reading and

writing but also with training church servants. Guaman Poma de Ayala includes a chapter on the *maestro de coro y de escuela* in his *Nueva corónica y buen gobierno*: the accompanying drawing shows the children seated at the foot of a music stand, learning to write under the watchful eye (and the whip) of the *maestro* (fig. 13). There is clearly no separation between the roles of choirmaster and schoolmaster in his mind.[41] Echoing the *Constituciones sinodales*, he writes: "In these realms, there should be a school in every village, big or small, and the boys and girls should all know how to read, write, and sing polyphony" (Guaman Poma de Ayala [1615] 1980, 634–35).

The post of parish *maestro de capilla* was therefore one of the highest to which an Andean could aspire, in any field of activity. The privileges and powers that accompanied it were allied to a salary or other rewards, giving the position economic as well as social weight. The *maestro de coro* in an Andean parish was far more than a choirmaster: he was the key indigenous figure in education and religion, a community leader, and an important point of contact between the Spanish and Andean republics. It served the interests of the church to have this post filled by a traditional yet acculturated figure of authority, and it served the interests of the indigenous nobility to consolidate its power within colonial society by establishing a foothold in the ecclesiastical hierarchy for its members, their kin, or their close associates.[42] It was logical that the priests should choose these new figures of authority from the ranks of leading indigenous families who were educated in music and inculcated with a Christian vision in the special *colegios de caciques* such as San Borja in Cuzco. These Andean nobles already had the allegiance of the populace, so the theory went, and having been indoctrinated by the friars, they could be relied on to serve the interests of the Catholic Church in their communities.

There was thus a particular link between the music profession and the minor nobility. The families of *caciques* had had a certain degree of power and privilege under the Inkas, but their authority diminished under Spanish rule. To the colonists, only the paramount *caciques*, perceived as key cultural intermediaries, were regarded as important. Their relatives risked being reduced to low ranking occupations as their privileges disappeared. The Andean nobility therefore sought to combine its traditional social advantages with the pursuit of new positions of responsibility and economic opportunities (Garrett 2005). Its members boosted their ceremonial roles by sponsoring or joining associations such as confraternities, but they were also active participants in the material, as well as the spiritual, economy. They tended to seek strength in diversification, both economic and religious, for in both respects their position might be considered precarious: they were neither "old Christians" nor, in many cases, conspicuously wealthy. Since inheritances were split evenly among the children of Andean elites, the assets of Andean noble families were often in fact modest (Garrett 2005, 139), obliging most to engage with the urban economy via a variety of trades, crafts, and investments. The attraction of the music profession to *principales* thus comes into view more clearly. The second son of a *cacique*, for example, would generally have inherited some money but little prospect of succeeding to his father's office. Such a minor noble had certain advantages and useful connections, but these required consolidation. The music profession offered prestige, thereby legitimating his social position; it offered a ceremonial role, and thus opportunities for the performance of authority; and it was a route to economic stability.

If education—learning to use the tools of the conquerors—was recognized as one way for the second tier of the native elite to counteract its declining status (Alaperrine-Bouyer 2002, 150), the music profession, too, served as an ideal means for its members to remain connected to the top echelons of society and to maintain their power and privileges. It also offered opportunities to some who had previously been excluded from the traditional social structure, opening up the possibility of "social climbing" (Spalding 1970).[43] Church music provided the minor elite with a chance to maintain its distinctive position in society by adapting to colonial realities, learning new skills, and occupying the new positions of authority that arose as a result of Spanish colonization. Kinship relations in themselves were no longer a guarantee of social status, but they afforded privileged access to positions of responsibility such as church office.[44] Andeans of medium to high social status were, of course, attracted to many other professions, such as painting and the decorative arts, but music offered particular advantages: whereas most native artists worked under Spanish *maestros*, many Andean musicians were *maestros* themselves and occupied the top musical positions in their respective institutions and communities. Music, then, offered Andeans the potential for leadership, independence, and benefits that was matched by few other professions.[45]

We should not, then, be surprised to find members of the upper strata of indigenous society occupying high musical posts in colonial Peru, yet existing musicological studies of urban centers have largely failed to take account of this key fact. A cathedral-centric approach, in focusing excessively on an institution that blocked opportunities for indigenous advancement, has reduced the role of indigenous musicians in urban institutions to that of permanent underlings. Those few native musicians who did climb the cathedral hierarchy in some Latin American cities are the exceptions that prove the rule that unequal colonial power relations extended to the musical organization of cathedrals. Archival evidence indicates that Andean cathedral musicians in Cuzco generally came from the social group known as *yanaconas*, roughly equivalent to servants, whereas parish *maestros cantores* were often leading figures in their communities. The possibilities for personal (and probably artistic) freedom were far greater for a high-ranking parish musician than for a cathedral *ministril*, and may have been greater still in rural parishes further from the center of colonial power.

It would therefore be more accurate to suggest that musicians' status within the Andean world was proportional to their distance from the colonial center than to assume that a post in the cathedral was the height of achievement. A centripetal model of musical organization, according to which the cathedral constituted the most desirable place of work, may be largely applicable in Spain but cannot account for patterns of employment among Cuzco's indigenous musicians. The musical hierarchy of the cathedral faithfully reproduced the colonial ideology of Andean subordination. In the parishes, however, the more complex realities of Andean life came into play: the Spanish enterprise depended on the collaboration of the indigenous authorities for its success, and in return it had to grant them certain privileges. The *maestros cantores* were the caciques of the cultural conquest—influential intermediaries in the subtle and complex process of the formation of colonial Andean culture. It is only when we look at Cuzco as a whole, and not simply at its cathedral, that we can see that Andean musicians constituted far more than a supporting cast in the city's musical life.

Case Studies of Indigenous Parish Musicians

ANDRÉS GÓMEZ

Don Andrés Gómez was a *principal* of the parish of Belén and *maestro cantor*, presumably at the parish church, in the year 1701. He had resided in the parish for at least fifteen years, having been described as "*maestro arpista* of the parish of Belén" in 1686 when he bought a house on the parish plaza from a priest named Francisco Menacho y Aguero. In 1700 he rented a house and land in the parish at a cost of 230 pesos for one year. He acted as the guarantor of a debt for one Sebastián Conde, and when the latter was imprisoned for nonpayment, Gómez paid off the debt of 112 pesos 4 reales. This repayment was itself guaranteed by Gómez's house on the plaza of

Belén, which was next door to that of the parish priest and free from any mortgage or *censo*. He was one of the executors of the will of Don Diego Ramos Tito, a *principal* of the village of Yaurisque. In 1690, he took on a seven-year-old apprentice named Blas Conde, agreeing to teach him music and to play the harp for a period of ten years.[46]

What does this tell us about Don Andrés Gómez? He was a *principal*, or community leader. His life revolved around the parish of Belén, where he was a figure of considerable standing. He bought his house from a clergyman, he lived next door to the parish priest on the plaza (the most desirable and prominent location in the parish), and he had close links with a fellow *principal* whose will he executed. He had money to invest in urban property and sufficient economic resources to act as guarantor of another's debts. These last two features, in particular, are found repeatedly in documents relating to urban musicians. Those who reached the level of *maestro* usually owned a house, and often land as well, something that was also frequently true of master artisans (Gibbs 1979, 46, 126). Property ownership was not only an investment of capital; it also served to generate cash flow since houses or land could be rented out to provide an annual income and could also serve as security for loans. Investment in property was therefore a gateway to full involvement in the urban economy and to the diversification of income, and it was characteristic of both Andean and Spanish elites in the seventeenth century (Garrett 2005, 54, 134). The first known examples of Andean musicians purchasing land date from the 1620s and involve the buying and selling of arable plots by the cathedral cornettist Pedro Juan Tinco and the shawm player Nicolás Guaman.[47] In the following decade, however, parish singers and organists also began to engage in such transactions.[48]

There are many documents that detail musicians acting as *fiadores*, or debt guarantors, for their friends or colleagues. This indicates that musicians commonly had the financial resources or property, as well as a certain trust factor, to support such guarantees.[49] The implication of these documents is that musicians who reached the level of *maestro* were generally considered to be solvent, reliable, and solid citizens, and it is worth noting that Gómez had the resources to pay off the debt in question when called on. Certain legal decisions, such as the appointment of the executors of a will or the guarantors of a debt, carry implications concerning the perceptions of the selector toward the selected. The right choice of debt guarantor, for example, could make the difference between liberty and imprisonment in the event of financial difficulties. It is perhaps surprising that indigenous Peruvian parish musicians were regarded as suitable for such roles: many of the documentary traces left by their peninsular counterparts, even those who worked in cathedrals, concern their financial difficulties, implying that musicians in Spain at this period were rarely considered as solvent or as suitable candidates to guarantee debts.[50] These *fianzas* (security bonds) also give clues to the social milieu in which musicians lived. They must have had close ties both to those whose debts they were prepared to guarantee, as they were legally required to cover the debts in the case of nonpayment, and probably also to their fellow *fiadores*, when more than one was required. For example, Don Antonio Cusi Guaranca, *maestro cantor* of the parish of San Sebastián, joined together with a silversmith and a tailor to guarantee the debt of Don Joseph Titu Atauchi, cacique of the village of Caycay (Paucartambo). Don Juan Poma Cusi, *maestro cantor* in the parish of Hospital de los Naturales, agreed to pay off the debt of an imprisoned friend, along with Don Juan Sutic Guaman, cacique of Guanoquite, while Don Fernando Asensio Amau, *maestro arpista y cantor ladino en la lengua castellana*, bailed out Don Lorenso Poma, the governor and *cacique principal* of the village of Sorite (Abancay) who was being held in the city jail.[51]

The involvement of these musicians in the economic affairs of caciques, the highest figures in indigenous society, once again indicates high socioeconomic standing and close connections to the Andean nobility: it is significant that two of these caciques turned to musicians in times of trouble. The profession of silversmith was one of the most prestigious, though associations with trades such as tailor and barber are more common. In addition to the tailor mentioned above as *fiador*, one Lucas de los Santos, *maestro organista*, joined a tailor to guarantee a debt of one hundred pesos in 1665.[52] The link between the professions of musician and barber appears to have been particularly close, as it was in Europe, and it is illustrated in a number of documents in Cuzco's archives.[53] In 1786, a document concerning tribute payments was produced by the Andean guild of barbers and musicians, demonstrating a formal connection between the professions, which were, in some cases, practiced simultaneously. The confraternity of the Archangel San Miguel in Huayllabamba, a village in the Urubamba Valley near Cuzco, was founded in 1695 by Don Juan Quispe, *cantor y maestro barbero*, while there is a mid-eighteenth century reference to the sale in Cuzco of an African slave named Antonio, described as "of Portuguese caste, who practices the trades of barber and trumpeter."[54] Martin Minchom (1994, 86–90) describes barbers in the Andean city of Quito as "an urban group which was virtually a distinct social category"—indigenous, but belonging to the Spanish world. The Spaniard Antonio de Ulloa ([1748] 1990,

1:349–51) perceived them as part of the acculturated Andean elite and noted their elegant Hispanicized dress. While the highest-ranking musicians were among the leaders of their communities, then, many moved in the company of middle-ranking, Hispanicized artisans and professionals, forming part of the mediatory class of *indios ladinos* who stood between the Andean and Spanish republics.

MATÍAS DE LIVISACA

Don Matías de Livisaca, a resident of the parish of Santa Ana, was variously described as *maestro de música* and *maestro compositor de música*. Livisaca was a name traditionally associated with musicians in this parish and, while the exact kin relationship is unclear, Don Matías appears to have been preceded in his profession by at least two generations of his family. In 1667, Don Juan Livisaca, *maestro cantor* from the parish of Santa Ana, guaranteed a debt repayment with a house in the parish. Twenty-five years later, Don Luís Livisaca, a *principal* of Santa Ana and *maestro cantor* in the parish church, founded a *censo* of five hundred pesos on houses and land that he had bought in the parish. Don Matías, the third member of the family, lived in the same parish in the early eighteenth century. Like his predecessors, he was involved in property investments, selling a house and land on the plaza of La Almudena for 1,050 pesos in 1717. He was given power of attorney in 1708 by one Miguel de Estrada, an indication that he was considered a man of influence and solid reputation.[55]

More information can be gathered from Livisaca's will, drawn up in 1722.[56] He owned two haciendas, both some distance from the city, which he had inherited from his second wife. He also owned the large house in which he lived in the parish of Santa Ana. He was active in the spiritual economy, having been a member of the confraternity of Nuestra Señora del Milagro in the monastery of San Francisco for more than forty years, and having served as *patrón* of the chantry founded in memory of his second wife.[57] Livisaca also had convent connections: he was owed thirty-five pesos by Doña Francisca Olaya, *vicaria* of the convent of Santa Catalina, for two psalms that he had composed. Even more interestingly, from a musical point of view, Livisaca owned three music books—two copies of Domenico Pietro Cerone's *El melopeo y maestro* (1613) and a copy of Andrés Lorente's *El porqué de la música* (1672)—as well as unspecified "music papers." He instructed that these should be handed over to Don Nicolás de Torres y Portugal, who was to keep the music but was to take the books to Don Antonio Durán de la Mota, *maestro de capilla* at the cathedral in Potosí, presenting a rare and fascinating example of the circulation of music materials between identifiable musicians in the Andean region.

The case of Livisaca raises both new and familiar issues. He and the preceding generations of his family were firmly rooted in the parish of Santa Ana; two of his predecessors had been *maestros cantores*, at least one of them in the parish church, while one was also *principal*, and all carried the honorific title "Don." There was evidently a high degree of continuity of profession and socioeconomic status within the family, as well as a low degree of mobility, and they had all invested in property in the city. Other signs of Don Matías's status are his ownership of haciendas outside the city and of a house in a prime location in the parish of Hospital de los Naturales, the power of attorney that he was granted, and his position as the *patrón* of a chaplaincy. While this confirms the high socioeconomic standing to which leading parish musicians might aspire, there are also certain elements that appear striking. First, it seems that Livisaca was primarily a composer. Second, judging by his ownership of books, he was literate and well instructed in European music theory. Third, he had a personal connection with one of the most important composers of his age in the entire Andean region.

There are many things that we do not know about Livisaca, such as for whom he composed his music. It is clear from his will that he wrote for the convent of Santa Catalina, and there is circumstantial evidence of his musical activities in the monastery hospital of La Almudena (see chapter 3), but he must have had more customers than these. We also do not know what portion of Livisaca's time was spent on composing, directing, and performing music, or how much of his income derived from these different activities. Nevertheless, the fact that he describes himself in his will as *maestro de música* and that in another document he is described as *maestro compositor de música* is unusual, implying that he was primarily a composer and director rather than a performer. This makes Livisaca an important discovery since little evidence of the existence of indigenous composers has been found in South America, let alone information about their background and lives. This is no doubt due partly to the fact that the majority of studies have focused on cathedral archives, which clearly reflect the careers and output of Hispanic composers. Few indigenous cathedral musicians rose above the lowest rung of the institution's musical hierarchy, the post of *ministril*, let alone learned the skills of composition or heard their music performed by their Spanish "masters."

The fact that Livisaca owned copies of music treatises by Cerone and

Lorente, implying that he was well grounded in music theory, indicates a notable level of musical sophistication in a provincial indigenous composer.[58] Both colonial sources and modern music historiography have tended to emphasize the enthusiasm and skill of indigenous performers, but the idea that they might have possessed noteworthy creative abilities or a serious conceptual knowledge of music has rarely been entertained.[59] No music from Andean parish churches has been found in Peru, and therefore there has been little discussion of Andeans' compositional capabilities, but the example of Livisaca is perhaps a warning that they should not be underestimated. This impression is bolstered by evidence that he sold liturgical compositions to the convent of Santa Catalina, a bastion of Hispanic culture, suggesting complete fluency in European idioms; we should be wary, therefore, of assuming that music produced at the interface of Spanish and Andean cultures is necessarily hybrid or "mestizo baroque" (Quezada Macchiavello 2004, 83–86). On the contrary, it seems probable that Livisaca's success within a cultural sphere dominated by the Hispanic church was due to his mastery of the European musical language. The fact that he wanted his music books to be given specifically to the Potosí maestro de capilla Antonio Durán de la Mota, one of the most important composers in the Viceroyalty of Peru in the eighteenth century (Stevenson 1995), suggests that he formed part of a professional milieu of the highest caliber.[60]

Livisaca came from a good family, owned urban and rural property, was musically well connected and well instructed, and made his living at least partly from composing. To say that indigenous composers like Livisaca have been overshadowed by their Spanish counterparts in the eyes of musicologists would be a serious understatement. Yet despite this neglect, it is clear from this case that an indigenous composer in early-eighteenth-century Cuzco could make a good living from working for Hispanic institutions and could aspire to a comparable socioeconomic and artistic level to that of a Spaniard. It is interesting to compare Livisaca's will with that of the cathedral maestro de capilla Juan Lázaro Gallegos, drawn up two years later in 1724.[61] This comparison reveals Livisaca to have been in a markedly better economic position than his Spanish contemporary, who occupied what is standardly regarded as the top post in the urban musical hierarchy. This supports the notion that a purely centripetal model misrepresents the nature of the music profession in colonial Cuzco. Once we become aware of figures such as Don Matías de Livisaca, our understanding of the social, economic, and artistic possibilities for Andean musicians outside the orbit of the cathedral is greatly expanded.

There is evidence that Livisaca's case was not unique. The only indigenous composer previously identified in Cuzco, Ignacio Quispe, is known solely because of the survival of one of his pieces in the seminary archive.[62] This piece, a rare example of a composition that can be firmly attributed to an indigenous composer, has gained a certain mythical status among musicologists. It is not known when Quispe lived, when the piece was written, or how it ended up in the library of a Hispanic institution. There are, however, documents in the Archivo Departamental del Cuzco (ADC) that may give further clues about its composer. There is an element of uncertainty as the name "Quispe" is the Andean equivalent of "Smith," but it is tempting to believe that the Don Ignacio Quispe, *maestro compositor*, who was given power of attorney in 1710 by Bernardo Quispe was the composer of the piece in the seminary archive.[63] The same Don Ignacio Quispe was described as *maestro arpista* in an earlier document concerning a loan of two hundred pesos that he had made to Bernardo.[64] Quispe drew up his testament on 9 May 1719 and died sometime before 24 October 1720, when the executor of the will, a *maestro pintor* named Don Matías Núñez, sold some houses that Quispe had bought twenty-five years earlier in the parish of Hospital de los Naturales. He is again described as *maestro arpista* in this document.[65] Whether or not these two Quispes are actually one person, there are nevertheless clear parallels with Livisaca. Both cases involve indigenous composers who were financially solvent, who had invested in urban property, and who were considered of sufficient social status to be given power of attorney by others, the main difference being that Quispe combined his compositional activities with playing the harp.[66]

This same mixture of activities is evident in documents relating to another indigenous composer, Don Tomás de San Bernardo, who is described twice as *maestro compositor*, once as *maestro de música* in the parish of San Blas, and once as *maestro organista*. San Bernardo was less solvent than his fellow composers—three of the four surviving documents concern the repayment of debts of between two and four hundred pesos. However, he owned a house in his native parish of San Blas, which he used to guarantee the loans, thereby demonstrating one of the main advantages of investing in property. His debts probably indicate poor cash flow rather than poverty, and he used his property in order to gain credit. On one occasion, the debt was guaranteed not only with the house but also with twelve mules. This evidence that San Bernardo was involved in nonmusical activities is strengthened by the fact that he rented land in the parish of San Jerónimo for the purpose of sowing potatoes, vegetables, and grass for a period of nine years at twenty pesos per year.[67] This is one of a number of archival traces indicating that many middle- and low-ranking musicians supported themselves in part through agriculture.

A final series of documents further illustrates the tendency of musicians to diversify income, whether through property investments or commerce, and the themes of continuity of profession within a family, the low mobility of musical families, and the connection between the music profession and high social status. Juan Domingo Guaman Topa, *indio organista* and resident of the parish of San Cristóbal, left traces of repeated property dealings, selling a plot of land and a house in the parish in 1626, another house in 1633, and buying land elsewhere in the city in 1639. More than eighty years later, Don Francisco Guaman Topa, *maestro de capilla* and native of the same parish, sold a tannery that he owned to a priest named Don Juan Dias de Alda for 220 pesos. This tannery, along with a house, had been passed on down the family from his grandfather, Don Juan Guaman Topa, who was cacique of the village of Yaure.[68]

It is clear, then, that by the mid-colonial period the upper echelons of the music profession in Andean parishes had attained a socioeconomic position on a par with that of the city's medium-level Spanish inhabitants. These indigenous musicians were playing a full part in the urban market economy, and playing it with some success. There is even a record from 1633 of an Andean organist named Diego Felipe who hired an indigenous couple to work as his servants at a cost of sixty pesos for one year, a strong indication of his position in Cuzco society.[69] It is probably the case that many such musicians enjoyed their socioeconomic position as a result of the status of their family, in which case it would be fair to say that the music profession attracted successful individuals as much as it created them, strengthening or legitimating previously existing authority. There is, however, also sufficient evidence to suggest that lower-ranking Andean musicians were able to use their tribute and labor exemptions, together with occasional payments or other rewards, to escape from a subsistence level of existence and become more fully involved in the Spanish urban economy.

The Eighteenth-Century Economic Crisis

Parish churches suffered along with other ecclesiastical institutions in the economic crisis that reduced Cuzco to "the poorest town in all of Spain and the Indies" in the late eighteenth century (Concolorcorvo 1965 [1773], 264).

Many were obliged to cut the inducements offered to their employees, in some cases—such as that of Ignacio Rocca, the organist of San Jerónimo forced to give up his job after seven years of unpaid work—to nothing. The impact of the worsening economic climate on Andean musicians can be seen repeatedly in the accounts of Rocca's parish. Payments were made to the musicians of San Jerónimo at Christmas for many years between 1740 and 1767, but these are then absent until the pointed entry in 1797 of twelve reales paid "to the musicians for Holy Week, the only reward given to them all year," followed by this revealing note by the church's administrator:

> Although I do not find any payments to musicians in the accounts of my two immediate predecessors, I do find them in those of Juan de Dios Pereyra and his predecessors under the name of "musicians and shepherds at Christmas," not only the small sum of 12 reales, but also 2 and 4 pesos. These musicians, at present two violinists and a harpist, serve the whole year without any form of pay or compensation, and as they are unhappy at not receiving what was previously normal, they threatened to leave the service of the church, and I had no right to demand that they continue. Therefore I had to agree to give them 12 reales, as used to be the case, for Holy Week, 4 reales for each one, which does not even cover the cost of strings.

Clearly an absence of payments to musicians does not imply an absence of musicians, who were simply suffering by this time from the informality of their long-standing nonprofessional arrangement. It is not clear how the musicians at San Jerónimo were expected to support themselves, given that they "serve the whole year without any form of pay or compensation." Perhaps they were among the musicians who, according to a 1796 entry in the accounts of the church of San Pedro, "as they have no land which might provide them with food, support themselves with their voices, doing the rounds of the churches." Apart from painting a rather sorry picture of the circumstances of these musicians, this entry also implies that they would normally have expected to survive on the produce of land that they cultivated, revealing that musicians had also operated as subsistence farmers. The scribe goes on to give details of the earnings of the *cantores* of San Pedro: there were eight of them, who earned thirty-one pesos four reales each per year, but who sang for free on Saturdays, Sundays, and fiestas "since they are appointed to this church."[70] This salary was low by most standards—though not by those of San Jerónimo—and it is clear that the *mayordomo* who wrote this entry thought the musicians were not being sufficiently rewarded for their efforts.[71] In the church of Belén, payments to musicians at Easter and Corpus Christi cease to be recorded in 1796, and there are no references to music after 1800, yet the inventories indicate not only that the church had an organ, a harp, a *bajón*, drums, and bird-whistles but also that the organ and harp were in regular use well into the nineteenth century.[72]

The state of economic decline among the parish churches and their musicians is eloquently expressed in two *libro de fábrica* entries from the end of the colonial period. San Jerónimo was forced to undertake organ repairs that it could ill afford because the organ pipes were continually being stolen by boys from the city. Meanwhile, the *mayordomo* at San Pedro included a note in the church accounts in 1815 revealing that the organist and *cantor* were unpaid and that he had therefore had to "help them with their most urgent needs." The former organist and singer, Antonio Bello, had been given an occasional item of clothing, while his successor had been helped with various small necessities, just sufficient to prevent him from abandoning the church. The scribe also noted that the *cantores* were paid the sum of two reales each at Easter, a sum unlikely to have made a large impact on their "most urgent needs."

There is a stark difference between the elite musicians described in the previous section, all of whom flourished between the mid-seventeenth and early eighteenth centuries, and the landless and low-paid singers who wandered between churches in search of work a century later. The fact that urban musicians were "doing the rounds of the churches" suggests that mobility increased markedly in the late eighteenth century as the stability and dependable rewards associated with the profession ebbed away; more evidence of this late colonial upheaval will emerge in the examination of rural musicians that follows in the next chapter. The decline in the profession is also evidenced by the virtual disappearance of musicians from the notarial records during the eighteenth century. The quantity of documents pertaining to musicians peaks between 1650 and 1700 then declines slowly between 1700 and 1720, after which date there are very few such records.[73] While far from conclusive in itself, this quantitative trend implies that the role of musicians in the urban economy diminished as the eighteenth century progressed. However, this decline involved both Spanish and indigenous musicians, reflecting wider developments in Cuzco's economic fortunes. The deprivation of Andean musicians described in the parish *libros de fábrica* at the end of the colonial period is matched by that of the Spanish musicians who competed for posts in Cuzco Cathedral around this time.

Indeed, musicians were suffering financially in many Spanish colonies, as well as on the Iberian Peninsula, as the economic fortunes of the Spanish empire waned. The state of the music profession at the end of the colonial period should not therefore detract our attention from the fact that indigenous parish musicians played a major part in, and reaped the rewards of, Cuzco's artistic golden age.

Conclusion

A focus on parish churches, religious institutions that have been marginalized within Hispanic and Latin American musicology, allows a glimpse of the possibilities that the music profession opened up to Andean elites within colonial society. There are certain parallels between these findings with regard to parish musicians and Burns's (2002) study of Cuzco's *beaterios*. Just as *beaterios* allowed indigenous women from prominent Andean families to exercise a degree of authority and responsibility that they could never have in convents, even holding the position of mother superior or abbess, parish churches provided native musicians with the possibility of ascending to the top post of *maestro de capilla*, something that was impossible in the cathedral. If *beaterios* provided opportunities for indigenous women to hold high religious rank, there were no equivalent institutions for indigenous men, who could not therefore become fathers superior of a religious establishment. The post of *maestro de capilla*, as the deputy of the parish priest, then takes on added significance as being the closest that a male Andean could come to holding religious office or directing a religious institution before the mid-eighteenth century, and the music profession thus appears as one of the primary ways for indigenous men to construct a "decent," honorable Christian identity.

Rather than regarding indigenous parishes as less important or as marginal in relation to Hispanic institutions, we should perhaps view them as semi-autonomous spaces within which Andean elites could exercise their limited power with greater freedom. This picture upsets a simple center-periphery model, for the so-called periphery here appears not as a pale reflection of the center but as a place of greater opportunity. *Beaterios* are often portrayed negatively in Hispanic documentary records and are marginalized in comparison with Hispanic-dominated convents, but it does not follow that they were less significant, certainly not from the point of view of the Andean nobility, and our understandings of parish churches, too, need to be reviewed in this light. The intermediary role of the Andean nobility has long been recognized as vitally important: Garrett (2005, 3) writes that "given the dual nature of the colonial order, their very liminality placed them at the center of colonial society." Such a claim rings especially true for the parish *maestros de capilla*, key members of this native elite who were located at the interface of Spanish and Andean religion, education, and culture.

CHAPTER FIVE

The Rural Doctrinas de Indios

In 1790 a Spanish geographer named Pablo José Oricaín visited the village of Andahuaylillas, to the southeast of Cuzco. There he composed a "Brief Compendium of Various Discourses on Different Matters," which included his impressions of music making in the rural parish churches of the region: "I cannot gloss over the fact that on Christmas Eve in general, and especially in the villages, those who play the instruments in the choir disturb the faithful at the moment of the mass, as they are not well versed in musical compositions suitable for divine worship, but rather adapt them, with four or six [musicians] who do not even perform them half-decently; and to vary, they introduce profane *contradanzas*, minuets, *yaravís*, and lascivious songs" (Maurtua 1906, 338–39).[1] He went on to express his fear that this secularized music conjured up worldly images in the imagination of the congregation.

This account was written by a Spanish outsider at a time when the intense cultural conservatism of the late eighteenth century was at its peak. If we put the author's severe value judgments to one side, however, we might catch faint strains of lively, hybrid musical practices, combining European dance music and Andean songs, that had become part of the religious and cultural traditions of indigenous communities. We might also perceive a remarkable continuity of parish music making over two and a half centuries of colonial rule, immune even to the huge social and political disruptions that had spread across the region in the wake of the Túpac Amaru rebellion a decade earlier. The value judgments themselves, meanwhile, are also noteworthy, for music making appears here as a source of disharmony between colonists and the colonized. Oricaín's account gives a glimpse of a thriving rural tradition with both European and Andean roots which came under intense scrutiny by Spanish authorities in the late eighteenth century, and his tone is indicative of a dramatic change of outlook on the part of the colonial elite whose ancestors had sown the first seeds of musical hybridity.

Some of the earliest interactions between native Andeans and Spanish missionaries in the sixteenth century involved musical performance, but while the Spaniards' attitudes to European music were generally positive, their views on native music were more ambivalent. At first, many saw indigenous music as essentially harmless, or even as a potentially beneficial source of diversion, and felt that it was enough to change the texts and the objects of worship in order to convert native songs *a lo divino* (to the divine). The repressive side of the Spanish conquest also manifested itself in the musical sphere, however, as a later wave of churchmen tried to force the indigenous population away from their traditional songs, dances, and instruments. The most extreme saw idolatry at every turn, and aimed at the total eradication of indigenous musical practices.[2]

Prominent among the former category was the Jesuit José de Acosta, who wrote about native music and dance in tolerant terms in his *Historia natural y moral de las Indias* (1590). Acosta, who had spent time in Cuzco, argued that "it is part of good government that the republic [of Indians] be allowed its recreations and pastimes." While he recognized that "many of these dances used to be performed in honor of their idols," he suggested that they were also "a source of recreation and joy for the people," and he advised that "it is therefore not a good idea to take them away from the Indians, but instead to ensure that no superstition is mixed in." He felt that it was better to allow supervised public displays than to ban them and thereby drive them underground, arguing that, as far as possible, native Americans should be allowed to continue with any artistic expressions that did not "mix their former errors," noting that priests adapted the doctrine to the natives' manner of singing (Acosta [1590] 1987, 432–35).

At the other end of the spectrum was the investigator Pablo de Arriaga, also a Jesuit, who published his *Extirpación de la idolatría del Peru* in Lima in 1621. The mood of the church authorities had changed substantially in the intervening decades: the broad campaigns to extirpate idolatry instigated by the Jesuits in the early seventeenth century now included efforts to "conquer" indigenous musical practices, though the account of the Jesuit-sponsored fiestas in Cuzco in 1610 suggests that political imperatives could outweigh cultural suspicion, allowing Andean music to continue to flourish in the former Inka capital even as the extirpation campaigns started to uproot native culture in the archdiocese of Lima (see chapter 1). Arriaga saw "dissimulation and boldness" in native ceremonies, recognizing that indigenous instruments had symbolic value and that their sounds and even the instruments themselves were intimately associated with indigenous religion. He implicitly criticized the permissiveness of those such as Acosta, writing: "No one who saw them performing these celebrations thought there was any malice in it but considered them pastimes, traditional dances and so forth" (Arriaga [1621] 1968, 70). Arriaga clearly disagreed with these "neutral" interpretations, and, as well as rooting out native instruments on his visits to native villages, he published "regulations to be left by the visitor in the towns as a remedy for the extirpation of idolatry," which included the instruction that "from now on in no case nor for any reason will the Indians of this town, whether men or women, play drums, dance, or sing and dance at a marriage or town festival, singing in their mother tongue as they have done up to now. For experience has shown that in these songs they invoke the names of their *huacas*, the *malquis*, and the lightning, which they worship" (170).[3]

Thus during the first century of colonial rule, music was seen as a double-edged weapon: it was a potential means of bringing Andeans into the flock, but there was also widespread suspicion that music could be, and often was, a key means through which indigenous religion might be perpetuated. Even Acosta ([1590] 1987, 433) recognized that "the majority [of native dances] were superstition and a source of idolatry, as this was how they worshipped their idols and *huacas*." Where Arriaga and Acosta disagreed was over the question of whether indigenous music and dance could be pruned of former associations and thereby recuperated. Arriaga clearly felt that the permissiveness of earlier missionaries had given Andeans free rein not only to maintain their cultural and religious expressions but to do so under the very noses of their colonial masters. That he viewed indigenous music and dance as conscious cultural resistance to Spanish indoctrination is evident from terms like *dissimulation* and *pretext* that pepper his diatribe, and he claimed that "the fact that these activities were passed over and little or no notice was taken of them has led the Indians to keep them up and perform them with impunity" ([1621] 1968, 70).

There is evidence that, in rural communities, indigenous religion was indeed perpetuated through music and dance, both in disguise, under the gaze of the Spanish, and in secret. According to witnesses questioned during a religious inspection of the village of San Francisco de Otuco near Cajatambo in 1656, many traditional rituals, dances, and songs were still being performed in honor of Andean deities out of sight of the Spanish authorities (Duviols 1986, 52, 60). Even more sinister was the notion that the Spanish were being hoodwinked by the native population. According to a report written by Francisco de Ávila in 1611, villagers in the diocese of Lima conflated their own ceremonies and festivals with those of the Catholic Church, thereby continuing their traditional practices under a thin veil of conformity (Duviols and Arguedas 1966, 255–59). Where some observers saw the days of drinking, dancing, and music making as harmless recreation, Ávila saw open defiance.[4]

The religious authorities were thus much concerned with indigenous music making, but not only in the field of traditional music, for alongside the attempts to control native musical practices ran sustained efforts to train Andeans in the performance of European ecclesiastical music. Music had been harnessed to the imposition of colonial rule from the outset as an evangelical tool, a weapon in the struggle to conquer the hearts and minds of the Andean population. It was perceived as an ideal way of teaching doctrine, since song had been an important form of recording and passing on histories and information in a culture that, prior to the Spanish conquest, had no writing system. The friars thus merely adapted an existing educational tool. Furthermore, by training Andeans to fill musical posts and thereby officiate in church ceremonies, missionaries sought to inspire devotion and commitment on the part of their charges. Music therefore formed part of a program of cultural indoctrination that aimed to seduce as well as to silence. The organization of music in indigenous parish churches was a question of policy, dictated by secular and sacred authorities including the crown and successive viceroys and bishops. The fact that such high authorities devoted their time to the organization of music indicates clearly that Acosta was in a minority in regarding it as a mere pastime, and that most legislators recognized music as an arena in which colonial power could be both imposed and contested.

Music in the Doctrinas de Indios

With the notable exception of studies of music in the Bolivian Jesuit missions, little sustained attention has been paid to rural music making in colonial Latin America.[5] The urban focus of colonial ideology has been largely maintained by musicologists' privileging of elite city institutions. Yet toward the end of the colonial period—the only time for which reasonably accurate statistics are available—around 85 percent of the population of the diocese of Cuzco lived in rural areas (Unanue [1793] 1985, 178; Brisseau Loaiza 1981, 22). If the musical experiences of the majority of inhabitants of the diocese are not to be sidelined, then a detailed examination of the organization of music in the *doctrinas de indios*, or rural Andean parishes, is a sine qua non.

The *doctrinas* were not fundamentally distinct from Cuzco's urban parishes, though they were more numerous, more remote, and significantly larger than their urban equivalents.[6] The key Spanish officials in the *doctrinas* were the *doctrinero*, or parish priest, and the *corregidor de indios*, a secular provincial magistrate; in some remote areas, however, their presence was nominal and limited to occasional visits. The traditional indigenous power structure of a cacique who ruled his subjects and organized tax collection and the provision of communal labor remained in place, though with an overlay of colonial laws and obligations (Stavig 1999, xxviii). The degree to which Spanish power depended on the cooperation of the caciques can be judged from the fact that parish priests might expect to have four hundred Andean parishioners under their supervision in the principal village alone, and many more in nearby annex villages (*Actas del III Congreso Internacional*, 695). Cooperation was quite often granted, since there were incentives for caciques to conform to a system that maintained many of their traditional privileges over their subjects. Yet as well as relying on self-interest, the Spanish opted also for indoctrination and persuasion as a means of creating and preserving their desired sociopolitical system.

THE *MAESTRO DE CAPILLA* AND EDUCATION

Visual and aural pomp were considered vital elements in convincing the local population of the superiority of the new faith. An indigenous musical hierarchy was thus installed by Spanish priests in the newly created *doctrinas de indios* in order to ensure that Catholic ritual maintained its appeal. At its head, as in the urban parishes, was the *maestro de capilla* or *maestro de coro*: indeed, the rural parishes had much in common with their urban counterparts with regard to musical organization. The *maestro de capilla* was responsible for ensuring that the village church had the music necessary for important occasions in the religious calendar, and his duties typically included directing rehearsals and performances—according to Guaman Poma de Ayala ([1615] 1980, 636), he was to lead the singers every morning, at the afternoon Salve, and at evening vespers—and teaching music to the children of the *doctrina*. Although some rural *maestros* were capable of composition, there are also many references to the copying and purchasing of music.[7] The church of Yucay in the Urubamba Valley recorded regular expenditure in the late seventeenth and early eighteenth centuries on "paper for copying the music for the church" and on payments to the *maestro de capilla* for this service. The church's *mayordomo* spent twelve pesos in 1697 on "music and paper that I bought for the singers," suggesting that the *maestro* of the church at this time was not a composer.[8] The church of Sumaro (Chinchaypugio) had an active *maestro de capilla* in the 1680s: the church paid one peso two reales in 1681 for two *manos* (quires) of paper in order to copy out some ferial antiphons for the church, and a further one peso four reales in 1684 to the village *maestro* for having copied out the music of the Passion and the offices for Holy Week.[9]

The post of *maestro de capilla* involved more, however, than simply organizing musical activities, for the *maestro* often fulfilled both religious and educational roles alongside his musical duties. From the early colonial period onward, the clergy was drawn increasingly toward urban institutions, which offered more attractive career opportunities, and by the end of the sixteenth century most friars and priests spent the majority of their time in cities (Ganster 1986, 142). This clearly left something of a vacuum in and around many rural churches, one which the head musician often filled. In 1687 Bishop Mollinedo ordered the creation of a school for the children of the *doctrina* of Calca, "and the *maestro de capilla* shall teach them every day to pray, read, and sing."[10] A similar decree was issued to the *doctrina* of Oropesa in the same year, ordering the establishment of a school where the village children were to learn to read, write, sing, pray, and speak Spanish, and the *maestro de capilla* was to instruct the singers for at least an hour every day.[11] Parish education was particularly crucial in peripheral regions, where the alternatives for Andeans were minimal. The *maestro de capilla* was clearly a pivotal figure in the *doctrinas*: the education of future generations—and therefore, to a large degree, the success or failure of Spanish cultural colonization in rural areas—often lay in his hands. Guaman Poma de Ayala ([1615] 1980, 635) concludes his chapter headed "Maestro de coro" with the words, "If possible, there should be a school and Christianity and *policía* in every village, large or small, throughout the realm." If this was the responsibility of the choirmaster, then his importance in the development of colonial Andean society and culture could hardly have been greater.

Archival evidence confirms that the enthusiasm of church authorities for musical education was borne out in practice in the *doctrinas de indios* and that indigenous *maestros de escuela* taught music alongside basic literacy, as Guaman Poma de Ayala had illustrated. In 1627, an Andean from the Cuzco parish of San Blas named Don Juan Guari Tito was hired by the cacique of San Juan de Totora in the province of Cotabambas to teach the children of the village to read, write, sing plainchant and polyphony, and play shawms, for a period of one year.[12] The church *fábrica* and the Cofradía de Santa Ysabel in Sumaro both made payments in 1679 "to the *maestro* who teaches the children to read and to perform music in the church," while Don Francisco Guaman Topa was paid by the church of Lamay-Coya in 1710 to teach the boy sopranos music and reading.[13]

If the dominant role played by the church in the education of Andeans is well documented, the extent to which its initiatives were placed in the hands of indigenous *maestros*, above all in rural areas, has been less widely recognized.[14] Furthermore, some scholars have concluded that educational efforts were largely unsuccessful because the enthusiasm of churchmen for rural education declined after the early years of missionary fervor, except in isolated cases in which individual *doctrineros* showed a particular interest (Brisseau Loaiza 1981, 92; Macera 1967, 331; Vidal 1985, 100). The evidence from Cuzco presents a rather different picture. The notion that the church lessened its educational efforts after the sixteenth century is undermined by evidence that Bishop Mollinedo had a clear interest in the establishment of schools in the *doctrinas*. More importantly, since education relied to a significant degree on indigenous *maestros*, the suggestion that efforts to educate rural Andeans were a failure due to a lack of priests is untenable. In some cases the funding of the key post of *maestro de coro* was in the hands of the native leaders rather than those of the church, as we shall see below, and therefore enthusiasm for education on the part of individual caciques played a significant part in determining its success. Such enthusiasm can be seen in a letter to the king in 1601, in which Andean nobles sought to hasten the foundation of Cuzco's *colegio de caciques* (Alaperrine-Bouyer 2002, 157). The upper levels of indigenous society saw benefits in education and played a key part in implementing and supporting educational and musical programs in the *doctrinas*: the instruction of rural Andeans in music, literacy, and doctrine should not therefore be seen simply as a function of Spanish efforts.

There is evidence, however, that Andean musicians' involvement in general education, once fundamental, declined after the mid-eighteenth century. Two documents dating from 1795, relating to proposals for the establishment of schools in the districts of Chumbivilcas and Urubamba, give detailed accounts of the current state of education and the nature of the intended programs, yet neither makes any reference to music or musicians.[15] This would have been hard to imagine a century earlier. According to these late colonial documents, however, there were no local candidates who could teach the children of the villages as the church servants were illiterate, and Spanish *maestros* from other areas were being sought to take charge of the proposed schools. The majority of the local population is described as ignorant of Spanish and of the most basic tenets of Christianity. The implication of these documents is that a rupture in the educational process had occurred during the eighteenth century: these late colonial efforts were not a continuation of earlier, church-sponsored initiatives, but formed part of a renewed, Enlightenment-inspired educational program with new aims and methods. Whereas seventeenth-century *doctrina* schools were generally run by Andeans for Andeans, the late colonial educational initiatives were part of a top-down approach that met resistance from both potential teachers and students (Van Oss 1986, 137, 142–45).

The second half of the eighteenth century also saw a decline in the power associated with minor church office and therefore in the attractions of the post of *maestro de capilla*. Karen Spalding (1984, 237), writing about the Huarochirí region to the north of Cuzco, puts this down to the increasing control exercised by both religious and secular colonial authorities:

> The Indian nobility on the provincial level in 1750 showed considerable reluctance to become involved in the structure of civil or religious government, in contrast to the pattern of the sixteenth century. Few of the people listed as noble in the census of 1751 held community or parish office. Those offices had become essentially positions of servitude under the control of priest and corregidor, and the Indian elite withdrew to exercise what authority it still commanded in the local community outside the structure of colonial government.

The suggestion that the power structure of Andean society was changing from the mid-eighteenth century onward is taken up by Scarlett O'Phelan Godoy (1997). The *cabildo indígena*, or indigenous council, made up of the elected *alcalde de indios* and his assistants, began to take over from caciques as the official voice of indigenous communities, in some areas eclipsing the latter altogether. These Andean officials were closely linked to the church, as their election was supervised by the priest, and they took over many of the peripheral religious duties that had once fallen under the remit of the *maestro de capilla*: calling villagers to mass, supervising confessions, organizing the church servants, and so on. This restructuring of the Andean officeholding system accelerated in the aftermath of the 1780 Túpac Amaru rebellion, which cast many caciques in a poor light, and it may well have played a role in the reduced influence and visibility of musicians, as the *maestros de capilla* were part of the old order, the amalgamation of traditional and colonial power structures that emerged in the early days of the colony.

As the power of the caciques declined and the institution was reduced to a state of crisis by the end of the eighteenth century, priests began to use *cabildo* members as intermediaries with the local population, and the *maestro de capilla* lost out to the *alcalde* as a key religious and political go-between.

A final nail in the coffin of the post of *maestro de capilla* may well have been the emergence of a limited number of native clergymen in the second half of the eighteenth century. A royal decree of 1697 supporting the right to indigenous ordination, reiterated by the viceroy in 1725, finally began to bear fruit toward midcentury, by which time several important indigenous lineages had managed to place sons in the clergy (O'Phelan Godoy 1995; Garrett 2005). Whereas second sons of caciques might previously have become *maestros de capilla*, a new pattern began to emerge from the 1730s onward, with the oldest son succeeding his father as cacique, as before, while the second son sought to join the priesthood. A church career was attractive to the native elite, not least because of the economic rewards on offer. When the powers of caciques were curbed after the 1780 rebellion, this toehold in the church allowed Andean nobles to maintain a degree of influence over their communities. The priesthood thus emerged as an alternative to the *cacicazgo* and became a strategy on the part of the native nobility for retaining authority. Once the possibility emerged for Andean nobles to become priests, it is not surprising that the attractions of the post of *maestro de capilla*—the priest's unofficial deputy—declined.

The ordination of Andeans was part of a general trend in the late colonial period in which the leading indigenous families moved toward increasing assimilation into Hispanic society. Legislation opened up fresh avenues of advancement for Andean elites, with new offices emerging; some members of the indigenous elite even moved into peripheral branches of the state administration (Garrett 2005). The other side of the coin was that criollos and mestizos, encouraged by the crown after 1780, increasingly coveted *cacicazgos* and the land and manpower that went with them. Their success in appropriating these positions of leadership contributed to the breakdown in traditional social structures at the end of the eighteenth century (Cahill 1999). Among these seismic changes, the position of *maestro de capilla* seems to have lost its privileged role as a route to power.

THE *CANTORES*

The *maestro de capilla* was in charge of the *cantores* of the parish, who standardly numbered around four to six and were exempt from tribute payments and personal services (see chapter 4). There are, however, some discrepancies in the sources with regard to the size of *doctrina* musical forces. Guaman Poma de Ayala ([1615] 1980, 630) writes of "the four *cantores*"—the logical minimum for the performance of polyphony—though his accompanying drawing shows five musicians playing recorders. While other sources propose that *doctrinas* should have between three and six musicians (see Baker 2003b), in practice, musical forces in the Cuzco region sometimes exceeded these official recommendations. Indeed, Viceroy Toledo's instruction in 1570 to leave only the necessary number of musicians in each church, "reducing any superfluity that you may find," suggests that churches tended to err on the generous side when it came to musical employment.[16] A report from the village of Guanoquite in 1689 stated that its church was served by a dozen musicians; the report from Guancaguanca, while complaining of the church's poverty, nevertheless recorded "a number of *cantores*, sacristans, and other officials" (Villanueva Urteaga 1982, 434, 438). The *doctrina* of La Asunción de Nuestra Señora de los Papres (Quispicanchis), considered below, had eighteen choir members in 1687.[17]

The *cantores* doubled up on wind instruments, the quantity of which in many church inventories implies a sizeable complement of players. The church of Chinchero possessed three *bajones*, two *bajonetes*, four shawms, and a cornett, according to a 1718 inventory, while the *doctrina* of Huayllabamba spent thirty-nine pesos in 1683 on "seven *bajones*, large, medium and small."[18] In 1647, the church of Soraya (Aymaraes) listed in its inventory a new organ, a set of shawms, two *bajones*, a sackbut, a cornett, and a consort of seven recorders and a *bajonçillo* (small *bajón*).[19] Similar inventories show that such impressive collections of wind instruments were found in many *doctrinas*, and there is evidence that organs and harps were found not just in most parish churches, but even in the chapels of remote haciendas.[20]

Two villages in the province of Cotabambas, Mamara and Turpai, had two organs each, in the style of major Hispanic churches (Villanueva Urteaga 1982, 45), and the church of Andahuaylillas still preserves its pair of colonial-period organs today. Bernardo Illari (2001, 112) illustrates the contrast between cathedral and parish churches in La Plata by underlining the principal church's possession of two organs, but it appears that this distinction is less applicable in the diocese of Cuzco. Certainly, if the music making in the church of Andahuaylillas came even close to matching the splendor of its decoration—and with two experienced musicians among its early *doctrineros*, this seems more than likely—there would have been nothing undeveloped or provincial about the sounds that filled its magnificently painted walls.[21] The *doctrinas* of Pichigua and Acos spent 2,000 and 2,500 pesos, respectively, on purchasing their organs, in both cases exceeding the sum that Cuzco Cathedral spent on a new instrument in 1654.[22]

The presence of so many musical instruments in rural parishes not only suggests the employment of many musicians but also implies that these musicians performed polyphony. This was certainly the intention of the church authorities: Franciscans such as Jerónimo de Oré ([1598] 1992, f.51) and Diego de Córdova Salinas ([1651] 1957, 159) both exhorted and recorded the performance of polyphony with instruments in the *doctrinas* of their order. Secular clerics, too, encouraged polyphony. Juan Pérez Bocanegra, the priest of Andahuaylillas, included in his *Ritual formulario* of 1631 the first piece of polyphony to be printed in the New World, the four-part "Hanac-pachap" with a Quechua text. Bocanegra had served for a dozen years as a singer at Cuzco Cathedral; formerly the priest of the urban parish of Belén, he spent more than forty years in the Cuzco region teaching doctrine to the native population (Stevenson 1976; 1980a). He thus had a deep knowledge of the musical capacities of Andean parish church musicians, for whom this piece was intended. The promotion of polyphony was not, however, restricted to Spanish churchmen: the Andean Guaman Poma de Ayala ([1615] 1980, 635) wrote that "boys and girls should know how to read, write, and sing polyphony," an instruction that is mirrored in contracts drawn up by caciques to hire village music teachers.

The Economics of Doctrina Musical Provision

Despite all this evidence of musical activity in *doctrina* churches, the church account books show few signs of payments to *cantores*. On the other hand, these books record many payments to specialist instrumental players; up to the mid-eighteenth century, organists, harpists, and *bajoneros* were hired frequently, while after this date violinists are found with increasing regularity, sometimes in combination with harp and harpsichord players. Payments to *maestros cantores* are also found in many *doctrina* records, and there are examples of all these principal musicians receiving annual salaries. Throughout the colonial period, one can find payments to drummers and trumpeters for their participation in religious ceremonies; these sounds seem to have been an indispensable feature of Andean church festivals, much as they are today. Nevertheless, the records are full of gaps and inconsistencies, and no pattern emerges in any one institution, let alone in the *doctrinas* in general.

A brief entry in the *libro de fábrica* of the village of Accha helps to illuminate the issue of musicians' financial rewards. The church made no payments to musicians except for a one-off fee in 1743 of six pesos "to the *maestro cantor* Nicolás Joseph, as he has been contracted [*concertado*] and is an outsider [*forastero*]."[23] That the musician was only paid in cash by the church *fábrica* because he was contracted, and that he was only contracted because he was a *forastero*, or Andean who had left his home *ayllu*, highlights issues explored in the previous chapter. Again, it appears that local musicians might not be paid in cash from the church *fábrica*; indeed, they might not be paid at all. Almost all the examples cited in this chapter involve the hiring of outside musicians for limited periods or for single events. It appears that musical services were regarded in different ways depending on the contexts in which they were performed. Ward Stavig (1999, 129) writes that in the Cuzco region Andeans were reluctant to work outside their communities unless they were well compensated, but that working *within* their communities was considered very differently, as communal labor was a long-standing feature of Andean society. This would seem to go a long way toward explaining the frequent absence of musicians from the church account books and the fact that most music contracts involved the hiring of *forasteros*: the relationship between a musician and his home community was often not a commercial one.

An examination of the *libros de fábrica* reveals the extent of musical activities in the *doctrinas* as much through inventories and repeated expenditure on musical hardware (new instruments, repairs, harp and violin strings, paper for music) as through direct payments to musicians. The church singers—the mainstay of *doctrina* music making—are mentioned only occasionally and obliquely, when the *fábrica* paid out for their musical necessities such as candles or a music stand. A late-eighteenth-century inventory at Andahuaylillas shows a sizeable collection of music books, yet those who performed the music are absent from the yearly accounts; they are only mentioned in a subsequent inventory noting that some of the books "had been lost by the singers."[24] *Cantores* were not salaried, at least not from the church *fábrica*, although in some *doctrinas* they received occasional payments for special functions, such as confraternity services. The most they could normally expect was a single payment for the fiesta of the patron saint of the village, at Easter, or for another feast of equal importance.

Maestros cantores, organists, harpists, *bajoneros*, and violinists appear with some regularity in the church accounts. They were hired at times when no cheap or free option was available, and they were closer to a modern conception of a professional musician than were ordinary *cantores*. They were more mobile, sometimes signing short-term contracts with institutions outside their own communities in return for a mixture of cash and other benefits such as food and lodging. Alongside these short-term opportunities, some were also paid salaries by their own churches over longer periods of time. The accounts of the church of Lamay-Coya show that the organist, the harpist, the *bajonero*, and the *maestro cantor* were regularly paid in corn or wheat in the late seventeenth century and first half of the eighteenth. However, there were also instrumentalists who differed little from the *cantores*, and whose existence is evident only from payments to cover expenses. The only financial reward received by the harpist and violinist of the church of Chinchero between 1769 and 1782 was one peso for strings "for the whole year," implying that, while they performed with some degree of regularity, they could hardly be considered professional musicians.

There was, therefore, a two-tier system in the rural parishes: the *cantores* made up the lower level, the *maestro de capilla* the upper, and the key instrumentalists might occupy either tier, depending on whether they were local or *forastero* and on the economic circumstances of the church, priest, and cacique. A musician's place in this two-tier structure was based on both his skills and his connection to his place of work, a system whose gradations and variations illustrate the partially developed state of market relations in rural areas and the persistence of older conceptions of reciprocal exchange. Workers were often employed on radically different terms on the same projects in colonial Latin America, and a mixture of salaried and servile labor was commonplace (Stern 1993, 156–57). No clearer example of this system could be found than the accounts of the church of Andahuaylillas for 1822, which record the payment of twenty-two pesos to the musicians who performed during Holy Week: two violinists and a keyboard player, as non-locals, were paid six pesos each, but the two harpists, "as they are servants of the church, were paid only 2 pesos each."

As in the case of urban parish musicians, exemption from tribute payments and community services was the primary form of reward for rank-and-file musicians, explaining their sporadic appearance in church records.[25] For musicians in a rural subsistence economy, the time and expense thus spared would have been a considerable incentive to participate in the ecclesiastical musical structure. Faced with the choice between fulfilling their community obligations in the church choir or in the mines, textile mills, or haciendas, it is not hard to see why many Andeans might have opted for a musical career. The *mita* to the silver mines at Potosí is the most notorious, but the draft to the mines at Huancavelica and Cailloma was equally feared, as was the *mita de coca* in the province of Paucartambo. Conditions in many of the region's textile mills were little better, and all these forms of labor left large numbers of Andeans dead or crippled by disease and injury (Villanueva Urteaga 1982, 6–13; Juan and Ulloa [1749] 1978, 136). Exemption from tribute would also have spared musicians the wage labor to which many Andeans were driven in order to pay their taxes. Wages for manual work were supposed to be two reales per day (Macera 1968, 132–44). The *tasa*, or tax, in the Cuzco region was around five pesos, which would theoretically equate the tribute exemption with about twenty days' labor. However, according to Jorge Juan and Antonio de Ulloa (1978, 128, 136), who were familiar with practice in the *audiencias* of Lima and Quito, hacienda workers earned fourteen to eighteen pesos per year, textile mill workers earned one real per day, and tribute was eight pesos per year. Accordingly, some individuals may in fact have worked a significant portion of the year in order to pay their taxes; the incentive of tribute exemption should therefore not be underestimated.

It is perhaps not surprising, then, that some *doctrinas* had large musical forces. In 1687, the *doctrina* of Papres sent seven *mitayos* (mita workers) to the silver mines at Potosí and five to a textile mill, while the eighteen *cantores* were joined in the service of the church by twelve *mayordomos* and two sacristans, and seven more Andeans occupied posts as community officials. In other words, nearly two-thirds of those available for community service were able to take the "soft option" of church employment, with around a third occupying musical posts. Other nearby villages also had impressive musical forces: the village of Marcaconga supported twelve *cantores*, Poma-canche thirteen, and Acopia ten.[26] These villages, too, were subject to the *mita*. If we consider the position of *cantor* in the context of other forms of community service, we may suspect why the musical forces in *doctrinas* often exceeded those set down in the official recommendations. These suspicions are confirmed by Guaman Poma de Ayala ([1615] 1980, 736), who claimed that caciques used community posts—including that of *cantor*—as an officially sanctioned way of shielding their friends and allies from the *mita*.

From the perspective of musicians themselves, paying tribute in the form of labor instead of taxes was much closer to the Inka model to which Andeans were accustomed. The tribute system changed under the Spanish from one based on labor or produce to one paid in cash, forcing indigenous communities to sell their labor and produce in the marketplace (Ramírez 1996, 119). In a cash-poor rural environment where most people lived by agriculture, and where transactions traditionally took the form of reciprocal arrangements, exchange, or services, it is understandable that exemptions from tribute would have played a much larger part in musicians' remuneration than cash, and such exemptions may ultimately have been more useful. For many rural Andeans, the principal need for cash was to pay their tribute, and if musicians were exempt, their need for financial rewards was low. Since musicians were excused from the two greatest burdens on the Andean population, the *mita* and wage labor, many may have seen exemptions as sufficient recompense for their services.

It should also be noted that the clergy had nothing to gain from the *mita*, a mechanism for state appropriation of indigenous labor. On the contrary, priests benefited from keeping Andean laborers close to the *doctrina* church, where they might be of use to the *doctrinero* himself, and therefore probably supported all of this musical activity wholeheartedly. From a less cynical perspective, the antipathy of village priests to the *mita* is clear in their 1689 reports: many were clearly appalled by the decimation of their communities and the depopulation of rural areas, both of which much reduced their capacity to spread the faith (Villanueva Urteaga 1982, 6–13). From either point of view, it was not in the clergy's interest to preside over a disappearing parish, so their support for musicians' right to exemption might be assumed.[27]

Higher-level musicians such as *maestros de capilla* would generally have expected more substantial rewards than *cantores*. The irregular appearance of such rewards in the *libros de fábrica* suggests that they were sometimes provided not by the church *fábrica* but by the community and its leaders. Viceroy Toledo, in his *ordenanzas* to the province of Charcas, recommended an annual salary from community resources of two items of clothing, six *fanegas* of corn or potatoes, and twelve rams (Levillier 1925, 359–60), and contracts in Cuzco's archives confirm this kind of practice. Don Juan Guari Tito was hired to teach the children of San Juan de Totora by Don Josefe Felipe Matará, the *cacique prinicipal*, not by the *doctrina* priest; he was to receive a salary of seventy pesos, twelve *cargas* of corn, twelve rams, twelve fleeces, two plots of land for sowing corn, and a pair of servants.[28] Three caciques of the village of Urcos hired the organist Juan Bautista de León in 1629 "in our name and in the name of our subjects, the other Indians of this village," to play in the church and to teach several pupils to fill his role after his departure.[29] It is specified three times that his payment—one hundred pesos, twenty rams, twenty *cargas* of corn, and two plots of land sown with corn—was to be met by the caciques and the community, who were even responsible for cultivating and harvesting the corn and transporting it to the organist's house. Such conditions of employment were well suited to the resources available in rural communities, and these employees may well have left no trace in church accounts.

These caciques valued their musicians' services much more highly than either Toledo or Guaman Poma de Ayala ([1615] 1980, 635) had recommended. A decree issued in 1687 by Bishop Mollinedo to the parish of Calca insisted that the *maestro cantor* and the organist's salaries from the church should be capped at twenty pesos, and that any additional costs should not be passed on to the *fábrica*.[30] Up to that date the salaries had been around one hundred pesos; although they dropped after the bishop's order, they soon rose back to around fifty pesos, confirming that in some *doctrinas*, at least, musical services were worth more in practice than in theory and were supported partly or entirely from local, nonecclesiastical sources. The sponsorship of culture by the native nobility was not new to Peru since its authority before the Spanish conquest had rested not just on its members' hereditary rights and abilities but also on their capacity to provide entertainment, food, and *chicha* at festivities (Ramírez 1996, 21). By subsidizing church music, caciques continued this tradition of festive munificence, looking after their subjects while setting down a marker (whether collaborative or competitive) to their parish priests.

The village leaders and community not only met the cost of hiring musicians but also on occasion paid for the construction or repair of organs, a burden that one might expect to have fallen on the church *fábrica*. The caciques and villagers of Acos hired the master organ builder Gabriel Cabezas in 1634 to provide their church with an organ, at the considerable cost of 2,500 pesos. The contract was signed by the *kuraka* (native leader) and *segunda persona* (deputy), "in the name of the other Indians and *principales* of the village."[31] The *mayordomo* of the church of San Juan Bautista de Catca in the province of Paucartambo noted in his accounts for 1743 that he had collected 346 pesos 4 reales in alms from the villagers in order to build a new organ for the church, and there is a reference in the accounts of the *doctrina* of Calca in 1771 to "the collection that the *ayllus* made for the construction of the organ by the *maestro* Don Ygnacio Vidaure."[32]

Evidence of funding from sources other than the *fábrica* raises the question of parish churches' capacity to pay for music. The alternative arrangements that were made may reflect the fact that although music was a fundamental part of Spanish evangelical efforts, some churches were simply unable to afford to pay musicians a sufficient salary or to provide them with the necessary instruments. In 1689, most parishes, both urban and rural, complained of having little income and very few resources (Villanueva Urteaga 1982). As a result, some of the more dedicated priests contributed to the cost of music out of their own pockets. The priest of Capacmarca claimed to have personally paid for musicians and instruments as part of his efforts to improve the *decencia del culto divino* (Villanueva Urteaga 1982, 310). In another case, dating from 1729, the caciques of Quiquijana stated that their priest "has a school and pays the *maestros* from his own money and also teaches [the Indians] to write, and some to play the harp, or other instruments, and others to sing so that they may serve the church" (Colin 1966, 92).

These cases are a valuable reminder that the initiative of individual priests, as well as of caciques, would have played a significant part in determining the scale of musical activities within a *doctrina*. Bishop Mollinedo, famous for his patronage of the visual and plastic arts in the late seventeenth century (Villanueva Urteaga 1989), also contributed to an increase in musical provision. While his letters to the king focus on his extensive efforts to build and decorate churches, his 1687 "Summary of the Ecclesiastical Inspection," focusing on the Cuzco diocese, includes instructions to various *doctrinas* concerning the organization of music.[33] He ordered the priest and caciques of the *doctrina* of Oropesa to share the cost of paying the salary of the *maestro de capilla* of Andahuaylillas, and gave instructions for the establishment of a school in which the teaching of music was to play an important part. He issued similar instructions to the *doctrina* of Calca, insisting that the *maestro de capilla* teach the village children to read, write, and sing, and intervening over musicians' salaries. He presided over the appointment of the *maestro de capilla* in Maras, ordered that the church of Quiquijana replace its decrepit organ, and requested that the caciques of Checasupa provide two boys who might learn to play the organ. His influence over Cuzco's musical life may not have matched his efforts in other artistic fields, but he clearly took steps to ensure that villages in his diocese were musically equipped.

If the role of both caciques and priests in financing musical activities in rural churches is taken into account, colonial musical culture begins to look less like an instrument of domination or a cultural invasion by the Catholic Church than like the result of negotiations between colonial religious authorities and indigenous leaders. In many ways, the two groups' objectives coincided since a flourishing musical life benefited both the priests, who could take pride in the celebration of the *culto divino* in their churches (while impressing inspectors and boosting their chances of promotion), and the caciques, who could use the church *capilla de música* to enhance their prestige and reinforce their authority. It also benefited the musicians themselves, who reaped the variety of rewards discussed above. The musical life of Cuzco's *doctrinas* seems to have been considerably richer than that of comparable rural parishes in Spain, reflecting both colonial policies and the economic and material support that Peruvian communities gave to their musicians, something that undoubtedly grew out of ancient Andean traditions of reciprocity, exchange, and community provision for religious personnel.

CONFRATERNITY MUSIC IN THE *DOCTRINAS DE INDIOS*

Confraternities took a significant burden off the *fábrica* of rural churches by paying musicians to participate in their ceremonies and even contributing to the cost of musical instruments. Many more confraternity account books survive from the *doctrinas* of the Cuzco region than from the city parishes or monasteries. Whereas the accounts of seven confraternities survive from the parish of San Jerónimo, and only one or two volumes from the other urban parishes, the *doctrina* of Calca has preserved the accounts of sixteen confraternities, and the nearby *doctrinas* of Yucay and Chinchero ten volumes each. Given that most confraternities paid the church musicians on at least one occasion per year, these societies were an important way for indigenous communities to channel resources toward musicians. They undoubtedly made a notable impact on musicians' earnings and occupied an important place in their professional and ceremonial lives, while considerably augmenting the quantity of music in and around churches. Most confraternities employed *maestros de capilla* and *cantores*, and in many accounts instrumentalists such as harpists and organists also appear. Their services were required for the confraternity feast day, sometimes for the weekly confraternity mass, and also on important occasions such as the days of *finados* and *aguinaldos*, Holy Week, and Corpus Christi. Those better endowed owned their own instruments and had salaried musicians who played at all confraternity functions; others brought in musicians from Cuzco as required.

In Calca, the Cofradía del Señor de la Resurección possessed five recorders, a set of shawms, a German sackbut, and another set of ten "fine recorders," according to a 1610 inventory, and it had added a *bajón* and a cornett by 1646. In 1616 the confraternity paid five pesos to a *maestro cantor* "to instruct the singers," implying either that it had its own group of musicians or that it trained the regular *doctrina* musicians specifically for confraternity events: both might imply that the confraternity used a distinct repertoire.[34] The Cofradía of Nuestra Señora de Belén in Calca owned a new harp and a small organ in 1751; the *mayordomo* of the Cofradía del Rosario in Urubamba spent twenty-nine pesos in 1655 on "a large harp that I bought for the *cofradía*"; and the Cofradía de la Asunción in Santiago de Hacca (in the *doctrina* of Accha) bought a drum in 1708 "to play during the fiesta inside the church."[35]

The only pattern that emerges from all these records is one of musical proliferation: every confraternity seems to have had its own distinctive requirements in terms of musical personnel and occasions, but the one universal feature is that music was a desired part of confraternity celebrations. The minimum requirement seems to have been a full-scale performance on the confraternity feast day. The Cofradía del Dulce Nombre de Jesús in Urubamba hired various combinations of harpist, organist, singers, drummer, and trumpeter for its feast day every year between 1697 and 1715. Wealthier confraternities might have salaried musicians: the Cofradía de Nuestra Señora del Rosario in the same village had sufficient funds to hire a harpist on an annual salary of between twenty and thirty pesos during the years 1705 to 1728 to perform at "masses, Salves, and other confraternity functions throughout the year," a tradition that stretched back at least half a century. For much of the eighteenth century, the Cofradía del Santísimo Sacramento of Urubamba hired both salaried musicians to perform at the weekly Thursday mass (harpists, organists, drummers, and trumpeters predominate) and freelance musicians for the functions surrounding Corpus Christi. This seems to have been a common pattern among the more financially secure confraternities. One solution for confraternities that could not afford to pay a salary on their own was to combine forces with others, as did the four confraternities in Pisac, which paid ten pesos each toward the organist's salary in 1678. Where there were no local musicians, confraternities made considerable efforts to hire outsiders at least on their feast day. The Cofradía de Nuestra Señora de la Limpia Concepción in Sumaro paid musicians to come from Cuzco from 1657 to 1660, while the Cofradía de Nuestra Señora de la Asunta in Calca brought in musicians—including violinists, harpists, a clarinetist, and a horn player—from Cuzco almost every year between 1795 and 1812 for its fiesta, at a cost ranging between fourteen and fifty pesos, a considerable outlay for a rural confraternity.

The Cofradías del Santísimo Sacramento were among the most active in the rural parishes, much as they were in the city. In Vilque (*doctrina* of Accha), the partial surviving confraternity constitutions reveal that on the Day of the Dead, the *cofrades* were to pay for a sung requiem mass with its response for their dead brothers "with much devotion and solemnity." Although direct payments to musicians appear only infrequently, there is regular outlay on buying and repairing instruments including the organ, *bajón*, shawms, harp, and drums, and on providing the organ repairer with potatoes and the singers with food; music was clearly not lacking. In Calca, too, constitutions survive, though in poor condition. They reveal that Corpus Christi was celebrated with vespers, a procession, and a mass to be sung "with great solemnity," and that there was to be a sung requiem mass and response for each cofrade who died, repeated with added peals of bells on the Day of the Dead. The confraternity in Huayllabamba made regular payments to singers, a harpist, and a salaried organist from around 1690 to 1750, when drummers and trumpeters start to appear in force, especially at the weekly confraternity mass and at Corpus Christi.

The accounts of rural confraternities are distinguished from their urban counterparts not only by their number but also by occasional payments to dancers and for chanzonetas on the feast of the patron saint.[36] The Cofradía del Santísimo Sacramento in Calca made several such payments in the 1710s, including one "to the maestro cantor for the dances and music," and another to the nearby village of Coya "for some entremeses and dances that they brought on the day of the fiesta."[37] In the village of Huayllabamba, the Cofradía de la Virgen Purificada paid for chanzonetas from 1679 to 1682 and from 1690 to 1693, while the Cofradía del Santísimo Sacramento made similar payments in 1687 and 1689. The Cofradía del Dulce Nombre de Jesús in Urubamba sponsored dances on its feast days in 1715 and 1716. Such records provide evidence of the breadth of the responsibilities of rural maestros de capilla; they also imply that some confraternities developed their own distinctive repertoires of vernacular songs and dances.

These records shed light on the tension between officially propagated orthodoxy and popular devotional practices in confraternities discussed in the previous chapter. The evidence from the Constituciones sinodales of 1591 and 1601 suggests that confraternities, and particularly their ceremonies, had been adopted enthusiastically by the Andean population. There are many reasons why this might have been so. There were parallels with pre-conquest social and religious practices, in particular with those of the basic unit of indigenous society, the ayllu (Meyers 1988; Moreno Chá 1992). Each ayllu was a small community responsible for the veneration of a particular sacred huaca; members of the ayllu were linked by their worship of this holy object, venerated as a supernatural mediator. There are thus clear similarities between the ayllu and the confraternity, unified by a saint or Catholic image. Moreover, as Andeans were excluded from the clergy for much of the colonial period, confraternities offered important opportunities for popular involvement with Catholic ritual. With the traditional forms of worship that accompanied ayllu membership regarded as idolatry and therefore strictly forbidden, confraternities constituted the prime ceremonial outlet for many Andeans. Participation in confraternity rituals allowed the indigenous population to "familiarize" the Catholic faith (Dean 2002) and gave Andeans a fair degree of autonomy in their religious observances.[38] The focus of confraternities on mutual support in life and death meshed with traditional Andean concepts of communal obligations and ancestor worship. Andeans were accustomed to treating the dead and the living as a spiritual and even physical community: joining confraternities in order to pray for and to recently departed *cofrades* would have been but a small step.[39]

Confraternities also flourished because caciques and other prominent members of indigenous communities realized that social prestige could be gained from occupying positions of leadership in these organizations. Founding a confraternity or acting as its *mayordomo* provided a means for Andean elites to consolidate their status and authority within their communities, to forge social connections across community lines, and to take a leading role in religious ceremonies. Confraternity elders accrued both spiritual and political benefits, which may explain why a power-hungry individual such as Don Bartolomé Tupa Hallicalla, the *cacique principal* and governor of the village of Asillo in the province of Azángaro, was *mayordomo* of all but two of the village confraternities in the 1670s.[40]

Priests, on the other hand, benefited in more tangible ways from the activities of confraternities. They could expect to be paid a fee for each said or sung mass that was celebrated by a *cofradía*, and they might receive further contributions such as food, wine, or agricultural produce from its *mayordomo* and members. In the mid-eighteenth century, the Spaniards Jorge Juan and Antonio de Ulloa ([1749] 1978, 104) were scathing about the ways in which members of the secular clergy enriched themselves in their parishes by exploiting the brotherhoods. Despite the efforts of Bishop Antonio de la Raya to restrict the number of confraternities and the scale of their activities in the *Constituciones sinodales* of 1601, these societies flourished in great numbers, for a large number of active *cofradías* meant considerable extra income for the *doctrina* priest; indeed, in some areas the parish priests came to depend on confraternities as the mainstay of their income.[41]

The fact that by the start of the seventeenth century confraternities were already threatening to escape the control of the Church lends credence to the idea that they were adapted to suit the needs of Andean communities, and that their original indoctrinating function was soon at least partially reversed. Through these lay societies, the indigenous population was able to introduce its traditional beliefs and rituals, particularly drinking and dancing, into orthodox Christianity, creating hybrid religious practices. The tension between official religious control and popular devotion in European confraternities thus resurfaced in Latin America, where an instrument of colonial power was partially transformed into a consolidator of Andean identity and ritual practice. The financial dependency of the priest on confraternities added a particular twist to this tension. While the priest might in theory resist deviation from orthodoxy, in practice his personal benefit was directly linked to the popularity of confraternities. There is a suspicion, therefore, that in areas that were more distant from the centers of colonial power, especially the rural *doctrinas* in which the village priest was the only permanent representative of colonial authority, a quid pro quo may have been established according to which the priest turned a blind eye to certain ceremonial practices in return for a steady flow of cash and gifts. It is thus hard to determine to what extent the clergy controlled the confraternities and to what extent the reverse held true. Juan and Ulloa ([1749] 1978, 118) certainly felt that, for all that priests might exploit their parishioners, the clergy were tied by the fact that confraternities held their purse strings: "Priests cannot condemn the orgiastic proceedings because they grow rich from these fiestas, and since the clergy sponsor these celebrations, they must excuse what goes on." It would appear that a balance or compromise was often achieved, and that, for the right price, a middle way between religious orthodoxy and popular observance was found.

It is significant, therefore, that dancing and the performance of secular influenced *chanzonetas* made their way into official confraternity account books as part of the duties for which *maestros de capilla* were paid. These activities, associated with popular religious observances, were to become prime targets in the late-colonial orthodoxy drive exemplified by the cathedral *Regla consueta* and the account of Pablo José Oricaín. That these cultural forms appeared even in official church records suggests that rural confraternities allowed considerable freedom of religious expression to their members, providing officially sanctioned spaces at the interface of popular and official Catholicism for the creation of distinctive, hybrid ceremonial practices, shaped to a large degree by their Andean Christian participants.

CONFRATERNITY MUSICIANS: EMPLOYEES OR BROTHERS?

While the channeling of economic resources to musicians through confraternities helps to explain the gaps in church *fábrica* accounts, many confraternity records are equally skeletal with regard to the compensation of musicians. In some cases, the explanation may be the same—payment in kind or from another source—but another reason for this lack of direct evidence of musical provision is that musicians were sometimes members of these associations and, as such, offered their services for free or were paid only for special events such as Corpus Christi or the annual confraternity feast day. By donating their services to a confraternity in this way, musicians were not only performing an act of devotion to the confraternity's saint but were also contributing to the spiritual assistance of *cofrades* past and present—thereby ensuring that they themselves would receive a decent burial and postmortem support in the passage of their soul through Purgatory. In a sense, confraternity activities thus constituted a form of spiritual investment, and musicians, in some cases, approached their confraternity duties from this perspective, rather than from a commercial one.

The best indication of the kinds of arrangements that musicians might have made when joining a confraternity appears in the constitutions of the Cofradía del Santísimo Sacramento in the urban parish of San Cristóbal: "If the singers wish to commit themselves to joining as *cofrades*, on the condition of singing for free the masses that are prescribed by this confraternity, they may enter without paying a membership fee, and if they wish to pay this fee like the others, they should be paid four reales for each mass and its vigil, or two reales without the vigil, unless they have not sung the prescribed mass that they should perform daily, in which case they should be given no more than two reales."[42] It would seem logical for musicians to pay their dues to the confraternity in musical form—and if they took the first option, they would not have appeared in the confraternity accounts—but unfortunately, very little information about *cofradía* membership survives, and it is therefore hard to see this kind of arrangement in action. However, the records of the Cofradía de Santa Isabel in the *doctrina* of Chinchaypugio are most unusual in that they contain a list of *cofrades* who joined and details of the dues that they paid to the confraternity on entry. The following is an excerpt from the list:

1700—the boy Bernabel Toyro joined as a trumpeter
1704—Francisco Vallpa joined as a drummer
1707—Blas Mulle with trumpet
1714—Pasqual Incaica joined as a brother with the obligation to help us out at the time of our fiesta with his instrument
1728—Andres Quiño joined with his drum

Thus several *cofrades* paid their membership fees with their services as trumpeter or drummer. The accounts of confraternity expenditure include payments to singers and a harpist, but none to drummers or trumpeters; this provides solid evidence of a quid pro quo between a confraternity and its musical members, and it indicates that some confraternities were partially self-sufficient. This, of course, makes the process of reconstructing the musical activities of confraternities somewhat complicated. The fact that musicians sometimes performed in return for spiritual, rather than financial, credit means that an account book showing just one payment per year to musicians may be concealing the fact that musicians performed all year round for free and were given a bonus just on the saint's day. The Cofradía de Nuestra Señora de Belén in Calca, for example, owned a new harp and a small working organ in 1751, yet it did not pay a harpist or an organist, the only mention of music in the accounts being the annual payment of one peso to the singers for the fiesta. In Cuzco's archives only account books, rather than lists of *cofrades*, survive, with two noteworthy exceptions: in both these cases there is firm evidence that musicians were members of the confraternities in question and that they paid their dues in kind.

In the second example, musicians seem to have played more than just a supporting role in the confraternity. There is reason to believe that the Cofradía del Arcangel San Miguel in Huayllabamba was established principally by and for musicians.[43] The confraternity was founded in 1695 by two musicians and a third person whose profession is not recorded. The lists of *cofrades* imply that many members were musicians and that they paid their dues to the confraternity with their musical services. On one page there is a list of twenty-nine names that appears to be a list of *cantores* who joined the confraternity over a period of some thirty years, starting from the foundation of the society and continuing until at least 1727. The first names on the list are:

D.n Alonso Quispe maestro
D.n P.o Juares
D.n Ju.o quispe el mayordomo
Sebastian yupanqui
D.n bentura pablo harpista
D.n salbador paullu el bajonero

Juan Quispe, *cantor y maestro barbero*, and Sebastián Yupanqui were two of the confraternity's founders. Alonso Quispe was presumably the *maestro cantor*, and the fact that he and the church harpist and *bajonero* joined the new confraternity implies a high concentration of musicians among the *cofrades*. The names Bernabel Paucar Tito and Gabriel Marca Pillaca both appear

further down the page of *cantores*, and both became *mayordomos* of the confraternity. Next to most of the entries are the words "dentro por cofrade con
su trabajo" (joined as a brother with his work). As this confraternity included a number of musicians, it would be reasonable to assume that *trabajo*
in this case often signified musical services. This hypothesis is strengthened
by the following entry: "Don Josep Cusi Paucar, *maestro de capilla*, entered as
a brother with his work." The confraternity accounts show that payments
were made to musicians, but the amounts are so small that these must have
been bonus payments for specific events rather than a salary.

Confraternities, like churches, sometimes paid their musicians in forms
other than cash. The same confraternity discussed above made donations to
the singers in the form of food, and in one year paid the *maestro cantor* and
the organist in corn. Another confraternity in the same village, the Cofradía
del Dulce Nombre de María, made a small annual outlay "to feed the singers
on the day of the fiesta," and while the Cofradía del Santísimo Sacramento
in Urubamba retained an organist, harpist, and drummer on salaries in the
years 1773–94, the musicians who performed at Corpus Christi were fed
rather than paid. These practices have clear pre-Hispanic precedents in the
agricultural taxation that supported Inka temple personnel and provided
refreshments on holidays, as discussed in chapter 4. There are also examples of musicians being compensated for their services with *chicha*, shoes, or
accommodation. Such examples support the contention that many parish
musicians fell into a semiprofessional category, meaning that much musical
activity once again falls through the cracks of the financial records. The
accounts of the Cofradía de la Asunción in Santiago de Hacca (Accha) show
almost no signs of musical activity over the course of an entire century, yet
when the *doctrinero* inspected the accounts in 1744 and questioned the confraternity's official about the harvest, the latter replied that four *cargas* of
potatoes had been given to the *cantores* and other servants for their assistance at the fiesta. The fact that this information only came to light during
an inspection suggests that while compensation in kind to musicians is
occasionally noted in the relevant confraternity accounts, many *mayordomos*
would have provided food and drink for their musicians at important functions without feeling the need to enter details in the confraternity records.

Thus musicians found opportunities to supplement their income and to
participate in popular devotional activities through confraternities, thereby
gaining both financial and spiritual rewards. Music—alongside charity,
prayers, and good works—was no doubt seen to benefit both the giver and
receiver: if the souls of dead *cofrades* were helped on their journey through

Purgatory by prayers rising to the sound of instruments and voices, musicians, too, were investing in their own smooth passage to the next world when the time came.

TRAINING AND EMPLOYMENT

Like the city parishes, rural *doctrinas* aimed for musical self-sufficiency, and musicians were normally trained by a local *maestro de coro* within the parish. However, gaps in the musical personnel inevitably appeared at times, and music was considered sufficiently important that outsiders were sometimes brought in to fill them. Pedro Miguel, an Andean organist who had previously worked for the monastery of San Francisco, traveled to the *doctrina* of Ollantaytambo in 1663 at the behest of its priest to serve as the organist in the village church for a year, for which he was to receive eighty pesos, two fields of corn, a house, and one real for every sung mass.[44] Where possible, the incoming (and expensive) musician was contracted to train the village boys in his art, so that the *doctrina* could return to self-sufficiency and cut its wage bill after his departure. When Pedro Miguel, now described as *maestro cantor y organista*, was hired by the priest of Coporaque in the province of Canas y Canchis in 1670, he was required to teach rather than perform: his contract was "to go to the village and teach the boys who are handed over to him to sing, ensuring that they learn to sing on their own as *maestros*."[45] He was to be paid one hundred pesos for this work, and agreed a contract on the side for another one hundred pesos with a certain Pantaleio de Sieva to teach his daughter to play the organ, a sign of the lucrative possibilities opened up by the music profession. Sieva no doubt hoped to place his daughter in a convent one day, and he was planning ahead to reduce her dowry. For reasons that are not clear, four days after this contract was signed, the priest of Coporaque drew up a new agreement with two Andean musicians from the Cuzco parish of Santiago who were hired for one year "to serve in the village, Sebastián Atau Poma as *maestro de capilla* in the church and Diego Callo as *cantor*, and to teach the children to sing."[46] Atau Poma was to receive seventy pesos, four plots of land sown with potatoes, and a ram each week, Callo forty-five pesos plus the same benefits.

The *libros de fábrica* of the village churches confirm this occasional practice of hiring outside music instructors. Nonlocal teachers, though expensive, could ensure the long-term musical future of the *doctrina*; they tended to be hired for a year, although if their charges were not trained to a sufficient standard by the end of this period, the contract might be extended. The church of Yucay paid eleven pesos in 1666 "to the *maestro* who is teaching a boy to play the organ for the church," and ten pesos in 1699 "to Juan Usno, *maestro cantor*, for teaching the shawm players, as those who used to play them died, and therefore they were lacking."[47] Huayllabamba paid eighty-three pesos three reales in 1683 "to a harpist, so that he might teach two *cantores* from this church for a period of one year."[48] The church of Calca frequently hired music instructors in the first part of the eighteenth century: the organist who was hired at fifty pesos a year between 1704 and 1708 "taught an Indian from the village, who now plays the organ."[49] Around 1710, the church paid forty pesos "to Antonio Quispe, *maestro cantor*, for the year and a half that he trained the *cantores* and sopranos of this church." The years from 1713 to 1718 include payments to the same *maestro de capilla* for teaching solfa to the village singers, and to Antonio Caigualpa, *maestro organista*, "who I hired at 50 pesos a year as the village organist had died; he came to play and teach."

When a musician could not be brought to the *doctrina*, a local boy might be sent instead to a *maestro* in the city, usually at the cost of the church. A young Andean, Juan Yucra, was sent to Cuzco in 1749 by the priest of Catca to train as a singer and church organist. He was taken on as an apprentice for one year by the *maestro organista* Gabriel Joseph Altamirano, who agreed to teach his pupil "to perform in any choir, and at any holy office, such as masses, vespers, and other offices which are held in church."[50] In 1803, the priest of Andahuaylillas noted in his accounts that he could not continue paying an organist himself and that this expense was also too onerous for the church, so he had sent a local boy to Cuzco for lessons at three pesos a month so that the village might have an organist in the shortest possible time, thereby saving on this outlay. Within three years, the sizeable payments to the organist cease, suggesting that the boy had finished his training in the city.

If teachers were normally hired for a year, performers were often brought in for a single occasion, and Holy Week in particular stands out as a time when greater quality or quantity of musical forces was sought. The church of Chinchero contracted a harpist from Cuzco for Holy Week in the years 1754–59 and 1766–74.[51] The village of Calca also brought in outside musicians: from 1782 to 1788, violinists and harpists were hired from Cuzco for the Passions and Lamentations of Holy Week and the three days of the Forty Hours Devotion, while in 1789, a harpist and a violinist were brought from nearby Huayllabamba for the period between Palm Sunday and Easter.[52]

The records of the village of Sumaro, annexed to the *doctrina* of Chinchaypugio, permit a reconstruction of these processes in the late seventeenth

century. The accounts of the Cofradía de Nuestra Señora de la Limpia Concepción note a payment of three pesos in 1657 to the organist who played on
the day of the fiesta, another three pesos the following year also to an
organist, and seven pesos in 1660 to the unspecified musicians brought
from Cuzco.[53] The Cofradía of Santa Isabel from the same village paid
outside singers on the confraternity's feast day in 1673, as there were none
in Sumaro.[54] Local resources were clearly rather threadbare. In 1679, however, the church took the decision to hire a maestro. In that year the fábrica
paid four pesos four reales to the maestro who taught reading and music to
the village children, and the Cofradía of Santa Isabel gave him a further
three pesos.[55] Entries in the libro de fábrica for 1681 and 1684 concerning the
provision of paper for copying music reveal that efforts to develop the
doctrina's musical life continued, and the effectiveness of these measures can
be seen in the regular references to cantores and a harpist—who were apparently local, judging from the amounts expended—in the account book of the
Cofradía de Nuestra Señora de la Limpia Concepción from 1689 to 1720.
Inventories throughout the seventeenth and eighteenth centuries show that
Sumaro had an organ, a harp, a number of wind instruments, and music
books, yet payments to musicians from the fábrica are lacking apart from the
early cases above, indicating that the decision to hire a temporary maestro
from outside in 1679 had had the desired effect of catalyzing the long-term
musical self-sufficiency of the village. The doctrina priest claimed in 1689
that the church was extremely poor and depended partly on alms from the
village: here, musical services were clearly part of the support that the community lent to its church, rather than a source of income for villagers.

THE MOBILITY OF MUSICIANS

Ordinary cantores were trained in the doctrina schools, and it was therefore rare
that villages needed the services of outside singers. The musicians of the
urban parish of Santiago were hired on one occasion by the Cofradía del
Santísimo Sacramento of the village of Pisac, and there are other scattered
examples of the movement of cantores, but this seems to have been the exception rather than the rule.[56] The training of an organist or harpist was, however, a more specialized process that would have been restricted to a few individuals, and in the event that a village's key instrumentalist died, fell ill, or
moved away, the church would have been left in need of a maestro to train his
replacement. Maestros and instrumentalists were more mobile than singers
because their skills were more specialized and less widely available. The doctrina of Livitaca had eight musicians in 1689 (Villanueva Urteaga 1982, 319–

25): the *bajonero*, two *cantores*, and three boy sopranos (one of whom was the son of a cacique) were from local *ayllus*, while two musicians—the *maestro de capilla* from Quiñota and a singer from Chivay—were *forasteros*. The training of local singers by a nonlocal *maestro* provides an example of the limited circulation of high-level musicians amid the general stasis of ordinary *cantores*.

Some musicians relocated temporarily or permanently from the countryside to the city, seeking opportunities for education or employment. One teaching contract drawn up in the city reveals both parties to have originally been rural dwellers: in 1687, Juan Ramos Suclli from the village of Coporaque hired Juan Estevan, *maestro arpista* from Laurisque, to provide him with six months of harp lessons.[57] More commonly, however, urban musicians moved from the city to the rural parishes in order to instruct local musicians or provide their musical services at specific events, such as parish fiestas. While many urban parish musicians were employed primarily by their local church, some apparently worked on a freelance basis, offering their services to any institutions, whether urban or rural, that found themselves short of personnel. The Andean organist Pedro Miguel, for example, was hired by two different *doctrina* churches, as well as by the monastery of San Francisco.

This circulation of musicians appears to have been normally a short- or medium-term process, rather than the long-term relocation of the kind seen among ambitious musicians in Spain (Torrente 1996–97). Opportunities for temporary movement generally arose because of the lack of a suitable local alternative. The rewards for such short contracts were high and must have appealed to musicians, but local candidates were generally preferred by the *doctrinas* for economic reasons. The circulation of musicians in Spain was maintained as much by the willingness of institutions to hire outsiders and their search for musical talent as by the desire of individuals to improve their lot. Smaller Peruvian institutions, which tended to rely on cheap or free local labor and paid village musicians at least partially in kind, appear to have regarded the hiring of outsiders as a painful last resort, limiting the movement of musicians to a necessary minimum.

Both lower-level musicians and priests had more to gain from a static arrangement. Given the pressures on rural communities and widespread depopulation, priests had good reason to support music ensembles within their *doctrinas*, for church servants, along with other officeholders and minor nobles, formed a stable core of the male village population. Through these minor positions of responsibility, Andean males were afforded a degree of influence over village life, and it might therefore be assumed that few would have been inclined to move. Guaman Poma de Ayala recognized the power that musicians had within their communities, though he did not regard the influence of the *cantores* and other church servants as entirely benign: on several occasions he denounces them for corrupting the village women, especially when their husbands were away on community duties like the *mita*, and stealing from their fellow Andeans. If the chronicler is to be believed, the musicians, sacristans, *fiscales*, and other minor church officials acted in some *doctrinas* like a local gang that knew how to exploit its central position in village life, and the contrast between the localism of these officeholders and the (often enforced) mobility of other rural Andeans is striking (Guaman Poma de Ayala [1615] 1980, 816, 824, 864). This negative perception notwithstanding, the commitment to musical provision by *doctrinas*, although instituted by the crown, might be seen as a way for both local communities and parish priests to combat the decimation of the Andean male population—a kind of "social glue" in the face of the pressure to migrate away from harsh forms of community service and rapacious colonial officials.

That said, the circulation of musicians appears to have increased substantially in the second half of the eighteenth century, a period of rising migration across Latin America (Szuchman 1996, 10). More than half of the members of Cuzco's guild of barbers and musicians were listed as absent in 1786, implying that many musicians had left the city in search of work. The cacique of the guild speaks of "the miserable state" in which its members found themselves, and evidence was presented in the previous chapter that urban parish musicians were going through hard times in the late colonial period, "doing the rounds of the churches" in order to make ends meet. References to *violinistas forasteros* (nonlocal violinists) in the accounts of the *doctrinas* of the Urubamba Valley in the 1780s confirm the impression that musicians were increasingly leaving their place of origin around this time. Most surviving contracts to teach music date from the period 1620–1720, whereas payments to outside musicians to perform at one-off events are concentrated in the late eighteenth century. This suggests that a rupture in the system of music education and self-sufficiency occurred during the eighteenth century, leading to greater dependence on freelance musicians.

There is limited evidence that musicians' exemption from tribute payments—the foundation on which parish music was built—was eroded in the late eighteenth century. The year 1779 saw the reform of the tribute system as royal officials sought ways to increase state revenue. As a result, *indios reservados*, who had for so long been exempt through filling community posts, were increasingly obliged to pay tax. In 1785 the *subdelegado* (subdele-

14. Felipe Guaman Poma de Ayala, 1613, folio 661,
Fiscal, cantor, sacristán.

gate) of Aymaraes claimed that church servants and community officeholders in his district were now all paying tribute (Cahill 1984, 251–52). This
suggests that the basic system of compensating musicians may have been
substantially undermined, and it would explain why music became markedly more professionalized in rural areas around this time. Musicians were
obliged to become less dependent on a single church to support them and
more like modern freelance musicians, traveling in order to earn fees. The
church still played a significant part in supporting musicians, but if tribute
exemptions were eroded, the profession must have lost much of its stability.[58] In the late colonial period, rural fiestas seem to have required more
music than those in the city, as they were more insulated from the restrictive
impulses of late-colonial officials, and musicians consequently headed to
the *doctrinas* in search of earnings. Regular expenditure on hiring musicians
is testimony to the continued role of music in the lives of rural dwellers, but

the capacity of *doctrinas* to meet their own musical needs seems to have declined.

Music in the Doctrinas in the Late Colonial Period

In 1782, the captain Don Juan Gonzáles de Villagra hired a harpist, a keyboard player, and two violinists to come to Paucartambo for the Christmas season. The captain was to pay the musicians and provide food, lodging, and mules for their transport, and they in return would perform at all the events connected with the festivities.[59] This contract reveals some noteworthy shifts in musical culture and patronage over the course of the century. Mid-colonial music contracts were normally agreed between the village priest or cacique and a musician to provide sacred music at vespers, masses, and processions. In this instance, however, a music ensemble was hired by a private citizen, with no mention of religious services and the only specific type of event being *comedias*, a genre of musical-theatrical performance that had come under increasing suspicion in Cuzco and had been banned in the city's seminary more than a decade earlier.

Most work on rural music making has focused on the first century of colonial rule during which the foundations of *doctrina* music were established (e.g., Stevenson 1976; Estenssoro 1990; Turrent 1993). This is largely due to the accessibility of sixteenth- and early-seventeenth-century printed sources and missionary chronicles, which tended to concentrate on the process of spiritual conquest. Research on the mid- to late colonial periods depends on the holdings of local archives, which have been little studied by musicologists. We have seen evidence, however, that music continued to flourish in Cuzco's *doctrinas* throughout the colonial period, and there are indications that these rural parishes became the most dynamic spheres of musical activity in the region in the late eighteenth century.

I noted the effects of the mid-eighteenth-century Bourbon reforms on popular religious observances in chapter 1. Increasing official disapproval of popular culture and religiosity manifested itself as attempts to root out secular or carnivalistic influences from church ceremonies and fiestas, leading to a gradual separation of the elite and popular cultures that had been so entwined for much of the colonial period. In Lima, the suppression of theatrical elements of religious rituals and the banishment of dramatic musical genres like the *comedia* and villancico from sacred contexts simply fed the popularity of the theater itself (Estenssoro 1989, 96–97). In the case of Cuzco, this separation took on more of a geographical dimension, as popular elements of civic and religious rituals banned by the authorities in the city simply flourished in the rural *doctrinas*, away from the center of colonial power and out of sight of colonial officials.[60] When Cuzco was restructured as an *intendencia* (intendency) in 1784, the *corregidores* who had exercised such control over rural areas were replaced by less influential *subdelegados*; while royal authority was thus strengthened in the center, it was weakened at the periphery. Priests, who continued to be the principal colonial authorities at the margins of the diocese, depended on the fees and gifts they received at fiestas for a significant portion of their income. As such, many were undoubtedly persuaded to turn a blind eye to popular festive practices, and some may even have encouraged the celebration of fiestas for economic reasons. Indeed, the removal of the *corregidores* and the end of the *repartimiento*, a system of forced sales to Andean communities, allowed priests to extract even more parochial fees from their parishioners (Cahill 1984, 246–47). In 1785 the *subdelegado* of Calca, who had enforced a prohibition on dancing issued by Cuzco's *intendente*, Benito de la Mata Linares, received a letter from the priest of Lamay-Coya begging him to allow the custom of dancing and fireworks in *doctrina* fiestas to continue.[61]

The *libros de fábrica* from rural churches and confraternities, unlike those of their urban counterparts, show no sign of a diminution in musical activities or expenditure in the late eighteenth century. There is less evidence of formal music education within *doctrinas* in the late colonial period—prospective musicians were more commonly sent to the city to take lessons—but musical performances show no signs of having lost popularity. The decree that banned festive dancing throughout the *intendencia* of Cuzco in 1793 appears to have been much less effective in rural areas than in the city (Espinavete López 1795, 152; Cahill 1996, 97), suggesting that the reduction of opportunities for musical performance and festive behavior in the city was offset by the continued vitality of popular observances in the countryside, stimulating the movement of musicians between the city and the provinces. The willingness of *doctrina* churches to pay for music may also reflect the importance, both religious and economic, of attracting the widely dispersed rural population to the seasonal festivals of the church. Fiestas took on the character of trade fairs, increasing ecclesiastical revenues (of benefit to both priest and church) and stimulating the local economy (Cahill 1996); the outlay on music may thus have been a worthwhile investment (see Kümin 2001, 80). The abundance of rural confraternities, meanwhile, suggests that the efforts of successive bishops to control their number were generally unsuccessful, and that popular religious practices flourished more abundantly where colonial authority was weaker.

Urban environments witnessed a growing official antipathy toward secular or popular cultural influences in sacred contexts. In the *doctrinas*, however, the erosion of this distinction only increased under the influence of rising migration and the consequent hybridization of Hispanic popular music, Andean traditions, and religious genres. The impression that secular influenced musical forms may have been banished from the city churches but lived on in the periphery is strengthened by the Paucartambo contract in 1782 in which the captain ordered *comedias*, a genre that had fallen out of favor with the church authorities in Cuzco. The constitution of the ensemble, too, hints at a blurring of the line between sacred and secular that may be observed in other *doctrina* festivities toward the end of the colonial period. The combination of violin, harp, and harpsichord, which became increasingly common in late-eighteenth-century religious entertainments, was employed by rural churches such as Yucay, Calca, Chinchero, and Andahuaylillas to play during Holy Week, traditionally the most solemn occasion of the year, yet it was also associated with popular secular music. A late colonial painting, "Fiesta en el campo," shows a harpist and a violinist in an apparently secular scene (Mesa and Gisbert 1982, 597), and the same instruments were employed specifically as symbols of worldliness in the late-eighteenth-century fresco in the convent of Santa Catalina in Cuzco discussed in chapter 1 (Sebastián López, Mesa, and Gisbert 1985–86, 2:555–56). Thus, while secular influences were being frowned on and increasingly extirpated from religious music in the city—witness the prohibition of "theatrical" musical styles and "worldly songs" in the 1780 *Regla consueta* of the cathedral—it seems that sacred and secular cultures were in fact drawing closer together in the provinces. This impression is further reinforced by Pablo José Oricaín's account of rural church music written in 1790 in the village of Andahuaylillas. As seen at the start of this chapter, the author complained that musicians who were not familiar with religious music performed dances such as the minuet, traditional *yaravís*, and other "lascivious songs" during the mass, blending sacred and secular, Andean and European.

For much of the colonial period, the authorities had waged battles against the persistence of supposed idolatry. They had seen their hegemony threatened by the celebration of "superstitious" Andean rituals and had thus promoted the lively ecclesiastical music found throughout the Hispanic world, such as villancicos with roots in popular dance music, in order to attract the indigenous population into church. The Jesuits had even translated traditional, secular Spanish songs into Quechua and taught them to the Andeans as part of their Hispanizing mission, as well as propagating Spanish and African dances among their native charges (Estenssoro 1992a, 379; 2003, 304–7; Guaman Poma de Ayala [1615] 1980, 730–31). Garcilaso de la Vega's early account of music at Corpus Christi states that during the festival in 1551 or 1552, the cathedral chapel master, Juan de Fuentes, adapted an Inka victory song called a *haylli* for polyphonic performance by eight mestizo choirboys in native costume, an occasion that was greeted with great enthusiasm by Spaniards and Andeans alike (Stevenson 1976, 288). Underlying such scenes was a sense that the juxtaposition of elements from popular and elite cultures, from Europe and the Andes, would not undermine the clear distinctions so important to Hispanic conceptions of a hierarchical society but, on the contrary, would strengthen the desired social order. From around 1750, however, hybridity and popularization were increasingly seen as threats to Hispanic culture that needed to be curbed. The distinctive, colorful performances that had so impressed the early colonists and had formed part of Spanish cultural policy across the Americas were now seen as prejudicial to the colonial order.

Having introduced European musical forms and instruments to the native population as part of their acculturating mission, the Spanish found that their capacity to control the resulting proliferation of music when the intellectual and political climate changed in the mid-eighteenth century was limited, since Andean communities had incorporated these forms and instruments into their traditions. Whereas the sound of indigenous musicians performing European music had once delighted Spanish observers, it now provoked profound anxieties. In the late colonial period, as Spanish attitudes to the intrusion of secular elements into church music hardened, the perceived threat now came not from native culture but from the very practices—hybrid, secular-tinged, even heterodox—that had been instilled by the Spanish in the sixteenth and seventeenth centuries.

Andahuaylillas, once a model *doctrina* under the guidance of the distinguished priest and church musician Juan Pérez Bocanegra, reappears as the village in which Oricaín composed his late colonial critique of rural musical decadence. Yet it was not the nature or vitality of indigenous music making that had changed in the intervening period, so much as the attitude of Spanish observers. It is worth recalling that the performance of *chanzonetas* was recorded in official documentation from rural confraternities in the late seventeenth and early eighteenth centuries. According to the early seventeenth-century *Tesoro de la lengua castellana o española* of Sebastián de Covarrubias ([1611] 1995, 432), "Chanzonetas are villancicos that are sung on Christmas Eve in churches in the vernacular, with a particular kind of lively and joyful music." What Oricaín described had thus been normal practice in the diocese of Cuzco—and across the Hispanic world, for that matter—for over a century: that this practice was now perceived as a worrying symbol of decadence reveals the profound change in the cultural climate that had occurred. If the Catholic Church began the colonial period by sowing its culture among native Andean communities, it ended it by rejecting the unwelcome fruits of this cultural experiment.

The colonists' concern was thus no longer idolatry or resistance to Hispanic culture but rather a perceived over-fondness for profane *contradanzas*, minuets, *yaravís*, and lascivious songs, all with clear European origins or influences—in other words, the hybrid popular expressions flourishing on the margins of the diocese. By comparison with the city, the peripheral rural parishes emerge as areas of relative cultural freedom, even of heterodoxy, and of continued interrelation between Spanish and Andean traditions, where the effects of growing Spanish intolerance of popular religion and music—as manifested by Oricaín—were softened by the distance from the centers of colonial power.

The Sounds of Authority

Rural *doctrinas* were competitive environments in which localized, personal struggles were played out among leading figures, principally the priest, the cacique, the *encomendero*, and the *corregidor*. Since many parishes were far from the center of colonial authority, the balances and imbalances of power were regularly contested and redefined, arguably more so than in the city parishes. Due to poor communications and a difficult terrain, the rural parishes at times resembled independent fiefdoms, controlled only by the occasional inspection (Brisseau Loaiza 1981, 154; Van Oss 1986). Music was harnessed by leading individuals as an aural manifestation of power, a means of bolstering their prestige and authority in ways perhaps harder to achieve in more closely supervised urban contexts.

Visits by high ecclesiastical authorities were to be greeted by a procession with dances, *taquis*, and peals of bells (Guaman Poma de Ayala [1615] 1980, 642), a privilege that the church attempted to reserve for its own representatives, though with limited success. The Third Council of Lima (1582–83) banned secular *corregidores* from such ceremonial receptions by church servants (Vargas Ugarte 1951–54, 1:360), and this ban was reiterated in the 1591 *Constituciones sinodales* issued in Cuzco, which claimed that the earlier decree was not being followed (Lassegue-Moleres 1987, 49). Furthermore, the *encomenderos*, an elite Spanish group who were granted vast tracts of land and rights to Andean labor in the earliest days of the colony, took on the trappings of native lords: "They are carried around on litters like the images of saints in processions. They are received with *taquis*, and dances and *saynatas* [indigenous dances] and *hayllis* [Inka victory songs]. In other words, they are carried around like Inkas" (Guaman Poma de Ayala [1615] 1980, 524). Native leaders continued to command such sonic displays of status after the conquest, as did lesser lords who seized the opportunity to advance their claims to authority by adopting the accouterments of power that had formerly been the preserve of the principal cacique (Ramírez 1996, 29–30).

Music was thus a symbol of authority utilized by many of the leading players vying for position in the early colonial period: it had the power to legitimate the claims to authority of aspirational individuals. As a result, there was competition for the services of musicians. The claims of the priest were strong, for the musicians were, after all, officially *los cantores de la santa iglesia* (the singers of the holy church) and their social and economic privileges derived from their position as church functionaries; Guaman Poma de Ayala ([1615] 1980, 555, 585) tellingly includes musicians among the *doctrinero's* assistants or servants. However, the link between *doctrina* musicians and caciques was also close. Musicians were, in many cases, either subjects of the cacique or paid by him. The cacique at times regarded the church musicians as servants who could be called on when so desired in order to bolster his prestige. The painting of the Virgin of Monserrat by Francisco Chihuantito, preserved in the church of Chinchero, shows the cacique, Pascual Amau, processing in front of the village church in 1693 to the accompaniment of a group of musicians that, although somewhat indistinct, appears to consist of a harpist, three shawm players, and five singers with sheet music (Kagan with Marías 2000, 133) (fig. 15). While this presents a harmonious picture of the relationship between the church and the native leader, power struggles were also common and could lead to attempts by the cacique to control the *doctrina* musicians, for example by taking them away on his travels (Estenssoro 1990, 19). To avoid such partisan manipulation, Guaman Poma de Ayala ([1615] 1980, 635) recommended that the *maestro de coro* should be hired not by the priest or cacique, but by the *corregidor* or the administrator of the church.

In 1616, the cacique of a *doctrina* in the Cuzco region celebrated the

15. Francisco Chihuantito, 1693, *Virgen de Monserrat*, detail of musicians, church of Chinchero. Photo by Stella Nair.

completion of a new house. He waited for the priest to leave the village and then organized a fiesta that included traditional dances, as well as the ringing of the church bells and the playing of shawms.[62] An equally pro- prietorial but rather more violent attitude toward church musicians was shown by Don Pascual Corimanya, the cacique of the village of Lamay. In a legal case brought against him, Corimanya was accused of assaulting those responsible for organizing the dances in village fiestas; he was apparently unhappy that they had not performed at his house before going to the church. Nor were the village musicians immune from such treatment: Cor- imanya attacked the *maestro de capilla* and the singers during the Salve be- cause they had not waited for him.[63] He clearly felt that the musicians' and dancers' loyalty should be to him before the church.

Certain types of music had particularly strong associations with authority, above all the sounds of church bells, trumpets, and drums, all of which represented the twin pillars of sacred and secular power in sonic form. The appropriation of power could therefore be dramatized through the appropriation of these sounds. The 1591 Cuzco *Constituciones sinodales* refer to the misuse of church bells by secular authorities such as *corregidores* (Lassegue-Moleres 1987, 49). In a later case, a local dispute ended with the *corregidor* attempting to strip the parish priest of his rights and duties: the magistrate drew up a decree and then gathered drummers and trumpeters who accompanied the town crier as he proclaimed the judgment on every street corner.[64] The *corregidor* clearly believed that this music lent his actions a vital air of legitimacy at a time when his authority needed to be asserted. A similar line was taken by the *cacique principal* of Andahuaylillas in the 1790s who bolstered his image by making use of the sounds and trappings of military power. According to local witnesses,

> not only on Sundays, but also on certain local fiesta days, the Indians who live in his *parcialidad* [faction] come with their arches of branches and line up on either side of their cacique, Visente Choquecahua, who comes out of his house and goes among them dressed like a military man with his staff of command and his sword. As he takes his first step into the street, they begin to play the drums and trumpets and to fire a salute. With this accompaniment they bring him to the church with his dancers and dances in front. . . . All his Indians call him by the title of Inka. (Stavig 1999, 137)

Thus even in the absence of the colonists, elements of the Hispanic sound world, such as church bells, shawms, and military instruments, were included voluntarily, indeed enthusiastically, alongside traditional Andean features such as dances. The adoption and absorption of Spanish sonic tools were not signs of cultural acquiescence: rather than disputing the value of European cultural symbols, Andean leaders joined the various Spanish figures of authority in competing for ownership of these symbols (Harrison 1995). Intriguingly, the reverse also held true, for, as Guaman Poma de Ayala notes, *encomenderos* were carried around "like Inkas," and both they and leading churchmen were received with indigenous dances and music. The meeting of two cultures increased the range of aural symbols of power, and Spanish and native leaders appropriated each other's traditions to bolster their prestige among both republics. By utilizing both Andean and European symbolic resources, these figures of authority emphasized the span of their ambition.

It has become apparent during the course of the past two chapters that European music, while introduced to Peru by Spanish missionaries, flourished in large part because of its multifaceted appeal to Andean communities and individuals. The Spanish friars were intent on replacing old rituals with new, and in the early days of the colony, they generally opted to follow the path of least resistance. They observed Andean enthusiasm for ritual and display, their fondness for "making a song and dance of their religion" (Clendinnen 1990, 115), and resolved to make use of this enthusiasm in the conversion process. There is thus a marked element of cultural accommodation in early missionary efforts, as evidenced by José de Acosta's ([1590] 1987, 433) remark that "our priests, who go among them, have tried to put the tenets of our faith to their way of singing." Spanish observers were continually impressed by Andeans' musical exuberance; some chose to see this as a sign of the success of their evangelical program, though others were less convinced. It may simply reveal the extent to which the process of conversion was conditioned by Andean cultural and religious practices. The analogy with the broader process of incorporation of Christianity into the Andes suggests that the introduction of European music should not be seen in terms of Spanish domination and native resistance or the imposition of cultural practices on an unwilling populace. Just as Kenneth Mills (1994; 1997) found widespread evidence that Catholicism was incorporated into Andean religion as a new and complementary set of symbolic and sacred resources, European church music seems to have flourished alongside traditional Andean music, adopted and assimilated in ways meaningful to indigenous communities.

Many Andeans saw the music profession as a means of obtaining privileges in the new society emerging after the conquest. These benefits might have taken material form, especially in the city, allowing the holders to prosper in the colonial urban economy; but in rural contexts, connections and influence often had a greater bearing on individuals' lives than straightforward wealth. Andean society "was a highly competitive one in which rank and prestige were important counters in the struggle for position. In a system in which property accumulation was limited, . . . wealth was measured more in what we think of as intangibles" (Spalding 1984, 56). One of these intangibles was religious responsibility. In many rural areas, the Spanish colonial enterprise rested largely on the Catholic Church, and the pursuit of music gave Andeans the opportunity to occupy a position in the ecclesiastical hierarchy. The more remote *doctrinas*, or those under the control of a less diligent priest, saw indigenous assistants take over much of the day-to-day running of the church and thereby access a prime source of colonial power.

Other benefits of the music profession contributed to its attractiveness as a career. For ordinary *cantores*, exemptions from tax and personal services would have removed a significant and unwelcome burden, and they also carried symbolic value as badges of social status, placing musicians in the same company as the native nobility and community officers. Senior music posts constituted a particularly attractive option for minor members of the native nobility; if leading musicians of the city parishes were often *principales* in their communities, there is ample evidence that the same held true in the *doctrinas* around Cuzco.[65] The position of the lesser nobility under Spanish rule proved ambiguous: its members might retain certain privileges, but their inherited authority was contested and insecure. Exemptions from tribute and labor levies, one of the prime markers of nobility, were normally restricted to the cacique and his eldest son (Garrett 2005, 35). The risk of downward social mobility thus hung over the minor elite, for whom losing the right to exemptions, and thereby being consigned to the ranks of the "tributary Indians," was a form of "social death" (Cahill 2000, 145). Younger sons and other relatives of caciques needed to secure this right in other ways and thereby defend their position within the slippery field of colonial power relations. After the conquest, as David Cahill (2000, 95) notes, "the surviving Inca nobility discovered Spanish institutional templates that were ready-made conduits for the preservation of at least some vestige of their pre-conquest, social and ritual roles," and church service emerged as a major such template. As a class, the Andean nobility survived Spanish colonial rule, but many individuals had to fight to maintain their status and rights (Garrett 2005, 259), and the music profession served as a useful weapon. Occupying a post like that of *maestro de capilla* allowed *principales* to occupy an important symbolic and ceremonial role, providing community leadership and cementing their privileges at a time when only caciques retained their traditional status.

It is clear, then, that a *doctrina* music post placed the incumbent at the heart of the rural power structure and opened up avenues to increased wealth, influence, and prestige. It would be a mistake, however, to view Andean enthusiasm for European music as purely strategic. Performance and ritual were also central to Andean religious traditions, and so from the earliest days of the conquest, many members of the native population gravitated, with the encouragement of the Spanish friars, toward music, processions, and confraternities. Many aspects of colonial music practices show continuities with pre-Hispanic traditions, suggesting that they were understood in Andean terms and shaped by their Andean practitioners, who were of course far more numerous than the churchmen who served as the initial conduit for European culture.

The colonial system emphasized the idea of parish musicians as privileged officials, giving personal services to the church and state, but these notions were not new to Peru's indigenous inhabitants. The chronicler Pedro Cieza de León noted that music was associated with important royal occasions in Inka society; performers, in particular trumpeters, enjoyed high honors, considerable rewards, and superior status (Stevenson 1976, 276, 298). He gave further evidence of the links between music and nobility in pre-Columbian Peru, stating that native leaders were celebrated in songs after their death (Estenssoro 1990, 11; Ramírez 1996, 176). Continuity between Inka and Spanish practices is particularly apparent in the use of music in rituals of death. In many pre-Hispanic cultures in Peru, wind instruments were associated with death, transcendence, or communication between mortal and immortal realms (Olsen 2002). After the conquest, wind instruments became a characteristic feature of Andean church music, as Guaman Poma de Ayala's drawing of the parish *cantores* underlines, and it was noted in the previous chapter that one of the prime responsibilities of indigenous parish musicians was the collection and burial of the dead.

There are also indications of continuities between Inka and colonial-period practices in the provision of musical services. In pre-Hispanic times, the *ayllu* paid tribute to the Inka rulers in the form of services or goods, and certain *ayllus* became associated with particular skills. In 1689, the village of Capacmarca was divided into three large *ayllus*, each of which was subdivided into several smaller "sub-*ayllus*" (Villanueva Urteaga 1982, 299–301). One of the smaller units had the name Los Cantores and included five musicians; another was labeled Los Sacristanes. The fact that the musicians and sacristans were listed in exactly the same way as the smaller *ayllus* suggests occupational specialization by particular social groups, while the linking of the musicians and sacristans together within the same large *ayllu* suggests a similar pattern on a larger scale, namely, that church service in general was the preserve of a distinct social sector. This large *ayllu* was headed by the "cacique and governor of all the *ayllus*," confirming earlier suggestions that church servants were often chosen from among the cacique's kin group. In this case, at least, the pre-Columbian specialization of certain *ayllus* in particular services seems to have continued well into the

16. Andean wind instrumentalists performing in traditional and Catholic contexts. Felipe Guaman Poma de Ayala, 1613, folio 324, *Fiesta de los collasuyos*, and folio 666, *Los cantores de la santa iglesia*.

colonial period, indicating that church service may have been regarded as an extension of earlier forms of tribute and may have formed part of the *ayllu*'s identity. In short, there is sufficient continuity between the pre- and post-conquest roles of music and musicians to suggest that the attractions of a musical career to Andeans were manifold and complex, and that the successful incorporation of European music derived in large part from its compatibility with traditional Andean sociocultural patterns.

This causes problems with attempts to reconstruct musical practices in Andean parishes from Hispanic economic records: such efforts rest largely on the idea that musical services formed part of commercial transactions. As we have seen, this tended to be the case primarily when nonlocal musicians were required, but financial records fail to take account of local traditions of donations, offerings, and communal labor that had been part of the Andean way of life for centuries. Both before and after the Spanish conquest, individuals expected to spend part of their time working for their communities in order to ensure collective well-being, and the rewards of religious services were not seen primarily in material or personal terms (Glave 1992, 126; Wightman 1990, 1–2). The transformation of the focus of Andean society from communal benefit to individual profit occurred at different rates and to different degrees depending on the local circumstances. While many urban musicians adapted to the new economic reality and contributed to the professionalization of music, most rural musicians appear to have retained a somewhat more community-oriented view. According to Ann M. Wightman (1990, 145), the period from 1570 to 1720 witnessed "the preeminence of private contracts over community obligations, the rise in the individualization of labor relationships, and the commodification of labor." This was true, to a large degree, of the upper tier of the music profession, occupied by better educated, more Hispanicized Andeans more attuned to the monetary value of their skills, but it appears that the concept of community obligation survived in many *doctrinas*, and especially among the lower tier of the music profession. Parish music was provided through a mixture of wage labor and community service, and just as the labor market was uneven and full of inconsistencies, so, too, are the surviving sources on the remuneration of musicians.

Music was thus much more than a profession. In the population lists in the 1689 reports for Bishop Mollinedo, individuals' professions are not normally noted; the fact that musicians *are* often recorded as such indicates that "musician" was seen as an office (like *alcalde*, cacique, and so on) rather than as a simple occupation. In a sense, the very absence of music from so many economic records also tells us something important about the way music was regarded and supported. Though these kinds of documents— virtually the only ones we have—sometimes barely overlap with Andean musical activity, their silences may speak volumes about the ways in which musicians perceived their duties and the ways in which the patronage of music was drawn partially away from the church into the hands of leading figures in colonial society.

Conclusion

If we focus on the aspirations of Andean musicians and the needs of Andean communities, the widespread adoption of European music should not be regarded as simply a triumph of colonial religious and cultural policy. Indeed, the evidence suggests that many parish churches could not afford to maintain musical forces alone and were only able to do so as a result of the support of Andean leaders. The dependence of the *culto divino* of most rural churches on the labor and goods provided by Andean communities is evident throughout the reports produced for Bishop Mollinedo in 1689. Similarly, a substantial part of the burden of supporting musical activities fell on the community rather than on the church: musicians had to be provided for, yet they contributed no taxes. Without the willingness of Andean leaders and villages to support musicians, and without the widespread understanding of musical skills as a form of communal service, music would not have flourished in rural areas, let alone to a degree apparently unprecedented in Spain.

We should perhaps regard the introduction of European music to the Americas as providing new, if circumscribed, opportunities rather than as a "musical conquest" (Turrent 1993). David T. Garrett (2005, 45–46) writes that Andean civilization "suffered from the imposition of many aspects of Spanish civilization . . . both through aggressive, sporadic campaigns and a gradual, and more profound, permeation." It could be argued, however, that more emphasis should be given to the agency of Andean elites who were active in "working the system to their minimum disadvantage" (Eric Hobsbawm, qtd. in Stavig 1999, 83). As Garrett himself explains (2002; 2005), the Catholic Church, although the most global symbol of colonial authority and a tool of Spanish hegemony, allowed indigenous elites to strengthen their position in Andean communities by placing themselves at the center of public life and ceremonies. The colonists' policy of structuring colonial Andean society around the parish church and its rituals provided the native nobility with a new set of symbolic resources with which to perpetuate and underline its superior social status. Andean nobles not only participated in the church music profession, maximizing the benefits offered by senior parish musical posts, but they also stimulated the artistic economy through the patronage of musicians and bolstered their authority through sponsoring fiestas and processions. They made pious donations and took leading roles in confraternities: one Andean *mayordomo* spent thirty-three years in charge of the Cofradía del Santísimo Sacramento in the parish of Santa Ana in the late eighteenth century, paying out of his own pocket for the wax and music during the Corpus Christi festival every year. Such activities reveal the importance of externalizing devotion to Andean elites (O'Phelan Godoy 1995, 60–61). Sponsored cultural displays of this kind underlined the authority of native leaders in the eyes of Spaniards, as well as in those of Andean communities: they not only manifested their status and provided for their own people but they also confirmed their aptitude for power by showing the Hispanic authorities that they were enthusiastic Christians capable of looking after their communities.

Religious ceremonies and fiestas thus served as "rituals of rule" (Beezley, Martin, and French 1994) for indigenous elites as well as Spaniards. The indigenous nobility asserted its difference from, and superiority to, Andean commoners through its Spanish trappings: dress and material goods, but also language, education, culture, and tastes. The proliferation of European-derived church music in indigenous society rested as much on its usefulness in demonstrations of authority by caciques—in expressing the Hispanism and "decent" Christian identity important to their success—as on the evangelical efforts of Spanish clerics. By taking musical patronage into their own hands, leading Andeans turned it to their advantage, incorporating music into the resources that were available to promote their own interests and shore up their position in the colonial social hierarchy (Burns 2002; Dean 2002). The colonists clearly did not impose harmony alone.

The development of European-derived music in indigenous parishes cannot, then, be slotted into a vision of colonial power relations based on the polarities of "Spanish domination" and "Andean resistance." There is ample evidence that its adoption was negotiated rather than straightforwardly imposed. The Spaniards depended on native intermediaries to spread their music through the region, while the music profession, if we may call it such, featured as an important way for Andeans to seek greater involvement with the Catholic faith. Juan Carlos Estenssoro (2003) has argued convincingly, if controversially, that the history of Andean Christianity is not one of forcible Spanish imposition and native resistance (or even grudging and superficial acceptance). Rather, he claims, much of the indigenous population strove to be recognized as Christian and to access the symbolic and institutional resources of Catholicism, while the Spaniards broadly resisted this integration, since inviolable difference was fundamental to the colonial project. With the colonial church keeping the Andean population at arm's length through the extirpation of idolatry and through its refusal, until the mid-eighteenth century, to countenance a native clergy, music emerges as a prime means for Andeans to approach the religion of the colonists and participate in its rituals and institutions, just as, in the political field, Andean nobles laid claim to symbols of prestige, seeking equality of status that would bridge the gap between indigenous and Hispanic elites (Cahill 2000, 149). Following a musical career path allowed Andeans to dissolve, at least partially, the cultural differences that the colonial church was in other ways so keen to essentialize and to pursue the social harmonization and "reconciliation of the colonial condition," to quote Cahill (149), that was sought by the Andean nobility.

Finally, this examination of rural music making also allows us to approach the fundamental issue of the nature of urban musical experience. In comparing urban and rural parishes, we notice striking similarities in terms of musical provision and performance; indeed, the rural parish *capilla de música* was conceived in exactly the same way as the urban one. There is ample evidence of polyphony with voices and instruments, in some cases accompanied by two organs, in Cuzco's *doctrinas*. These sounds have generally been considered a distinguishing feature of urban musical practices within the Hispanic world, as "sounds of the city," yet while there was undoubtedly a difference in terms of complexity and scale of music making between, say, the seminary and a rural parish, the same kinds of music were heard throughout the diocese of Cuzco.[66] In broader terms, the urban focus of Spanish *letrados* was not matched by the Andean population's more rural outlook and its traditional connection with the countryside: where Spaniards saw the rural expanses as "vast, alien, and hostile spaces . . . capable of engendering only barbarism" (Rama 1996, 12–13), most Andeans saw richly detailed "namescapes" and texts of social memory (Robinson 1989). A comparison of the Cuzco city plans discussed in chapter 1 is revealing (figs. 1 and 2). The Spanish illustration shows Cuzco as a (fictional) walled city: outside lies nothing of any significance, with culture and society contained firmly within the city limits. Guaman Poma de Ayala's drawing, however, places Cuzco at the juncture of the four *suyos*, or Inka realms, portraying the city as a microcosm of the entire pre-Hispanic state of Tahuantinsuyu (Locke 2001). Rural areas are thus not only represented but also connected to the city.

An excessive focus on urban music making, combined with assumptions that rural music was its poor relative, does not therefore do justice to Andean practices or experiences. A clear division between urban and rural may have been characteristic of the outlook of colonial *letrados*, but it is unrepresentative of the reality of musical culture in the diocese of Cuzco, supported as it was by the Andean population. Certain differences have indeed emerged between urban and rural parishes, but a center-periphery musical distinction was not pronounced, partly because the colonial church and crown dictated policy for the diocese as a whole, and partly because rural communities had the labor resources and social structures in place to support musical training and performance even in remote areas. What distinguished urban musical culture was not primarily the musical sounds, but rather the concentration of patrons and opportunities, the dense networks of institutions and individuals, and, above all, the grand civic ceremonies like the Corpus Christi procession, designed as a showcase of colonial Andean culture.

Conclusion

Having begun by following Viceroy Toledo on his route from the Andean countryside into the heart of the colonial city, this study has made a somewhat slower return journey to the rural *doctrinas de indios* via the central Hispanic institutions and the *parroquias de indios* that surrounded them. At a number of points along the way, questions have been raised about centers and peripheries, and above all about the relationship between geographical and cultural marginality. The *doctrinas* showed intriguing signs that cultural freedom and vitality may have been greater in rural than urban areas, especially in the conservative climate of the late colonial period; there is little doubt that the sonic heterodoxy and hybridity that so disturbed Pablo José Oricaín were less audible in the city in the 1790s, the time when he was writing, than in the countryside. More broadly, as the preceding pages have revealed, the musical experiences of the majority of Cuzco's inhabitants, and the professional lives of its indigenous musicians, revolved around parish churches, monasteries, and confraternities, or convents and *beaterios* in the case of women, rather than around the cathedral, the institution that lies at the heart of most musicological accounts of colonial Latin America. The decentralized panorama that has emerged calls into question the usefulness of the geographical and political hierarchy conceived by the Spanish colonists—a dominant cathedral surrounded by peripheral urban parishes and even more marginal rural *doctrinas*—as a model for Latin American historical musicology. Many scholars of colonial Latin American music, in their implicit acceptance of this hierarchy, have arguably perpetuated the Hispano-centric ideology of the colonial elite: by focusing on elite institutions and generally failing to take account of the musicians—in many cases indigenous and African—who made up the majority of the musical workforce, they have reinforced the historical marginalization of these social actors and have thereby produced a somewhat unbalanced picture of urban musical life. A decentered view is, however, vital if we are to take account of the perspectives of native populations on the geographical margins and thereby create a distinctively Latin American historical musicology, rather than a reflection of European musicology and its concerns.

European musicologists have tended to concentrate on towns and cities, focusing on urbanization as a process that brought about the concentration of artistic talents and provided the circumstances in which musical culture could flourish (Kisby 2001). In Latin America, however, two parallel developments occurred at the start of the colonial period. Musicians came from Spain to work in the newly founded cathedrals, an influx of labor that was clearly urban in orientation, exemplifying the economic and social attraction exercised by cities. But the second process—the teaching of music to indigenous populations as part of the evangelical drive—was as much rural as urban. The link between music and evangelization led to quite distinct developments in Latin America, with much more sophisticated musical activity on the periphery than in early modern Europe. Musical growth at the margins was further stimulated by the opportunities that music provided for ambitious individuals. Cuzco's musical decentralization thus resulted from a concentration of indigenous power and missionary activity in parish churches on the urban periphery and in rural areas. Rather than regarding parish churches as a pale reflection of the center, we should view them as places where colonial Andean culture was forged through complex and nuanced negotiations, not a simple cultural "conquest," and where the possibilities for indigenous musicians were greatest.

While many colonial Spaniards focused their attentions on the city, the locus of "civilization," with secular churchmen aspiring to urban parish benefices or cathedral posts and their regular brethren concentrated in the city's monastic houses, it could also be argued that this was a society in which a considerable amount of power was exercised at the periphery by parish priests, *corregidores*, and native leaders. Although there is justification for regarding cities as centers of culture and education (Hoberman and Socolow 1986, 12–13), this view needs to be qualified by the evidence of a developed musical culture and of indigenous *maestros de coro* in rural areas. Furthermore, the weakening of royal authority in rural areas and the apparent flourishing of parish culture in the late colonial period suggests that the concentration of native authority and cultural vitality in the geographical periphery only increased under the stricter political climate of the Bourbon reforms. The impression of colonial Peru as a centripetal society is thus belied by the exercise of power by both Andeans and Spaniards outside the city and—from a cultural perspective—by the thriving rural musical life uncovered in this study. Most Europeans viewed the countryside as plainly uncivilized (Rama 1996, 12–13), but just as Andean sources of sacred and secular power were spread across the landscape, so, too, was Andean cultural activity, blurring the oft-assumed distinctions between urban and rural music making.

If the decentralization of musical life is an indication of its vitality (Kendrick 2002, 22), then the importance of peripheral churches in the musical economy reveals Cuzco to have been an unusually musical diocese. With so many musically trained students at the Seminary of San Antonio Abad and the colleges of San Bernardo and San Borja, many members of the upper strata of Spanish and Andean society must have been musically literate, no doubt stimulating the cultivation of music throughout the bishopric. Music education was not, however, confined to these institutions: musicians were also trained in parish churches and convents, while others studied privately in their homes or as apprentices to master musicians. This wealth of educational possibilities is likewise a potent indicator of the breadth and depth of musical development in this Andean region. Within the city, decentralization was hastened by the weakening of the cathedral music establishment from the early seventeenth century onward and the corresponding rise in importance of the seminary, displacing the center of Hispanic musical activity away from its traditional focal point, the cathedral *capilla de música*. Though extremely active in central institutions and urban spaces, seminary musicians had only limited influence across the wider city due to the constraints on their time: they were, after all, seminarians rather than professional musicians. The combination of colonial policies and distinct professional organization thus contributed to an unusual breadth of musical development.

This musical richness, remarkable from a European perspective, is intimately linked to the issue of professionalism. One model of Hispanic musicology has at its core a *capilla de música* of professional musicians, employed by one principal institution, usually the cathedral, and available for hire by others. Another model is that of convent and monastery musicians, who were largely nonprofessional and inward-looking, producing music primarily for their own communities and congregations. Latin America, meanwhile, saw a flowering of mission music: amateur native musicians trained to perform in mission churches by (usually Jesuit) friars. The detailed examination of musical employment in Cuzco presented here, however, has produced a complex variety of overlapping pictures. Most churches in the diocese of Cuzco employed a range of musicians who fell somewhere between the poles of "professional" and "amateur," with varying degrees of professionalism coexisting within the same group of musicians. Most importantly, the fact that many musicians who worked in churches across the diocese were not paid salaries greatly increased the numbers that could be employed, and thus the potential for musical splendor.

There are many possible definitions of the word *professional*: it may relate to earning a living, to the quantity of time devoted to music, to the standard of performance, or to issues of perception and self-perception. Ruth Finnegan's (1989, 14) description of professionalism as a "complex continuum" is very apposite to Cuzco, where most church musicians earned some money from music, but only a minority earned their living, and most devoted considerable time to nonmusical activities. There were many musicians who performed at a professional standard, but who received limited tangible rewards and who may not have considered music to be their primary activity. Some followed the Spanish cathedral model for part of their careers only to abandon music in favor of other ecclesiastical activities. Others, especially Andeans who described themselves as *maestros*, may have regarded their music making in professional terms, but their musical performances frequently overlapped with the realms of religious devotion and communal duty.

Clear distinctions of professional and amateur have little relevance to Andean parishes, where local traditions of tribute provision and community service survived alongside the partial development of a market economy. The same complexity applies to the Hispanic musicians in Cuzco. Because of the centrality of the Seminary of San Antonio Abad, an arrangement that was highly unusual in the Hispanic world, the main musical force in Cuzco Cathedral for two-thirds of the colonial period was made up not of professional musicians but of trainee priests. To a degree, singing in the cathedral was thus part of their identity as prospective clergymen, rather than as professional musicians; it was, at least in part, a route to subsidizing their education and improving their ecclesiastical career chances, rather than simply the best paid or most prestigious musical post available to them. The fact that the seminary musicians were not professional (in an economic sense) had repercussions beyond the worlds of the cathedral and the seminary. It meant that the high mobility traditionally attributed to Spanish musicians by scholars played little part in Cuzco's mid- to late colonial musical life. Furthermore, there is no evidence of the hiring of cathedral musicians by other churches, a practice recorded so frequently in Europe. They were sent to sing at convent and monastery feast days, in a gesture of solidarity by the cathedral chapter, but apparently they were not hired as such. Indeed, their onerous duties and long hours as trainee priests prevented them from taking on many musical activities outside the cathedral and seminary.

It was not just the seminary singers but also the Hispanic cathedral musicians proper who showed little inclination to move in search of more prestigious musical appointments. They, too, devoted much of their attention to nonmusical activities, whether seeking to promote their ecclesiastical careers, engaging in business, or fulfilling their duties as parish priests, seminary teachers, or university administrators. Unlike their peninsular colleagues, Cuzco's Spanish musicians occupied an elevated position in society in the sixteenth and seventeenth centuries, and they were able to use this position to their advantage, exploiting the opportunities for socioeconomic advancement through nonmusical avenues. The restricted range of employment prospects within the music profession, coupled with the ample opportunities outside it, seems to have made music more like part of a priest's training and professional life and less like a specific vocation. A musical post was often a preliminary or intermediate stage in an ecclesiastical career, or part of a kind of portfolio of religious duties, rather than an exclusive end in itself. Hispanic cathedral musicians in Cuzco collected their incomes from a variety of sources; "musician" therefore lost some of its definition as a distinct profession and, perhaps for this reason, very few cathedral musicians described themselves as such, preferring the title of priest. This dilution of the Hispanic music profession contributed to the unusual balance of musical power between cathedral and parishes: the proliferation of Andean musicians probably had as much to do with the limited ambitions of the cathedral musicians and seminarians as with the sheer number of opportunities in other city churches.

While the development of music in Cuzco shows striking differences to Spanish models, it has much in common with that of the diocese of Tucumán in modern-day Argentina, one of the very few provincial centers to have been studied in South America (Illari 1996). Of particular relevance is the importance of the seminary as a training ground for musicians and a source of musical personnel for the cathedral, as well as the tendency of musicians to hold second jobs and, in the case of those of good social standing, to seek promotion to prebends and other nonmusical posts in order to pursue their careers within the highest levels of the clergy. In addition, the cathedral *capilla de música* in Tucumán disappeared due to the regional economic malaise in around 1705, very close to the date on which the last references to cathedral singers have been found in Cuzco's archives. This supports the tentative conclusion that a similar development may have occurred in Cuzco, perhaps in response to the 1720 plague and subsequent economic decline, with the salaried singers replaced by the seminary music scholars who had been boosting their numbers for over a century. While there is still woefully little evidence on which to draw, both in Cuzco and elsewhere, these features may be characteristic of provincial cities in South America, and they may therefore point to some of the ways in which Spanish organizational models were adapted in the far-flung reaches of the empire. The partial deprofessionalization of musical careers and the reliance on a local institution to maintain a supply of musicians, rather than seeking candidates through the sending out of edicts to distant towns, as was the custom in Spain, were probably responses to problems of distance, poor communications, and insufficient income to pay travel expenses for external candidates and musicians' salaries. The inclination on the part of individuals to seek second jobs and promotion outside the music profession, meanwhile, reflects both the economic realities of colonial society and the status of Hispanic musicians as part of a small white minority that had a monopoly on high office and a stranglehold on the economy of the colonies, and that therefore had varied options for advancement and self-enrichment outside of music. They were born into a position of privilege, unlike their peninsular counterparts, and the pursuit of a musical career was often subsidiary to the exploitation of the socioeconomic possibilities of this position.

Despite the illuminating parallels with Tucumán, the organization of music in the city of Cuzco as a whole reveals a unique character. The symbiotic relationship that developed between seminary and cathedral music establishments reflects a conglomeration of institutional, legislative, and economic changes that coincided in Cuzco in the early seventeenth century. Meanwhile, music flourished in the Andean parish churches and confraternities of the diocese under the direction of indigenous *maestros*, descendants of traditional elites who sought in the music profession a route to maintaining their privileges in colonial society. Music policies were implemented by the Spanish crown and Catholic Church across the Americas, but distinctive local adaptations took place in Cuzco, where a sense of local identity emerges clearly.

Signs of local identity have been sought in the music that survives in the seminary archive (Quezada Macchiavello 2004), but to date such efforts have been unsubstantiated and unconvincing. A thorough analysis of this repertoire may reveal traces of distinctive compositional techniques, but as yet, little evidence of local inflection has been found and none at all of musical *mestizaje*. Such fusion remains unsurprisingly elusive in the repertoire produced by a colonial institution like a seminary, dedicated to the reproduction of European cultural values, in a city where elite Hispanic conceptions of colonial culture centered on highlighting rather than blurring difference. The concept of *mestizaje* may be valorized today, but the same did not hold true for the Hispanic population of seventeenth- or eighteenth-century Cuzco. Indeed, it is precisely the lack of identifiably Andean features in these musical works that stands out: like the churches studied by Fraser (1990, 156), they reveal their "colonialness" through absences and silences. Rather than searching for Andean elements in a colonial repertoire written to be performed largely or entirely by Spaniards, rather than imagining the presence of the indigenous population in such cultural products, we should note their exclusion or suppression. More importantly, we should recognize that indigenous influence on colonial musical culture was to be found away from the musical notation, in the much more fundamental spheres of professional organization and performance.[1] Furthermore, the evidence that Andeans wanted to learn European music, both as a professional strategy and as an aspiration to *decencia*, and were very skilled in so doing, suggests that within the realm of urban church music, at least, local stylistic adaptation was probably limited. Andeans like Matías de Livisaca, who sought to sell their musical services or compositions to Hispanic institutions like convents and monasteries and to the confraternities that they housed, had little to gain from musical *mestizaje* and much to lose.

If distinctiveness is to be located in the seminary repertoire, it is rather in the institutional and civic religious identities encapsulated in the pieces' dedications—the honoring of saints, protectors, and patrons of local significance through musical means. It may also be identified in the theatrical repertoire of San Antonio Abad, for it was unusual for a church *capilla de música* to have such a prominent role in the performance of dramatic music. The availability of numerous highly trained seminarians offered unusual possibilities, as their priorities and capabilities were quite different from those of most cathedral choirs. There were sufficient numbers of students to provide actors and musicians for large-scale dramas: the witness to the *comedias* performed in 1713 reported a cast of 140, including 50 students with musical instruments and costumes on stage. Viewed as a whole, then, the seminary repertoire shows quite distinctive characteristics, revealing the varied roles played by the musicians of San Antonio Abad within urban musical culture.

The characteristic local features of musical organization had a significant impact on the sounds of Cuzco. The seminary *capilla de música* could perform the compositions for seven choirs found in its archive—the largest works located in South America—because most of its musicians were funded by scholarships, chantries, or second jobs. The richness of musical life in the urban and rural parishes depended on the availability of cheap or free musical labor from the Andean population, something only possible in a society with a tradition of community service. Because of a combination of local customs and colonial policies, many Andean villages maintained sizeable contingents of trained musicians and performed polyphony with many musical instruments. Even in the more professionalized music market of the city, the availability and affordability of Andean musicians encouraged a flourishing musical life in the churches of the religious orders. If I began by echoing Valerie Fraser's question "where are the Indians?," the answer has become clear: they are everywhere, if we know where to look for them. Just as with the construction of the early colonial churches, the Andean presence is to be found in the labor contracts, in the sheer quantity of production, in the proliferation and richness of musical culture.

Cuzco's musical identity may thus be located above all in the imposing sound of fifty seminary singers performing seven-choir compositions and of rural musicians performing polyphony with instruments, accompanied by two organs. The frequency and grandeur of such musical displays would have put most of their peninsular equivalents to shame. If today there is a tendency to fetishize stylistic difference, colonial-era observers of music, for their part, frequently sought to emphasize sameness: the highest praise that could be bestowed on musicians was that they were indistinguishable from a European cathedral choir. Criollo competition with the old continent was often expressed through attempts to outshine Europeans, but on European terms. The distinctiveness of seminary music making therefore lies in the size of its musical forces and the scale of its performances rather than in any particular stylistic features of the music. Ricardo Miranda (2005) has described the exuberance and hyperbole of sacred music in New Spain as "el delirio criollo novohispano" (a Mexican criollo delirium), the result of competition and self-justification in relation to Old Spain expressed through an almost obsessive desire to reiterate and demonstrate religious devotion. This desire, born out of an awareness of marginality with regard to the original holy places, scriptures, and saints of Christianity, was manifested in extravagant demonstrations of faith and fervor. In music, it appears as a distinctively criollo combination of orthodoxy and exaggeration that is far

Conclusion   245

from cultural *mestizaje*, both in conception and realization. Bernardo Illari (2001) rightly punctures the myth of the giant scale of the *capilla de música* of La Plata Cathedral, but the opposite is true in the case of Cuzco, where the musical forces apparently outshone those to be found anywhere else on the continent. Cuzco's seminary repertoire is Hispanic music writ large, enlisting the numerous nonsalaried but highly trained musicians to push the polychoral ideal to its limits. This, like the proliferation of Andean musicians, is what distinguishes the colony from the metropolis: Cuzco's imposing harmony.

Negotiating Harmony

Reading early colonial instructions and reports about the establishment of European music in the New World, it is striking that the aptitudes and inclinations of the native populations are given a prominent place. The rationale given by early churchmen for using music in conversion was not that it was the most orthodox or most "holy" manner of teaching, but that it was the most effective, since it was the one for which indigenous peoples showed the greatest affinity. From the beginning, then, the language of the missionaries was one of seduction and attraction, of adapting their methods to the inclinations of the colonized. For all that Lourdes Turrent (1993) writes of a "musical conquest," this was not an iron-fist approach: negotiation and accommodation were evident from the earliest musical efforts. Andeans were attracted to European music not just for its parallels with traditional practices but also because of the advantages afforded by participation in the church music profession. Musical proliferation in native parishes was as much a response to colonialism as a reflection of the success of colonial policies, and the large numbers of indigenous Americans flocking to the music profession in the first decades of Spanish rule suggest that they saw it as a potential means to soften the blow of the conquest.

Moving into the seventeenth century, European-derived music became increasingly bound up with the question of the formation of a "decent"—in other words, honorable and Christian—identity by native elites. Some of the most incisive recent studies of Andean history, in particular several of the essays in Jean-Jacques Decoster's edited volume *Incas e indios cristianos* (2002), have explored the variety of ways in which Andean elites constructed such an identity, consolidating their privileges using the tools provided by the institutions and rituals of the Catholic Church. They acquired education in the Jesuit *colegios de caciques*, founded and joined confraternies and beat-

erios, and, from the middle of the eighteenth century onward, were ordained as priests, if only in small numbers. Church music was a potent symbol of both the Catholicism and the Europeanized culture that were so important to many native leaders in colonial Andean society, embodying their aspirations to both piety and Hispanism. Identification with this music, either professionally or as a sponsor, constituted a route to *decencia*, or power, as it would be called today (Burns 2002, 132), a channel for consolidating both indigenous authority and Christian identity and a means of bridging the cultural gap between colonizers and colonized. The crucial intermediary role of Andean elites in the formation of colonial Andean Christianity and culture is illustrated by the instruction of the indigenous founders of the Beaterio de la Santísima Trinidad that the *beatas* should learn "to read and write and sing and play some musical instruments with the aim that, with the brightness of their voices, the unbelieving Indians who have still to be conquered may be drawn into the Christian faith" (Burns 2002, 127). If music was indeed a weapon of conquest, then it was not only the Spaniards who were doing the conquering. As the indigenous *beatas* sang and played instruments, "creating great harmony, admiration, and devotion" (127) they fulfilled the Andean founders' aim to play a leading role in the propagation of harmony.

The characterization of music as a tool of colonialism thus needs to be qualified. Music can provide ethnic groups with means to manage unequal, changing relationships with the outside world, and incorporating other musics can thus be a route to power and strength rather than loss (Stokes 1994, 17). In colonial Peru, the "European" music profession was a prime "contact zone" (Pratt 1992) between the Spanish and Andean worlds, one which was a potential source of advantage to the native population. The music profession combined the acquisition of European cultural skills with active involvement in the Catholic Church, while familiarity with European music, along with language and clothing, was an outward sign of belonging to the privileged category of *indio ladino*, the native elite that moved between the Spanish and Andean republics. European music was far from a neutral sound in colonial society; rather, it was associated with advancement and high social standing.

Bearing in mind the centrality of Andean performers, directors, and composers in colonial musical culture, yet their elision in surviving musical sources, it is instructive to compare the imposition of harmony in the New World with that of the written word. Édouard Glissant has claimed that "it is against [the] double hegemony of a History with a capital H and a Literature consecrated by the absolute power of the written sign that the peoples who until now inhabited the hidden side of the earth fought, at the same time they were fighting for food and freedom" (qtd. in Mignolo 1995, 127). This same hegemony is reproduced in the writing of music, for "whatever surfaces in notation has undergone the preventative censorship of what one might call the imperialism of Western literacy" (Middleton 1990, 111). Critiques of the privileging of text over performance by scholars such as Richard Middleton (1990) and Tim Carter (2002) are highly pertinent to colonial Latin American musicology, where a focus on musical works has perpetuated this literary imperialism. Colonial musical culture has been cleansed of most features that do not fit standard European models: first, in the notation of the music and texts by colonial composers and authors, and second, through modern scholarly methodologies derived from Spanish musicology. It thus behooves us to resist this hegemony of the written sign by broadening our approaches to colonial music making without resorting to fanciful notions of a supposed mestizo baroque. If musical notation may be included among the tools of empire, however, it is far from clear that European musical culture as a whole should be bracketed with History and Literature when considering the relations between native peoples and Europeans in colonial Latin America. To a large extent, it was indigenous elites who enabled the propagation of European music in the hemisphere. Unlike literature or history, disseminated through writing or printing, music required constant recreation through performance and could not therefore be maintained as a tool for domination by a small European elite. Native participation was essential to the consolidation of European music in a way it never was for literature or history: the written word could be imposed, but harmony could not.

Notes

Introduction

1 I will use the term *Andean* to refer to those of indigenous descent, as an equivalent of the colonial category *indio*. *Spaniard* here refers to those of European descent, whether born in Spain (*peninsulares*) or Peru (criollos). A distinction between the latter two categories will be made clear where relevant.

2 His idea that the seminary repertoire reflects an "American manner"—a manner that nevertheless leaves no traces, it would appear—is derived from Seoane and Eichmann 1993, a work which has been effectively critiqued by Bernardo Illari (2001, 106–7). The risks of nationalist influence on musicological research are evident in these studies, which are infiltrated and distorted by the politically correct discourse of *mestizaje*. One of Illari's important contributions has been to shift the focus of attention from an imagined *mestizaje* to the much more real *criollismo* that underpinned much of the cultural production by Hispanic institutions in the Andean region.

3 Despite the analytical problems mentioned above, Quezada Macchiavello's catalogue is the most thorough to date, and his numbering system will be used here.

4 The ADC was renamed the Archivo Regional del Cuzco shortly before the publication of this book.

5 Transcriptions of various notarial records of relevance to this study can be accessed at my professional Web site (www.rhul.ac.uk/Music/Staff/GeoffreyBaker .html).

ONE The Urban Soundscape

1 The description comes from an early seventeenth-century document in the Biblioteca Nacional in Madrid, Chapter XXII, "Del viaje del Visorey hasta el Cuzco y recibimiento que se le hizo." All translations are by the author unless otherwise indicated.

2 General studies of colonial urban history, such as Hoberman and Socolow 1986 and Kinsbruner 2005, have devoted little or no attention to music or musicians, despite their discussion of an array of social actors.

3 The close link between music, education, and the imposition of *policía* is made

explicit in Felipe Guaman Poma de Ayala's ([1615] 1980, 635) instructions with regard to native *maestros de coro* (choir masters) in Andean villages, discussed in chapters 4 and 5.

4 Attention to the sound of bells has been a hallmark of urban musicology ever since they announced Reinhard Strohm's pioneering study of medieval Bruges (1985). The reflections of Jacques Attali (1985, 6) on noise are particularly relevant to the sound of Cuzco's church bells: "It is what links a power center to its subjects, and thus, more generally, it is an attribute of power in all its forms. . . . Equivalent to the articulation of a space, it indicates the limits of a territory and the way to make oneself heard within it."

5 AAC, LXXX, I, 13. For example: "A la primera, que se dice del Alba, se daran quince campanadas, primero a pausa, despues quince corridas, y a lo ultimo, tres a pausa, cuya repeticion se ordenaria sin duda, para dispertar a los que duermen, siendo mas facil oirse el signo a los demas tiempos meridiano, y vespertino. A las ocho de la mañana se tocara la campana mediana, que llaman la Gorda, corrida-mente, como quando dexan a Misa, por un breve espacio: despues seguira esta misma campana a pausas, hasta la media, golpe por golpe. A la media entrara la menor que llamamos la Chica, tocada corridamente con algunos intervalos, hasta los tres quartos, en que se tocara el esquilon, que llaman Segundilla, sin cesas hasta las nueve: dadas estas, se tocara la Gorda, como a las ocho por un breve rato, y luego la Chica del mismo modo; observese todo el año este orden."

6 See, for example, ADC, Flores de Bastidas, Leg. 98, 1654–5, ff.368 and 370. In September 1654, the cathedral commissioned new bells to be made by Andeans from the parish of Santiago, one of whom was the *cacique principal*. Were these among the bells consecrated by Bishop Isaguirre in 1663?

7 My understanding of these paintings and of the Corpus Christi festival in general owes a great debt to the studies of Carolyn Dean (1990, 1999). The majority of the paintings are currently housed in the Museum of Religious Art in Cuzco.

8 AAC, Cuentas de la Cofradía del Santísimo Sacramento fundada en la Catedral del Cuzco y en San Francisco, 1644–73.

9 My thinking here is influenced by studies of colonial Mexico such as Lafaye 1976 and Lechner 1988.

10 The relationship between corporate organization and cultural display in Corpus Christi is evident as early as the city council meeting on 14 May 1548: "Se ordeno a los gremios residentes en esa ciudad que aprestasen danzas e invenciones para solemni-zar la festividad [de Corpus]" (ADC, Libro de Actas del Cabildo I, 1545–1551, f.64).

11 Lewin 1973, 167: "También celarán los ministros, corregidores, que no se repre-senten en ningún pueblo de sus respectivas provincias *comedias u otras funciones públicas, de las que suelen usar los indios para memoria de sus dichos antiguos Incas* . . . . Del propio modo, se prohiben y quiten las trompetas o clarines que usan los indios en sus funciones, a las que llaman *pututos* y son unos caracoles marinos de un sonido extraño y lúgubre con que anuncian el duelo, y lamentable memoria que hacen de su antigüedad."

12 AAC, XLIII, 3, 53.

13 ADC, López de Paredes, Leg. 155, 1671, f.258; ADC, Bustamente, Leg. 14, 1683, f.250.

14 ADC, Básquez Serrano, Leg. 48, 1700–1, f.184. See also Messa Andueza, Leg. 189, 1658, f.1080v: the inventory of goods for the dowry of Doña Juana Portillo includes a harp with its tuner, worth twenty-five pesos.

15 ADC, P. Gamarra, Leg. 159, 1747, f.409.

16 ADC, Cabildo, Justicia Ordinaria, Causas Criminales, Leg. 92, 1740–59, Cuaderno 9, f.12.

17 ADC, J. B. Gamarra, Leg. 142, 1767–9, f.s/n.

18 ADC, Escribano de Naturales, Leg. 315, 1677–1705, f.243. The musician was paid thirty pesos for the year and received clothing, food, and a good trumpet; AGI, Mapas y Planes, Perú y Chile, 220.

19 It is also worth noting, in the light of the arguments advanced above, that the author hints at the aspirational aspect of European-derived music: for an Andean, learning a European instrument, like wearing Hispanic clothes, appears to have formed part of adopting a more cosmopolitan identity.

20 AAC, LXVIII, 2, 35, f.2v.

21 AAC, XI, 2, 23.

22 ADC, Xaimez, Leg. 313, 1692–3, f.81 [1/7/1692]: "Para efecto de enseñar tocar la harpa todos los sones que se usan de manera que quede diestra que los enseñara dentro de seis meses y por su trabajo y ocupasion se le a de dar quinsse pesos." The words "todos los sones que se usan" are intriguing, though highly ambiguous; they may imply popular tunes, perhaps associated with dances.

23 ADC, de Oro, Leg. 267, 1634, f.1027.

24 Guitars are occasionally found in church inventories. For example, in 1687 the *doctrina* of Coporaque is recorded as owning two harps, two *bajones*, and four guitars (AGI, Lima, 306).

25 ADC, Corregimiento, Causas Ordinarias, Leg. 46, 1763–5, Doc. 1025: "1765— Autos sobre la numeración de indios del Ayllu Yanaconas reducidos al curato de indios de la Santa Iglesia Catedral del Cuzco y de sus gremios." One of the guilds mentioned is that of *guitarreros* (f.8v). In ADC, Pérez de Vargas, Leg. 270, 1686, f.680, two Andean *maestros guitarreros*, both named Pedro Quispe, guaranteed to repay a debt of forty-one pesos owed by Sebastián Davalos, also an Andean guitar maker, to Joseph de Herrera.

26 ADC, D. Gamarra, Leg. 125, 1752–4, f.597.

27 ADC, Solano, Leg. 306, 1674–6, f.s/n [damaged—obligas.n—9/6/1674] refers to Don Francisco Osorio, "Prinsipal de [la pa]rroquia del ospital de los naturales de . . . y maestro guitarrero."

28 ADC, de Oro, Leg. 262, 1629, f.1439. A *discante* is a small guitarlike instrument. Miguel Poma, "yndio maestro carpintero natural de la parroquia del ospital de los naturales desta ciudad . . . otorgo se concertava y concerto con Joan de la Cruz que esta presente por tiempo de un año que corre desde oy dicho dia en el qual dicho

tiempo se obligo de hacer y que hara tres dozenas de discantes medianos y una dozena de viguelas medianas con haros de haya nogal o burne seis harpas de alto de una bara y media de cedro y nogal y pino y le a de dar el sussodicho para los dichos discantes y viguelas la madera que para ello fuere necesaria y para los dichos discantes la a de poner el." De la Cruz agreed to pay one peso per *discante*, two and a half pesos per vihuela, and eighteen pesos per harp.

29 ADC, Quiñones, Leg. 279, 1659, f.310. The inventory includes

- veinte y dos guitarras pequeñas
- veinte y çinco guitarras menores y unas pequeñas
- catorze guitarras chiquitas
- una guitarra grande—y otra mediana
- cuerdas para guitarra

30 It is interesting, therefore, that the maker Miguel Poma, referred to above, recorded his profession as *maestro carpintero* rather than *maestro guitarrero*. Gutiérrez (1979, 4) found evidence of a combined guild of Andean carpenters, instrument makers, and distaff makers at the end of the eighteenth century.

TWO *The Cathedral and the Seminary of San Antonio Abad*

1 AGI, Lima, 526.

2 Juan de Fuentes, who became *maestro de capilla* at Cuzco Cathedral, traveled to Peru in 1535, making him one of the first church musicians in South America (AGI, Contratación 5536\L.3\1\296).

3 AAC, LXXX, 1, 13.

4 AAC, LXXX, 1, 13, chapter 30: "Mandamos q.e el Mrõ de Capilla disponga sus composiciones, de modo, q.e sean serias y deuotas, pero de ningun modo profanas y conducentes al gusto de los hombres mal dispuestos . . . ; en cuia conformidad, quedan prohividas aquellas inflecsiones de voces y modulaciones q.e llama Teatrales, . . . esas atenuaciones de voces, q.e parece han pasado de los estrados de mugeres, al Sagrado lugar de la Iglesia."

5 AAC, Libro de Fábrica de la Santa Iglesia Catedral del Cuzco, 1800–14.

6 ADC, Messa Andueza, Leg. 227, 1681, f.635v.

7 The cathedral employed three singers in 1598 (AGI, Lima, 305) and four in 1607 (AGI, Lima, 312).

8 BNP, Ms. B25, f.iv: "Yran a la yglesia cathedral, y asistiran con sus sobrepellices todas las fiestas de guardar, y domingos de entre año, y las fiestas principales de primera, o segunda clase, y patrones de la ygl.a o de la ciudad. Yran a primeras visperas, y segundas en algunas dellas: y los semaneros, que seran quatro yran siempre a segundas visperas: y en la yglesia sirviran siempre que fueren quatro en el altar por el orden que el Rector diere. Yran tambien a maytines a la yglesia todos los collegiales en las fiestas de Navidad, Resurrection, y Semana Sancta."

9 According to a report by the seminary's rector in 1669, cathedral service was the principal purpose of its foundation and its main priority (AGI, Lima, 340).

10 AGI, Lima, 305: "A mas de catorçe años . . . acuden estos collegiales al seruiçio desta sancta Igl.a y su culto diuino a visperas salues y misa todos los dias por sus turnos y los Jueues de todo el año que se dize la missa del ssmo sacramento y quando sale a los enfermos van salmeando y cantando a canto de organo cossa que edifica mucho al pueblo."

11 AGI, Lima, 312.

12 Hipólito Unanue ([1793]1985, 249) states that in 1793, Cuzco's seminary had 122 students, including 23 who served the cathedral and 12 who were instructed in music. His accounts of the seminaries of Lima, Arequipa, Huamanga, and Trujillo make no mention of musical services.

13 AGI, Lima, 312. Ocón is credited for his attention to the organization of music in the cathedral and for his devotion to the seminarians, for whom he even obtained musical compositions from the Capilla Real in Madrid (Esquivel y Navia [c.1749] 1980, 2:104; Contreras y Valverde [1649] 1982, 144–45).

14 AGI, Lima, 333: "Tienen capilla de musica formada en el dho colegio con su maestro de capilla con mas de treynta musicos que continuamente se estan exerçitando en seruiçio desta Santa Ygleçia cathedral por lo qual es la mas bien seruido y de mayor lustre que ay en todo este reyno del piru a lo qual se junta el salir por deuoçion el dho colegio en comunidad a acompañar el santiss.o sacramento con su capilla de musica todas las veçes que se lleua a los enfermos con notable consuelo y edificassion de los fieles, y que ademas desto asisten todos los Juebes del año en la misma forma a la missa que en la dha cathedral se canta descubierto el santissimo."

15 AGI, Lima, 312

16 AGI, Lima, 340: "Tienen acompañando al santisimo sacramento con solemne musica de todos los cantores y demas colexiales quando se lleua a los enfermos pues no se tiene notiçia que en ciudad alguna se lleue el señor con tanto acompanamiento de solemnidad y musica como en esta . . . y son mas de cinquenta colejiales los cantores que sirben en la dha Yglesia y la administran en todas las desta ciudad con mucha solemnidad y pompa." Again, a witness confirmed that the seminarians sang polyphony in other churches on the feast days of their patron saints.

17 According to Lassegue-Moleres 1987, 63, priests were banned from attending "comedia alguna si no se presentare en las iglesias, y con nuestra licencia la qual no se concedera si no fuere para representar cosas de la Sagrada Escritura, y otras conforme a la religion, y buenas costumbres con que en las dichas comedias no representen mugeres, ni se hagan mientras se celebran los divinos oficios, lo qual cumplan so pena de ocho pessos, y dos dias de carcel." A *comedia* performed during Corpus Christi in 1651 took place in the cemetery of the cathedral, no doubt due to the effects of the recent earthquake (AGI, Lima, 306).

18 AAC, LXXX, I, 13, f.20.

19 The terms *loa* and *entremes* both refer to relatively broad genres with roots in staged drama. A *loa* was usually a spoken or sung act of homage, often serving as a

prologue, while an *entremes*—originally performed between the acts of a play—tended to have a popular or comic flavor and might involve songs, instrumental music, and even dancing.

20 Exceptionally, the civic celebrations in 1713 to mark the successes of the Spanish armies at Villa-Viciosa included two large-scale performances of *comedias* by the students of San Antonio Abad (AGI, Lima, 526). After the religious celebrations came "los temporales regosijos çiudadanos, que en dos Comedias representaron los Collegiales de la R.l Universidad Seminario de San Antonio, que consta de mas de çiento y quarenta, siendo en ellas en su primera salida musica a las tablas mas de çinquenta con instrumentos vistosos y vesturarios."

21 Doubts about *comedias* were apparently already circulating in Cuzco well before the royal decree of 1770 (see Esquivel y Navia [c.1749] 1980, 2:46, 281). *Comedias* were suppressed in the late colonial period as the church retreated into restrictive orthodoxy, rooting out the secular features that had characterized church sponsored music since the beginning of the colonial period.

22 ADC, Messa Andueza, Leg. 227, 1681, f.636v.

23 ADC, López de la Cerda, Leg. 131, 1696, f.658: "Yten quiero y es mi voluntad para quitar toda confusion que en la capellania o capellanias que dejo fundadas para el coro de la santa yglecia cathedral de esta ciudad sea sin el grauamen de misas por quanto su fin es, que los capellanes canten en el coro en las festiuidades que ubiere assi de canto llano como de organo por el mucho trauajo que considero." Earlier in his will, he had founded a *capellanía de coro* with two hundred pesos of income "para un capellan de coro que tenga la mejor vos que ser pueda y sepa bien de punto para que pueda juntamente cantar canto de organo y acompañar la musica de dha Yglecia en las festiuidades y demas funciones que ubiere."

24 ADC, Messa Andueza, Leg. 219, 1675, f.325.

25 ADC, Messa Andueza, Leg. 226, 1745–7, f.601.

26 ADC, P. Gamarra, Leg. 171, 1765, f.51.

27 The long-term inaccessibility of the cathedral archive means that any conclusions must be drawn from other sources and are thus tentative.

28 ADC, P. Gamarra, Leg. 149, 1729–31, f.340. Don Pedro Carasa, *presbítero*, sold "unas Haciendas nombradas Guamantiana que estan en terminos de la Parroquia de San Sevastian de esta dicha ciudad que lindan por una parte con las tierras de los Indios Cantores de la Santa Iglesia Cathedral de esta ciudad."

29 The *ayllu* was the basic traditional unit of Andean society. Robinson (1989, 161) translates *ayllu* as "kin-territory," in other words a combination of social and spatial relations. *Yanaconas* were Andeans linked by special service relationships to private individuals or institutions (Stevenson 1980a, 3; Wightman 1990).

30 ADC, Corregimiento, Causas Ordinarias, Leg. 46, 1763–5, Doc. 1025.

31 ADC, Corregimiento, Causas Ordinarias, Leg. 21, 1679–80, f.5.

32 ADC, Pérez de Vargas, Leg. 271, 1686–7, f.574.

33 AGI, Lima, 312; AAC, Cuentas de la Cofradía del Santísimo Sacramento fundada en la Catedral del Cuzco y en San Francisco, 1644–73.

34 AAC, Libro de Fábrica de la Santa Iglesia Catedral del Cuzco, 1800–14. The second document, produced by the Andean guild of barbers and musicians in 1786, is discussed in chapters 4 and 5 of the present volume.

35 For a positive evaluation of Andean voices by a Spaniard who arrived in Quito in 1560, see Stevenson 1980c, 20. Judging from chapter 30 of Cuzco's 1780 *Regla consueta*, it appears to be the case that those who had taken minor orders were preferred for cathedral singing posts. As very few Andeans were able to take holy orders, their disadvantaged position within the cathedral music hierarchy was reinforced.

36 An account of the Indian Mass, which included music with instrumental accompaniment, can be found in a report by the bishop dating from 1713 (AGI, Lima, 526).

37 The cathedral of Trujillo in northern Peru employed native singers at the end of the seventeenth century, but this seems to have been a decision born out of desperation and financial need, judging from the disparaging tone of the chapter acts in 1699 (Stevenson 1960, 95).

38 ADC, Quiñones, Leg. 279, 1659, f.353. See also ADC, D. Gamarra, Leg. 123, 1756, f.87; ADC, Fernández Escudero, Leg. 102, 1724, f.486.

39 Further evidence of ceremonies in the cathedral involving singing by the Mercedarians and Franciscans can be found in Esquivel y Navia [c.1749] 1980, 2:307, 420.

40 AAC, Parroquia de Belén, Cofradía de Nuestra Señora de Belén, 1746–1838.

41 AAC, Catedral del Cuzco, Cofradía del Señor de los Temblores, 1782–7; AAC, LIX, 2, 28.

42 ADC, Acuña, Leg. 1, 1760–1, f.140.

43 ADC, Saldaña, Leg. 294, 1677–8, f.370: "Este testigo vio rretratado al dho thomas de herrera en san lorrenso del Real el escorial de su Magestad por uno de los hombres insignes asi en la composiçion de la musica como en el organo de que estubo mas tiempo de sesenta anos en dho exerçiçio con toda puntualidad estimado de todos los señores obispos y prebendados que fueron desta ciudad y saue que el dho thomas de herrera retrataba como perssona noble acompañandose con caballeros y lustres desta çiudad." Herrera's salary at the cathedral was quite impressive at eight hundred pesos a year (ADC, de Oro, Leg. 259, 1627, f.70). The family also had dealings in textiles (ADC, Quiñones, Leg. 280, 1660–1, f.327v) and land (ADC, Maldonado, Leg. 197, 1701, f.209).

44 ADC, Beltrán Lucero, Leg. 10, 1646–9, f.129. Herrera stated: "Me obligo de enseñar y que enseñare a un hijo suyo nombrado Alonso Lopez Ponce colegial del Colegio Seminario de San Antonio desta ciudad el canto y a componerlo y echar el contrapunto y todo lo demas tocante a lo susodicho . . . y al fin del año lo tengo de dar maestro y que sea mediano compositor y en qualquier libro de canto llano pueda contrapuntear . . . y ansimismo le tengo de enseñar a tocar en discante y que sea diestro en cantar y en el templar y por el trabajo y ocupacion que en ello e de tener me a de dar y pagar la susodicha duzientos y ochenta pesos corrientes . . . y

con esto me obligo de le enseñar los dichos cantos en la forma referida dandole sus liciones cada dia."

45 See chapter 3 for the texts of these contracts.

46 ADC, López de Paredes, Leg. 145, 1662, f.882. Similar clauses are found in a number of other contracts.

47 AGI, Lima, 235\N.1\1. A *ración* was a cathedral office with a stipend attached, and therefore synonymous with a prebend. It was the lowest of the three levels of cathedral offices. The highest were the five *dignidades*, or dignitaries, which included the *chantre*. The middle level was occupied by the canons, of whom there were to be ten, according to the cathedral's foundation, although in practice there were far fewer. The third level was occupied by the *racioneros*, six of whom were to hold full *raciones* and six half *raciones*, although again, these were never all occupied due to a lack of funds.

48 AGI, Lima, 305; AGI, Lima, 312; AGI, Cuzco, 65.

49 AGI, Lima, 249\N.14. This document was drawn up on 11 June 1657. *Informaciones de oficio y parte* was the name given to a document drawn up when a resident of the Americas requested a concession, such as a promotion or new appointment, from the Spanish crown. Secular clergy in the Americas were subject to royal patronage, thus many Hispanic church musicians had to request such documents when they sought promotion (Gembero 2005, 274).

50 AGI, Lima, 249\N.14. Zúñiga's date of birth is given as 1625 and 1628 in different sources; the former date seems more plausible.

51 ADC, Pérez de Vargas, Leg. 234, 1701–3, f.585.

52 AGI, Lima, 531: "El Licenciado Alonso de Çuniga y Anaya hijo legitimo de padres nobles natural de la dicha çiudad criose desde niño en el colegio de San Antonio del Cuzco donde estudio la Gramatica, facultad de Artes y la Theologia moral. Es de edad de 50 años y 26 de sacerdote A sido uisitador y juez ecclesiastico en la Probincia de Canas y Canches deste obispado y en el exerçiçio della dotrino a los Yndios con desuelo y a probechamiento de sus almas por lo qual le honrraron los Prelados y de todo lo que a estado a su cargo a dado buena quenta. A 31 años que esta continuamente exerciendo el officio de Maestro de Capilla desta Cathedral es muy diestro en la Musica en que a sacado diçipulos muy abiles. . . . este sujeto, señor, es buen estudiante virtuoso y de singular exemplo, es ya de edad y se halla rendido con el exerçiçio de la Musica es digno de que V.M. le honrre con una Prebenda desta Yglesia para que con este exemplar otros trauaxen y se adelanten en la Mussica para poder seruir dicho offiçio."

53 See the requests for prebends for musicians in AGI, Lima, 305. Many prebends were left vacant during the colonial period due to a lack of tithe income to support them; see letters in AGI, Lima, 305 and 312, and chapter 10 of the 1780 *Regla consueta*.

54 See Stevenson 1980a, 6–9. At least eight cathedral singers—Hernán Rodríguez Pacheco, Gaspar de Villagra[s], Victorian[o] Rubio, Juan de Oliva, Bartolomé de Contreras, Alonso de Buytrago, Juan Pérez Bocanegra, and Luis de Aranda—were

parish priests in the years around 1600. See ADC, Salas, Leg. 293, 1600–1, f.211; Olave, Leg. 243, 1600–12, f.296; Carrera, Leg. 54, 1604, f.132v and 276; Montoya, Leg. 230, 1613, f.66; ADC, Montoya, Leg. 231, 1613–14, f.47. Villagra was simultaneously *maestro de capilla* and priest of Santa Ana.

55 AAL, Apelaciones del Cuzco, Leg. XVII, Doc. 11.

56 AGI, Quito, 209, L.1\1\302–3; ASFL, Reg. 15, Section 5, f.701–11.

57 Given that many ordinary singers had been given urban parishes at the start of the century, the fact that, even as *maestro de capilla*, Zúñiga was not granted one is perhaps a sign that the status of cathedral musicians was just beginning to slip at this time.

58 AGI, Lima, 305. The first includes the following analysis: "En esta yglesia se ha acostumbrado dar a los Cantores de ella las Dotrinas de la mesma çiudad porque el salario q les da la fabrica no es bast[ante] para sustentarse, y porque estos dos offiçios de Cura y Cantor pareçen en parte imcompatibles, y sin duda se seruirian mejor las dichas Dotrinas por otros clerigos que no tengan esta obligaçion de acudir a cantar a la yglesia mayor, espeçialm.te que no todas vezes los cantores han estudiado lo que es menester para ser curas de animas ni se aplican a ello: Si V.M. fuese seruido anexar las quatro raçiones de esta yglesia para los quatro cantores como en la de Granada y capilla real lo estan, y probeer las tres q aora ay bacas en Victorian Rubio tenor, y Bar.me de Contreras tiple, y Al.o de Buytrago contralto q son muy benemeritos y ha dias que siruen a esta yglesia estaria mejor seruida y ellos remunerados y honrrados, y la fabrica se ahorraria el salario q les da demas de 400 ducados cada año para emplearlos en otras cosas de que tiene mucha neçesidad, y las dotrinas que aora tienen se proueerian en quien no teniendo otra oblig.n cumpla mejor con la de Cura de animas."

59 See letters dated 1612, 1615, 1619, 1621, 1622, and 1625 in AGI, Lima, 305 and 312.

60 ADC, Saldaña, Leg. 303, 1694, f.391; ADC, López de la Cerda, Leg. 125, 1687, f.418.

61 ADC, Bustamante, Leg. 60, 1700, f.1032. See also ADC, López de la Cerda, Leg. 194, 1702, f.366.

62 ADC, López de la Cerda, Leg. 126, 1688, f.299 and f.539; Leg. 127, 1691, f.312; Leg. 131, 1696, f.92.

63 AAL, Apelaciones del Cuzco, Leg. XXIII, Doc. 1; ADC, López de la Cerda, Leg. 131, 1696, f.651.

64 ADC, Saldaña, Leg. 299, 1687–8, f.625v; ADC, Pérez de Vargas, Leg. 232, 1701–3, f.52; ADC, Messa Andueza, Leg. 227, 1681, f.532v.

65 ADC, Solano, Leg. 306, 1674–6, f.518; ADC, Bustamante, Leg. 61, 1701, f.959v; ADC, Messa Andueza, Leg. 221, 1676, ff.1315 and 1318.

66 ADC, Cáceres, Leg. 29, 1683, f.78; ADC, Bustamante, Leg. 21, 1690, f.58.

67 See ADC, Bustamante, Leg. 63, 1703, f.s/n [8/11/1703]; and ADC, Cáceres, Leg. 30, 1684, f.250.

68 For examples of loans to a lawyer, a priest, and a captain, see ADC, Bustamante, Leg. 62, 1702, f.941; ADC, López de la Cerda, Leg. 192, 1700, f.1060; ADC, Messa

Andueza, Leg. 219, 1675, f.720. For slave purchases, see ADC, Saldaña, Leg. 296, 1685, f.177; ADC, Pérez de Vargas, Leg. 272, 1689–92, f.271; ADC, Messa Andueza, Leg. 219, 1675, f.810; ADC, Messa Andueza, Leg. 214, 1671, f.781.

69 ADC, Libro de Actas del Cabildo Libro 18, 1689–94, f.87; Libro 20, 1712–19, f.62v.

70 ADC, Pérez de Vargas, Leg. 232, 1701–3, f.205.

71 ADC, Bustamente, Leg. 27, 1697, f.165.

72 I borrow the term *spiritual economy* from Burns 1999.

73 ADC, Bustamente, Leg. 15, 1685, f.297.

74 ADC, Pérez de Vargas, Leg. 271, 1686–7, f.574; ADC, Pérez de Vargas, Leg. 273, 1690–6, f.810. The name Jospeh Ygnacio is shared by two prominent Cuzqueño musicians. A second, later Joseph Ygnacio (Mayta) is discussed in the following chapters.

75 ADC, Bustamente, Leg. 27, 1697, f.1090 and f.1096.

76 He claimed not to owe any money himself, suggesting that he had been able to repay the sizeable loans that he had taken out some years earlier (ADC, Pérez de Vargas, Leg. 271, 1686–7, f.574; ADC, Pérez de Vargas, Leg. 273, 1690–96, f.810).

77 AGN, Eclesiásticos, Obispados, Cuzco, Leg. 9, Cuaderno 107, 1774, and account book from the cathedral for the years 1772–9; ASSAA, uncatalogued document.

78 AAC, VII, 3, 59, f.244v.

79 ADC, Villavisencio, Leg. 284, 1769–70, f.242; ASSAA, uncatalogued document.

80 ADC, Acuña, Leg. 6, 1767–8, ff. 550, 732, 749, 768.

81 ADC, Asuntos Eclesiásticos, Leg. 11, 1788–9.

82 AAC, VIII, 2, 39.

83 His will can be found at ADC, Fernández Escudero, Leg. 105, 1724, f.569.

84 Pérez de Vargas's will can be found at ADC, Arias de Lira, Leg. 24, 1739–40, f.204. See also ADC, Unzueta, Leg. 266, 1718, f.238. For more information on Pérez de Vargas and Gallegos, including the latter's will, see Baker 2001.

85 In 1703, Gallegos applied for an arts professorship at the university, though he was eventually awarded the lesser position of "master of students of arts and theology," which involved the teaching of philosophy, theology, and literature. He went on to rise up in the university (Valcárcel 1953, 11–19).

86 ADC, García Rios, Leg. 182, 1756–9, f.198.

87 AGI, Lima, 531.

88 AAC, LIV, 2, 39.

89 AGN, Eclesiásticos, Obispados, Cuzco, account book from the cathedral for the years 1772–79.

90 Attitudes to the practice of providing salaried musicians with *capellanías de coro* seem to have been inconsistent. For every example of such a practice, there is counterexample in which it is discouraged.

91 For example, Asensio Vera, a *seise* in the cathedral, applied for a singing scholarship at the seminary in 1738 (AAC, XIV, 5, 85). Vera was examined by the cathedral *maestro de capilla* "en la voz y auilidad de cantar para que pueda ocupar plasa de musico q estas son las Vecas, q consiguen los familiares de dha S.ta Yglesia por

cuya rason los examinan primero en la voz, para q puedan seruir en el coro." See also AAC, LVI, 2, 27: "Informasion de Legitimidad, costumbres y natales de Matias Aramburo para entrar al Real Colegio Seminario de San Antonio Abad" (1793). Theodoro Gamarra, *sochantre*, testified that Aramburo had served three years as *seise* in the cathedral, "los q.e son nesesarios segun la costumbre p.a ser admitido en el Seminario." The rector of the seminary wrote: "Es cierto q el Colegio a recibido a los clericulos q an servido en la S.ta Yglesia Catedral en calidad de seises siendo desentes, y legitimos, y se les a destinado beca de Cantores."

92 AAC, LXVI, 2, 21; AAC, XX, 3, 49. These documents are discussed in detail in Baker 2001.

93 AAC, Libro de Fábrica de la Santa Iglesia Catedral del Cuzco, 1800–14, Recibo No. 76.

94 The origins and early career of Estaban Ponce de León are still not known with any certainty, despite the investigations of Samuel Claro (1969a), but the scarce available evidence suggests that he may at least be considered an "adopted son" of Cuzco.

95 James Saunders's (2001) work on "moonlighting" by cathedral musicians in early modern England paints a similar picture.

THREE *Convents and Monasteries*

1 ADC, Solano, Leg. 305, 1671–3, f.s/n [Reg.2 – 9/6/1673]. Francisco Auca Tinco, Don Antonio León, and Don Francisco Jacobi, *maestros cantores* "se obligaban y obligaron de acudir al combento y hospital de San Juan de Dios . . . a cantar en esta manera = Los lunes a la misa de las Animas y los Juebes, viernes y sabado a las ocho de la mañana an de acudir a las missas que se an de Desir los dhos y los dhos Dias de Sabado a las quatro de la tarde a la salbe de nrã señora = y los viernes de la quaresma asi a la misa como al ensierro del santo xpto. a de llebar sus chirimias y el Juebes santo a la noche an de acudir a la prosecion y el dia de Domingo de rramos y viernes santo an de acudir a la misa de la pacion = y a las Bisperas y missa de la fiesta de Señor san Bartholome = y asimesmo an de acudir a los tres dias del Jubileo de nuestro Padre San Juan de Dios tarde y mañana que es la misa y ensierro y la mañana de pasqua de Resurecion an de acudir a la Prosecion = y a las Renobaciones del señor ansimesmo an de acudir llebando las chirimias = y asimesmo an de acudir a cantar a los entierros que vbiere de Religiosos en el dho combento y a las demas Relijiones que se ofresieren y para todas estas Musicas y Dias Referidos an de llebar los dhos Maestros los oficiales siguientes = organista. harpista. bajon. y corneta = Dos contra altos Dos thenores. seys tiples. Dos segundos."

2 ADC, Bustamante, Leg. 11, 1676–8, f.12–17: "En la ciudad del Cuzco—La Señora Doña Ysabel de Tapia, Priora del santo Monasterio de Santa Catalina de esta dicha ciudad, con las señoras Madres de consejo y demas señoras religiosas atendiendo

a las buenas prendas de Doña Josefa Maria de Santa Cruz y padilla y q.e desde q.e nacio se ha criado en este monasterio, y q.e le ha dado nr̃o. señor buena voz, y q.e hiciera falta a la musica del coro si saliese del conbento, y la llebase a Lima el señor Dean Doctor Don Alonso Merlo de la Fuente su tio y padrino de bautismo de la dicha Doña Josefa, a quien reconocemos particulares obligaciones por el afecto con q.e nos ha acistido desde q.e llego a esta ciudad = En cuya consideracion la dicha señora Priora Doña Ysabel de tapia, y las madres de consejo, y demas religiosas de comun acuerdo y consentimiento digeron, q.e se dicho señor Dean gustase le darian luego de gracia y sin dote el abito de hermana de belo blanco a dicha Doña Josefa, y la recibirian para cantora, y q.e solamente acudiese al coro los dias de fiestas solenes de canto de organo, y q.e la reserbarian de todos los oficios, y serbidumbres a q.e acuden todas las religiosas asi de velo negro como de velo blanco, y q.e desde luego le concederian, q.e durmiese en su celda por q.e las indias no le hurtasen su ropa: y q.e si Dios se sirbiese de quitarle la voz, no por eso se le quitarian los privilegios, q.e se le conceden q.e goce desde luego para sienpre de ellos."

3 This is symptomatic of a wider neglect, according to Kathryn Burns (1999, 1), who states that convents have been "marginalized mostly by omission" from colonial historiography. These institutions have traditionally occupied a somewhat peripheral place in Spanish and English musicology (Marín 2002, 121; Burgess and Wathey 2000, 18).

4 The most comprehensive discussion of music in Lima's convents is Estenssoro 1990, 396–440; see also Stevenson 1960, 56–57; Estenssoro 1989, 87–89; Sas 1971; and Martín 1983. Lima's convents have yielded little in the way of surviving music (García 1976).

5 This section draws extensively on Burns 1999, a pioneering study of Cuzco's convents.

6 Stevenson (1960, 56) and Martín (1983, 212) describe the regular attendance of large congregations drawn to Lima's conventual churches by the elaborate musical programs on offer. The Dominican friar Reginaldo de Lizárraga's (1987, 112) report of the crowd-pulling capacity of music at the convent of La Encarnación, Lima, in the early seventeenth century is especially revealing: "El cuidado en celebrar los oficios divinos, la solemnidad y concierto, con tanta musica de voces admirables, y sobre todo los sabados a la Salve, donde concurre la mayor parte del pueblo y de las Ordenes muchos religiosos a oirla. Yo confieso de mi que si todos los sabados, hallandome en esta ciudad, me diesen mis prelados para oirla, no la perderia. Los señores inquisidores muchos sabados no la pierden y los Virreyes hacen lo mismo." There is no reason to suppose that Cuzco's convents were any less successful in attracting sizeable and distinguished audiences. Mendoza ([1665] 1976, 70) implies their presence when he writes of the "exemplo a todos los que oyen, y atienden a lo deuoto del rezo, y suaue del canto" in Santa Clara in the mid-seventeenth century.

7 Diego de Mendoza's account of musical activities is framed by a description of the

physical structure of the convent church: "Tiene Coro alto, y baxo, donde se cantan, y rezan las diuinas alabanças, a todas horas; a que acuden en comunidad todas las Religiosas, rezan segun estilo de la Orden, con mucha deuocion, y estudio del canto llano, y de organo, las festiuidades clasicas, Visperas, Maytines, y Missa con la solemnidad, que en nuestra Religion se acostumbra, y exemplo a todos los que oyen, y atienden a lo deuoto del rezo, y suaue del canto . . . . Ponen las Religiosas especial cuidado en celebrar sus festiuidades, y Pasquas, con mucha musica, suaue en las vozes, y sonora por la mucha destreza adquirida en el continuo exerçiçio de estudio del canto, y en tañer con magisterio todos los instrumentos musicos, a mayor harmonia de las vozes." The author also mentions that the convent possessed a fine organ.

8 ADC, Messa Andueza, Leg. 197, 1664, f.418: "De enseñar a las monjas profesas y nobicias cantoras que nombrare hasta doce la señora abadeza la musica de canto sin cubrir las cosa ninguna y darles toda la musica que fuere menester para las festibidades que se ofresiere en el dho monasterio y asi mismo les a de enseñar y adieztrar las musicas de organo y harpa acudiendo a la dha enseñanza todos los dias."

9 Fernando García (1976, 11) mentions a prohibition order dating from 1775 that refers to comic music and secular dances performed by day and by night in Lima's convents.

10 ADC, Solano, Leg. 306, 1674–6, f.519.

11 The nuns of Lima were accused of performing satirical songs about the viceregal government in 1669; and a battle that continued for many years between the abbess of Santa Catalina and the archbishop of Lima during the 1790s saw the latter "ridiculed in songs and poems in the cloisters of Santa Catalina" (Martín 1983, 240).

12 AAL, Apelaciones del Cuzco, Leg. VI, Doc. 1: "Doña Juana de los Remedios, religiosa del convento de nra sra de los Remedios de la ciudad del Cuzco, contra Doña Mençia de San Bernarda, religiosa del dho convento, sobre que se de por nula la eleccion de Priora del dho convento que se hizo." One of the accusations was, "Para que botasen por la dha doña mencia Prometio a muchos oficios en el convento y sobornos y rregalos teniendo ya preuenidas como para cossa hecha y cierta musicas y saraos Por la dha doña mencia." Music also played a part in electioneering in Lima's convents, to judge from the order of Archbishop Melchor Liñán y Cisneros in 1703 that "las elecciones en los conventos de religiosas se llevasen a cabo con mayor secreto y seriedad, evitando escandalos y prohibiendo que los partidos manifestasen sus pasiones con clarines, caxas y matracas" (Sas 1971, 1:36).

13 The verses include

Sepan pues q mi abadesa es un çielo una deidad / Y esto lo diçe quien puede y asi todas lo diran (verse 3)

Bien se a bisto en su eleccion pues a sido singular / Q todas los coraçones le ofreçen con voluntad (verse 4)

Mas todo te lo mereses porque al fin sabes pagar / Y sabras reconoser lo que tus
hijas te dan (verse 5)

Q prelada tan amada echa a nuestra voluntad / Es mui digna de alabansa aunq
alabada se esta (verse 7)

Y a mi vicaria tambien el parabien le e de dar / Encargando q este coro sea
bentaje a los demas (verse 9)

14 Male musicians also participated in convent music in Lima (Sas 1971, 1:39) and
Ávila, Spain (Vicente Delgado 1989, 18–21).

15 ADC, Raya y Andrade, Leg. 240, 1722–3, f.297.

16 ADC, Bustamente, Leg. 22, 1694, f.897.

17 ADC, Flores de Bastidas, Leg. 98, 1654–5, f.419: Herrera "conserto con el L.do
juan de pancorbo presuitero administrador del monesterio de monjas de santa
catalina de esta ciudad por tiempo de dos años que an de correr y contarse desde
seys deste dho mes para efecto de enseñar a una niña que se esta criando en el dho
monasterio nombrada ana maria carrillo a tocar tecla y cantar canto de organo
con todos los rrequisitos que tiene el arte de musica y se obligo a darle todos los
dias de trauajo una liçion y no a de tener obligacion a darsela los dias de fiesta de
guardar ni los domingos. y por la ocupacion y trauajo que en ello a de tener le a de
dar y pagar çiento y ueinte pesos en cada uno de los dhos dos años."

18 ADC, López de Paredes, Leg. 141, 1656, f.446: Herrera "conserto con el Licensiado
juan de pancorbo presuitero para enseñar a una niña que tiene en el monasterio de
nrâ señora de los Remedios en la tecla a raçon de siento y beynte pessos cada año a
lisionarla y ducomentarla en contrapunto y compusision en la musica y le a de dar
a entender todo el juego del organo con que la a de dejar que sepa conoser
entender y sacar el proceder y de todos los tonos y sus diapacones a contento de
qualquier maestro y por la ocupasion del contrapunto y compossesion le a de dar
siento y sinq.ta pesos de a ocho y de la dha compusision reciue agora setenta y
sinco pesos de a ocho que es la mitad de los dhos ciento y sinquenta y lo demas a
un año y antes si antes ssupiere el dho contrapunto y compusision = Y por el
trauajo de la dha compusision y de lisionar la en la dha tecla le a de dar y pagar
siento y beynte pesos por un año en que le a de enseñar los susodho pagados
cada seis meses adelantados la mitad y confeso aber receuido los sesenta pesos
dellos."

19 ADC, Solano, Leg. 306, 1674–6, f.13. Achasa agreed "de ensenar a doña sisilia de
pas que esta en el monesterio de santa Catalina en el baxon y organo dando dos Lis-
iones todos los dias y asimesmo a doña sebastiana muchacha en el baxon." His salary was fifty pesos, less than half of Herrera's. The *bajón* was undoubtedly an important instrument in convents, as it could compensate for the lack of lower voices.

20 Mendoza [1665] 1976, 71: "En lugar aparte dedicado para Nouiciado, assisten las
Nouicias, y recien professas, que estan a la obediencia de la Maestra de Nouicias;
aprendiendo las ceremonias de la Religion, rezado mayor, y menor, canto llano, y
de organo, y las muchachas que necessitan de leer, y escriuir, y tañer los instrumentos precisos para la musica del Coro."

21 ADC, Asuntos Eclesiásticos, Leg. 3, 1739–50, Doc. 10.

22 ADC, Básquez Serrano, Leg. 55, 1708–9, f.210. The abbess told the convent's senior nuns "que Antonia Viacha yndia nobicia en este dho monasterio estaua Para professar de velo blanco y para ello auia de dar un mil seis cientos sinquenta y seis pesos y Dos rreales de Dotte y que la susso Dicha en tantos años como a estado en el dho monasterio enseñando a ottras de bajonera por que no ayga falta en este dho combento por cuyo trauaxo y servicio ttan dilatado como el que a tenido seria Muy justo el que se le rremunerasse en alguna manera lo mucho que a servido a este monastterio y que assi a pedido la sussodha le perdonen los seis-cientos sinquenta y seis pessos y dos rreales y que dara un mil pessos corrientes de a ocho rreales de Dotte para professar de belo blanco." She went on to mention the "trauaxo tan exsesibo que tiene de baxonera en el coro." The one thousand–peso dowry was to be paid out of the legacy left by her uncle, Don Gaspar Viacha.

23 ADC, Tapia Sarmiento, Leg. 256, 1767–71, f.174v: "Una niña . . . de edad de dies y seis años nombrada Maria Eulalia Solorsano . . . q.e desde su tierna edad la á criado en este monasterio la madre Manuela del Christo, se le dé el Avito de Religiosa de Velo negro, obligandose el, por la media Dote que son un mill seiscientos sesenta y dos p.s cuatro rr.s condonandosele la otra mitad por la asistencia q.e ha de haser la dha. Maria Eulalia, al choro en el Exercisio de Organista en el que actualm.te está de un año á esta parte á lo que condesendieron dhas. R.das madres Priora, y de consejo p.r ser util, y nesesaria en el referido choro, y organo la mencionada Maria Eulalia Solorsano."

24 Alfonso de Vicente Delgado (1989, 14–15) quotes a 1729 report by the bishop of Ávila that, as well as confirming dowry exemptions, describes privileges similar to those offered by Santa Catalina in Cuzco: "En algunos conventos se estila música de religiosas, y cantan versos en lengua vulgar, y especialmente en las mayores solemnidades y en la fiesta del Santísimo Sacramento, de que se sigue que los seglares más van por oir cantar las monjas que por devoción, y ellas se desvanecen por vanidad de su canto, y se admiten sin dote las músicas y no se les da oficios porque no malogren la voz con el trabajo."

25 ADC, Flores de Bastidas, Leg. 92, 1645, f.s/n. [23/12/1645]. Candidate agreed to teach Francisca de Vega de Buerres: "Que sepa oficiar una misa asi de canto llano como de organo. Que sepa oficiar unas visperas y bertear con el coro que sepa un tiento de mano asentada = otro de rompido = dos motetes entre ellos la Susana = un tiento de dos tiples = Un medio registro = otro de un tiple = otro baxo = que sepa cantar canto de organo de manera que sepa tañer a quatro boces de concierto dandole un maestro qualquier paso sobre qualquier tono de los ocho todo lo qual se obligo de enseñarlo dentro de dos años que a de correr desde oy dia de la fecha desta escritura y qualquier maestro deste arte o monxa que entienda la apruebe." The contract was to run for two years, and the musician was to be paid the considerable sum of three hundred pesos. Juan Cadidato de Cárdenas subse-quently moved to La Plata, where he was *maestro de capilla* at the cathedral from 1654 to 1656, and then organist (Illari 1997, 99; 2001, 33).

26 ADC, Arias de Lira, Leg. 27, 1745–6, f.4: "Otorgaron que el dho Dn Miguel Cano de Contreras hase concierto con el dho Dn Augustin Apomayta para que a la referida su hija D.a Maria Rosalia Cano le enseñe el Monacordio y puntos de solfa hasta bersos de todos los salmos . . . al fin de dos años a de estar muy perfecta en dha Muçica sin ignorar Claues ni resetados ora este afuera o en qual quier Monasterio sprê a de correr este consierto." Apomayta was to be paid fifty-two pesos per year. He was *principal* of the *ayllu* of Matará in the Hospital de los Naturales parish, home to a number of musicians.

27 ADC, Villavisencio, Leg. 283, 1766–8, f.288.

28 ADC, J. B. Gamarra, Leg. 132, 1749–52, f.s/n [7/7/1750].

29 ADC, López de Paredes, Leg. 151, 1667, f.218.

30 ADC, Bustamente, Leg. 14, 1683, f.242: "Yten declaro que en ensenarle y darle instrumentos como son de harpa monacordio Banduria y en todo lo que sabe cantos y puntos mi hija catalina de samudio tengo gastados siento y ochenta y sinco p.s."

31 This piece includes a part (the "papel del francés") with an alternative text that refers to "los religiosos" rather than "los mayordomos" and includes a dedication "to the provincial" instead of "to the Sacrament." The first part also includes a variant in which the Spanish-speaking character asks the Frenchman, "what does monsieur think of this *convento real?*"

32 ADC, Messa Andueza, Leg. 182, 1653, f.2688.

33 ADC, Flores de Bastidas, Leg. 98, 1654–5, f.359.

34 ADC, Messa Andueza, Leg. 183, 1654, f.425.

35 ADC, Messa Andueza, Leg. 184, 1654, f.1426.

36 This information appears in ADC, Arias de Lira, Leg. 25, 1741–2, f.329, a contract to build an organ worth 680 pesos for the church of Usicayos in the province of Carabaya.

37 AAC, Parroquia de San Jerónimo, Libro de Fábrica, 1672–1814.

38 AAC, LIV, 2, 39. See chapter 2.

39 AAC, XX, 3, 49.

40 Information about organ builders active in Cuzco's monasteries and across the diocese can be found on my professional Web site at www.rhul.ac.uk/Music/Staff/GeoffreyBaker.html.

41 ADC, Diez de Morales, Leg. 75, 1631, f.12.

42 ADC, Flores de Bastidas, Leg. 102, 1662, f.108.

43 ADC, Messa Andueza, Leg. 200, 1663, f.1310.

44 ADC, Messa Andueza, Leg. 214, 1671, f.190.

45 ADC, Beneficencia, Leg. 42, 1781, "Gastos diarios del Convento de San Agustín."

46 BNP, Ms. B271, f.3: "Expediente sobre el escándalo fomentado por los padres franciscanos en su convento del Cuzco." See also Esquivel y Navia [c.1749] 1980, 2:139.

47 ADC, Messa Andueza, Leg. 212, 1670, f.1167.

48 ADC, Messa Andueza, Leg. 176, 1649, f.1886.

49 AGI, Lima, 306. This period includes the 1673 contract, which specified an outlay of 250 pesos for a year's musical services.

50 The physiological and medicinal effects of music were discussed by Spanish music theorists of the fifteenth and sixteenth centuries, who drew on ancient sources (León Tello 1962, 215; Otaola González 2000, 93). The accounts of San Juan de Dios reveal that such ideas informed actual medical practice: the friars invested consistently in the services of professional musicians, who must therefore be considered key hospital employees.

51 ADC, Beneficencia, Pergamino 24, 1709, "Datas de Limosnas-misas-entierros."

52 AAC, LXXVI, 1, 4.

53 The account books for this period can be found in ADC, Colegio de Ciencias. At the time of research, this series was somewhat disorganized, and there were two numbering conventions. The information was found in Leg. 58, 1698–1734; Leg. 78, 1715–1816; Leg. 61 (33), 1699–1729; Leg. 59 (32 A), 1733–1799; Leg. 65 (35), 1751–1809.

54 A distinction between "musicians" and drummers or trumpeters often appears in such accounts, implying that the former term was used primarily for those who possessed more specialized skills, such as musical literacy and the capacity to perform polyphony.

55 ADC, Colegio de Ciencias, Leg. 13, Cuaderno 1, Cuerpo 1, f.4.

56 AAC, XLVIII, 3, 52.

57 ADC, Colegio de Ciencias, Leg. 15, Cuaderno 5, "Libro de visitas generales de 1751, Convento de la Almudena," f.6, 8.

58 ADC, Beneficencia, Pergamino 23A (1708), "Libro de Gastos del Hospital de San Andres"; 25 (1718), "Gastos diarios del Hospital San Andres"; 27 (1724), "Gastos diarios del Hospital San Andres."

59 Ygnacio's will (ADC, Quintanilla, Leg. 235, 1741–9, f.599; transcribed in Baker 2001) reveals him to have been a maker of keyboard instruments and harps—his house was full of instruments at various stages of completion—and an individual of considerable social and economic standing.

60 AGI, Lima, 306; ADC, Beneficencia, Leg. 45, 1786[–92], "Libro de entradas y gastos del Hospital San Andrés."

61 Ibid., f.51v, note 2: "Que siendo notorio q.e se han establecido las misas de Ntro Amo todos los dias Jueves del año: las renobaziones: las Quarenta horas, en las que se vela Ntro Amo descubierto; el Novenario de corpus: el Septenario de Dolores: cuyas fiestas se han hecho con el mayor lusim.to y desencia asitencia de Saserdotes, Sirbientes del Altar Musicos, Cajas, Clarines, chirimias, y cohetes en el tiempo q.e se husaban: se debe adbertir se causan, no cargo al Hospital ni un Sentabo, por q.e he costeado en estos dos años, y p.a lo susesibo costeare de mi dinero, y con la limosna q.e junte p.r mi p.a ayudarme, y mobiendo a algunos Piadosos."
Note 6: "Que siendo publico q.e el dia en q.e cumplen las enfermas con la Sta Madre Yglesia costeo Musica flores, fruta, cajas, clarines, y chirimias p.a las enfermas, y la comida se doi como de boda no le cargo el costo."

62 Ibid., f.73, note 3: "Que diciendose todos los dias Jueves del año una misa cantada a las seis de la mañana en la Yglecia, con musica completa, toque de cajas y clarines y asist.a de sobrepellises, tampoco cargo un centabo de gasto al Hosp.l como igualm.te de las renovaciones."

Note 4: "Que velandose nr͠o Amo Sacramentado en los tres dias de Carnestolendas con musica muy cumplida, tampoco cargo un centabo al Hosp.l sus gastos."

63 ADC, Beneficencia, Leg. 44, 1785, Libro de la Administración del Hospital Real de Naturales, f.57; ADC, Asuntos Eclesiásticos, Leg. 12, 1790–6, f.171, ff.188–9.

64 AAC, LXXII, 2, 37. A slightly earlier document issued by the secular authorities suggests that the church and state fought over the assets of the dying (ADC, Intendencia, Leg. 134, 1785, N.235). If the church, naturally, encouraged expenditure on a lavish funeral, the state issued regulations that attempted to discourage "los excessivos gastos q.e en los Lutos, Funerales, y Exequias de los Difuntos se havia introducido con notable detrimento de los Havitantes de este Reyno." Clearly, the conversion of wealth into spiritual credit sat uneasily with the rigorous efforts to increase state revenue in the last quarter of the eighteenth century.

65 ADC, Beltrán Lucero, Leg. 5, 1638, f.888: Juan Candidato (discussed in note 25, above), "se obligaua y obligo de acudir al colegio rreal de san bernardo de esta ciudad tiempo de un año cumplido . . . a donde enseñara a cantar la musica a los colegiales que el padre geronimo ermenegildo rretordel le señalare acudiendo cada dia a darles una licion eceto los domingos pasquas y una fiesta si hubiere mas en la semana."

66 ADC, Beltrán Lucero, Leg. 9, 1644–5, f.79: Juan Blas, *indio ladino en la lengua española*, "se concertaba y concerto con el padre Cristobal Luzero de la Compañía de Jesus rector del colegio de San Bernardo desta ciudad por tiempo y espacio de un año cumplido que corre y se quenta desde primero dia del mes de junio deste presente año de mill y seiscientos y quarenta y cinco en adelante hasta ser cumplido y se obligo de acudir todos los dias al dicho colegio desde las doze horas del dia hasta la una a tocar el bajon y enseñar a los colegiales ecetos los dias de domingos y fiestas de guardar sin hazer fallas y por la falla que hiziere se le a de descontar a dos reales y juntamente a de acudir con los dichos colegiales a las partes donde fueren a cantar pagandole su trabajo por el rector del dicho colegio y asimismo si acaeciere que el dicho Juan Blas concurriere a la yglesia mayor el susodicho a de buscar quien acuda al dicho colegio."

67 ADC, Cáceres, Leg. 37, 1691, f.250.

68 AAC, Parroquia de San Jerónimo, Libro de Fábrica de la Iglesia, 1672–1814.

69 The annual letter written by the head of the Jesuit order in Peru to his European superiors in 1620 describes the aim of the *colegio de caciques* in Lima as "imponerlos en buenas costumbres y apartarlos de sus padres, . . . y volviendo después à sus pueblos puedan enseñarles lo que han aprendido" ("Letras anuas" 1900, 58).

70 ADC, Fernández Escudero, Leg. 95, 1713–4, f.834. Cortés took on Quispe "para efectto de enseñarle a ttocar el organo con ttoda perfecssion y asseo de suertte que al fin de dichos dies años pueda ser ofissial enttendiendo de punttoi y de ofisiar la

missa y demas oras canonicas sin que ygnore cossa alguna por cuia enseñanssa no le a de pagar cossa alguna y solo si en el ttiempo rreferido de dhos dies años se a de seruir del dho Ygnacio quispe ocupandole en su lugar para que asistta en el coro en ttodas las funssiones que se ofresieren y de Vesttir a de tener cuidado el dho su padre de darle y el hermano Joseph Corttez solo le a de dar el susttentto nattural en su selda."

71 ADC, Maldonado, Leg. 205, 1713, f.506.

72 The most comprehensive study of colonial Latin American confraternities is Meyers and Hopkins 1988, while Varón 1982, Moreno Chá 1992, Dean 2002, and Viñuales 2004 examine Andean confraternities in varying degrees of detail; none of these works, however, tackles the subject of music. Music played an important part in the activities of confraternities throughout Europe, and musicologists have shown increasing interest in reclaiming a central role for these lay societies in urban soundscapes (Strohm 1985; Williamson 2001; Marín 2002; Glixon 2003), though as yet with limited impact on studies of the Hispanic world.

73 Vargas Ugarte 1948, 42–43: "Aquí todos los días del mundo rezan la Doctrina Cristiana, y la cantan, con otras coplas devotas y motetes, los ciegos y pobres, cosa que ha causado y causa admiración y algunos de ellos son diestros en la música, sin poder haber aprendido más que de oídas, y por no tener ojos toman de memoria los responsos e Himnos y Epístolas de San Pablo, para cantar en sus fiestas y en las misas que dicen aquí por sus difuntos. Todos los sábados cantan en esta capilla, la Salve de Nuestra Señora con su letanía, a canto de órgano, y así en estos días, como en sus fiestas y procesiones, y en las de nuestro Colegio, tocan los ministriles de la dicha cofradía, sus orlos, flautas, chirimías y trompetas, y esto con destreza."

74 ADC, Calvo, Leg. 46, 1641, f.786.

75 ADC, Messa Andueza, Leg. 205, 1666, f.1106: Don Juan de Soria Puma Cusi, *maestro cantor, natural de la parroquia del hospital de los naturales*, "dijo que por quanto los cantores de la parroquia de santiago de esta ciudad estan consertados con la cofradia del santo cristo de los españoles fundada en el ospital de San Juan de Dios de san bartolome de esta ciudad . . . para cantar en la dha cofradia con toda la musica en las missas y ffestibidades del año y entre ellos estaua concertado martin ataupuma contraalto y se les auian de pagar por año ochenta pesos y aora esta conbenido y consertado con los dhos cantores de que en lugar del dho contraalto a de entrar a serbir el dho Don Juan de Soria Puma cusi en cuya conformidad otorgo que se consertaba y se conserto con los cantores de la parroquia de santiago y con manuel martinez sequeyro mercader mayordomo de la cofradia del santo cristo de los españoles fundada en la yglesia de san bartolome ospital de san Juan de Dios de esta ciudad por maestro Cantor y contraalto de los dhos cantores." The musicians were to attend every Friday and at all festivities, "acudiendo con su musica y cantando." The group of singers is described as a *gremio*, or guild, which indicates a highly stable and coherent musical ensemble: "Los dichos cristobal chauca Don simon cusi mango Diego concho y lucas rramos cantores lo

açetaron y rresçiuieron en su gremio al dicho Don Juan puma cusi soria por contralto."

76 ADC, Bustamente, Leg. 16, 1686, f.582.

77 ADC, Fernández Escudero, Leg. 88, 1707, f.1034. The named musicians were Joseph de Medina, *pardo libre* (free African), Baltasar Chalco, a harpist from the village of Quiñota, Miguel Apac Tupa, a *bajonero* of the parish of Santiago, and Baltasar Guaman, an organist of the same parish. This final contract involves a group that has the appearance of a "music company," with musicians of different ethnic and geographical origins. Viewed together, the four contracts seem to imply a change in the corporative structure of Andean ensembles from a parish model in the seventeenth century to a more freelance arrangement. Independent music companies grew in importance in many parts of the Hispanic world during the eighteenth century, challenging the position of the traditional *capillas de música*.

78 ADC, Messa Andueza, Leg. 212, 1670, f.1167. The music profession was clearly a family affair in the parish of Santiago, as Don Cristóbal Chauca was succeeded as *maestro cantor* by Don Tomás Chauca (see the 1686 contract above). The musicians of Santiago seem to have been in demand by confraternities in the late seventeenth century: they were hired by the Cofradía del Santísimo Sacramento in Pisac in 1676 to provide music for the Corpus fiesta (AAC, Pisac, Cofradía del Santísimo Sacramento, 1664–1780).

79 AAC, Iglesia de San Francisco, Cofradía de Jesus Nazareno, 1720–63.

80 AAC, Cuentas de la Cofradía del Santísimo Sacramento fundada en la Catedral del Cuzco y en San Francisco, 1644–73.

81 The cacique Don Gaspar Viacha left one thousand pesos to support his musical niece in Santa Clara. After her death, half the money was to be donated to each of these two confraternities to support their annual festivities.

FOUR The Urban Parishes

1 There were no Spaniards in San Sebastián at this time, only three families of Spaniards in San Jerónimo, and five in Belén. Even in the parishes in which Spaniards had gained more of a foothold, they probably numbered no more than 10–15 percent of the population.

2 AAL, Apelaciones del Cuzco, Leg. xv, Doc. 11 (1659), f.328.

3 AAC, Parroquia de San Pedro, Libro de Cabildo, 1602 [–1625]. The entry for 1609 is particularly evocative of the cultural variety of these parish fiestas: "En este cau.do mandaron que aya cinco ynbençiones de taqueis de los yn.os guanocos y guancas e yungas y los collas e aymaras y pomatambos cada uno de su naturaleza e danças como es costumbre en cada año para la dha fiesta y proçesion." The priest Bernabé Cobo provided a description of Cuzco's seventeenth-century church fiestas that tallies precisely with the information from the Hospital de los Naturales records: "Tenían los indios del Cuzco para todas sus obras y faenas sus cantares y bailes propios, y cada provincia de todo el imperio de los Incas tenía su

manera de bailar, los cuales bailes nunca trocaban; aunque ahora cualquiera nación, en las fiestas de la Iglesia, imita y contrahace los bailes de las otras provincias" (qtd. in Estenssoro 1990, 72–73). This suggests a somewhat complex relationship between performance and indigenous identities, though this phenomenon was apparently limited to the city: Guaman Poma de Ayala wrote in around 1613 that the individuality of dances and songs prevailed in every *ayllu* to the southeast of Cuzco (Stevenson 1976, 297). For a discussion of the blurring of cultural distinctions within Andean society, see Estenssoro 1992a.

4 AAL, Apelaciones del Cuzco, Leg. XV, Doc. II, f.321, 327.

5 Notable exceptions are Illari 1997, which focuses on the indigenous musicians at La Plata cathedral, and Bermúdez 2001.

6 Tibesar (1953, 77) quotes a Franciscan report from 1563: "Teniendo ciertos frailes de la dicha Orden a su cargo la doctrina de una parroquia de naturales en la ciudad Cuzco . . . doctrinandolos a que sepan ayudar a Misa y a vestir los sacerdotes, rezar oras, cantar el coro, oficiar una Misa y visperas cantadas y tañer flautas y violones."

7 The parish of San Pedro was also known as Hospital de los Naturales in the colonial period; I will henceforth refer to the church by the former name and to the parish by the latter.

8 Vargas Ugarte 1951–54, 374: "Es cosa cierta y notoria que esta nacion de yndios se atraen y provocan sobremanera al conocimiento y veneracion del summo Dios con la cerimonias exteriores y aparatos del culto divino; procuren mucho los obispos y tambien en su tanto los curas, que todo lo que toca al culto divino se haga con la mayor perfeccion y lustre que puedan, y para este effecto pongan studio y cuydado en que aya escuela y capilla de cantores y juntamente musica de flautas y chirimias y otros ynstrumentos acomodados en las yglesias."

9 Qtd. in Estensoro 1990, 92: "Ansi mesmo dexareis en las iglesias el numero de cantores y musicos para el culto divino necesarios, acortando la superfluidad que hallareis, y queriendo los tales cantores y musicos permanecer en el servicio de las dichas iglesias provereis que los corregidores ni caciques no se los puedan quitar: y al maestro dellos señalareis un salario competente de la comunidad, segun y como en el capitulo antes deste se declara [es decir: "con que pudiesen pagar sus tributos y sustentar sus personas y casas"], y a los demas los reservareis de los servicios de mitas y tambos y otros servicios de la comunidad todo el tiempo que se ocupasen en esto." The *mita* was the most notorious kind of tribute exacted from the Andean population, involving forced labor in the mines, textile mills, and coca plantations. *Tambos* were travelers' inns.

10 Guaman Poma de Ayala [1615] 1980, 631: "Los cantores de la yglecia an de lleuar de salario los quatro cantores rrata por cantidad que pagare de cada pueblo. Los mayordomos de la yglecia y de cofrade, a cada yndio doze pesos en plata y la comida de la ofrenda. Pag[u]en los dichos padres a cada yndio sey medias de mays y seys medias de papas en cada año en este rreyno. Y ci fuere tributario pague su tributo y las obligaciones y *mitas* y minas, plasa y acuda al oficio que por eso le paga."

11　Philip III's decree, included in the 1618 *Recopilación de leyes de los reynos de las Indias* (book 6, title 3, law 6), reveals that musical provision was, in a sense, key to the definition of a *pueblo*. The arguments to which he was responding concerned the fact that the church saw music as central to its evangelical campaign, and therefore wanted the services of musicians who were old enough to have been fully trained but not so old that their health was failing—in other words, Andeans aged between eighteen and fifty. This was the same sector of the population, however, that formed the labor force on which Spanish wealth depended, for most male Andeans between these ages, known as *tributarios*, owed taxes and labor service to the Spanish state. Disputes arose because some members of the Spanish secular elite were opposed to any reduction in the number of "tributary Indians" in order to provide church assistants. Guaman Poma de Ayala ([1615] 1980, 629, 649) insisted that *cantores* should not be chosen from the tributary population, but should be young, old, infirm, or disabled.

12　BNP, MS. B853.

13　AAC, Parroquia de San Jerónimo, Libro de Fábrica de la Iglesia, 1672–1814; Parroquia de Belén, Libro de Fábrica, 1743–1894, and Libro de Inventarios, 1743–1869; Parroquia de San Pedro, Libro de Fábrica de la Iglesia, 1681–1775, and Inventarios y Cuentas, 1788–1865.

14　The parish church of Belén and a confraternity that it housed, the Cofradía de Nuestra Señora de Belén, made payments to a *vicaria de coro* between 1757 and 1796 (AAC, Parroquia de Belén, Libro de Inventarios, 1743–1869; Cofradía de Nuestra Señora de Belén, 1746–1838). The musician in question was apparently a nun, "la madre vicaria de casa hermana Paula de buen Pastor," who donated a *bajón*, two bird-whistles, and three drums to the church. This is a rare example of a nun-musician active outside a convent in colonial Peru.

15　For example, the entry for 1699: "Gastamos sesenta pesos en treintta y seis papeles de Musica de Tropas, quatros y Duos, y dos misas que nrõ Cura nos trajo Comprados de Lima."

16　ADC, Flores de Bastidas, Leg. 96, 1649–51, f. 309 [30/5/1650].

17　An example of a private endowment that included a provision for music in the parish church of San Pedro can be found in the will of Don Bernardo Cayetano Orco Guaman y Diaz, an Andean *principal* of the parish of Belén: "Yten declaro que por la mucha devocion, y beneracion que tengo a la Soberana ymagen de Nrâ Señora de la Concepcion fundada su cofradia en la Yglecia de dho ospital de Naturales me he dedicado a darle culto, y mandar decir una miza cantada en el dia del ensierro de su octauario cada año dando la limosna de quatro pesos y costeando su musica sera y flores para el adorno del Altar" (ADC, Arias de Lira, Leg. 33, 1759, f.314).

18　Indigenous cathedral servants, including musicians, from the *ayllu yanaconas* were also exempt from tax and labour levies (ADC, Corregimiento, Causas Ordinarias, Leg. 46, 1763–5, Doc. 1025).

19　The entry for 1676 "reads": twenty-six pesos two reales "al harpista que ha servido en el coro un año, y dos meses en las partidas siguientes seis p. y dos R.s con que le alquilaron cinco topos de tierras a dies R.s topo, veinte R.s de una carga de semilla de mays, veinte R.s de alquiler de Yndios reras y bueyes, quatro p. de zapatos que se le han dado, dos p. que se han gastado en cuerdas y nuebe p. en generos que se le han dado para su sustento."

20 Peter Marzahl (1978, 50) sums up the problems of research in areas in which an exchange economy prevailed due to a scarcity of cash and a long history of reciprocity: "The tendency to do without cash, to discount payments against one another, must have been strong. Notions of what is fit and due depend not on an exchange of cash but on a system of accounting that need not be on paper. It is not the worker who is shortchanged necessarily, but the historian."

21 The problems encountered by Clive Burgess and Andrew Wathey (2000, 27–36) in their study of English parish music are remarkably similar. Their discussion of churchwardens' accounts, the main source of information on parish expenditure, recalls the issues surrounding the libros de fábrica from Cuzco, in particular the division of musical patronage between the church and community leaders. The authors stress that churchwardens were not responsible for everything: much musical activity seems to have been paid for by others, probably those higher up the hierarchy known as "the masters" or "the worshipful," yet evidence of provision by these figures has rarely survived. The churchwardens' accounts seldom mention musicians' salaries: instead, they focus on the acquisition of instruments and written music, and payments to musicians at major feasts such as Christmas and Easter. The wardens took care of what might be considered the musical extras, while the masters of the parish shouldered the main burden. If we substitute the term caciques for masters, this would seem to be an accurate assessment of the financial organization of many Andean parishes.

22 AAC, Parroquia de San Cristóbal, Cofradía del Santísimo Sacramento, 1685–1773.

23 ADC, Colegio de Ciencias, Leg. 13, Cuaderno 1, Cuerpo 1.

24 ADC, Solano, Leg. 305, 1671–3, f.19.

25 AAC, Parroquia de Belén, Cofradía de Nuestra Señora de Belén, 1746–1838; Parroquia de Santiago, Fábrica, 1733–53 (in fact contains the accounts of Cofradía de la Purificación de Nuestra Señora, 1710–51); Parroquia de San Pedro, Cofradía del Santísimo Sacramento, 1681–1715 (in fact 1681–95); Parroquia de San Pedro, Libro de Cofradía del Santísimo Sacramento, 1715–82.

26 Aguinaldo signifies a gift or offering, and it is associated with the Christmas period. Evidence from monastery records presented in chapter 3 suggests that aguinaldos was celebrated between Christmas Eve and Epiphany in colonial Cuzco.

27 AAC, Parroquia de San Cristóbal, Libro de la Cofradía del Santíssimo Sacramento y Animas del Purgatorio, 1662–1741; Parroquia de San Cristóbal, Cofradía del Santísimo Sacramento, 1685–1773.

28 Confraternities dedicated to the Eucharist were particularly encouraged by the church after the Council of Trent in order to educate the faithful about the importance of the dogma of transubstantiation (Dean 2002, 174). Under pressure

from the Reformation, the Council of Trent recommended the foundation of a confraternity of the Holy Sacrament in every village; see Lassegue-Moleres (1987, 67) for a similar recommendation in the 1601 *Constituciones sinodales* in Cuzco.

29 On Spanish parish church music, see Casares Rodicio 1980; Zudaire 1987; Pavía i Simó 1993; Gembero 1998; and Marín 2002. Juan Ruiz Jiménez (1997) reveals the dependence of most churches in Granada, a city larger than Cuzco, on just three music ensembles.

30 AAC, Parroquia de San Pedro, Inventarios y Cuentas, 1788–1865.

31 New World cathedrals were founded according to the Sevillian model and can therefore be seen as an extension of the Spanish church, with the exception of that of La Plata in the sixteenth century (Illari 1997).

32 There were also skeptics: see reports by eighteenth-century Guatemalan priests in Van Oss 1986, 20–22.

33 Granada shows certain similarities to Cuzco in terms of decentralization. This city, a contact zone between Christian and Muslim populations, was another important evangelical center; this further suggests an underlying connection between the diffusion of musical culture and the prominence of evangelical imperatives (Ruiz Jiménez 1997).

34 The crown's defense of musicians' rights can also be seen in a letter from the king to the *audiencia* of Quito in 1647 (AGI, Quito, 209, [L.21458]); see my chapter 5.

35 For 1676, the entry reads: three pesos four reales "que han dado a cuenta de su salario por lo que ha de auer de su concierto al Mro de Capilla que se trajo concertado del Cuzco por no auerle en el pueblo para que enseñasse a los muchachos tiples en plata un p. y veinte R.s en una carga de mays."

36 In 1689, for example, the priest of San Jerónimo described his church as virtually destitute and struggling by on the produce from a few patches of church land (Villanueva Urteaga 1982, 219). This would explain why the accounts show unavoidable expenditure on items of musical hardware (instruments and music) but no musicians' salaries around this time. The priest stated that the Andeans worked on church lands for free, as an offering to the church, which raises the possibility of Andean musicians serving their parish on the same terms.

37 In the Pamplona parish studied by María Gembero, the professional head musicians (*maestro de capilla* and organist) participated in the circulation of musicians between establishments in search of better pay and working conditions. The cleric-singers (known as *beneficiados* or *coristas*) were not professional musicians and therefore did not circulate in the same way, and they were generally chosen from among the residents of the parish itself.

38 ADC, Solano, Leg. 306, 1674–6, f.s/n [28/6/1674]; ADC, Solano, Leg. 305, 1671–3, f.76; ADC, Arias de Lira, Leg. 27, 1745–6, f.4. The name "Ynga" indicates a person of considerable social status, as does the prefix "Apu-." Joseph Ygnacio Mayta, an organist mentioned in chapter 3, also records his name in his will with the "Apu-" prefix; he may have been related to the musician noted above. His

father carried the name Don Francisco Xavier Viracocha Ynga, again suggesting a kinship relation with the native nobility.

39 Juan Carlos Estenssoro (1989, 70) quotes a traveler's report from late eighteenth-century Lima: "No se conocen ahora más que dos caciques, que son el de Miraflores y el de Surco, tan miserables, que están reducidos a vivir del exercisio de enseñar en Lima a tocar instrumentos." Apparently caciques also retained their affinity for music until the end of the colonial period in the capital.

40 Nancy Farriss (1984, 305), writing about colonial Maya society, goes further still, stating that "the vast majority of curates continued to leave the catechism completely to the Maya *maestros cantores*." The native *maestro cantor*, one of the local principal men, carried out all religious and ritual functions except that of the Eucharist: the priest "was a visiting Spaniard with a supervisory role who offered additional ritual services in return for some steep fees and taxes" (Restall 1997, 150–51). Highland Peru had more in common with Mayan areas than with central Mexico in that the number of priests was woefully inadequate for the area and number of inhabitants in question (Boxer 1978, 115). Priests were disproportionately highly represented in cities, and therefore *maestros cantores* in Cuzco's urban parishes are unlikely to have played as significant a role in religious ceremonies as their rural counterparts. Nevertheless, it is illuminating that in 1682 the caciques of the city parish of San Sebastián, located only a couple of miles from the Plaza de Armas, went to Cuzco to complain that their former priests had never lived in the parish, preferring to stay in the center (Colin 1966, 103).

41 In colonial Yucatán, Mexico, "*maestro cantor, maestro de escuela*, and *maestro de capilla* were merely three different titles for what in reality was one position" (Collins 1977, 243).

42 Guaman Poma de Ayala ([1615] 1980, 736) reveals the power of Peruvian caciques to allocate posts—including that of *cantor*—to their friends and thereby to ensure that they maintained allies in positions of authority: "Los caciques principales y alcaldes destos reynos, reservandose ellos los que no tienen titulo y a sus amigos alcaldes y fiscales y cantores y sacristanes, enbian a los ninos y muchachos de la dotrina de poca edad y a los biejos pasados a las dichas minas de azogue y de plata."

43 Guaman Poma ([1615] 1980, 857) includes *cantores* among his examples of the proliferation of "Inkas"—in other words, the creation of new elites—after the conquest.

44 According to Karen Spalding (1984, 221–22), "kurakas (native leaders) initially responded eagerly to the lure of participation in the colonial system, actively seeking offices and privileges in the same fashion as their European counterparts." New colonial officials often came from the families of these traditional leaders: in Huarochirí, the son of one of the caciques served as *alcalde* (mayor) and then as *cantor*.

45 Clearly the *maestros cantores* were at the top of their profession, so it would be a mistake to assume a connection between high social status and the music profession across the board. Many ordinary parish musicians were undoubtedly of

average social rank by birth; however, their position as *indios reservados* and participators in Catholic ritual ensured a certain rise in social status, and some were able to accrue economic benefits (Spalding 1970). According to David T. Garrett (2005, 43), "while the social space of the Indian elite remained largely unchanged for almost two centuries, the determination of who occupied that space, and possessed its privileges, was constantly challenged and changed." Church musicians were certainly among those who competed for access to this space, with a considerable degree of success.

46 ADC, Básquez Serrano, Leg. 48, 1700–1, f.711; ADC, Cáceres, Leg. 32, 1686, f.s/n; ADC, Escribano de Naturales, Leg. 315, 1677–1705, f.827; ADC, Bustamente, Leg. 27, 1697, f.1122; ADC, Bustamente, Leg. 20, 1690, f.624.

47 ADC, de Oro, Leg. 252, 1620, f.72; ADC, Lucero, Leg. 163, 1623–1624, f.231.

48 See, for example, ADC, Beltrán Lucero, Leg. 1, 1630–1631, f.364; ADC, Beltrán Lucero, Leg. 3, 1634, f.248; ADC, Beltrán Lucero, Leg. 4, 1636–1637, f.225 and 592.

49 For further examples of musicians as *fiadores*, see ADC, Xaimez, Leg. 314, 1694–6, ff. 94 and 155. In these cases, two *maestros cantores* agreed to pay off debts of 150 pesos and 100 pesos, respectively.

50 To take one example, the *maestro de capilla* of Granada Cathedral from 1592 to 1627, Luis de Aranda, was *fiador* for a singer who died owing money to the cathedral chapter, but Aranda was unable to pay the singer's debt (Ramos López 1994, 175). It is intriguing, and perhaps unexpected, that Andean *maestros cantores*, despite their multiply marginalized position as colonized subjects employed by minor institutions on the periphery of a provincial city in the Americas, were often in much better financial condition than the chapel master at a major peninsular cathedral.

51 ADC, Xaimez, Leg. 314, 1694–6, f.195; ADC, López de Paredes, Leg. 151, 1667, f.633; ADC, Arévalo y Ayala, Leg. 22, 1714–21, f.132.

52 ADC, Solano, Leg. 304, 1664–7, f.45 [2nd foliation]. See also ADC, Flores de Bastidas, Leg. 106, 1668, f.11 [final *registro de indios*, 20/3/1668], in which Juan Saqui Cuya, *maestro cantor* in the parish of Santa Ana, was jointly responsible with a tailor from San Blas for the repayment of a debt of three hundred pesos.

53 Antonio Corona Alcalde (1999, 96–97) stresses the strong historical association between guitar playing and the profession of barber-surgeon in Spain, writing that "this instrument became practically a symbol of their trade, as much as the barber's bowl." The connection between these professions also spread to colonial Brazil, where bands of barber-musicians, known as *barbeiros*, played at the doors of churches (Fryer 2000, 140).

54 ADC, uncatalogued loose document: 'Expediente promobido p.r Jose [Cana]tupa Casique de los Gremios de Barbero . . . y Mucicos sobre que se le dedusgan bar[ios?] Yndios que alega estar ausentes' (Cuzco, 27 May 1786); AAC, Huayllabamba, Cofradía del Arcangel San Miguel, 1695–1764; ADC, D. Gamarra, Leg. 126, 1756, f.87.

55 ADC, Solano, Leg. 304, 1664–7, f.4 (4th foliation—11/1/1667); ADC, Bustamente,

Leg. 22, 1692, f.881; ADC, Arevalo y Ayala, Leg. 22, 1714–21, f.61 (more information can be found in ADC, Ximénez Ortega, Leg. 301, 1719, f.295); ADC, Arévalo y
Ayala, Leg. 21, 1707–13, f.35.

56 ADC, Raya y Andrade, Leg. 240, 1722–3, f.297.

57 There is a hint that he might have provided his musical services for this confraternity, "en donde ê sido esclauo a mas de quarenta años y seruido en el y en toda[s]
las funsiones que se an ofresido." The word *seruido*, though ambiguous, may
imply musical participation, rather than mere attendance.

58 It is of course impossible to know for certain that Livisaca had read these treatises.
Nevertheless, the fact that only three books are mentioned in the will, and that
Livisaca made special provision to have them sent across the Andes to Potosí,
implies that the books had special importance for him. These were not the only
copies of Cerone's book in Cuzco: the cathedral *maestro de capilla* Alonso de Zúñiga
bought a copy from the priest and musician Juan de Pancorbo in 1674 (ADC,
Solano, Leg. 306, 1674–6, f.520). Cerone's treatise—a complex, erudite work—
was very influential in the Hispanic world and was also known in colonial Mexico:
it left its mark on the noted composer Francisco López Capillas, and Sor Juana
Inés de la Cruz is known to have owned a copy (Brothers 1993).

59 An insight into colonial-era perceptions of Andeans' musical abilities can be
found in a report written by the Jesuit missionary Bernardo Recio in 1774 (Stevenson 1980c, 33), in which the author describes the interaction between the Jesuits
and the musicians of Quito, "entre los cuales, hay indios bellos remedadores"
(among whom there are fine Indian imitators). The word *remedadores*, from the
verb *remedar* (to imitate, mimic, ape), carries the dismissive connotation that the
native musicians were little more than skilled parrots. A similar view is expressed
by another Jesuit, Francisco Eder, writing this time about the missions of Moxos
in Bolivia in the mid-eighteenth century. He credits the indigenous musicians
with technical and imitative skill, but goes on: "No han podido aprender el arte de
composición, lo cual parece provenir de los estrechos límites en que se halla encer-
rado su ingenio, así como, ejerciendo un arte toda su vida, en nada lo perfec-
cionan, sino que su última obra de arte será enteramente igual a la primera"
(Claro 1969b, 12). The Spanish made a clear distinction between skill and art;
native peoples were seen as possessing the former in abundance, but not the latter
(Fraser 1990, 35).

60 How Livisaca and Durán de la Mota knew each other is a mystery. However, while
the latter's origins are unknown, at least three of his works are conserved in the
seminary archive in Cuzco, and Bernardo Illari's work in progress on the Cuzco
repertoire is providing circumstantial evidence that Durán may have been a *colegial*
at San Antonio Abad and may therefore have received his musical training in the
city. Furthermore, Livisaca's bequest of his music books could imply that he had
in fact been Durán's teacher, raising the intriguing possibility that one of the
greatest eighteenth-century Hispanic composers of the Andean region may have
been educated by an indigenous musician.

61 ADC, Fernández Escudero, Leg. 105, 1724, f.569–573.

62 This piece, entitled "A señores los de buen gusto," is listed by Samuel Claro (1969a), but it is now reported to be missing from the archive (Quezada Macchiavello 2004, 154).

63 ADC, Arévalo y Ayala, Leg. 21, 1707–13, f.273 [4/7/1710].

64 ADC, Arévalo y Ayala, Leg. 21, 1707–13, f.243 [19/11/1709].

65 ADC, Fernández Escudero, Leg. 101, 1720, f.860. Quispe's will could not, however, be located.

66 Another Ignacio Quispe was taken on as an apprentice by the Franciscan friar and organist Joseph Cortés in 1714; see my chapter 3.

67 ADC, Cáceres, Leg. 38, 1692–3, f.475; ADC, Xaimez, Leg. 312, 1687–91, f.3; ADC, Saldaña, Leg. 300, 1690, f.257; ADC, Fernández Escudero, Leg. 94, 1713, f.772.

68 ADC, Lucero, Leg. 164, 1625–1626, f.114 and 357; ADC, Beltrán Lucero, Leg. 6, 1639, f.730; ADC, Diez de Morales, Leg. 77, 1633, f.917; ADC, Fernández Escudero, Leg. 97, 1716, f.696. This is probably the same Don Francisco Guaman Topa who guaranteed the repayment of a debt of five hundred pesos in 1702 with two houses that he owned (ADC, Bustamente, Leg. 62, 1702, f.s/n), and who was paid by the church of Lamay-Coya in 1710 to teach the boy sopranos music and reading (AAC, Lamay-Coya, Fábrica/Inventarios, 1676–1756).

69 ADC, Beltrán Lucero, Leg. 2, 1633–34, f.550.

70 "Yt. el gasto de Cantores no se puede negar es evidente, porq.e en la Ciudad y Parroquias aunque eran sacados p.r el Rey a este fin, como no tienen chacras de donde comer se mantienen p.r la voz dando vueltas por las Iglesias, se les paga solam.te los Jueves por la misa de ntrô. Amo a 2 r.s incluso el organista, y los Domingos en la prim.a misa por el canto de Sacris Solemni en Lengua y el Himno de Eterne Deus q.e sirbe de grande instruccion a la feligrecia otros 2 r.s son 4 r.s p.r semana, 2 p.s p.r mes y 24 p.r año. Aqui se juntan los tres p.s que se dan por las Lamentaciones y Paciones, para cuerdas, y por los tres dias de Espiritu S.to q.e velan a ntro. Amo todo el discurso del dia son 7 p.s 4 r.s y con los 24 hazen 31 p.s 4 r.s p.r año y en los ocho importan 252 p.s los que doy en descargo. Ni esta paga tampoco compensa a la asistencia a todos los Domingos a la misa combentual del medio dia, y todos los savados del año en todos los dias de fiesta q.e todo lo hasen devalde por estar señalados a esta Yg.a" (AAC, San Pedro, Inventarios y Cuentas, 1788–1865).

71 As a point of comparison, the viceregal government issued guidelines in the seventeenth century on how much indigenous manual laborers should be paid: workers in obrajes (textile mills) in the Cuzco region were to receive an annual salary of forty-eight pesos four reales or fifty-six pesos four reales, depending on the type of job, plus food (Macera 1968, 132–44). Working in an obraje was one of the hardest and lowliest forms of labor.

72 An 1837 inventory includes "organo corr.te; una Harpa que sirve al continuo uso."

73 The cutoff date of 1720 may not be coincidental, given that half the population of the bishopric of Cuzco died in the plague of that year.

FIVE *The Rural Doctrinas de Indios*

1 The *contradanza* derived from the French *contredanse*, which had its origins in the English country dance. The *yaraví* was a kind of traditional Andean song.

2 The literature on the struggles over indigenous religion and culture in the sixteenth and early seventeenth centuries is extensive: see, for example, Duviols 1971, 1986; Estenssoro 1992a, 2003; Ramos and Urbano 1993; and Mills 1997.

3 A *huaca* was an idol or sacred object. A *malqui* was the mummy of an ancestor.

4 Recent historiography has questioned the intentions of Spanish inspectors and the accuracy of their reports, suggesting that ecclesiastical politics, personal ambition, and attempts to polarize the colonists and their subjects (in other words, the deliberate construction of difference) were behind many of the "findings" (Ramos 1993; Estenssoro 2003).

5 For brief but illuminating details on rural parish music, see Bermúdez 2001, 175–78; and Stevenson 1976, 277–88.

6 The diocese of Cuzco consisted of 137 parishes after its division in 1609, of which 112 were controlled by the secular clergy and 25 by the regular orders (Villanueva Urteaga 1982).

7 Clive Burgess and Andrew Wathey (2000, 40) stress the importance of music copying in English parish churches, which "were arguably more active as users of performed polyphony than as producers of high-art composition in its written form."

8 AAC, Yucay, Libro de Fábrica de la Iglesia, 1660–1727.

9 AAC, Chinchaypugio, Sumaro, Fábrica, 1646–1700.

10 AAC, Calca, Fábrica/Inventario, 1664–1730: Mandato 2; AGI, Lima, 306.

11 AGI, Lima, 306: "Que aya escuela de muchachos, para lo qual el cura y su theniente los pongan en memoria, y obliguen a que acudan a ella sin falta, y se les enseñe a leer, escreuir, cantar, reçar, y hablar en lengua castellana, y que los cantores despues de prima todos los dias pasen por lo menos una hora para que se adestren en la musica en lo qual ponga todo cuydado el maestro de capilla." Guaman Poma de Ayala ([1615] 1980, 636) tells a (rather unflattering) story about a *maestro de coro* who had been hired in Santiago de Qeros to teach reading, writing, and singing for a salary of eighty pesos and his food.

12 ADC, de Oro, Leg. 259, 1627, f.860.

13 AAC, Chinchaypugio, Iglesia del Pueblo de Sumaro, Fábrica, 1646–1700; AAC, Chinchaypugio, Cofradía de Santa Ysabel, 1646–1697; AAC, Lamay-Coya, Fábrica/Inventarios, 1676–1756.

14 See, for example, Galdo Gutiérrez 1970 and Brisseau Loaiza 1981, 155. Yet both secular and religious authorities promoted the involvement of Andeans in education from the early colonial period: in 1575 Viceroy Toledo recommended the establishment of a school in every district, "para lo cual se procure un indio ladino y hábil, de que hay bastante número en todas partes que sirva de maestro en la dicha escuela" (Levillier 1925, 359–60), and Jerónimo de Oré ([1598] 1992, f.55)

suggested that doctrine should be taught by the best-instructed Andean children except on Sundays, when the priest should take this role.

15 BNP, Ms. C1290 and Ms. C3988.

16 See Stevenson 1976, 167–69, and Estenssoro 1990, 30–31, on the problem of excessive numbers of indigenous church musicians in Mexico and Peru.

17 The four churches in the *doctrina* also recorded impressive collections of instruments in inventories drawn up in 1689 (Villanueva Urteaga 1982, 145, 149, 152, 154).

18 AAC, Chinchero, Cuentas, 1718–82; AAC, Huayllabamba, Libro de Fábrica, 1676–1760. See also Villanueva Urteaga 1982, 334.

19 AAC, Soraya (Aymaraes), Fábrica/Inventario, 1641–1754.

20 ADC, Quintanilla, Leg. 237, 1755–62, f.70v (Hacienda of Mandurque): "Una harpa corriente en el Coro." ADC, Asuntos Eclesiásticos, Leg. 2, 1735–9, 1708 (Hacienda of Casinchigua): "Un organo realejo con sus fuelles." There is also evidence that haciendas participated in rural religious festivals: Bishop Mollinedo, as part of his inspection in 1687, ordered *hacendados* in the Oropesa vregion to send dancers to participate in *doctrina* ceremonies on three major feast days (AGI, Lima, 306).

21 The *doctrinero* of Andahuaylillas at the end of the sixteenth century, Alonso Catalan, introduced "todo genero de mussica" (AGI, Lima, 322, qtd. in Estenssoro 1990, 218). His post was later occupied by Juan Pérez Bocanegra, discussed below.

22 Villanueva Urteaga 1982, 251; ADC, Diez de Morales, Leg. 80, 1634, f.1719; ADC, Flores de Bastidas, Leg. 98, 1654–5, f.618.

23 AAC, Accha, Fábrica/Inventarios, 1688–1794.

24 San Pedro de Andahuaylillas, Libro de Fábrica, 1759–1822 (held privately).

25 Exemptions did not always work as well in practice as in theory. Musicians from the *doctrina* of Yucay were forced to appeal directly to the bishop in the 1660s in order to receive even this most basic form of compensation for their musical services (AAC, Yucay, Libro de Fábrica de la Iglesia, 1660–1727, f.76). See Baker 2003b, 192–93. Communities' tax and tribute obligations rarely kept up with the changing demographic and economic reality: as more individuals migrated, the burden on those who remained became heavier, so there was also more pressure on caciques to ignore exemptions (Wightman 1990, 18–19). In some cases they may have been applied selectively: the village of Chuquinga in Aymaraes had just two *reservados*, an organist and a *bajonero*, but there is no mention of exemptions for singers (Villanueva Urteaga 1982, 364). This may reflect the practice, common in some areas, of choosing singers from among the younger and older (and therefore nontributary) members of the community in order to spread the tax burden more evenly, as Guaman Poma de Ayala ([1615] 1980, 629, 649) recommended. Of the eight musicians listed in Livitaca in 1689, for example, only two fell within the tributary age range of eighteen to fifty years old: three were boys and three men were aged fifty or above (Villanueva Urteaga 1982, 319–25). In other cases, musicians may have simply been obliged to pay tribute by unsympathetic caciques (e.g., Stavig 1999, 35).

26 ADC, Corregimiento Provincial, Leg. 61, 1679–1705 [1687], Mita de Quispican-chis. See Stavig 1999, 131.

27 The church's defense of musicians' privileges in the face of pressures from secu-lar leaders, both Spanish and Andean, can be seen in a letter from the king to the *audiencia* of Quito in 1647 (AGI, Quito, 209, [L.2/1/458]): "Fr diego de Vcles, General de la orden de san francisco de esa Prouincia se me ha echo Relacion que en todas las Iglesias de las doctrinas de ellas ay seis Indios que siruen de cantores y acuden al culto diuino y con el salario que por esta ocupacion se les da pagan los tributos y viuen con comodidad y sin embargo dello y de las cedulas que estan dadas para que los dhos Indios sean bien tratados y Viuan sin que sean forcados al seruicio personal las Justicias y caciques deesas prouincias los sacauan de los Lugares donde auitauan y las lleuaban a partes asperas y remotas a trauajar por cuya Causa y de los malos tratamientos que les hacian."

28 ADC, de Oro, Leg. 259, 1627, f.860. A *carga* was the "cargo" of one mule.

29 ADC, Solórzano, Leg. 309, 1626–39, f.392 (transcription by Gabriela Ramos): "Sepan quantos esta carta vieren como nos Juan Bautista de Leon yndio ladino en lengua española natural del pueblo de Guancabelica maestro organista de la una parte y de la otra don Felipe Yanyache y don Diego Quispi Unpiri y don Francisco Pillaca caciques principales deste pueblo de Urcos desta provincia de Quispi-cancha por nos y en nombre de los demas yndios a nos subjetos deste dicho pueblo y decimos que por quanto todos somos combenidos y concertados en que yo el dicho Juan Bautista de León me obligo de asistir y que asistiré en este dicho pueblo tiempo de un año cumplido que corre y se a de contar desde el dia que se cumpliere otra escriptura que tengo fecha ante Francisco de Belasco escribano de Su magestad en que me obligue de tocar el organo deste dicho pueblo en todas las ocasiones que se ofreciessen de los oficios divinos y de enseñar dos yndios can-tores hasta que supiesen tocar en el dicho organo con destreza en todos los dichos oficios divinos como parece por la dicha escriptura a que me refiero y por averme pedido me quede otro año mas con el concierto que de suso yra declarado por no aver thenido efeto todo lo que me obligue en el dicho concierto ni aver acavado de salir aviles y suficientes los dichos yndios en la destreza que se requiere para tocar el dicho organo me obligo de estar y que estare el dicho año mas en este dicho pueblo teniendo a cargo el dicho organo como le e tenido hasta aquí y de enseñar los dichos dos yndios que no an quedado diestros y mas otros dos yndios de nuevo durante el dicho año . . . y por el trabajo y ocupacion que en ello e de tener se me an de dar y pagar por los dichos curacas cient pesos corrientes de a ocho reales pagados como los fuere sirviendo y mas veinte carneros de Castilla y veinte cargas de maiz y ansimismo se me an de dar dos topos de chacara de maiz barvechada sembrada almeada y calcheada y puesto el dicho maiz en grano en mi cassa todo a costa de los dichos curacas y comun."

30 AAC, Calca, Fábrica/Inventario, 1664–1730.

31 ADC, Diez de Morales, Leg. 80, 1634, f.1719.

32 AAC, Catca, Libro de Inventarios de la Iglesia Parroquial de San Juan Bautista de Catca; AAC, Calca, Inventarios/Fábrica, 1696–1775.

33 AGI, Lima, 306.

34 This impression is strengthened by the accounts of the Cofradía de Nuestra Señora de la Purificación in Pocoray, which show payments every year for "paper for the music": pieces were apparently composed or copied specifically for confraternity functions (AAC, Accha, Pueblo de San Juan Baptista de Pocoray, 1718–1727).

35 AAC, Calca, Confradía de Nuestra Señora de Belén, 1751–1843; AAC, Urubamba, Confradía del Rosario, 1650–1767[–1669]; AAC, Accha, Pueblo de Santiago de Hacca, Confradía de la Asunción, 1688–1787.

36 The term *chanzoneta* is roughly synonymous with villancico, that is, a paraliturgical composition with a vernacular text, though the former tended to have a more popular character.

37 AAC, Calca, Cofradía del Santísimo Sacramento, 1711–1847.

38 Ercilia Moreno Chá (1992, 414) even sees a polarization between the *doctrina* and the *cofradía*: "Doctrinas and *cofradías* became antagonistic power centers that stood for opposing symbols of authority: The *doctrina* represented the clergy and the official church, while the *cofradía* stood for the lay religion of the masses."

39 Mummies were often included in pre-Hispanic ceremonies. The sixteenth-century chronicler of Inka history Juan de Betanzos (1996, 79), wrote: "After Viracocha Inca died, Inca [Pachacuti] Yupanque honoured him greatly, having his body brought in a well-adorned litter as if he were alive, coming to the city of Cuzco whenever there were fiestas."

40 AAL, Leg. XXV, Doc. 2, 1675/7, f.144. One of the two *cofradías* that the cacique did not control was led by the *maestro de capilla*, Don Fernando Ortiz.

41 See Van Oss 1988, 44–45, with reference to Guatemala. In 1775, the Bishop of Guatemala claimed that the whole parish structure would have decayed without confraternity revenues.

42 AAC, Parroquia de San Cristóbal, Cofradía del Santísimo Sacramento, 1685–1773.

43 AAC, Huayllabamba, Cofradía del Arcangel San Miguel, 1695–1764.

44 ADC, López de Paredes, Leg. 146, 1663, f.689.

45 ADC, López de Paredes, Leg. 152, 1670, f.56.

46 ADC, Messa Andueza, Leg. 213, 1670, f.416.

47 AAC, Yucay, Libro de Fábrica de la Iglesia, 1660–1727.

48 AAC, Huayllabamba, Libro de Fábrica, 1676–1760.

49 AAC, Calca, Fábrica/Inventario, 1664–1730.

50 ADC, J. B. Gamarra, Leg. 135, 1749–52, f.s/n [31/5/1749].

51 AAC, Chinchero, Cuentas, 1718–82.

52 AAC, Calca, Libro de Fábrica, 1772[–1802].

53 AAC, Chinchaypugio, [Pueblo de Sumaro], Cofradía de Nuestra Señora de la Limpia Concepción, 1649–.

54 AAC, Chinchaypugio, [Pueblo de Sumaro], Cofradía de Santa Ysabel, 1646–1697.

55 AAC, Chinchaypugio, Iglesia del Pueblo de Sumaro, Fábrica, 1646–1700.

56 AAC, Pisac, Cofradía del Santísimo Sacramento, 1664–1780 (1676): Fifteen pesos

"en que se alquilo la musica y cantores de la Parroquia de Santiago del cuzco para esta fiesta [de Corpus]."

57 Five months later, Suclli contracted another Andean teacher, Don Pascual de Pineda, this time from the city parish of Santiago, to help him become a *maestro* in his own right (ADC, Bustamente, Leg. 17, 1687, ff.590 and 631). Both contracts give unusual indications of the kinds of music to be learned by the apprentice harpist. The first specified "todas las entradas de tonos y puntos en canto y musica de horgano y sones graues," while the second listed "todos los sones graues y entradas y pasacalles tientos y ffantasias y juguetes de manera que sea maestro."

58 Some village churches may have opted to pay their musicians' tributes in order to retain their services. In 1796, for example, the church of Anta paid 3 pesos 5 reales for the tribute of the *cantor* Ygnacio Villca (ADC, Asuntos Eclesiásticos, Leg. 13, 1796–98: Cuentas, Iglesia de Anta), but many probably could not afford to do so.

59 ADC, Acuña, Leg. 16, 1782–4, f.252: "Asistir con la Musica en la festividad de la S.ta Pasqua de Navidad de este presente año que se celebra en dho R.l Asiento conforme a la costumbre obserbada, y asi mesmo a todo el Nobenario comedias, y ensayos de ellas, y a todos los actos anexos, y consernientes a dha festividad." The group included Tomás Grandón, "Negro libre Maestro Harpista," confirming that Africans made limited inroads into the music profession in the eighteenth century.

60 A similar kind of physical displacement took place in late colonial Mexico (Viqueira Albán 1987, 147, 161).

61 ADC, Intendencia. Leg. 133, 1785, N.89.

62 Alonso Ramos Gavilán, qtd. in Estenssoro 1990, 20: "Por los años de 1616, en cierta dotrina quatro jornadas del Cuzco, un Cazique aviendo acabado de cubrir una casa nueva, aguardó dia, y ocasión en que el Sacerdote que los doctrinava, se ausentase del mismo pueblo, hizo una gran fiesta, donde fueron muchos los bayles, y las supersticiones no pocas, renovando el uso antiguo dellos; por no aver quien le fuesse a mono, hixo replicar las campanas, y tocar las chirimías."

63 ADC, Corregimiento, Causas Ordinarias, Leg. 17, 1664–67; Exp. 348, Cuad. 7: "El dho cassique quando selebra algunas fiestas en el dho pueblo que los yndios mayores le hacen dançar y bailar le assota a los yndios mayores diciendo que por que no le acudia[n] primero con los dhos bailarines a su cassa y no a la iglesia . . . en dos ocassiones la una estando privado de su sentido dentro de la yglesia el dho curaca con los cantores que fueron Pascual Cuña, Franciso Llanos, Salvador Ninaca, Mateo Quispi, Nicolas Quispi, y Joan Roca ofiçiando la salve como a las siete de la noche entro a la dha yglessia diçiendo que por que no le esperaua los maltrato dando coses y puñetes los echo de la yglessia." Corimanya was also accused of encouraging prohibited native dances and music, suggesting that he took a catholic approach to colonial culture: "El dho curaca contrabiniendo al usso de su oficio debiendo escussar borracheras y taquies las tiene y acostumbra muy repetidamente en su cassa con atambores con los yndios forasteros todas la

noches escandolossamente." Musicians who fell foul of their caciques could end up in serious problems. Don Andrés Guaman Vilca, the *cacique principal* of the village of Umachiri, was denounced by the widow of Don Juan Poma Cusi, a harpist from the parish of Hospital de los Naturales. The musician had been teaching the singers in the village, but was treated so badly by the cacique that he was forced to flee without even collecting his pay from the priest. Not content with hounding Poma Cusi out of town, Guaman Vilca gathered a band of his subjects and descended on the harpist's house; not finding him at home, they instead stole most of his possessions (ADC, Saldaña, Leg. 296, 1685, f.597). On the other hand, a good relationship with a figure of authority could be extremely beneficial: Guaman Poma de Ayala ([1615] 1980, 636) recounts the story of a *maestro de coro* who was so thick with his local priest that he carried on receiving his salary despite neglecting his duties and devoting himself to worldly pleasures.

64 AGI, Lima, 526. According to the 1729 letter, the *corregidor* "juntó cajas, y clarines, pregonero, y toda la Justicia del Pueblo, y de este todo lo que agregó a la Justicia semejante inaudita novedad, y con este estruendoso aparato se pregonó, y publicó en las esquinas de la plaza, y calles publicas dho Auto."

65 In the legal case brought against the cacique of Lamay in the mid-1660s, discussed above, the *maestro cantor* Don Pascual Ninaca is described as "principal desde su origen." Native leaders were inclined to provide their children with a musical education. Don Joseph Chaguayra, the *cacique principal* and governor of Andahuay-lillas, hired the *maestro arpista y organista* Don Joseph Chávez to teach his two sons the harp and organ, respectively (ADC, López de la Cerda, Leg. 131, 1696, f.880). Don Asensio Rimache, the *cacique principal* of San Lorenzo, made a three-year apprenticeship agreement on behalf of his son, Agustín, with Don Andrés Ccacya Vilca, *maestro cantor*, to learn to play the harp and sing (ADC, Bustamente, Leg. 20, 1690, f.655).

66 Miguel Ángel Marín (2002, 41) describes polyphony as an urban phenomenon that Spanish rural dwellers would only have encountered on visits to the city: "Music amounted to a feature that distinguished towns from villages, and urban environments from rural ones, where sophisticated musical works were virtually unheard of." Looking at the Cuzco seminary repertoire, it may in fact have been *polychorality* that distinguished the sound world of the city, though I would suggest that multichoir writing marked out a division between Hispanic and Andean institutions more than between urban and rural ones.

Conclusion

1 Bernardo Illari's (2007) work in progress on the seminary repertoire has revealed signs of a local compositional practice in a set of pieces with important, virtuosic sections for two *bajones*. While there is nothing indigenous about this music in stylistic terms, it is nevertheless suggestive: if most *bajoneros* in Cuzco were Andeans, then this repertoire reveals not only an unusual level of instrumental skill

on the part of the city's indigenous musicians—these instrumental parts are more difficult than those found anywhere else in the Spanish empire—but also a relatively high profile for these *ministriles* in terms of performance, since *bajón* parts are prominent within the compositions. The native Andean contribution, invisible on the page, would thus have been clear in the act of performance.

References

Archives

AAC   Archivo Arzobispal del Cuzco
AAL   Archivo Arzobispal de Lima
ADC   Archivo Departamental del Cuzco
AGI   Archivo General de Indias (Seville)
AGN   Archivo General de la Nación (Lima)
ASFL   Archivo de San Francisco, Lima
ASSAA   Archivo del Seminario de San Antonio Abad
BNP   Biblioteca Nacional del Perú (Lima)

Textual Materials

Acosta, José de. [1590] 1987. *Historia natural y moral de las Indias.* Ed. José Alcina Franch. Madrid: Historia 16.

Actas del III Congreso Internacional sobre Los Franciscanos en el Nuevo Mundo (siglo XVII). 1991. Madrid: Editorial Deimos.

Agnew, John A., and James S. Duncan, eds. 1989. *The Power of Place: Bringing together Geographical and Sociological Imaginations.* Boston: Unwin Hyman.

Akkerman, Abraham. 2000. "Harmonies of Urban Design and Discords of City-Form: Urban Aesthetics in the Rise of Western Civilization." *Journal of Urban Design* 5 (3): 267–90.

Alaperrine-Bouyer, Monique. 2002. "Saber y poder: La cuestión de la educación de las elites indígenas." In *Incas e indios cristianos: elites indígenas e identidades cristianas en los Andes coloniales,* ed. Jean-Jacques Decoster, 145–67. Cuzco: Centro de Estudios Regionales Andinos Bartolomé de Las Casas.

Antelo Iglesias, Antonio. 1985. "La ciudad ideal según fray Francesc Eiximenis y Rodrigo Sánchez de Arévalo." *En la España medieval* 6:19–50.

Arriaga, Pablo José de. [1621] 1968. *The Extirpation of Idolatry in Peru.* Ed. and trans. L. Clark Keating. Lexington: University of Kentucky Press.

Attali, Jacques. 1985. *Noise: The Political Economy of Music.* Trans. Brian Massumi. Manchester: Manchester University Press.

Baker, Geoffrey. 2001. "Music and Musicians in Colonial Cuzco." PhD diss., University of London.

———. 2002. "Indigenous Musicians in the Urban *Parroquias de Indios* of Colonial Cuzco, Peru." *Il saggiatore musicale* 9 (1–2): 39–79.

———. 2003a. "Music in the Convents and Monasteries of Colonial Cuzco." *Latin American Music Review* 24 (1): 1–41.

———. 2003b. "La vida musical de las doctrinas de indios del obispado del Cuzco." *Revista andina* 37:181–205.

———. 2004. "Music at Corpus Christi in Colonial Cuzco." *Early Music* 32 (3): 355–67.

Beezley, William H., Cheryl English Martin, and William E. French, eds. 1994. *Rituals of Rule, Rituals of Resistance: Public Celebrations and Popular Culture in Mexico.* Wilmington, Del.: Scholarly Resources Books.

Beltrán y Rózpide, Ricardo. 1921. *Colección de las memorias o relaciones que escribieron los virreyes del Peru acerca del estado en que dejaban las cosas generales del reino.* Madrid: Imprenta del Asilo de Huérfanos.

Bermúdez, Egberto. 1999. "The Ministriles Tradition in Latin America, Part One: South America; 1. The Cases of Santafé (Colombia) and La Plata (Bolivia) in the Seventeenth Century." *Historic Brass Society Journal* 11:149–62.

———. 2001. "Urban Musical Life in the European Colonies: Examples from Spanish America, 1530–1650." In *Music and Musicians in Renaissance Cities and Towns*, ed. Fiona Kisby, 167–180. Cambridge: Cambridge University Press.

Betanzos, Juan de. 1996. *Narrative of the Incas.* Ed. and trans. Roland Hamilton and Dana Buchanan. Austin: University of Texas Press.

Black, Christopher. 1989. *Italian Confraternities in the Sixteenth Century.* Cambridge: Cambridge University Press.

Bombi, Andrea. 1995. "La música en las festividades del Palacio Real de Valencia en el siglo XVIII." *Revista de musicología* 18 (1–2): 175–228.

Bombi, Andrea, Juan J. Carreras, and Miguel A. Marín, eds. 2005. *Música y cultura urbana en la edad moderna.* Valencia: Universitat de València.

Bourligueux, Guy. 1970. "Quelques aspects de la vie musicale à Avila: Notes et documents (XVIIIe)." *Anuario musical* 25:169–209.

Boxer, Charles. 1978. *The Church Militant and Iberian Expansion, 1440–1770.* Baltimore, Md.: Johns Hopkins University Press.

Braun, Georg and Franz Hogenberg. 1572. *Civitates orbis terrarium.* Cologne: P. Gallaeum.

Brisseau Loaiza, Janine. 1981. *Le Cuzco dans sa région: Étude de l'aire d'influence d'une ville andine.* Lima: Institut Français d'Études Andines.

Brothers, Lester. 1993. "Musical Learning in Seventeenth-Century Mexico: The Case of Francisco López Capillas." *Revista de musicología* 16 (5): 2814–34.

Bueno, Cosme. [1768] 1951. *Geografía del Perú Virreinal (siglo XVIII).* Ed. Carlos Daniel Valcárcel. Lima: n.p.

Burgess, Clive, and Andrew Wathey. 2000. "Mapping the Soundscape: Church Music in English Towns, 1450–1550." *Early Music History* 19:1–46.

Burns, Kathryn. 1999. *Colonial Habits: Convents and the Spiritual Economy of Cuzco, Peru.* Durham, N.C.: Duke University Press.

——. 2002. Beatas, "decencia" y poder: La formación de una elite indígena en el Cuzco colonial." In *Incas e indios cristianos: Elites indígenas e identidades cristianas en los Andes coloniales,* ed. Jean-Jacques Decoster, 121–34. Cuzco: Centro de Estudios Regionales Andinos Bartolomé de Las Casas.

Cahill, David. 1984. "Curas and Social Conflict in the *Doctrinas* of Cuzco, 1780–1814." *Journal of Latin American Studies* 16:241–76.

——. 1986. "Etnología e historia: Los danzantes rituales del Cuzco a fines de la colonia." *Boletín del Archivo Departamental del Cuzco* 2:48–54.

——. 1996. "Popular Religion and Appropriation: The Example of Corpus Christi in Eighteenth-Century Cuzco." *Latin American Research Review* 31 (2): 67–110.

——. 1999. "Caciques y tributos en el sur Peruano después de la rebelión de los Túpac Amaru (1780–1830)." *Revista del Archivo Departamental del Cuzco* 14:111–27.

——. 2000. "The Inca and Inca Symbolism in Popular Festive Culture: The Religious Processions of Seventeenth-Century Cuzco." In *Habsburg Peru: Images, Imagination and Memory,* ed. Peter T. Bradley and Cahill, 85–150. Liverpool: Liverpool University Press.

Calvino, Italo. 1997. *Invisible Cities.* Trans. William Weaver. London: Vintage.

Carreras, Juan J. 2005. "Música y ciudad: De la historia local a la historia cultural." In *Música y cultura urbana en la edad moderna,* ed. Andrea Bombi, Juan José Carreras, and Miguel Ángel Marín, 17–51. Valencia: Universitat de València.

Carter, Tim. 2002. "The Sound of Silence: Models for an Urban Musicology." *Urban History* 29 (1): 8–18.

Casares Rodicio, Emilio. 1980. *La música en la catedral de Oviedo.* Oviedo, Spain: Universidad de Oviedo.

Castro, Ignacio de. [1795] 1978. *Relación del Cuzco.* Lima: Universidad Nacional Mayor de San Marcos.

Choque Canqui, Roberto. 2002. "Caciques de la provincia de Pacajes y la religiosidad cristiana." In *Incas e indios cristianos: Elites indígenas e identidades cristianas en los Andes coloniales,* ed. Jean-Jacques Decoster, 331–45. Cuzco: Centro de Estudios Regionales Andinos Bartolomé de Las Casas.

Claro, Samuel. 1969a. "Música dramática en el Cuzco durante el siglo XVIII y catálogo de manuscritos de música del Seminario de San Antonio Abad (Cuzco, Perú)." *Yearbook of the Inter-American Institute for Musical Research* 5:1–48.

——1969b. "La música en las misiones Jesuitas de Moxos." *Revista musical chilena* 23 (108): 7–31.

Clendinnen, Inga. 1990. "Ways to the Sacred: Reconstructing 'Religion' in Sixteenth-Century Mexico." *History and Anthropology* 5:105–41.

Colin, Michèle. 1966. *Le Cuzco à la fin du XVIIe et au début du XVIIIe siècle.* Paris: Institut des Hautes Études de l'Amérique Latine.

Collins, Anne. 1977. "The Maestros Cantores in Yucatán." In *Anthropology and History in Yucatán,* ed. Grant D. Jones, 233–47. Austin: University of Texas Press.

Concolorcorvo. [1773] 1965. *El Lazarillo: A Guide for Inexperienced Travelers between Buenos Aires and Lima, 1773*. Trans. Walter D. Kline. Bloomington: Indiana University Press.

Contreras y Valverde, Vasco de. [1649] 1982. *Relación de la Ciudad del Cusco*. Cuzco: Imprenta Amauta.

Corbin, Alain. 1998. *Village Bells: Sound and Meaning in the Nineteenth-Century French Countryside*. Trans. Martin Thom. New York: Columbia University Press.

Córdova Salinas, Diego de. [1651] 1957. *Crónica Franciscana de las provincias del Perú*. Washington: Academy of American Franciscan History.

Corona Alcalde, Antonio. 1999. "The Players and Performance Practice of the Vihuela and Related Instruments, the Lute and the Guitar, from 1450 to c. 1650." PhD diss., University of London.

Covarrubias, Sebastián de. [1611] 1995. *Tesoro de la lengua castellana o española*. Ed. Felipe C. R. Maldonado, rev. Manuel Camarero. 2nd ed. Madrid: Editorial Castalia.

Curcio-Nagy, Linda. 1994. "Giants and Gypsies: Corpus Christi in Colonial Mexico City." In *Rituals of Rule, Rituals of Resistance: Public Celebrations and Popular Culture in Mexico*, ed. William H. Beezley, Cheryl English Martin, and William E. French 1–26. Wilmington, Del.: Scholarly Resources Books.

Damian, Carol. 1995. *The Virgin of the Andes: Art and Ritual in Colonial Cuzco*. Miami Beach: Grassfield.

Davis, Natalie Zemon. 1974. "Some Tasks and Themes in the Study of Popular Religion." In *The Pursuit of Holiness in Late Medieval and Renaissance Religion: Papers from the University of Michigan Conference*, ed. Charles Trinkaus, with Heiko A. Oberman, 307–36. Leiden: Brill.

Dean, Carolyn. 1990. "Painted Images of Cuzco's Corpus Christi: Social Conflict and Cultural Strategy in Viceregal Peru." PhD diss., University of California, Los Angeles.

——. 1993. "Ethnic Conflict and Corpus Christi in Colonial Cuzco." *Colonial Latin American Review* 2 (1–2): 93–120.

——. 1999. *Inka Bodies and the Body of Christ: Corpus Christi in Colonial Cuzco, Peru*. Durham, N.C.: Duke University Press.

——. 2002. "Familiarizando el catolicismo en el Cuzco colonial." In *Incas e indios cristianos: Elites indígenas e identidades cristianas en los Andes coloniales*, ed. Jean-Jacques Decoster, 169–94. Cuzco: Centro de Estudios Regionales Andinos Bartolomé de Las Casas.

Decoster, Jean-Jacques, ed. 2002. *Incas e indios cristianos: Elites indígenas e identidades cristianas en los Andes coloniales*. Cuzco: Centro de Estudios Regionales Andinos Bartolomé de Las Casas.

Del Río Barredo, María José. 2005. "Cofrades y vecinos: Los sonidos particulares del Madrid barroco." In *Música y cultura urbana en la edad moderna*, ed. Andrea Bombi, Juan José Carreras, and Miguel Ángel Marín, 255–78. Valencia: Universitat de València.

De Oré, Fray Luis Jerónimo. [1598] 1992. *Symbolo catholico indiano*. Lima: Australis.

Díaz Rementería, Carlos. 1977. *El cacique en el Virreinato del Perú: Estudio histórico-jurídico*. Seville: Universidad de Sevilla.

Duviols, Pierre. 1971. *La lutte contre les religions autochtones dans le Pérou colonial: 'L'extirpation de l'idolatrie' entre 1532 et 1660*. Lima: Institut Français d'Études Andines.

——. 1986. *Cultura andina y represion: Procesos y visitas de idolatrías y hechicerías, Cajatambo, siglo XVII*. Cuzco: Centro de Estudios Regionales Andines Bartolomé de Las Casas.

Duviols, Pierre, and José María Arguedas, eds. 1966. *Dioses y hombres de Huarochirí: Narración quechua recogida por Francisco de Avila*. Lima: Instituto de Estudios Peruanos.

Eaton, Ruth. 2002. *Ideal Cities: Utopianism and the (Un)Built Environment*. London: Thames and Hudson.

Espinavete López, Manuel. 1795. "Descripción de la Provincia de Abancay." *Mercurio Peruano*, Tomo XII, 112–163. Lima: Imprenta Real de los Niños Huérfanos.

Esquivel y Navia, Diego de. [c.1749] 1980. *Noticias cronológicas de la gran ciudad del Cuzco*. Ed. Félix Denegri Luna, with Horacio Villanueva Urteaga and César Gutiérrez Muñoz. 2 vols. Lima: Fundación Augusto N. Wiese, Banco Wiese.

Estenssoro, Juan Carlos. 1989. *Música y sociedad coloniales: Lima, 1680–1830*. Lima: Editorial Colmillo Blanco.

——. 1990. "Música, discurso y poder en el regimen colonial." MA thesis, Pontificia Universidad Católica del Perú.

——. 1992a. "Los bailes de los indios y el proyecto colonial." *Revista andina* 20:353–89.

——. 1992b. "Modernismo, estética, música y fiesta: Elites y cambio de actitud frente a la cultura popular; Peru, 1750–1850." In *Tradición y modernidad en los Andes*, ed. Henrique Urbano, 181–95. Cuzco: Centro de Estudions Regionales Andinos Bartolomé de Las Casas.

——. 2003. *El paganismo a la santidad: La incorporación de los indios del Perú al catolicismo, 1532–1750*. Lima: IFEA/Pontificia Universidad Católica del Perú.

Farriss, Nancy. 1984. *Maya Society under Colonial Rule: The Collective Enterprise of Survival*. Princeton: Princeton University Press.

"Fiestas Incas en el Cuzco colonial." 1986. *Boletín del Archivo Departamental de Cuzco* 2:42–7.

Finnegan, Ruth. 1989. *The Hidden Musicians: Music-Making in an English Town*. Cambridge: Cambridge University Press.

Flynn, Maureen. 1989. *Sacred Charity: Confraternities and Social Welfare in Spain, 1400–1700*. London: Macmillan.

Fraser, Valerie. 1990. *The Architecture of Conquest: Building in the Viceroyalty of Peru, 1535–1635*. Cambridge: Cambridge University Press.

Fryer, Peter. 2000. *Rhythms of Resistance: African Musical Heritage in Brazil*. London: Pluto.

Galdo Gutiérrez, Virgilio. 1970. *Educación de los Curacas: Una forma de dominación colonial*. Ayacucho, Peru: Ediciones Waman Puma.

Ganster, Paul. 1986. "Churchmen." In *Cities and Society in Colonial Latin America*, ed. Louisa Schell Hoberman and Susan Migden Socolow, 137–63. Albuquerque: University of New Mexico Press.

García, Fernando. 1976. "En busca de música colonial sacra en los conventos de monjas limeños." *Boletín de música (Casa de las Américas)* 56:3–15.

Garr, Daniel, ed. 1991. *Hispanic Urban Planning in North America*. New York: Garland Publishing, Inc.

Garrett, David T. 2002. "La iglesia y el poder social de la nobleza indígena cuzqueña, siglo XVIII." In *Incas e indios cristianos: Elites indígenas e identidades cristianas en los Andes coloniales*, ed. Jean-Jacques Decoster, 295–310. Cuzco: Centro de Estudios Regionales Andinos Bartolomé de Las Casas.

———. 2005. *Shadows of Empire: The Indian Nobility of Cusco, 1750–1825*. Cambridge: Cambridge University Press.

Garrioch, David. 2003. "Sounds of the City: The Soundscape of Early Modern European Towns." *Urban History* 30 (1): 5–25.

Gembero, María. 1995. *La música en la catedral de Pamplona en el siglo XVIII*. Pamplona: Servicio de Publicaciones del Gobierno Foral de Navarra.

———. 1998. "El patronazgo ciudadano en la gestión de la música eclesiástica: La Parroquia de San Nicolás de Pamplona (1700–1800)." *Nassarre* 14 (1): 269–362.

———. 2005. "El compositor español Hernando Franco (1532–85) antes de su llegada a México: trayectoria profesional en Portugal, Santo Domingo, Cuba y Guatemala." *Latin American Music Review* 26 (2): 273–317.

Gibbs, Donald Lloyd. 1979. "Cuzco, 1680–1710: An Andean City Seen through Its Economic Activities." PhD diss., University of Texas, Austin.

Glave, Luis Miguel. 1992. *Vida símbolos y batallas: Creación y recreación de la comunidad indígena; Cusco, siglos XVI–XX*. Lima: Fondo de Cultura Económica.

Glave, Luis Miguel, and María Isabel Remy. 1983. *Estructura agraria y vida rural en una región andina: Ollantaytambo entre los siglos XVI y XIX*. Cuzco: Centro de Estudios Rurales Andinos Bartolomé de las Casas.

Glixon, Jonathan. 2003. *Honoring God and the City: Music at the Venetian Confraternities, 1260–1807*. Oxford: Oxford University Press.

Guaman Poma de Ayala, Felipe. [1615] 1936. *Nueva corónica y buen gobierno*. Ed. Paul Rivet. Paris: Institut d'Ethnologie.

———. [1615] 1980. *El primer nueva corónica y buen gobierno*. Ed. John V. Murra and Rolena Adorno. 3 vols. Mexico City: Siglo Veintiuno.

Gutiérrez, Ramón. 1979. "Notas sobre organización artesanal en el Cusco durante la colonia." *Histórica* 3 (1): 1–15.

Harrison, Simon. 1995. "Four Types of Symbolic Conflict." *Journal of the Royal Anthropological Institute* 1:255–72.

Hernáez, Francisco Javier. [1879] 1964. *Colección de bulas, breves y otros documentos relativos a la iglesia de America y Filipinas*. 2 vols. Vaduz: Kraus Reprint.

Hoberman, Louisa Schell. 1986. Conclusion to *Cities and Society in Colonial Latin America*, ed. Hoberman and Susan Migden Socolow, 313–31. Albuquerque: University of New Mexico Press.

Hoberman, Louisa Schell, and Susan Migden Socolow, eds. 1986. *Cities and Society in Colonial Latin America*. Albuquerque: University of New Mexico Press.

Illari, Bernardo. 1996. "La música que, sin embargo, fue: La capilla musical del obispado del Tucumán (siglo XVII)." *Revista argentina de musicología* 1:17–54.

———. 1997. "No hay lugar para ellos: Los indígenas en la capilla musical de La Plata." *Anuario del Archivo y Biblioteca Nacionales de Bolivia* s.n.:73–108.

———. 2001. "Polychoral Culture: Cathedral Music in La Plata (Bolivia), 1680–1730." PhD diss., University of Chicago.

———. 2007. "Composing the Local—With Two *bajones*: Cusco, Potosí, and Chuquisaca, c. 1650–c. 1750." Paper delivered at the Surviving Colonialism: *Indios, Criollos,* and Music in Pre-1800 Latin America conference, University of North Texas, Denton, March.

———. n.d. "Struggles over 'Performing Space': The Rise of Private Enterprise." Unpublished manuscript.

Juan, Jorge, and Antonio de Ulloa. [1749] 1978. *Discourse and Political Reflections on the Kingdoms of Peru: Their Government and Special Regimen of Their Inhabitants and Abuses Which Have Been Introduced into One and Another, with Special Information on Why They Grew Up and How to Avoid Them.* Ed. John TePaske. Trans. TePaske and Besse A. Clement. Norman: University of Oklahoma Press.

Kagan, Richard L., with Fernando Marías. 2000. *Urban Images of the Hispanic World, 1493–1780.* New Haven: Yale University Press.

Kendrick, Robert. 1996. *Celestial Sirens: Nuns and Their Music in Early Modern Milan.* Oxford: Clarendon.

———. 2002. *The Sounds of Milan, 1585–1650.* New York: Oxford University Press.

Kinsbruner, Jay. 2005. *The Colonial Spanish-American City: Urban Life in the Age of Atlantic Capitalism.* Austin: University of Texas Press.

Kisby, Fiona, ed. 2001. *Music and Musicians in Renaissance Cities and Towns.* Cambridge: Cambridge University Press.

Kreitner, Kenneth. 1992. "Minstrels in Spanish Churches, 1400–1600." *Early Music* 20 (4): 532–548.

Krims, Adam. 2002. "Rap, Race, the 'Local,' and Urban Geography in Amsterdam." In *Music/Popular Culture/Identities,* ed. Richard Young, 181–96. Amsterdam: Rodopi.

Kümin, Beat. 2001. "Masses, Morris and Metrical Psalms: Music in the English Parish, c.1400–1600." In *Music and Musicians in Renaissance Cities and Towns,* ed. Fiona Kisby, 70–81. Cambridge: Cambridge University Press.

Lafaye, Jacques. 1976. *Quetzalcóatl and Guadalupe: The Formation of Mexican National Consciousness, 1531–1813.* Trans. Benjamin Keen. Chicago: University of Chicago Press.

Lanuza y Sotelo, Eugenio. 1998. *Viaje ilustrado a los reinos del Perú en el siglo XVIII.* Ed. Antonio Garrido and Patricia Hidalgo. Lima: Pontificia Universidad Católica del Perú.

Lassegue-Moleres, Juan Bautista. 1987. "Sínodos diocesanos del Cusco, 1591 y 1601." *Cuadernos para la historia de la evangelización en América Latina* 2:31–72.

Lechner, Jan. 1988. "Colonial Literature and the Problem of Identity." In *Essays on Cultural Identity in Colonial Latin America: Problems and Repercussions,* ed. Lechner, 135–48. Leiden: TCLA.

León Tello, Francisco José. 1962. *Estudios de historia de la teoría musical*. Madrid: Consejo Superior de Investigaciones Científicas, Instituto Español de Musicología.

Leppert, Richard. 1987. "Music, Domestic Life, and Cultural Chauvinism: Images of British Subjects at Home in India." In *Music and Society: The Politics of Composition, Performance and Reception*, ed. Richard Leppert and Susan McClary, 63–104. Cambridge: Cambridge University Press.

"Letras anuas de la Provincia del Perú de la Compañía de Jesús: 1620 a 1724." 1900. *Revista de Archivos y Bibliotecas Nacionales* 5:35–140.

Levillier, Roberto. 1925. *Gobernantes del Peru: Cartas y papeles, siglo XVI*. Vol. 8. Madrid: Imprenta de Juan Pueyo.

Lewin, Boleslao. 1973. *Túpac Amaru: Su época, su lucha, su hado*. Buenos Aires: Editorial Siglo Veinte.

Lizárraga, Reginaldo de. 1987. *Descripción del Perú, Tucuman, Río de la Plata y Chile*. Ed. Ignacio Ballesteros. Madrid: Historia 16.

Locke, Adrian. 2001. "Catholic Icons and Society in Colonial Spanish America: The Peruvian Earthquake Christs of Lima and Cusco, and Other Comparative Cults." PhD diss., University of Essex.

Lockhart, James. 1992. *The Nahuas after the Conquest: A Social and Cultural History of the Indians of Central Mexico, Sixteenth through Eighteenth Centuries*. Stanford, Calif.: Stanford University Press.

López-Calo, José. 1963. *La música en la catedral de Granada en el siglo XVI*. 2 vols. Granada: Fundación Rodríguez Acosta.

———. 1990. *Documentario musical de la catedral de Segovia*. Santiago de Compostela: Universidade de Santiago de Compostela.

Lowe, Kate. 2005. "The Stereotyping of Black Africans in Renaissance Europe." In *Black Africans in Renaissance Europe*, ed. T. F. Earle and Lowe, 17–47. Cambridge: Cambridge University Press.

Macera, Pablo. 1967. *Noticias sobre la enseñanza elemental en el Perú durante el siglo XVIII*. Lima: Universidad Mayor de San Marcos.

———. 1968. *Mapas coloniales de haciendas cuzqueñas*. Lima: Universidad Mayor de San Marcos.

Madurell, José. 1948. "Documentos para la historia de maestros de capilla, infantes de coro, maestros de música y danza y ministriles en Barcelona (Siglos XIV–XVIII)." *Anuario musical* 3: 213–34.

Maravall, José Antonio. 1986. *Culture of the Baroque: Analysis of a Historical Structure*. Trans. Terry Cochran. Minnesota: University of Minnesota Press.

Marín, Miguel Ángel. 2002. *Music on the Margin: Urban Musical Life in Eighteenth-Century Jaca (Spain)*. Kassel, Germany: Edition Reichenberger.

Martín, Luis. 1968. *The Intellectual Conquest of Peru: The Jesuit College of San Pablo, 1568–1767*. New York: Fordham University Press.

———. 1983. *Daughters of the Conquistadores: Women of the Viceroyalty of Peru*. Dallas: Southern Methodist University Press.

Martín, Luis, and Jo Ann Pettus. 1973. *Scholars and Schools in Colonial Peru*. Dallas: Southern Methodist University Press.

Martín Hernández, Francisco. 1964. *1563–1700*. Vol. 1 of *Los seminarios españoles: Historia y pedagogía*. Salamanca: Ediciones Sígueme.

Marzahl, Peter. 1978. *Town in the Empire: Government, Politics and Society in Seventeenth-Century Popayán*. Austin: Institute of Latin American Studies, University of Texas.

Mateos, Francisco, ed. [1600] 1944. *Historia general de la Compañía de Jesús en la Provincia del Perú*. 2 vols. Madrid: Consejo Superior de Investigaciones Científicas.

Maurtua, Victor. 1906. *Obispados y audiencia del Cuzco*. Vol. 11 of *Juicio de límites entre el Perú y Bolivia*. Barcelona: Henrich y Companía.

Mendoza, Diego de. [1665] 1976. *Chronica de la Provincia de S. Antonio de los Charcas de Orden de Ñro. Seraphico P. S. Francisco en las Indias Occidentales, Reyno del Peru*. La Paz: Editorial Casa Municipal de la Cultura "Franz Tamayo."

Mesa, José de, and Teresa Gisbert. 1982. *Historia de la pintura cuzqueña*. Lima: Fundación Augusto N. Wiese.

Meyers, Albert. 1988. "Religious Brotherhoods in Latin America: A Sketch of Two Peruvian Case Studies." In *Manipulating the Saints: Religious Brotherhoods and Social Integration in Postconquest Latin America*, ed. Meyers and Diane Hopkins, 1–21. Hamburg: Wayasbah.

Meyers, Albert, and Diane Hopkins, eds. 1988. *Manipulating the Saints: Religious Brotherhoods and Social Integration in Postconquest Latin America*. Hamburg: Wayasbah.

Middleton, Richard. 1990. *Studying Popular Music*. Milton Keynes, Great Britain: Open University Press.

Mignolo, Walter. 1995. *The Darker Side of the Renaissance: Literacy, Territoriality, and Colonization*. Ann Arbor: University of Michigan Press.

Mills, Kenneth. 1994. *An Evil Lost to View? An Investigation of Post-evangelisation Andean Religion in Mid-Colonial Peru*. Liverpool: Institute of Latin American Studies, University of Liverpool.

——. 1997. *Idolatry and Its Enemies: Colonial Andean Religion and Extirpation, 1640–1750*. Princeton: Princeton University Press.

Minchom, Martin. 1994. *The People of Quito, 1690–1810: Change and Unrest in the Underclass*. Boulder, Colo.: Westview.

Miranda, Ricardo. 2005. "Éxtasis de luz y fe: La policoralidad en la Nueva España a través de la obra de Juan Gutiérrez de Padilla." Paper presented at the La tradizione policorale in Italia, nella penisola iberica e nel Nuovo Mondo conference, Fondazione Levi, Venice, October.

Monson, Craig. 1995. *Disembodied Voices: Music and Culture in an Early Modern Italian Convent*. Berkeley: University of California Press.

Moore, John Preston. 1954. *The Cabildo in Peru under the Hapsburgs*. Durham, N.C.: Duke University Press.

Moreno Chá, Ercilia. 1992. "Encounters and Identities in Andean Brotherhoods." In *Musical Repercussions of 1492: Encounters in Text and Performance*, ed. Carol E. Robertson, 413–27. Washington: Smithsonian Institution Press.

Morse, Richard M. 1972. "A Prolegomenon to Latin American Urban History." *Hispanic American Historical Review* (52) 3: 359–94.

Moseley, Michael. 1992. *The Incas and Their Ancestors*. London: Thames and Hudson.

Muir, Edward. 1981. *Civic Ritual in Renaissance Venice*. Princeton: Princeton University Press.

Muir, Edward, and Ronald Weissman. 1989. "Social and Symbolic Places in Renaissance Venice and Florence." In *The Power of Place: Bringing Together Geographical and Sociological Imaginations*, ed. John A. Agnew and James S. Duncan, 81–103. Boston: Unwin Hyman.

Olsen, Dale. 2002. *Music of El Dorado: The Ethnomusicology of Ancient South American Cultures*. Gainesville: University Press of Florida.

O'Phelan Godoy, Scarlett. 1995. *La gran rebelión en los Andes: De Túpac Amaru a Túpac Catari*. Cuzco: Centro de Estudios Regionales Andinos Bartolomé de Las Casas.

———. 1997. *Kurakas sin sucesiones: Del cacique al alcalde de indios (Perú y Bolivia 1750–1835)*. Cuzco: Centro de Estudios Regionales Andinos Bartolomé de Las Casas.

———. 2002. "'Ascender al estado eclesiástico': La ordenación de indios en Lima a mediados del siglo XVIII." In *Incas e indios cristianos: Elites indígenas e identidades cristianas en los Andes coloniales*, ed. Jean-Jacques Decoster, 311–29. Cuzco: Centro de Estudios Regionales Andinos Bartolomé de Las Casas.

Otaola González, Paloma. 2000. *Tradición y modernidad en los escritos musicales de Juan Bermudo*. Kassel, Germany: Edition Reichenberger.

Pavía i Simó, Joseph. 1993. "La música a la parròquia de Sant Just i Sant Pastor de Barcelona durant el segle XVII." *Anuario musical* 48:103–42.

Perdomo Escobar, José Ignacio. 1976. *El archivo musical de la catedral de Bogotá*. Bogotá: Instituto Caro y Cuervo.

Peters, Gretchen. 1997. "Urban Musical Culture in Late Medieval Southern France." *Early Music* 25 (3): 403–10.

Pratt, Mary Louise. 1992. *Imperial Eyes: Travel Writing and Transculturation*. London: Routledge.

Quezada Macchiavello, José. 2004. *El legado musical del Cusco barroco: Estudio y catálogo de los manuscritos de música del seminario San Antonio Abad del Cusco*. Lima: Fondo Editorial del Congreso del Perú.

Rama, Ángel. 1996. *The Lettered City*. Ed. and trans. John Charles Chasteen. Durham, N.C.: Duke University Press.

Ramírez, Susan Elizabeth. 1996. *The World Upside Down: Cross-cultural Contact and Conflict in Sixteenth-Century Peru*. Stanford, Calif.: Stanford University Press.

Ramos, Gabriela 1993. "Política eclesiástica y extirpación de idolatrías: Discursos y silencios en torno al Taqui Onqoy." In *Catolicismo y extirpación de idolatrías: Siglos XVI–XVIII*, ed. Ramos and Henrique Urbano, 137–68. Cuzco: Centro de Estudios Regionales Andinos Bartolomé de Las Casas.

Ramos, Gabriela, and Henrique Urbano, eds. 1993. *Catolicismo y extirpación de idolatrías: Siglos XVI–XVIII*. Cuzco: Centro de Estudios Regionales Andinos Bartolomé de Las Casas.

Ramos López, Pilar. 1994. *La música en la catedral de Granada.* Granada: Diputación Provincial.

———. 2005. "Música y autorrepresentación en las procesiones del Corpus de la España moderna." In *Música y cultura urbana en la edad moderna,* ed. Andrea Bombi, Juan José Carreras, and Miguel Ángel Marín, 243–54. Valencia: Universitat de València.

Relación del temblor, y terromoto que Dios Nuestro Señor fue servido de embiar a la Ciudad del Cuzco a 31 de Março este año passado de 1650. 1651. Madrid: Julian de Paredes.

Restall, Matthew. 1997. *The Maya World: Yucatec Culture and Society, 1550–1850.* Stanford, Calif.: Stanford University Press.

Robertson, Carol, ed. 1992. *Musical Repercussions of 1492: Encounters in Text and Performance.* Washington: Smithsonian Institution Press.

Robinson, David 1989. "The Language and Significance of Place in Latin America." In *The Power of Place: Bringing Together Geographical and Sociological Imaginations,* ed. John A. Agnew and James S. Duncan, 157–84. Boston: Unwin Hyman.

Rowe, John Howland. 1967. "What Kind of a Settlement Was Inca Cuzco?" *Ñawpa Pacha* 5:59–77.

Ruiz Jiménez, Juan. 1997. "Música y devoción en Granada (siglos XVI–XVIII): Funcionamiento 'extravagante' y tipología de plazas no asalariadas en las capillas musicales eclesiásticas de la ciudad." *Anuario musical* 52:39–75.

Sánchez de Arévalo, Rodrigo. [c.1454] 1944. *Suma de la política.* Ed. Juan Beneyto Pérez. Madrid: Consejo Superior de Investigaciones Científicas, Instituto "Francisco de Vitoria."

Santander, Joseph Antonio. 1748. *La lealtad satisfecha.* Lima: La Imprenta que esta en la Plazuela del pie del Cerro.

Sas, Andrés. 1971. *La música en la catedral de Lima durante el Virreinato.* 2 vols. Lima: Universidad Nacional Mayor de San Marcos/Casa de la Cultura del Perú.

Saunders, James. 2001. "Music and Moonlighting: The Cathedral Choirmen of Early Modern England, 1558–1649." In *Music and Musicians in Renaissance Cities and Towns,* ed. Fiona Kisby, 157–66. Cambridge: Cambridge University Press.

Sebastián López, Santiago, José de Mesa, and Teresa Gisbert. 1985–86. *Arte Iberoamericano desde la colonización a la independencia.* 2 vols. Madrid: Espasa-Calpe.

Seoane, Carlos, and Andrés Eichmann. 1993. *Lírica colonial boliviana.* La Paz: Editorial Quipus.

Siemens Hernández, Lotear. 1975. "El maestro de capilla Palentino Tomás Micieses I (1624–1667): Su vida, su obra y sus discípulos." *Anuario musical* 30:67–96.

Spalding, Karen. 1970. "Social Climbers: Changing Patterns of Mobility among the Indians of Colonial Peru." *Hispanic American Historical Review* 50 (4): 645–64.

———. 1984. *Huarochirí: An Andean Society under Inca and Spanish Rule.* Stanford, Calif.: Stanford University Press.

Stanislawski, Dan. 1947. "Early Spanish Town Planning in the New World." *Geographical Review* 37 (1): 94–105.

Stavig, Ward. 1999. *The World of Túpac Amaru: Conflict, Community, and Identity in Colonial Peru.* Lincoln: University of Nebraska Press.

Stern, Steve. 1993. *Peru's Indian Peoples and the Challenge of Spanish Conquest*. Madison: University of Wisconsin Press.

Stevenson, Robert Murrell. 1960. *The Music of Peru: Aboriginal and Viceroyal Epochs*. Washington: Pan American Union.

——. 1961. *Spanish Cathedral Music in the Golden Age*. 2nd ed. Berkeley: University of California Press.

——. 1976. *Music in Aztec and Inca Territory*. 2nd ed. Berkeley: University of California Press.

——. 1978. "Musical Life in Caracas Cathedral to 1836." *Inter-American Music Review* 1 (1): 29–71.

——. 1980a. "Cuzco Cathedral: 1546–1750." *Inter-American Music Review* 2 (2): 1–25.

——. 1980b. "Guatemala Cathedral to 1803." *Inter-American Music Review* 2 (2): 27–72.

——. 1980c. "Quito Cathedral: Four Centuries." *Inter-American Music Review* 3 (1): 19–38.

——. 1995. "Lírica colonial boliviana." *Inter-American Music Review* 14 (2): 105–6.

Stokes, Martin. 1994. Introduction to *Ethnicity, Identity and Music: The Musical Construction of Place*, ed. Stokes, 1–27. Oxford: Berg.

Strohm, Reinhard. 1985. *Music in Late Medieval Bruges*. Oxford: Clarendon.

Suárez-Pajares, Javier. 1998. *La música en la catedral de Sigüenza, 1600–1750*. Madrid: Instituto Complutense de Ciencias Musicales.

Szuchman, Mark. 1996. "The City as Vision: The Development of Urban Culture in Latin America." In *I Saw a City Invincible: Urban Portraits of Latin America*, ed. Gilbert Joseph and Szuchman, 1–31. Wilmington, Del.: Scholarly Resources Books.

Thompson, J. Eric, ed. 1958. *Thomas Gage's Travels in the New World*. Norman: University of Oklahoma Press.

Tibesar, Antoine. 1953. *Franciscan Beginnings in Colonial Peru*. Washington: Academy of American Franciscan History.

Torrente, Álvaro. 1996–97. "Cuestiones en torno a la circulación de los músicos catedralicios en la España moderna." *Artigrama* 12:217–36.

Torres de Mendoza, Luis, ed. 1867. *Colección de documentos inéditos relativos al descubrimiento, conquista y organización de las antiguas posesiones españolas de América y Oceanía*. Vol. 8. Madrid: Imprenta de Frias y Compañía.

Turrent, Lourdes. 1993. *La conquista musical de México*. Mexico City: Fondo de Cultura Económica.

Ulloa, Antonio de. [1748] 1990. *Viaje a la América meridional*. Ed. Andrés Saumell. 2 vols. Madrid: Historia 16.

Unanue, Hipólito. [1793] 1985. *Guía política, eclesiástica y militar del Virreynato del Perú, para el año de 1793*. Ed. José Durand. Lima: Corporación Financiera de Desarrollo.

Urteaga, Horacio, and Carlos Romero, eds. 1926. *Fundación Española del Cusco y ordenanzas para su gobierno*. Lima: Talleres Gráficos Sanmarti y Compañía.

Valcárcel, Carlos Daniel. 1953. *Libro de oposiciones de la Universidad de San Antonio del Cusco (siglo XVIII)*. Lima: Universidad Nacional de San Marcos.

Van den Berghe, Pierre L., and George P. Primov, with Gladys Becera Velazque and

Narcisco Ccahuana Ccuhuata. 1977. *Inequality in the Peruvian Andes: Class and Ethnicity in Cuzco*. London: University of Missouri Press.

Van Oss, Adriaan. 1986. *Catholic Colonialism: A Parish History of Guatemala, 1524–1821*. Cambridge: Cambridge University Press.

——. 1988. "Rural Brotherhoods in Colonial Guatemala." In *Manipulating the Saints: Religious Brotherhoods and Social Integration in Postconquest Latin America*, ed. Albert Meyers and Diane E. Hopkins, 35–49. Hamburg: Wayasbah.

Vargas Ugarte, Rubén. 1953. "Un archivo de música colonial en la ciudad del Cuzco." *Mar del sur* 5 (26): 1–10.

——, ed. 1948. *Historia del Colegio y Universidad de San Ignacio de Loyola de la Ciudad del Cuzco*. Lima: Instituto de Investigaciones Históricas.

——, ed. 1951–54. *Concilios limenses*. 3 vols. Lima: Tipografía Peruana.

Varón, Rafael. 1982. "Cofradías de indios y poder local en el Perú colonial: Huaraz, siglo XVII." *Allpanchis* 17 (20): 127–46.

Vásquez de Espinosa, Antonio. 1992. *Compendio y descripción de las Indias Occidentales*. Ed. Balbino Velasco Bayón. 2 vols. Madrid: Historia 16.

Vega, Garcilaso de la. 1964. *Commentarios reales*. Buenos Aires: Espasa-Colpe.

Vera Aguilera, Alejandro. 2004. "Music in the Monastery of La Merced, Santiago de Chile, in the Colonial Period." *Early Music* 32 (3): 369–82.

Vicente Delgado, Alfonso de. 1989. *La música en el monasterio de Santa Ana de Avila (siglos XVI–XVIII)*. Madrid: Sociedad Española de Musicología.

Vidal, Hernán. 1985. *Socio-historia de la literatura colonial hispanoamericana: Tres lecturas orgánicas*. Minneapolis: Institute for the Study of Ideologies and Literature.

Villanueva Urteaga, Horacio, ed. 1982. *Cuzco 1689: Documentos; Economía y sociedad en el sur andino*. Cuzco: Centro de Estudios Regionales Andinos Bartolomé de Las Casas.

——. 1989. "Los Mollinedo y el arte del Cuzco colonial." *Boletín del Instituto Riva-Agüero* 16:209–20.

——. 1992. *La Universidad Nacional de San Antonio Abad del Cuzco*. Cuzco: Editorial Universitaria de la UNSAAC.

Viñuales, Graciela M. 2004. *El espacio urbano en el Cusco colonial: Uso y organización de las estructuras simbólicas*. Lima: Epígrafe Editores.

Viqueira Albán, Juan Pedro. 1987. *¿Relajados o reprimidos? Diversiones públicas y vida social en la ciudad de México durante el Siglo de las Luces*. Mexico City: Fondo de Cultura Económica.

Vitruvius. 1999. *Ten Books on Architecture*. Trans. Ingrid D. Rowland. Commentary and illustrations by Thomas Noble Howe. Cambridge: Cambridge University Press.

Waisman, Leonardo. 2005. "La musica en la definición de lo urbano: Los pueblos de indios americanos." In *Música y cultura urbana en la edad moderna*, ed. Andrea Bombi, Juan José Carreras, and Miguel Angel Marín, 159–75. Valencia: Universitat de València.

Wightman, Ann M. 1990. *Indigenous Migration and Social Change: The Forasteros of Cuzco, 1570–1720*. Durham, N.C.: Duke University Press.

Williamson, Magnus. 2001. "The Role of Religious Guilds in the Cultivation of Ritual Polyphony in England: The case of Louth, 1450–1550." In *Music and Musicians in Renaissance Cities and Towns*, ed. Fiona Kisby, 82–93. Cambridge: Cambridge University Press.

Wittkower, Rudolf. 1998. *Architectural Principles in the Age of Humanism*. 5th ed. London: Academy.

Zudaire, Claudio. 1987. "La vida musical en la parroquia navarra de Falces (siglos XVII al XIX)." *Revista de musicología* 10 (3): 843–78.

Index

Clarinet, 209

Clavichord, 99, 157

Cofradía. See Confraternities

Colegio de caciques. See San Borja, Colegio de

Colleges. *See* Schools: for Andean and Hispanic elites

Colonialism, 2, 4, 30, 125, 169, 246, 247

Colonization, 2, 19, 20, 88, 178, 196

Comedia, 35, 41, 61, 64, 67, 72, 78–80, 116, 117, 222, 224, 244, 254 nn.20, 21. *See also* Theatrical music

Competition. *See* Rivalry

Composers: Andean, 120, 182–85, 195, 196; female, 121

Conde, Blas, 180

Confraternities, 1, 3, 7, 12, 15, 35, 37, 38, 54, 57, 58, 158, 159, 177, 238, 243, 244, 246, 267 n.72, 271 n.28, 280 n.38; in cathedral, 78, 84, 86, 90, 101, 141, 147; in convents, 147; in monasteries and schools, 43, 99, 132, 137, 144–48, 182; in rural parishes, 181, 202, 208–18, 223, 225; in urban parishes, 150, 152, 161–66, 235. *See also* San Bartolomé: Cofradía del Santo Cristo de la Coluna in; *Libros de cofradía*

Constituciones sinodales, 67, 79, 86, 152, 154, 158, 162, 176, 177, 210, 211, 227, 229

Contreras y Valverde, Vasco de, 157

Convents, 3, 10, 12, 15, 31, 49, 68, 77, 79, 87, 111–126, 128, 132, 142, 148, 161, 216, 238, 240, 241. *See also* Santa Catalina: convent of; Santa Clara: convent of; Santa Teresa: convent of

Conversion, religious, 19, 25, 49, 53, 88, 230, 246

Coporaque, 216, 219

Córdova Salinas, Diego de, 201

Corimanya, Pascual, 228

Cornett/cornettist, 111, 146, 166, 180, 200, 208

Corpus Christi, 35–42, 46, 49–55, 59, 62, 68, 71, 79, 84, 86, 90, 130, 138, 145, 150, 156, 162, 164–66, 188, 208–210, 213, 215, 225, 235, 237; paintings of, 37–40, 43, 51–56, 101, 128, 250 n.10

Corregidor: in rural parishes, 161, 195, 198, 223, 226–29, 239

Corsino Dávalos, Andrés, 105

Cortés, Joseph, 144

Cortés de la Cruz, Agustín, 81, 96–100

Countryside. *See* Parishes: rural

Coya, 210

Criollos, 2, 9, 11, 14, 47, 48, 57, 60, 80, 91, 108, 109, 114, 115, 199, 245, 249 n.2

Cusiguaman, Carlos, 137

Cusi Guaranca, Antonio, 181

Cusi Paucar, Joseph, 215

Cuyotopa, Carlos, 138

Cuzco: city council of, 18, 19, 33–35, 41, 45, 55, 57, 70, 80, 97, 98, 113, 138, 139; diocese of, 2, 4, 5, 10, 12, 15, 19, 61, 194, 207, 237, 240, 277 n.6; division of diocese of 95, 96, 106, 107; Spanish conquest of, 2, 3, 5, 19, 20; Spanish foundation of, 20

Dance, 18, 22, 35, 36, 39, 41, 43, 46, 47, 53, 59, 61–68, 71, 79, 114, 117, 150, 154, 193, 94, 210–12, 223–29, 269 n.3, 281 n.63. *See also Taqui*

Dávila y Cartagena, Juan Bravo, 79, 93

Death: music in rituals of, 134, 135, 140, 141, 151, 152, 164, 232

Debt guarantee, 69, 179–82, 274 n.50

Decencia, 124–27, 189, 236, 244–47

De la Nava, Melchor, 77, 120

De la Raya, Antonio, 67, 75, 76, 79, 94, 95, 211

De Oré, fray Jerónimo, 144, 154, 176, 201

Dixit Dominus, 10, 119

Doctrina de indios. See Parishes: rural

Doctrinero. See Parish priests

"Hanacpachap," 201

Harmony, 11, 20–30, 33, 44, 58, 64, 125, 169, 236, 246–48

Harp/harpist, 37, 55, 64, 65, 68, 69, 83, 84, 92, 99–101, 111, 116, 119, 120, 125, 135–38, 146, 156–60, 163–66, 170, 179–81, 185–88, 201–203, 207–210, 214–19, 222, 224, 227

Harpsichord, 98, 116, 201, 222, 224

Haucaypata, 19–20, 31

Haylli, 225, 227

Herrera, Tomás de, 90–92, 98, 99, 116, 120, 121, 131

Hispanicization, 19, 54, 56, 101, 112, 113, 127, 182, 225, 234, 236, 247. *See also* Acculturation

Holgado, Matías, 171

Horn, 86, 138, 209

Hospital de los Naturales, 41, 51–55, 62, 66, 94, 97, 100, 123, 130, 133, 139, 140, 149, 150, 154, 157, 163–67, 174, 181–88

Hospitals, 3, 127, 133–41, 158, 161. *See also* Hospital de los Naturales; La Almudena: monastery and hospital of; San Andrés: hospital of; San Bartolomé: monastery and hospital of

Huayllabamba, 181, 200, 210, 214, 217

Hybridity. *See Mestizaje*: cultural

Identity, 11, 22; Christian, 127, 236, 246, 247; criollo, 9, 47, 48; indigenous, 54, 55, 251 n.19, 268 n.3; local, 243, 245; urban, 31, 32, 35, 42, 56

Idolatry, 23, 49, 57, 60, 62, 168, 192, 193, 210, 224, 226, 236

Ignatius of Loyola, 39–43

Inkas, 4, 5, 17–20, 25, 31, 41–51, 55, 56, 59, 60, 112, 159, 177, 204, 215, 225, 227, 232, 237

Instrument makers, 68, 148, 265 n.59. *See also* Guitar maker; Organ builder

Instruments/instrumentalists/instru-

mental music, 2, 5, 25, 37, 39, 41, 48, 53, 61–68, 76, 83–85, 90, 111, 116, 121–25, 129–33, 138, 143–46, 152–57, 160, 171, 174–75, 191–93, 200–203, 206–208, 218, 229, 232, 237, 244–47. *See also Bajón/bajonero*; Clarinet; Clavichord; Cornett/cornettist; Drum/drummer; Guitar; Harp/harpist; Harpsichord; Horn; Organ/organist; Sackbut; Shawm; Trumpet/trumpeter; Violin/violinist

Isaguirre, Bernardo de, 32

Jaca, 7, 13, 106

Jacobi, Francisco, 259 n.1

Jesuit order, 30, 33, 39–43, 50, 51, 58–59, 87, 127, 142–147, 168, 174, 192, 194, 225, 240, 275 n.59; church of, 1, 86, 134, 145; college in Arequipa, 145; *Relación de las fiestas*, 39–43, 50, 59, 62, 89, 192. *See also* San Bernardo, Colegio de; San Borja, Colegio de; Schools: for Andean and Hispanic elites

Joseph, Nicolás, 202

Juan, Jorge, and Antonio de Ulloa, 67, 161, 204, 211, 212

Kuraka. See Elites: Andean

Kusipata, 19, 20, 31

La Almudena: monastery and hospital of, 70, 127, 130, 133–38, 141, 163, 183

Laetatus Sum, 119

Lamay-Coya, 197, 203, 223, 228

La Merced: monastery of, 1, 43, 86, 99, 127, 130, 131, 171. *See also* Mercedarian order

La Plata, 7, 9, 76, 82–84, 94, 106, 110, 125, 126, 174, 200, 246, 263 n.25

Las Nazarenas, Beaterio de, 101, 124

Lauda Jerusalem, 116, 119

Laudate Dominum, 10

Laudate Pueri, 119

Music: traditional Andean, 39, 42–56, 61–63, 150, 154, 192–94, 229, 230

Navarra y Rocafull, Melchor de, 168
Ninaca, Pascual, 282 n.65
Notarial records, 7, 12–14, 112, 153, 174, 188, 249 n.5
Núñez de Prado, Laurencio, 101–3

Ocón, Juan Alonso de, 77, 91, 253 n.13
Office of the Dead, 70, 89, 127, 138
Olazábal, María Teresa Juana de Dios, 123
Ollantaytambo, 216
Ondegardo, Polo de, 19, 154
Opera Serenata, 80
Oposición, 103–5
Oratory, 47, 64
Organ/organist, 13, 65, 83, 90, 92, 111, 116, 121–38, 142, 144, 146, 156, 157, 160, 164–66, 171–74, 180, 181, 185–88, 200–210, 214–18, 237, 245, 264 n.36; of cathedral, 73, 74, 90, 91, 101–5, 130, 131
Organ builder, 5, 98, 120, 128, 131, 134, 264 n.40
Oricaín, Pablo José, 191, 212, 224–26, 238
Oropesa, 196, 207
Otalora, Joseph, 69
"Oy cielo y tierra," 120

Pacheco Salazar, María, 123
Padilla, Bartolomé, 123
Pancorbo, Basilio de, 73
Pancorbo, Juan de, 92–97, 116, 121
Papres, La Asunción de Nuestra Señora de los, 200, 204
"Para entrarse monja," 119
"Para lograr las gracias," 119
Parishes: rural, 10, 15, 22, 39, 45, 61, 64, 89, 94, 109, 158, 172, 179, 191–240 passim, 245; urban, 1, 4, 5, 7, 10, 12, 15, 31, 35–46, 50, 51, 55–62, 71, 87–89, 134, 144, 147, 149–90 passim, 195, 208, 238, 242–45. *See also* Belén; Hospital de los Naturales; San Blas; San Cristóbal; San Jerónimo; San Sebastián; Santa Ana; Santiago
Parish priests, 195–99, 205–7, 211, 212, 215, 219, 220, 223, 226–29, 239; Andeans as, 175, 199, 236, 247; Hispanic musicians as, 94–96, 109, 110, 256–57 n.54
Parroquias de indios. See Parishes: urban
Paucartambo, 222, 224
Pérez de Oblitas, Fernando Joseph, 80
Pérez de Vargas, Tomás, 102, 108
Performance, 9, 20, 44–49, 55, 244, 248, 283 n.1
Periphery: centre and, 4, 5, 31, 44, 61, 71, 189, 223, 226, 237–40
Philip II, 25
Philip III, 41, 155, 169
Philip V, 34, 70, 71, 77, 80, 89, 90, 138
Pichigua, 200
Pineda, Pascual de, 281 n.57
Pisac, 209, 218
Plague, 33, 42, 43, 49, 56, 85, 102, 152, 243, 276 n.73
Plainchant, 36, 41, 43, 71–76, 81, 88, 89, 103, 116, 121, 122, 127–29, 133, 137, 141, 142, 147, 166, 167, 196
Plaza: de Armas, 1, 18–20, 31, 35, 42, 43, 71, 72, 77, 127, 149; of parish, 5, 150, 152, 179, 180; del Regocijo, 19, 31, 35, 77, 80
Policía, 23, 50, 196, 249 n.2
Policy: music and, 88, 168, 169, 194, 208, 225, 234, 237, 243–46
Polychorality, 116, 119, 120, 246, 282 n.66
Polyphony, 26, 30, 37–43, 49, 70–76, 80–82, 87–89, 98, 103, 105, 110–17, 121, 122, 125, 128, 129, 133, 134, 137, 141, 144, 145, 152, 166, 175, 177, 196, 200, 201, 225, 237, 245, 265 n.54, 282 n.66

Geoffrey Baker is a lecturer in the Music Department
at Royal Holloway, University of London.

Library of Congress Cataloging-in-Publication Data
Baker, Geoffrey, 1970–
Imposing harmony : music and society in colonial
Cuzco / Geoffrey Baker. Geoffrey Baker.
p. cm.
Includes bibliographical references and index.
ISBN 978-0-8223-4136-9 (cloth : alk. paper)
ISBN 978-0-8223-4160-4 (pbk. : alk. paper)
1. Music—Peru—Cuzco—History and criticism.
2. Music—Social aspects—Peru—Cuzco. 3. Cuzco
(Peru)—Social life and customs. I. Title.
ML236.8.C92B34 2008
780.985'37—dc22
2007038485